HOPE BEYOND BORDERS

HOPE BEYOND BORDERS

The Life and Letters of

Paul Fried

Stephen I. Hemenway

Van Raalte Press
Holland, Michigan

Van Raalte Press is a division of Hope College Publishing

Offices: Theil Research Center
             9 East 10th Street
             Holland, MI 49423

Mailing: Hope College
             PO Box 9000
             Holland, MI 49422-9000
             vanraalte@hope.edu

www.hope.edu/vri

Printed in the United States of America

ISBN 978-0-9891-469-0-6

Editor-in-Chief and Publisher
    Jacob E. Nyenhuis, PhD
Copy Editor
    JoHannah Smith
Layout and Cover Design
    Russell L. Gasero

Author's Biographical Note

Dr. Stephen I. Hemenway has been a professor in the Hope College English Department since August 1972. In 1976 Dr. Paul G. Fried selected Stephen to replace him and guide the Hope College Vienna Summer School in Austria. In 2015 Stephen plans to lead another group of students to Vienna for his fortieth consecutive year. He resides in Holland, Michigan.

Stephen received his AB in English from the College of the Holy Cross (Worcester, MA) in 1964, his MA in English from Boston College (Chestnut Hill, MA) in 1967, and his PhD in English from the University of Illinois (Urbana) in 1972. He taught in Jamaica, India, and Austria. He published *The Novel of India* in two volumes: *The Anglo-Indian Novel* in 1975 and *The Indo-Anglian Novel* in 1976 (Calcutta: Writers Workshop).

Stephen was awarded the Knight's Cross, First Class, Order of Merit of the Republic of Austria (1991). He was named Michigan Professor of the Year (1992) by the Council for Advancement and Support of Education. He was the first recipient of the Hope College Vanderbush-Weller Award for Extraordinary Contributions to the Lives of Students (1999).

Contents

Illustrations

Acknowledgments

One individual stands out as the person most responsible for this book: Paul G. Fried. His preservation of personal papers and thousands of letters made judicious selection of material difficult but rewarding. His legacy—as son and brother, soldier and translator, teacher and mentor, traveler and citizen of the world, bon vivant and excellent friend—is enormous.

The Theil Research Center on the Hope College campus houses the Joint Archives of Holland and the A. C. Van Raalte Institute. In this repository containing so many boxes of Fried papers, letters, and memorabilia, staff members work tirelessly to aid authors and other researchers. In the initial stages of my work, Geoffrey Reynolds and Lori Trethewey guided me daily with locating sources and scanning documents and photographs. In the pre-publication days, JoHannah Smith provided superb hands-on advice with every aspect of copy editing, style, format, and indexing. Jacob (Jack) Nyenhuis added so much professional expertise, especially in determining the look of the book. Elton Bruins and Robert Swierenga offered helpful suggestions on content and publication options.

In the English Department, now retired office manager Myra Kohsel transformed my early handwritten scrawls of the most intriguing paragraphs from Paul's letters into readable computer prose. Current office manager Sarah Baar solved every computer riddle, scanned and organized numerous photos, and transferred items back and forth from U-drives to CDs. Christina Van Eyl proved so valuable as the first copy editor and primary indexer. Kathleen Verduin, resident grammarian, helped solve many stylistic and linguistic problems. Gisela Strand and Brian and Barbara Gibbs translated important letters from German into English, and Brian located many references to the published works of Paul's mother and father. Carl Heideman identified years and models of Paul's automobiles. Chris Spencer and Charles Aschbrenner shared their boxes of Fried memorabilia willingly and let me copy documents and photos. Tom Renner supplied numerous photographs that he had taken of Paul at Hope for four decades. Martin Baierl gave me all of his notes from long interviews with Paul in the final decade of his life. Glenn Lowe, Paul's official guardian, also told me many stories of Paul's final days.

Several other people offered tangible help and encouragement in so many ways, and this partial list is by no means complete: Sharon Adcock, Jim Alexander, Kathleen and James Beyer, Stephanie Browne, Donald Bruggink, Leah Chase-Wallar, Shirley Dickman, Jan Evert, Maureen Geiger, Janis Gibbs, Paul Grande, Elisabeth Grosse, Jane and Stetson Hall, John Hanson, Clare Hemenway, Mary Ann Hemenway, Ruth Hemenway, Greg Holcombe, John and Winnie Hollenbach, Brigitte Marcher, Christa and Josef Mraz, Bill Moreau, Bruce Neckers, Thomas and Eva Nowotny, Kelsey O'Brien, Greg Olgers, Amy Otis-DeGrau, Judy Tanis Parr, Anna Peterson, Chelsea Poest, Lynne Powe, Richard Ray, Eva Sagastume, Peter Schakel, Mackenzie Schumborg, Gloria Shay, Bob and Rita Snow, Neal Sobania, John Tysse, Elizabeth West, Kendra Williams.

Preface

Dr. Paul G. Fried occasionally spoke of a desire to write an autobiographical memoir or a novel based on his wartime experiences, but he never completed this task. Indeed, he seldom even spoke about the many traumatic events that peppered his life from 1919 to 1945. In 1985 Dr. John W. Hollenbach published "Apostle for International Understanding," a superbly written twenty-four-page biography of Paul in the festschrift (a book of essays by several authors that is presented as a tribute) entitled *Into All the World* (edited by Robert J. Donia and John M. Mulder on the occasion of Paul's retirement from Hope College). Paul then thought that there was now no need to write his own memoir. He did, however, dutifully leave copies of most of his personal letters and papers to the Joint Archives of Holland at Hope College in 1998, just in case anyone ever decided to pull together the various strands of his life in ways that he had started but left unfinished.

I found that Paul's extensive autobiographical notes (especially his boyhood and World War II reflections), the carbon copies of at least ten thousand personal letters that he wrote and preserved, and other personal papers presented an opportunity for creating an edited version of the highlights of his life and career. Most of these documents are currently available in thirty-five boxes located in the basement of the Theil Research Center on the Hope College campus, but the files and folders labeled with the names of letter recipients are still undergoing reorganization. Paul signed over his legal copyright on all of these documents to the Joint Archives in 1998. In preparing this book, I have tried to keep this treasure trove of insights into the personality and achievements of Paul Fried in his own words as much as possible.

In a 5 June 1951 letter to Harvard roommate Bob Bernen, Paul stated, "I feel that interesting correspondence follows a pattern. It includes references to day-to-day matters of mutual interest, physical experiences, and, in its best form, a record of thoughts and mental activity." Several years later, in a 23 January 1965 letter to former student and art curator John Dryfhout, Paul said, "I am always somewhat aware of the historian's task. I don't think I ever had in mind the possibility of my letters being published as the value, for myself, of putting down on paper things I would otherwise easily forget." I, however, think that Paul's letters and autobiographical sketches do have incredible value in revealing the personality of a man who breathed "hope beyond borders" in all of his life's actions and passions.

Several of this book's chapters are very serious treatments of discrimination and persecution, refugee status, unsuccessful efforts to save family members, World War II exploits, the Nürnberg Trials, and philosophical and religious ideas. Other sections are narrations of Paul's academic adventures at Hope (as student and professor) and Harvard and the establishment of the Hope College Vienna Summer School and other international programs. Humor surfaces in many entries, but especially in those linked with Paul's passions for automobiles, exercise, food, travel, and his adopted town of Holland, Michigan.

In addition to Paul's own letters, I read at least five thousand other letters and cards written to Paul by numerous friends; they are carefully preserved in those same files and folders identified by each correspondent's name. For the most part, because of copyright legalities, I have used only brief synopses of or very short quotations from these letters to Paul in order to put certain experiences into the proper context.

I have taken liberties with correcting typographical and punctuation errors and altering a few awkward stylistic choices in the autobiographical pages. I have edited and heavily abbreviated the contents of letters in order to capture the best moments; in addition, I have often chosen only a few significant sentences from a long letter.

I have eliminated a few nonessential phrases, translated most German words within brackets, reduced several words to lower case, and opted not to use ellipsis marks in letters because there would be too many. I have also made decisions about a uniform way of indicating dates (day/month/year) and about when to use or not use umlauts or capital letters or italics in German words.

Many of the photographs in this book were undated and unlabeled in boxes and albums and not attributed to any particular photographer. Several appeared originally in Hope College publications, and many are from the files of Tom Renner, associate vice president for public and community relations at Hope. Quite a few early pictures are kept in the Joint Archives of Holland and in albums left by Paul to Chris Spencer and Charles Aschbrenner, and many are from my personal collection. In a few cases, I made "educated" guesses for dates and places.

Ideally, I hope that this biographical memoir will actually stand forth as Paul's own inspirational autobiography collated and interpreted and partially understood by a dear friend and colleague.

Timeline of Paul Fried's Life

Most of this information has been garnered from Paul's letters and curriculum vitae. The dates of deportations and deaths in various concentration camps were provided to Paul's friend Chris Spencer by the Holocaust and War Victims Tracing and Information Center through the American Red Cross. The Yad Vashem/Holocaust Martyrs' and Heroes' Remembrance Authority corroborated the information about Paul's father, mother, and younger brother inhabiting the Lodz ghetto.

20 July 1875   Paul (Pavel) Markus Fried (father) was born in Vienna, Austria, of Jewish parents. At age seven, he received Christian baptism together with his parents into the Evangelical Reformed Church. He became a doctor of philology, journalist, author, and teacher.

30 December 1885   Emilie Julina (nee Grünhaut) Fried (mother) was born in Czerna Ostrov, Russia. Both of

	her parents, originally Jewish, were received into the Lutheran Church prior to her birth. She became a doctor of medicine, specialist for women and children, and well-published author.
1911	Alfred Hermann Fried (11 November 1864 to 5 May 1921), cousin of Paul's father, bookseller, and journalist, received the Nobel Peace Prize.
2 September 1915	Paul's parents were married in Budapest, Hungary.
23 June 1916	Julius Markus Fried (Paul's older brother) was born in Berlin, Germany. He played cello and became a private teacher of language before imprisonment by the Nazis.
4 April 1919	Paul Viktor Georg Josef Jakob Fried was born in Leipzig, Germany.
14 November 1925	Felix Alexander Fried (Paul's younger brother) was born in Wiesbaden, Germany. He was a student until his imprisonment by the Nazis.
1929	Paul's parents co-authored *Liebes und Eheleben: Ein praktischer Berater für die gesunde und harmonische Ehe sowie für sexuelle Not-Fragen* (Love and married life: a practical advisor for healthy and harmonic marriage as well as for sexual emergency questions). The book was banned and probably burned but appears to have gone into at least twenty-seven printings, most of them published after their deaths.
April 1938	Paul was arrested by the Nazis and imprisoned in Vienna for about six weeks.
Summer 1938	Paul, stateless, was released from prison and dropped from a train near the Czechoslovakian border to escape from Austria. He lived as a refugee in Prague for the remainder of the year.

January 1939	Paul arrived in London and worked for the British Society for the Propagation of the Gospel among the Jews; his job was to find places for European refugees.
22 December 1939	Paul entered the United States aboard the SS *Veendam*.
23 December 1939	Paul arrived in Cleveland to work for the Hebrew Christian Mission.
13 July 1940	Paul's brother Julius was confined to Dachau Concentration Camp, Germany; his prisoner number was 13834.
16 August 1940	Julius was transferred from Dachau to Mauthausen-Gusen Concentration Camp, Austria; his prisoner number was 7507.
September 1940	Paul enrolled at Hope College on a full-tuition scholarship ($125).
21 August 1941	Julius was shot to death "while trying to escape" from Mauthausen-Gusen at 2:45 p.m.
16 October 1941	Paul's father, mother, and younger brother Felix were deported from Prague to the Litzmannstadt (Lodz) ghetto in Poland, with transport numbers A-710, A-711, A-712.
20 February 1942	Paul's father perished in the Lodz ghetto; the Polish Red Cross said that he died in the extermination camp in nearby Chelmno.
24 May 1942	Paul's mother and brother Felix perished in the Lodz ghetto.
15 September 1942	Paul was drafted into the US Army and later began military training for interrogation work.
1 June 1943	Paul became a naturalized US citizen in the district court of El Paso, Colorado.
1943-45	Paul served in Europe as an interpreter and sharpshooter for the army.

3 April 1945	Paul was awarded the Bronze Star Medal for meritorious service.
25 October 1945	Paul received an honorable discharge from the army at Fort Meade, Maryland.
June 1946	Paul received his BA (cum laude) from Hope College.
June 1947	Paul received his MA in modern European history from Harvard University.
1947-1949	Paul served as the chief of translation for Foreign Office Case #11 against Baron Ernst von Weizsäcker in the US Military Tribunals in Nürnberg, Germany.
August 1949	Paul received his PhD (magna cum laude) from the University of Erlangen, Germany. His dissertation, "Die tschechische Frage in den Akten des Auswärtigen Amtes" (The Czech question in the files of the German Foreign Office), examined German-Czech diplomatic relations from 1935 to 1939.
Sept. 1949-Jan. 1951	Paul did research in history and international law at Harvard University.
Jan. 1951-July 1953	Paul worked as a liaison officer (classified work) for the US Air Force to British Intelligence offices in Kiel, Essen, and Hamburg for the USAF Research Division (Germany).
July 1951-Apr. 1952	Paul taught two courses for the European program of the University of Maryland in Hof an der Salle, Germany.
September 1953	Paul began his teaching career in the Hope College Department of History.
Summer 1956	Paul brought his first group of students to Vienna and founded what would eventually become the Hope College Vienna Summer School.

18 October 1968	Paul received the "Goldene Ehrenzeichnen für Verdienste am die Republik Österreich" (Gold medal of merit from the Republic of Austria).
Summer 1981	Paul led an alumni/ae tour to Vienna to celebrate the 25th anniversary of the Vienna Summer School.
Spring 1984	Paul received the Hope College Distinguished Alumni Award. He retired and became professor emeritus.
1985	*Into All the World*, a volume of essays edited by Robert J. Donia and John M. Mulder, was published by former students to honor Paul.
24 April 1987	Paul received a Hope College honorary degree.
22 September 1990	The International Education Center at Hope was renamed in Paul's honor.
15 Jan.-4 Feb. 1996	"Visions from Vienna," showcasing parts of Paul's art collection, was on exhibit in Hope's De Pree Art Center. Paul later donated many pieces to Hope's permanent collection.
15 October 2005	The Fried-Hemenway Auditorium in Hope's new Martha Miller Center for Global Communication was dedicated.
24 July 2006	Paul Fried died at age eighty-seven; he was buried in Pilgrim Home cemetery in Holland, Michigan, and eulogized at a memorial service on 9 September 2006.

Fried family photo (ca. 1935). Paul Markus Fried with wife Emilie and sons (l-r) Julius, Felix, and Paul

CHAPTER 1

Boyhood in Germany and Austria (1919–38)

Paul Fried rarely talked about his youthful days in Europe, but from 5-7 January 1970, he wrote section one (1919-38) of what he termed "Notes for an Autobiography." Handwritten in blue ink on lined yellow legal-pad paper, Paul's manuscript has many crossed-out passages, but he provided comic and tragic glimpses into his early years. It is intriguing that he penned this segment on his boyhood a few decades after he had written about many of his later experiences.

German years

I was born, I am told, on a Sunday afternoon, not far from the main railway station in Leipzig. This was not the way my parents had planned things. But then my mother never was too good at mathematics.

In the spring of 1919, our family lived in Berlin. But with the war only just ended and the continued food shortage, it was decided that my mother should accept an appointment at a hospital in Switzerland. That way I would enter the world as a Swiss citizen and grow fat on milk, butter, and Swiss cheese in my diet.

1

My curiosity to find out what was going on outside forced my parents to break the journey in Leipzig. We stayed in the city of my birth for two weeks, and I have not been there since. I doubt if I would recognize the place now—fifty years later.

There followed a year of rich Swiss diet in Lausanne which endowed me with a comfortable upholstery. This has been helpful when rations were short but also seems to have prevented me from achieving any success in athletics or maintaining a trim figure.

There is not much I remember about the years from the time I was one to the time I was five when we lived in Berlin again. My father was editor of the *Nordddeutsche Allgemeine Zeitung* [North German general newspaper], my mother worked in a clinic, and my brother Julius (three years older) and I petted and tortured a huge St. Bernard. He [the dog] survived all of that only to succumb to a surfeit of chicken fat after he had eaten a large pot of this.

In 1924, when I was about five, my parents moved to Wiesbaden. As a result of some kind of investment, my father had ended up the responsible owner of a large brickyard outside of Wiesbaden. This necessitated enough trips to suggest that the whole family move there.

For some months we stayed in a hotel, and I remember that Julius and I developed great skill in climbing on top of the wardrobe chest, and like parachutists, jumping down onto the huge double bed. Before long the bed caved in. The management took a rather dim view of the matter, but I am not sure if we were punished. In those days our parents were modern and indulgent.

Eventually, we moved into a huge house which my father bought from Baron Auer von Herrenkirchen. The Baron's great pride was that Kaiser Wilhelm the Second had been a guest in this place on several occasions. A huge red carpet which could be rolled all the way to the sidewalk survived.

The first school I attended was in Sonnenberg, just outside of Wiesbaden. I am not sure that I learned much, and staying home for a year after that because of some sort of skin disorder made me forget most of what I might have learned. I re-entered school the following year and did so poorly that the teachers wanted me to repeat the second grade.

My father felt that the shame of having the son of a PhD and an MD fail in school was more than he could bear, so I was moved to a new school—for slow learners—where I entered third grade and did well. That led to my transfer to yet another regular school for the fourth grade, where I again had difficulties.

Over the objections of my teacher, who advised one more year in the Volksschule [elementary school], I entered the Gymnasium [secondary school stressing academics], having barely passed the necessary entrance exams. The results were possibly predictable. This time I would certainly have to repeat the year. Only at that point, before the end of the school year, my parents withdrew me from the public school and enrolled me in a private school for the rich and the dumb. I did well. In fact, at the end of the first year there, I advanced into the fourth class, skipping the third altogether.

Although my mother commented appropriately, "Among the blind, the one-eyed is king," my father thought it was time for me to get back into a public school. Since I had dropped out of the Gymnasium in Wiesbaden and could not go back there, I was now sent to a Realgymnasium [secondary school preparing students for university] in Mainz.

I think I might even have been able to stay in school there for more than a year if the advent of Hitler had not brought about a fundamental change in the life of my family. During the early summer of that year, my father was arrested and sent off to a concentration camp. After the Austrian government intervened for him, he was released on the condition that he and the family leave the country within two weeks.

In a dictatorship, no reasons are needed to expel an undesirable alien, but I suppose for the Nazis there were more than enough counts against my father. He had been active in the political campaign against Hitler; he was an Austrian, i.e., a foreigner; he was a Jew by birth, though his parents had joined the Reformed Church when he was only seven years old; and if that was not enough, he and my mother had jointly published a best-selling book advocating birth control.

So, early in September 1933, my parents, my two brothers (Felix had been born shortly after we moved to Wiesbaden), and I left Germany and went to Vienna. We traveled by train, and I remember our thirteen suitcases and boxes, which represented most of our possessions. For each of us, my father was permitted to take out one hundred Deutschmarks; the rest of his property had been confiscated by the German government.

Austrian years (with earlier Russian interludes)

In Germany, our family had been fairly well-to-do; in Austria, we were extremely poor, frequently forced to depend on the charity of relatives and friends. All of Austria was seriously affected by the Depression, and we were not alone in our poverty. But it hurt my father's pride to be unable to earn enough to support the family and to have to let my mother work as a night nurse just so we could eat.

Regardless of politics or poverty, I had to go back to school, and for once I was able to hang on in the same school for three years.

Not that I was a good student, but I liked history and English. French and mathematics were something else again. Thrice my grades in these subjects were so low that I had to spend the summer preparing for fall make-up exams, which I then passed by the skin of my teeth.

In the meantime, the political and economic situation of the country—and of my family—did not improve. The short but bitter civil war in February 1934 at the time impressed me mostly by the fact that we did not have to go to school. Since I had experienced a first-hand encounter with National Socialism before, the July Putsch during which Dollfuss was killed seemed a far more serious matter.

Since there seemed to be little hope of building a permanent home in Austria in the middle 1930s, the possibility of moving to Russia and settling there was frequently discussed by my parents. Here I had better back up to a time long before I made the scene, when my father was in Moscow as a foreign correspondent for a group of German and Austrian newspapers. The year was 1908. My father, an eligible young man from a wealthy Viennese family, became a frequent visitor in the home of my grandfather, who had come as a young doctor from Austria and had remained to become a prominent member of the Moscow medical community. Though all his children were born in Russia, my grandfather always remained an Austrian both in spirit and in law.

Soon my father began to court my mother's older sister. Though my mother enjoyed eating the candy father brought for his date, nothing came of the affair, which ended when my father's paper sent him to Turkey, Bulgaria, and other parts of eastern Europe. He did not return to Moscow until late in 1913 or early 1914. By that time, Aunt Nina was happily engaged to a Russian mathematician. Meanwhile, however, my mother had completed her medical training, and soon my father fell in love with the young girl he had ignored a few years earlier. The outbreak of war between Russia and the Central Powers almost ended this romance. My father left Russia and became a war correspondent on the Eastern Front. My mother finished her internship when she was assigned to the staff of a Russian military hospital.

Though Russia and Austria were at war, mail somehow apparently continued between the two countries. At any rate, the romance continued and flourished for my father was a persuasive writer. An engagement by mail followed and created a rather unusual situation. By the summer of 1915, my mother, daughter of an Austrian, was the fiancée of another enemy alien and was in charge of a large Russian military hospital since the male doctors had been sent to the front. When some Austrian prisoners escaped from this hospital and attempted to derail a Russian troop train, the charge that my mother was aiding the enemy was an obvious consequence.

Warned by my grandfather's Russian friends of possible repercussions and supplied with the necessary passes and identifying papers, my mother traveled westward with Russian troop trains and, on reaching the front, continued through the German-Austrian front lines, using identifying documents my father had secured for her. Without serious mishap, she arrived in Budapest in the late summer of 1915. One of my father's sisters, married to a Hungarian banker, lived in Budapest. On 2 September 1915, my parents were married in his sister's home.

By the time my older brother, Julius, was born in the summer of 1916, my father had exchanged his front-line war correspondent's assignment to head a newly formed news agency in Berlin. Also, by this time, the Czarist regime in Russia had been overthrown. Soon the Bolshevik Revolution followed and took Russia out of the war by the Treaty of Brest-Litovsk, which my father covered as a correspondent.

Despite the upheaval of the revolution, Germany and Russia were now no longer at war, so in the summer of 1918, my mother decided to take Julius to Moscow so my grandfather could see her firstborn. The journey through the war-torn areas of Poland and Russia must have been something less than comfortable for a woman traveling alone with a small baby. But grandfather was happy and so was my mother, for he passed away not too long after she returned to Berlin.

I think that throughout the 1920s and early 1930s my mother was able to correspond with her sister and two brothers, both of whom had adjusted to the new regime without too much difficulty. Travel between the two countries obviously cannot have been as impossible as one might assume today.

I recall that in 1925, when Felix was born, my mother's sister came to visit us in Wiesbaden and stayed for several months. Her brother, who was a member of a Soviet technical fundraising commission, also came to Wiesbaden on several occasions. My best memory is of this huge man entering the room where we were playing with two large shopping bags containing wrapped, filled candies. He turned them upside down, and a mountain of candy grew on the carpet!

By 1934, when the situation in Austria seemed to become more and more hopeless, my mother's brothers urged her to return to Russia and secured for her an appointment on the staff of the Moscow University Hospital. Hoping that this might be the first step toward establishing a new family home and that the rest of the family would soon be able to follow, she signed the three-year contract and left Austria in the summer of 1935.

Father Paul Markus

Mother Emilie

Before the summer was over, it became clear that it would not be easy for my father or Julius and me to be granted visas to Russia. Felix, on the other hand, being still under ten years old, was included on my mother's passport, and hence her visa was valid also for him, even though he did not travel with her initially. Since he had to get there before he reached his birthday in November, it was decided that he should join my mother at once. Hence, on a cold October day, we took him to the East Station; he was all bundled up and properly labeled and tagged, and we put him on the express train to Warsaw. Someone was to meet him there and see that he got on the right train, and someone else was meeting him at the Russian border where he again had to change trains. Apparently, he made the trip without any trouble and was safely united with my mother after he arrived in Moscow.

This now left my father, Julius, and me on our own in Vienna. The expectation was, of course, that we, too, would leave for Russia soon. But time went on, and month after month the Russian consulate said it had no news for us. Julius and I began to talk about emigrating somewhere else (Canada, South America, or the United States), and in time we visited most of the consulates. I am not sure how seriously the questions asked by two teenaged boys were taken, but in some places we were given lists to sign or forms to fill out. Though I was unaware of it at the time, I must have filled out an application for a quota number for emigration to the United States.

Meanwhile the three of us—my father, my brother, and I— shared a furnished room and apparently lived pretty much a day-to-day existence. My interest in school, never terribly great, further declined, and by the spring of 1936, I received a school-leaving certificate. By that time, I had been told that my visa for Russia would come in any day now, so there seemed to be no reason for me to plan on returning to school in the fall. In fact, during the summer of 1936, I was ready to go, even to the point of saying goodbye to some of my friends, only to learn that the promised visa had not come after all. It was not all that easy to go back to my friends and tell them I was staying!

Work for Swedish Missionary Society in Vienna

Most of that summer I spent in Meidling, near Vienna, in a summer home or camp maintained by the Swedish Missionary Society. An old established Protestant enterprise to bring the Gospel to the Jews in Vienna, this society had in 1934 come under the leadership of Pastor Frederick Forell, who made it a haven and cultural center for refugee families. A Lutheran clergyman from Breslau with some Jewish ancestors of his own, Forell was a dynamic preacher and a charismatic father figure for all who came under his spell in the Seegasse Center of the society.

To me, he was a modern Luther, and I began to spend more and more time at the Seegasse. With the guidance of a dedicated layman, Forell's two sons, his nephew, a few other boys, Julius, and I formed a local YMCA club both for fun and for Bible study. At first my father was pleased to see us thus engaged; later he worried that I might become too involved religiously. This led to many arguments, but in the end he gave up objecting.

Since I did not return to school in the fall of 1936, I could try to find work. For a while, I was a delivery boy for a goldsmith firm, then I worked in a mimeograph office, and eventually I ended up with a more-or-less full-time job working for the Swedish Missionary Society on Seegasse.

Early every morning, I carried a day's supply of wood and coal from the basement to the fourth floor apartment of our young Swedish assistant pastor, Rev. [Goete] Hedenquist, and stoked fires in the kitchen range and two tile stoves. In return for this, I received a generous Swedish breakfast which more often than not was my biggest meal of the day.

For the rest of the day, I worked as a general assistant for the director of welfare, a retired bank manager, who distributed food and clothing received from Sweden to needy members of the congregation and other applicants. By this time, my father had more or less moved to Bratislava, in Czechoslovakia, where he earned a meager income as a lecturer at the German-language evening college.

Julius, too, had taken a job; he combined the position of secretary to a textile merchant with that of tutoring the merchant's son. Between us, we earned just about enough to pay for the furnished room we shared and for some of our most essential needs.

Indirectly, working for the Swedish Missionary Society later helped me get out of a Nazi prison to spend a year in England and to immigrate to the United States. In the early summer of 1937, the society was headquarters for an extended meeting of the International Missionary Council, which brought delegates from all parts of the world to Vienna. Dr. Conrad Hoffmann Jr., who had charge of organizing the conference, came to Vienna about two months ahead of time, and I was assigned to assist him.

It was exciting work to prepare to house and feed so many people from different countries and to prepare papers, meeting places, name tags, meal tickets, and all the other things familiar enough to most American convention-goers today, but quite new to Austria and certainly to me. I worked long hours, but no matter how early I got to the office, Dr. Hoffmann was already there with a stack of handwritten notes ready to be marked. I admired him greatly, and I think he was pleased with my efforts.

Anyway, three years later, when the war had begun and I was stranded in England, he found someone willing to sponsor me as an immigrant, so I could come to the United States. Later, when I asked him for advice about attending college, his assistant [Rev. John Muilenburg] helped secure a tuition scholarship for me to attend Hope College.

The other significant meeting which came from this conference was with Rev. Arthur Parry, the general secretary of the British Society for the Propagation of the Gospel among the Jews. We exchanged only a few words on several occasions, but he remembered me well enough to send money to Pastor Forell when it became apparent that a small amount (20 pounds) would buy my freedom after Hitler had annexed Austria. Then, after I had made my way from Austria to Czechoslovakia, Rev. Parry offered me hospitality in his society's home in England and even sent the money for the air ticket from Prague to London.

This conference of churchmen in many ways widened my awareness of the outside world. In a way, it probably marked the point at which my own life as an individual began to be quite distant from that of my family. This was the period, too, when religious questions, doubts, and aspirations were of major importance to me. Perhaps this was related also to the time I spent at the church's summer home in Meidling. Not that this was a place of constant prayer and meditation. On the contrary, we had a good deal of fun, and there was even a fair amount of sexual experimentation.

Teenage heartthrob   *Teenage scholar*

Imprisonment and release

It is hard to say how my life would have developed had Austria remained free. As it was, the *Anschluss* [annexation of Austria into Nazi Germany] in March 1938 quickly ended that phase of my experiences. About 6 a.m. one morning, shortly after Hitler had arrived in Vienna, I awoke to find two plain-clothes policemen standing next to my bed. They confirmed that I was indeed Paul Fried and told me to get dressed and to come with them for an "examination." Since my father's name, which was also Paul, was on the Nazi blacklist, I expect they really wanted him. But he was safely in Czechoslovakia at that point, and even the wrong Paul Fried was probably better than to arrest no one.

On my way to the bathroom to get dressed, I managed to pick up the phone in the hall so I could call one of my friends and alert him in case I should not be back that day. As it turned out, it was to be six weeks before I left the police prison on Elisabethkai. But at least my friends knew where I was, and eventually a kindly old lawyer, who came to see me two or three times, arranged for my release by paying a small bribe. I later found out that the money for this had been provided by Rev. Parry, one of the men I had met during the conference the summer before.

During my six weeks in the police prison, the number of prisoners increased constantly. I was in a fairly large room which initially housed seventeen men. Before I left, there were eighty of us in the same room. Since almost everyone there was a political prisoner, there was a different tone about the place from that usually found in prisons. We played chess (boards drawn on tables and men made of scraps of paper), talked, and read what there was to read. I personally experienced no beating or brutality, though some of the more prominent "guests" did not escape as lightly.

When I was released six weeks later, it was on the condition that I leave Austria at once and promise not to return or make any claims against the government. I gladly signed the necessary paper, though leaving Austria was not that simple a matter. I did not have a passport, and anyway, with the annexation of Austria, I had become a stateless person. Thus, I could not apply for a visa to go anywhere or enter another country legally.

From the police point of view, however, this was not an important obstacle to having me leave the country. Early in the morning on the day of my release, two plain-clothes detectives took three others and me to the train station and went with us by train to a small village near the Czech frontier. We then walked for what seemed hours before coming to a forest, and there, one by one, we were told how to cross over into Czech territory. We were warned not to let the Czechs catch us since, if we were caught, they would lock us up for two weeks and then push us back into Austria. Our kindly escorts also warned me not to come back since the Germans were patrolling the border and had orders to shoot anyone attempting to cross illegally.

So, on a warm April day, I suddenly found myself free, walking across a plowed field inside of Czechoslovakia, but very much aware that I could be arrested at any moment. My dark suit, black oxfords, and heavy winter coat had seemed appropriate weeks earlier in Vienna. Now, as I was walking through fields, they seemed singularly out of place, and I felt that anyone looking at me would at once know that I was a stranger who did not belong here.

"A Refugee's Story"

This next article, "A Refugee's Story," conveys Paul's experiences from 1933 to 1938 in words fashioned from his presentation in England to "the boys at Wheatly House" about his earlier experiences. It appeared anonymously in the *Upper Holloway Messenger*, 15 October 1939.

A boy of fourteen arrives home from school one day in 1933 to find his comfortable home, a thirty-three-room house in a famous Rhine town, in complete disorder. The Gestapo have ransacked it and taken away letters and documents from his father's library. Father is an Austrian journalist, mother a doctor of Russian birth. Going to school the next day, the boy and his brother are sent for by the headmaster and told they must absent themselves from school pending the outcome of their father's trial. The trial ends in the expulsion of the father to Austria, and the family settles down almost penniless in Vienna. Here for five years they enjoy at least peace and quietness, but in 1938 Hitler turns his attention to Austria, and their troubles begin again.

His father loses his citizenship, although he fought in the last war as an Austrian soldier, and has to flee to Prague, where one son joins him. The mother is offered and accepts an appointment in the University at Moscow, while the other lad has to keep himself as best he can. This he does, first as a coal porter, carrying hods of coal up five flights of stairs at a time. Then he works as a cyclist messenger, then in a duplicating office. He next comes into contact with a Swedish mission working in Vienna and obtains a post as a secretary. One morning, however, he is awakened in his simple room to find a Gestapo agent, who orders him to dress while he searches his few poor possessions and then takes him off to prison, where he spends several weeks, herded in one room with all kinds of criminals, at first eighteen in number but as time goes on, as many as eighty! The lord mayor of Vienna is held captive in the same building.

The lad's next experience is of being taken from this place of confinement by two Gestapo men on a long journey to a place a few miles from the Czecho-Slovak border and being set free with instructions to cross the frontier as best he can, without passport or visa, and only a few coins in his pocket, a dangerous enough exploit, as those who have read the English story "The Escaping Club" will know. He succeeds, however, and after long tramps through woods and country roads, finds a bus to Prague, where he puts up in a cheap hotel for the night. To his amazement, the next morning as he leaves the hotel and steps into the street, he runs straight into his own brother.

Then comes the German occupation of Bohemia and Moravia, and once more our friend is on the move. This time he succeeds in escaping to England, where he has now been for seven months, hoping to go on to America and to training for the Christian ministry. And what was the crime that brought all the trouble to a united and devoted family? That there was Jewish ancestry on his father's side!

Interviews dealing with boyhood memories

At this point, Paul's boyhood and youth really ended. The years 1938 and 1939 became a period of uncertainty and desperation. In interviews conducted mainly in 1999 and 2003 by Martin Baierl, a Hope graduate (1994) from Germany, Paul offered other reflections

Friend and astute interviewer Martin Baierl (ca. 2003)

on boyhood memories about family, Leipzig, Wiesbaden, Vienna, and Bratislava. Many positive thoughts revolved around the staff of the Swedish Missionary Society which gave Paul spiritual direction and significant employment in Vienna. Baierl's interviews provided some additional information about Paul's boyhood.

In 1929 Paul's parents co-authored a book entitled *Liebes und Eheleben: Ein praktischer Berater für die gesunde und harmonische Ehe sowie für sexuelle Not-Fragen* (Love and married life: a practical advisor for healthy and harmonic marriage as well as for sexual emergency questions). After Hitler was elected in 1933, this book was supposedly put on the black list and burned.

Paul's Sunday birth in Leipzig in 1919 occurred with no doctor, but with a midwife in a pension. The family was en route to Switzerland, where Paul's mother had a one-year contract with a hospital. Paul's father was not good with finances. Paul and his older brother Julius were very close. Julius was a role model, a better student, three years older, taller, slender, and looked more like his dad. Paul and Julius stuck together against some of their dad's expectations and ideas and were disappointed that their dad was often away from the family. Paul's parents lamented: "Why can't you be more like Julius?" This attitude, however, did not alienate the brothers. Paul enjoyed playing chess with his mom. He was not as close to his younger brother Felix (b. 1925) due to the age difference of six years and long periods of separation; both older brothers patronized Felix who could not sleep without his little pillow.

According to Baierl, the Fried address in Wiesbaden was Schöne Aussicht 28, a large house with a "beautiful view." It now appears to be the address of a real estate company. The Frieds had a cook and service person. A Russian aunt came for Felix's baptism in 1925 and stayed for a while. Paul was in school in Wiesbaden from 1925 to 1932 and in Mainz from 1932 to 1933.

Paul told Martin a story about how Julius and he once saw people selling spring flowers at a market. Realizing that they had even nicer flowers in their own garden, they picked a bundle to sell in order to raise money to buy a Mother's Day gift. Their father got mad at them for doing this. Many guests from Russia—diplomats, writers of the pre-Stalin era—visited them in Wiesbaden. Lots of Russian was spoken, but Paul did not understand this language. His mom's jolly engineer brothers from Moscow visited often in Wiesbaden. The Fried family moved to a smaller place due to the depression around 1928. (In the book written by Paul's parents, the address of Dotzheimer Strasse 28 is provided on page 20, so this may be the smaller place or their office.)

Paul was initially attracted to the *Hitler Jugend* (Hitler Youth). He was very conscious of the Nazi campaign due to his father's activities and writing against Nazi propaganda. (In his oral history interview with Dr. John Hollenbach, Paul talked about how his dad had written with biting sarcasm of Hitler on the platform in the spring of 1932 and about how the Nazis could not forget that.) Paul's dad was arrested in June of 1933 and sent to a concentration camp with very primitive living conditions, but the family could visit him. Eventually, the Austrian consul arranged for Paul's father to leave the camp on the condition that the family would depart from Germany at once.

The brother and sister of Paul's dad lived in Vienna. The Frieds lived first with his sister and later moved to rented rooms in the flat of another family. Paul's mom worked as a nurse; being trained abroad in Moscow disqualified her for a physician's job in Vienna. Paul's dad contacted the Swedish Lutheran Church for financial support. This church was Paul's first connection with religion outside of school; it provided him with his first notion of organized religious participation. (A Lutheran chapel still functions today at the Seegasse address in Vienna.)

Paul had a close relationship with Pastor Forell's two sons and nephew. Paul found Forell, a Lutheran minister of German origin, warm and lively and a good preacher. Paul earned pocket money as an errand boy for Forell and for Fritz Neumann, a minister who was semi-retired due to not being fully Aryan. Paul was in school in Vienna from

1933 to 1936. At Paul's school, he could feel the anti-Semitic tendencies against all who were not pure Aryan.

Around 1935, Paul's mother moved to Moscow to stay with her two brothers and sister; Felix, Paul's younger brother, soon joined her. His dad moved to Bratislava, Czechoslovakia (an hour by train from Vienna; about half the population was German-speaking), to teach evening classes for adults in writing. His mom disliked Moscow under Stalin, so she eventually joined her lonely husband in Bratislava. Julius and Paul shared one room in Vienna and relied on each other.

Paul's report cards show that his studies in Wiesbaden, Mainz, and Vienna included: Bible, German, French, English, Latin, mathematics, mechanical drawing, history, geography, biology, chemistry, physics, shorthand, drawing, calligraphy, singing (music theory), and physical training.

Letters about boyhood memories in Germany and Austria

In excerpts from many later letters, Paul revealed other aspects of his boyhood and family life. These are arranged in the approximate chronological order of the boyhood experiences to which they refer.

To Dr. Max I. Reich, president of the [International] Hebrew Christian Alliance (probably July 1941):

My mother, doctor of medicine, was born in Czerna Ostrov, Russia, on 30 December 1885. Her father, an Austrian physician who practiced in Russia, and her mother were Hebrew Christians. My mother was brought up in the Lutheran faith and raised us in the same way. My father is also a second generation Hebrew Christian. While in Vienna, my mother attended the services of the Swedish Mission in Seegasse. I myself worked in the office of the same mission for Pastor Forell, then president of the Austrian Hebrew Christian Alliance.

To Jan Evert, 1957 Hope graduate and one of fourteen participants in the first Vienna Summer School of 1956, 14 December 1995:

One important building in Leipzig which does not appear in any guide book is the house on Bosestrasse 4 where I was born. Not even an historic marker! I didn't care for the place too much and told my parents to get on with the trip. I guess we should not insist that our guide take us there. I have seen the place, and think I made the right recommendation seventy-six years ago!

To Dr. Masanao and Kiyoko Kano, 26 May 1985:

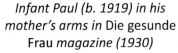

Infant Paul (b. 1919) in his mother's arms in Die gesunde Frau *magazine (1930)*

I must apologize for not getting the article on my mother to you on time. I found a picture which must have been taken some sixty-five years ago in which I was not as completely dressed as a college professor ought to be. [Paul appears clad in a diaper and lovingly held up by his mother's hands in this magazine photo.] It appeared in one of the issues of a short pamphlet which my mother and father were editing in the late 1920s or early 1930s. The magazine was *Die gesunde Frau* (The healthy woman), and the title of the article which it was intended to illustrate was "The Tasks of the Young Mother." Anyway, I had a copy made for you as a possible illustration for your article. I also thought that at age sixty-six, I had better send you a picture in which I am fully dressed. Then I began to feel that I really ought to make some efforts to "dig" at my roots rather than simply to pass on mainly childhood recollections or family lore. Since I am going to Europe for some nine weeks—leaving Holland tomorrow—I plan to spend some time in the newspaper archives in Wiesbaden to see if I can get some source references. I realize that this is mainly to satisfy my feeling that, as an historian, I should be able to cite sources to substantiate recollections.

From Esther M. Snow to her children, 27 August 1961:

We were happy to land at Wiesbaden, the base of the American Air Force in Germany. It is also Paul's former home, and he was stationed there for a time during the war, so he really knows the place. Next, we drove to see Paul's old home. I always feel so sorry for him when anything pertaining to his family comes up, but I think it is good for him to occasionally think out loud. This was really an estate in a very exclusive part of the city and clearly shows what kind of background he has. We then went to a huge country club to which his family belonged, where we had dinner in a huge dining room with music, flowers, and service plus. He had gone to various activities there as a child and seems to remember every detail.

From Margaret (Mrs. Herbert) Mills, 28 June 1945:

Margaret wrote to Paul almost weekly from 1942 to 1983; their combined letters read as diaries of their lives for about four decades. In this letter, Margaret expressed enjoyment in reading about Paul's trip to Wiesbaden and wondered if he had gotten any pictures of the exterior of his previous home. She was deeply moved by the lack of self-pity in his description of his return to Wiesbaden and praised his response "as a beautiful example of complete lack of hatred, bitterness, resentment, or regret over something that could not have been changed."

To Margaret Mills, 5 May 1947:

The first of May, more properly the survival of the pagan spring festival in Europe, has a special significance. We used to have maypoles and special fairs in the country towns. In the last thirty years, the first of May has become a political occasion, both for the Communists and for the Nazis. Both had parades, speeches, flags, and all the trimmings. I remember in 1933, we had to decorate the whole house; we had so much green that we couldn't find any room for flags.

To Marty Costos, Vienna Summer School participant and 1966 Hope graduate, 21 August 1996:

I don't know if I ever told you that way back in the dark ages, I was a student or rather *Schüler* in the *Realschule Schottenbastei* [in Vienna], so I do know the *Umbegung* [neighborhood], even though I do not have happy memories of that period. But I like the *Schottenstift* [monastery] and particularly enjoyed the tour Dr. Spitzmüller gave us this summer.

To Rev. Paul Gerhard Diez, 9 September 1955:

I wore lederhosen myself until I was about fifteen or sixteen. I think they are nice on young people. As with everything, Americans are inclined to go too far. I don't like to see fat old men in shorts.

To Dr. Gerda Ungar, 31 January 1955:

I went to Boyne Falls yesterday. Snow was very good; place was terribly crowded. None of the runs are as long as you would like. The whole thing is little more than that meadow a few steps from the end station (I think it was in Hütteldorf) where we used to go after school by streetcar.

To Margaret Mills, 7 January 1947:

Did I tell you the story about my first ball in Vienna when I took my brother's girl waltzing?

To Margaret Mills, 6 January 1948:

I guess we always expect others to see the full impact of something we had a hard time grasping. I had that experience during this vacation having these two young fellows with me. I wanted to see things, eat strange dishes, and get off the beaten track. They wanted to eat steak and French fries, go to the movies, and read western stories. *Exasperating* is the word I used to myself when we drove through the beautiful French countryside on a sunny day, and they were reading their silly books—once removed from the comics. Then I suddenly remembered a hot summer day in 1937, when my brother Julius and I made a trip to Pressburg [Bratislava], the beautiful Slovak city on the Danube. He wanted to see the cathedral and the castle, while I said that it was too hot and promptly went to a swimming pool where I read my book. I guess if he had known English well enough, he would have told me that I had *exasperated* him.

To Arthur Frederix, 16 April 1967:

Thank you for the most beautiful birthday present. I love the owl! He, named Julius as a tribute to my older brother, now sits on the corner of my desk in the office and is quite the conversation piece. He adds quite a bit of dignity to my plain steel desk.

Letters about the Swedish Mission and Paul's escape from Vienna to Prague

Paul became an administrative assistant at the Swedish Missionary Society in Vienna's Seegasse from autumn 1936 to April 1938. This society was supported by Protestant groups in Sweden to do missionary work and social service in Vienna. Paul's immediate supervisor was Fritz Neumann for two months in the summer of 1937. In preparation for an International Missionary Society conference in Vienna that year, Paul got assigned to help Dr. Conrad Hoffmann Jr., secretary-in-charge of Jewish Work for the Board of National Missions of the Presbyterian Church in New York City. Hoffmann would contact the right people in order to rescue endangered persons engaged in church work. Paul typed a three-hundred-page manuscript for him in English, although he did not know the meaning of most of the words.

Paul did not finish high school due to bad grades and financial difficulties. After his arrest and imprisonment in Vienna, Paul eventually was set free on the condition that he would never return to Austria. How he was actually set free is a bit of a mystery, though Paul often hinted that it involved bribery.

To Rev. Karl and Helen Goldberg, 20 April 1996:

I don't recall the fruit transport from Meidling to Seegasse, but I do have quite a few pleasant recollections of both Meidling and Seegasse. One incident I remember involved a bucket brigade to carry water from some overflow area up to the top of the garden. Rev. Hedenquist was sitting reading the paper when someone (intentionally?) dropped one of the buckets, and he got wet and dashed off to take a bath or shower, not knowing that that particular water was fresh from the tap. Of course, I don't think either you or I were involved in the deed. I also found some pictures which were taken in Meidling, probably in the summer of 1936 or 1937. They were given to me when I visited Vienna in 1948 or 1949 when I was working in Nürnberg. [Karl, a boyhood friend from Vienna, was Paul's guest when he spoke at Ventura Baptist Church on Quincy Street in Holland, Michigan, on 15 July 1979.]

To Margaret Mills, 29 June 1950 (Paul told her about seeing Karl Goldberg, then a married missionary with two daughters in Buffalo, for the first time in twelve years.):

Karl was the last person to see me in Vienna before I left. He had come to the station the morning I was released from prison and had slipped me a purse with some money and tickets to use from the Czech border.

In the notes left by Dr. John Hollenbach from his oral history interviews, Paul said:

Then one of these men took one of the guys, while the other one kept the three of us in place, and then he came back alone. We didn't know whether he might have shot him. They put us close to a border point and said, "Over there is Czechoslovakia; now go, and don't come back!" I was walking across a field on Czech farm land dressed like I'm going to an afternoon tea or something and smelling to high heaven because the Lysol or the disinfectant of the prison will stay in your clothing forever.

To Huntington Terrell, 20 February 1949:

There is a good chance that I may go to Vienna for a couple of days next week to meet my oldest friend—not in years but in time I have known him. Harry Hellmann went to school with me when I was about fourteen. He later went to Czechoslovakia and in Brunn [Brno] in 1938 gave me a room and bath and clean shirt when I came out of jail from Austria. Later he came to England and served in the British Army during the war. He now has his own import-export business in Manchester and will be in Vienna for a couple of weeks.

To Rev. Goete Hedenquist, pastor from the Swedish Mission in Seegasse in Vienna, 28 May 1980:

More significant are my recollections of the summer of 1937, when the Committee on the Christian Approach to the Jews met at Seegasse and I had the challenging experience of working with Conrad Hoffmann for quite a few weeks. I am most grateful for the many friends I made at that time who, directly or indirectly, helped me to make my way to the United States as the only survivor of my family. My thanks to you for your part in arranging to get me out of prison so I could make my way to Czechoslovakia.

To Hilda Cook, English friend, 24 August 1987:

I am particularly excited about spending a few days each in Norway and Sweden, which I have never seen before. The former assistant pastor of our church in Vienna, then in charge of our young people's group but now about eighty, lives in Stockholm. What makes me feel old is his reference to his oldest daughter, now forty-seven, who was not even born when we first met.

To John Anderson, 8 December 1987:

In October, I left for a six-week trip to Europe which included visits to many familiar places but also two firsts: Sweden and Norway. In both places, I saw old friends whom I had not seen since 1938 when I departed from Austria under the condition that I would never return there! When I met Bruno Kreisky in 1957, I told him that perhaps I should not tell him that I had signed that paper. His reply: "Don't worry; I did, too."

To Reinhard Grond, German friend, 4 February 1988:

In Norway, I visited the man who had helped get me out of the Vienna police prison after the *Anschluss*. I had not seen him since. In Sweden, I called on the eighty-year-old former assistant pastor of our church in Vienna.

Paul provided only an outline for Part 1, "Escape from Austria to Flight from Prague," from section two (April 1938 to December 1939) of his autobiographical notes. No date of composition is indicated. It briefly mentions his escape from Austria by walking over the border to Znaim (Znojmo), boarding a bus to Brunn (Brno), finding Harry Hellmann's hotel, meeting his brother Julius accidentally in Prague, and finally reuniting with his family.

CHAPTER 2

Refugee Status in Czechoslovakia and England (1938–39)

Interviews about Paul's life in Czechoslovakia

In-depth conversations between Paul Fried and his friend Chris Spencer in Holland, Michigan, indicated the stress and strain endured by the Fried family and others of Jewish origin during the Nazi era, particularly during their time in Czechoslovakia. Paul described how the family always tried to stay one step ahead of the Gestapo as the noose was tightening. The Nazis were adding new rules almost daily, and each rule demanded strict compliance. Posters were plastered all over cities, towns, and villages on walls, homes, and trees. They were forbidden to listen to a radio or use a telephone or to go to shops until closing time (when almost everything had been bought). Sometimes a storekeeper would hide some food for Paul's mother at the risk of being caught. They were in grave danger if caught in public places, such as parks.

Paul told Chris how the family would travel mostly at night and always be on the lookout for German sentries. They would hug the walls of buildings so as not to create shadows that could be seen from windows. Once when they were staying with some friends, they heard pounding two doors away with the butts of rifles as an entire family was arrested. When Paul's brother Julius disappeared, his father's inquiries at Nazi headquarters alerted officials to his own whereabouts.

Martin Baierl received additional information from interviewing Paul about his days in Czechoslovakia. From June 1938 to January 1939, Paul worked as a clerk and an errand boy for Ok Parfumerie, Narodni trida, Prague. He was introduced to the owner ("a very nice young lady") by some acquaintance. The customers wore rich costumes; they were tired of carrying their purchased items and had these delivered home. Paul was trusted with delivering precious goods. Mostly, housemaids opened the doors and took the goods. He got a small weekly wage and was sometimes tipped by customers. He also taught German and learned more English in Prague.

On one errand for Ok Parfumerie, Paul met Fred Bradley, an Englishman living at the Prague YMCA. A retired businessman, Fred was good company and worked as a freelance reporter for English newspapers with links to Reuters. Paul sifted through German-language newspapers to translate funny stories and strange events for Fred to rewrite in order to amuse his readers. At times, both used their hands and feet to communicate since Paul's English and Fred's German were not very good. Paul ran errands for Fred, and Fred instilled in Paul the desire to learn better English. "I might have been the son he never had," declared Paul.

Later letters about life in Prague

To Fred Bradley, 6 February 1947:

Many a time I have been asked where I learned to speak English and why I don't have as much of an accent as others. Usually, I end up talking about the months in Prague when I was supposed to be reading German papers.

To Margaret Mills, 27 April 1947:

I learned English just so I would not have to speak German any longer.

To Fred Bradley, 6 August 1947:

I hope I will be able to see [on Paul's planned visit to Prague] the last landlady of my parents and find out from her what happened, and if there are any personal effects still in her keeping.

Fred Bradley helped Paul in writing letters and contacting the appropriate religious organization in England to get permission for him to leave the country. Fred intervened with the British consul in

Prague when Paul and his brother Julius applied for visas as agricultural workers in Bolivia. Julius was too skinny to be accepted, but Paul's more bulky physique was considered beneficial. Fred helped Paul use the Bolivia visa as a way to get a visa to the United Kingdom. With help from Fred Bradley and Dr. Conrad Hoffmann Jr., Paul went by plane to London "to prepare my journey to South America." England did not usually take refugees at that time, but persons with visas to other places were admitted.

Paul's move to England without family

The Joint Archives at Hope College has a treasure trove of more than 150 letters in German from Paul's family members in Prague from 1939 to 1941. The letters were sent to Paul at various addresses in England and later in the United States. Most are currently in the first of two gray cardboard containers in box twenty-eight. One frequent Prague address was Prag 2, Klimentska 25, but other return addresses indicate that the family moved around. Most of the letters were addressed to *Lieber* or *Liebster* Pauli with such endearing variations as *Unserer Lieber Sonnenschein* Pauli; *Unser allerliebster* sunny-boy!; *Mein heissgelietes Kind!; Mein lieber, guter Junge;* and *Mein lieber, ernster Studiosus* Pauli. The second cardboard container in box twenty-eight includes numerous photographs and postcards, including a piece of "Prisoner of War Mail" (examined by Censor 62) from civilian internee Gerhard Muller, Camp "L," Internment Operations, Canada, who asked Paul for an affidavit and money and told him that he felt very alone.

A few letters (one dated 4 April 1941) from his parents are on formal stationery labeled:

MUDr. Emilie Friedova//em. Ordinatorka//moskevske univer- sity zenske kliniky
PhDr. Pavel Fried//redactor a spisovatel//PRAHA II. Klimentska 25

Numerous letters have been opened and inspected by Examiner #1608. Other letters have been examined by those numbered 3285, 5540, 378, 6841, 4999, 7150, 5895, and so on. The last letters from September and October 1941 were sent to Paul when he was attending Hope College; they arrived just before his parents and younger brother were deported to the Lodz ghetto in Poland.

From January to December 1939, Paul worked for the British Society for the Propagation of the Gospel among the Jews, in London, as an interpreter and administrative assistant for European refugees (especially picking up refugees at train stations and placing needy children from German-Jewish homes into Christian families). Paul moved about on bicycle and streetcar, got to know England well, and became fluent in English. Dr. Conrad Hoffmann Jr. recommended Paul to the Cleveland Hebrew Christian missionary group and helped him get an immigration visa.

From the Under Secretary of State, Home Office (Aliens Department), 7 September 1939:

The Under Secretary of State is directed to inform the British Society for the Propagation of the Gospel among the Jews with reference to their letter of the 4th instant regarding Mr. Paul Fried that the Secretary of State does not desire to raise objection to his remaining in the United Kingdom till 31st March 1940. This communication must be shown at once to the police registration officer of the registration district in which the holder is resident.

A document dated 20 November 1939, from the Metropolitan Police on Caledonian Road, asked Paul to appear at the Hornsey Road L.C.C. Schools on Thursday, 23 November 1939:

Tribunals have been appointed to examine the position of all Germans and Austrians over the age of sixteen in this country and to consider which of them can properly be exempted from internment and which of those exempted from internment can be exempted also from the special restrictions which are imposed by the Aliens Order on enemy aliens, i.e., the restrictions on travelling without a travel permit, on change of residence without the permission of the police, and on the possession without a police permit of certain articles, including motor cars, cameras, etc.

Jewish Missionary Herald article on Paul

The following article, probably written by Rev. Arthur G. Parry, general secretary of the British Society for the Propagation of the Gospel among the Jews and Paul's immediate supervisor in England, appeared in the *Jewish Missionary Herald*, January 1940.

The New Year finds some of our refugee friends making a fresh start in life, and may 1940 be much brighter for them than 1939 proved to be.

It will be remembered that Mr. Exley and I visited Vienna two-and-a-half years ago and spent a week there with colleagues in the good work of preaching the Gospel "to the Jew first." The visit proved to be one of those journeys planned of God for the purpose of bringing two lives into touch with each other. In Vienna I crossed the path of a young lad whose initials are P. F., and he crossed with mine. We met once or twice in the Swedish Mission in Seegasse and on each occasion struggled for a little while to understand one another. When the day came for Mr. Exley and me to return to England, I was on the way to Vienna West Station, when P. F. met me once again, and we had just a few minutes' chat together in the street. I learned then that, like so many thousands of others, P. F. was separated from those whom he loved the most, and, like his parents and his brothers, wanderers in one country and another, he was a refugee in Austria as it was then. He had no home, therefore, and of course no work; his prospects were of the poorest. Apart from the devoted workers of the Swedish Mission, I suppose I can safely say he had no friends. I shall never forget our conversation in the street, though I shall not write concerning the tenderness and intimacy of that talk. When at length I said good-bye to him, I was sure in my own heart that God would enable me to help him. But a week or so ago, he referred to that never-to-be-forgotten chat in the street of Vienna and told me that as he turned from me to resume his way that noon-day, he was convinced that he had said farewell to the man whom God would use to bring him to his desired haven. Neither of us was mistaken. Step by step, the Lord led him and led me, and finally, twelve months since, I had the joy of meeting P. F. at Croydon airport. He has remained with us for the twelve months. As a member of our Home, and as a helper in the office, he has proved himself to be one of the finest Christians it has been our privilege to meet. He has, therefore, gained for himself our deepest esteem and indeed won our love. We cannot speak too highly of our P. F. Just a week ago, we said good-bye to him once again, for he has gone to Cleveland, Ohio, to become a member of the staff of Cleveland Hebrew Mission. Three or four times our colleagues in that mission wrote me concerning P. F., and at length he felt constrained to accept the invitation which they gave him to enter their mission. He has gone forth, therefore, to make a new beginning at the beginning of the New Year, and I am sure that not only shall we follow him in our prayers, but you, dear readers, will do the same.

Paul came to the United States through the intervention of Rev. Frederick C. Imhof, the superintendent of Cleveland Hebrew Mission. Paul provided only an outline for part two, "England to USA," of section two (April 1938 to December 1939) in his autobiographical notes. In the outline, he mentions his attempts to rescue his family members, the homes of Rev. Arthur Parry and Mrs. Edith Lambotte, blackouts, gasmasks, ditches in Hyde Park, and his miraculous affidavit to come to the United States.

Paul in England, 1939
(Mindel and Faraday, London)

Later letters about life in England

To Hilda Kloucek, 4 August 1994:

I still have a fairly clear memory of all the complications of getting Kenneth and his brother out and Rev. Parry's willingness to pick up his hat and umbrella and take off for Germany, if that seemed the only way to get something done. In any case, I have had a couple of days to recall my very busy but also pleasant experiences in the ten or eleven months I spent in England in 1939 and the wonderful friendships I made there during that time.

To Edith Lambotte ["My beloved English mother" was Paul's salutation to her in most of his letters; she addressed him as "My dearest Paul" or "Paul, Beloved Son" or "My Darling Paul." She was the widow of a missionary to the Congo and more or less in charge of the place where Paul lived in London.], 6 May 1946:

The regulations on the mailing of packages have changed, so that now I can send eleven pounds. I should like to get something special for your birthday. I wonder if you could send me the measurements for a nice summer dress, or if you would rather have me send some material so you can have something made in British style.

To Edith Lambotte, 13 August 1947:

I hope you will accept the enclosed little birthday gift as a token of my love. I am not sure about the pattern, but it was the only real silk I could get.

To Edith Lambotte, 19 November 1949:

I would very much like to come and fix your garden wall. I imagine the leaves need raking.

To Edith Lambotte, 1 July 1951:

I am still looking forward to a leave starting about September 1st and would love to have you for company on it. The trip to England in the summer fell into the channel (to use a German idiom).

From Gerhard Muller, writing to Paul about the death of Mrs. Lambotte a week earlier, 1 May 1974:

She loved you and me like sons. There was not a single occasion when she did not talk about you with love and affection.

To Gerhard Muller, 25 June 1974:

I think the best way we have of showing our gratitude to Mrs. Lambotte is to try, in some small way, to pass on some of her interest and concern for others.

To Frank Exley, in regard to Rev. Arthur G. Parry's death from a very malignant form of cancer, 2 January 1950:

Mr. Parry's death was not unexpected, and for some time I have been wondering whether there should not be some way of providing a memorial to him. I had thought of a number of things: a memorial fund to help Jewish or Hebrew Christian boys or DP children; a material remembrance, such as a plaque; or perhaps only an article in the *Magazine*. I feel that I, who, but for the grace of God and the kind hand of Mr. Parry, might well have perished in an extermination camp together with my family, do have a debt of gratitude which I would like to express in some form. The obvious answer came to me only after much futile thought. I am an historian. Why not a biography of Arthur Parry? No doubt, stories of missionaries and clergymen are plentiful, yet this is the talent I have, and perhaps his life would provide interesting material for a serious historical study of his time and of the work he was trying to do. [In a letter dated 23 January 1950, Exley described to Paul the decision to raise funds for a Parry Memorial House.]

CHAPTER 3

Work for Cleveland Hebrew Mission (1939–40)

Paul traveled to New York by the steamer *Veendam* with money from Dr. Conrad Hoffmann Jr., a bicycle, and almost no other possessions. Hoffmann picked him up and let him stay at his home. In Cleveland, Paul saved money in an attempt to get his family to the United States, and he applied for US citizenship. Paul was very grateful to the Cleveland Hebrew Mission for accepting him and thus securing his entrance into the United States. Later, he had serious questions about the organization's effectiveness and learned that a missionary life was not for him.

"An Urgent Need: Help a Hebrew Christian Refugee"

This undated and anonymous article headlined "An Urgent Need: Help a Hebrew Christian Refugee" probably appeared in 1939 in a magazine entitled the *Trumpeter for Israel*.

In November of 1937, we were urged to have come to this country a young Viennese refugee who was then temporarily employed by the Swedish Jewish Mission. The young man was highly recommended by the

29

Immigrant Identification Card to enter the United States,
22 December 1939

secretary of the International Mission Council who had met him in Vienna a number of times and became much interested in him.

As a result of the absorption of Austria by Germany, this young Hebrew Christian was arrested and thrown into prison. Through the help of friends, he was able to get to Czechoslovakia and finally was brought to London by the British Society for the Propagation of the Gospel among the Jews. By very reliable sources, this young man is brought to our attention again and highly recommended as a missionary. At present he is on a temporary (six-month) transit visa in England, which will expire soon. Because of the emergency, and the fact that we need a Jewish young man to work among the thousand refugees already here in Cleveland, we are appealing to our friends and prayer helpers to assist us financially in this effort to bring him to our city. We are now negotiating with immigration authorities for his entrance to this country. By aiding this young man, we will be helping a worthy and desirable refugee and also promoting the cause of missions among the Jews.

Letters about emigration from England to the United States

To Rev. Fred Imhof, 29 June 1939:

Thank you for all the efforts you have made in order to get me to the United States. I hope it is now only a matter of a short time before I have all the papers ready. I want to say how glad I am that you are willing to take me on the staff of your mission. After all I have heard from Dr.

Conrad Hoffmann about Cleveland and especially about you and your work, I am looking forward with much pleasure and hope to my new work.

To Rev. Fred Imhof, 20 November 1939:

Owing to the war, it will be impossible to give you the exact date of arrival or even the name of the ship, but Mr. Parry will send you a wire as soon as I leave. As soon as I get to New York, I will send you a wire or phone you. I will also call at Dr. Hoffmann's office in case you want to leave a message for me there.

To Han W. Hünd, 18 March 1940:

I feel almost ashamed for not having written to you before. My only excuse is that I have been overwhelmed with work from my very first day in this country. I left England some ten days later than I was supposed to, and after a rather stormy and cold crossing, I arrived here just before Christmas.

To Helen Kirkwood, 15 May 1940:

Thank you for your kind wishes in regard to my work here. I hope to be able to help others here, although I am not so sure whether I will stay in this work as the conditions are not very satisfactory.

Upper Holloway Messenger article about Paul

This anonymous article about Paul appeared in the *Upper Holloway Messenger*, 21 April 1940.

Cleveland, Ohio, is now the home of our friend, Paul Fried, who is working for Cleveland Hebrew Mission, and he sends us a most interesting account of his surroundings, colleagues, and activities: "Cleveland is among the largest cities in the States, with more than a million inhabitants. It is a beautiful city with wide avenues and many parks. There are four broadcasting stations in the city, so one can always have just the program one wants! The remarkable—and I think unique—thing about our congregation is that it consists of seventeen different nations. Germans, Englishmen, Frenchmen, Italians, Russians, Poles, Swedes, Czechs, Irish, Swiss, Hungarians, and even Negroes come to our meetings, not to forget the Jews." Paul also sent us a copy of the mission magazine, *The Trumpeter for Israel*—like most American literature an excellent piece of work. It contains a photograph of Paul, with a short account of his experiences under the *Anschluss*, his conversion, and his stay in London, together with a message from Paul to the readers of *The Trumpeter*. We shall follow his work with prayerful sympathy and interest, remembering the good times some of us had with him while he was in Holloway.

Cleveland Hebrew Mission

From December 1939 to September 1940, Paul served at Cleveland Hebrew Mission as a missionary student in refugee and relief work. He spoke in churches in Ohio, Michigan, New York, Pennsylvania, and West Virginia. Lida Imhof directed many of his speaking activities. Paul received a card accepting him into full membership of the Hebrew Christian Alliance of America on 1 June 1943.

On 23 December 1949, Paul wrote these early pages of section three (December 1939 to December 1944) in his autobiographical notes.

Ten years ago tonight, I arrived in Cleveland, after just one short stop in New York where I had briefly stopped to see Dr. Hoffmann in his office. At that time, he was the only man on the whole continent of America whom I had known in Europe. He had arranged for my transportation and secured a position for me with Cleveland Hebrew Mission as a junior missionary or student. Arriving in Cleveland, I was met by Rev. Howard Kramer, who cordially welcomed me and drove me out to the mission. There I met Mr. Imhof, the superintendent, his wife (a comfortable German American housewife), his daughter Lida, and two sons, Ezra and Erwin. I also met the mission staff and the Harwoods, who were to become "my step-parents" Hulda and Florence.

My room was ready on the top floor of the mission and next to the Harwood apartment where I was to have my meals. The room was nice and large, though impersonal, but had the advantage of a private bath. Lida found an old radio for me and did several nice things to make me a bit more comfortable as time went on. Of course, a day or two before Christmas, there was a continuous round of activities (Sunday school plays, etc.), and I had my first two or three dreadful experiences giving "testimonies" to the mission assembly. But there was compensation in that the people were all very nice and friendly and sympathetic. From that first Christmas, I remember quite a number of families, though most of them I got to know only later on.

Christmas day I was invited to dinner with the Imhof family. I never saw so much food; we ate in the basement. There were the wives (Marion and Violet) of the two boys and three grandchildren (Jackie and Henry and Roberta). Also present was Erwin Gerhard, the rich but damned nephew. I think I found more enjoyment in the company of the two boys, Jackie and Henry, than in the company of the adults. Still, of the tribe, aside from Lida (whom I got to know a great deal better later on), Erwin seemed the most pleasant and sane—the all-American ex-football player with a crooked but pleasant grin who plays with his children as a boy among boys.

I ended up with quite a number of minor presents, mostly last-minute but pleasant all the same. That and the continued round of Christmas and New Year's activity helped make me feel at home, or at least less strange during my first week in the States. Very nice were the Kramers, who were living in a small apartment not far away. There was quite a group of fellows but mostly too much concerned with appearing very religious. I found the constant emphasis on salvation and conversion quite embarrassing, probably because I felt I should have to point to some specific experience by day and hour. I compromised by referring to the summer of 1937, when I really had a very great interest in specific religious questions, some of them emotional.

After New Year's, the life at the mission settled down, and I began to feel the routine of things. First, I found out not to take too seriously promises made. Mr. Imhof had said something about getting me a suit, but he never did; nor was there ever any talk of a salary. First payday I got $2 for two weeks' pocket money, I guess. Lida added something once in a while from her meager pay of $25 a week, and even poor Florence, who was keeping her old mother, slipped me a dollar now and then. But all in all, I think I just had enough for streetcar and postage the first two weeks or even months. Oh, yes, and for the collections in church.

The work, which I had never really seriously thought about when I was still in England, turned out to be mostly house-to-house calling, mostly with Henry, but now and then (and those were the better days) with Howard Kramer. There were a few refugees about, and by asking for other names—I was very eager to prove my worth then—we soon found quite a number, some of whom began to come to the mission. But Mr. Imhof was really not the man for them. He was too concerned about the congregation, about proper evangelism, and too German. Being a simple man himself, he could not see any way except coming right to the point very crudely. After one or two experiences, I began to invite people to [visit] the Kramers, and before very long he kept having a house full on the North Side. Those evenings at his home became a real pleasure. I guess what I had in mind mostly was the spirit of Forell and the Seegasse in Vienna.

Before many weeks had passed, Mr. Imhof started to take me out to show me off and have me give little speeches to young people's groups and later to the churches. At first I was afraid, but when I saw how people responded to a change from the standard service, I began to enjoy it.

*Working for the Hebrew Christian
Mission in Cleveland, 1940*

Also, of course, it meant relief from the routine of sweeping the stairs and cleaning the auditorium and calling on people, wondering how long the day would take to pass. Besides, when we were on the road, Mr. Imhof was always at his best—the genial old gentleman who could be very kind and entertaining. In the early months of our travels, I thought much of his sermons. They were good, but soon I had heard most of them.

On 11 January 1950, Paul continued writing about his Cleveland experiences in section three of his autobiographical notes.

At first I spoke only at small gatherings, Sunday schools, and young people's groups, but by and by, I was given more than a few minutes in the main service. I remember one Sunday in Wheeling, West Virginia, when Mr. Imhof was suffering from a gall bladder attack, and I had to carry the whole afternoon meeting. Mr. Smelzer was the pastor, and we got along fine. The church had a slanting auditorium, and I stood in front of the first row speaking uphill, but it came off. On another occasion, we drove to Buffalo in bitter cold to meetings at the church of Rev. Beacon, who had announced my coming in great letters. Imhof spoke for hours, making everyone restless. When he finally sat down, I got up and spoke for another twenty minutes. But I was mad. I think the old man was getting envious and did not like the fact that Beacon had asked his people to come and hear me speak.

The trips I enjoyed best were with Lida and Hulda. Once we went through quite a number of towns in Pennsylvania, spending some seven days on the road. We spent a couple of days in cabins at Cook Forest. A real rest, and I think that is one time I might have gotten close to Lida, had I wanted to or known how. This was where I started praising Kramer's work on the East Side and got my first contribution for the refugee fund. The other long trip was up into Michigan, and this was lots of fun. One little country church was on a crossroad with moonlight and a warm spring evening and a swing outside. Later we went to Grand Rapids and then to Holland where we stayed with the Beerthuises. I don't think I even saw anything of Hope College then, but a lot of people apparently remembered me when I came back a few months later.

Kramer's work on the East Side was wonderful. I tried to tell him something of the Seegasse work and had gone out to locate a few refugees, but the credit really was his. He combined a rational outlook on life with the compassion of a Jew and the faith of a true convert. His sermons and Bible classes always showed his real soul was in the work in Cleveland—not like Imhof, who preached his best sermons on deputation trips. A few of the families—the Bergmanns, Steins, Sophers—were contacted by me. Henry also liked it better to work on the East Side.

Meanwhile we were going out to Kidron every time we had a chance and working on the buildings there, painting, hammering, and sweating. The food was good, but the atmosphere that of a concentration camp; a laborer is worth his hire—or should be—even in the mission fields. Still, there is something pleasant about seeing progress in physical work. The camp time could have been very nice, but my position, as so often, was between two chairs. I should have been one of the young people, but was not really, since I was a worker, and I was not in the inner circle of the older counselors either. So, all I can remember is buying a pair of tennis shoes for Freddy Stein with some of the money Mrs. Pulliam had sent.

When we were in Cleveland, the routine became more than dull. In the mornings were the long and tiring workers' meetings and prayers and the harangues by Imhof about the work, the Jews, the people in the church, and mostly, the workers. There was revolution in the air with Mrs. Harwood doing much of the talking and even Lida siding against her father. But in the end, everyone backed out except Kramer, who was left holding the bag. I still remember the morning Mussolini declared war on France—the stab in the back—when Kramer and I were in my room while Imhof was holding a meeting to which neither one of us had been asked. The break came, but I did not go with him, mostly because I still felt I owed the mission something for bringing me over. Also, I was looking for a way out of the whole mess.

I had written Dr. Hoffmann about my problem, and much to my surprise the answer came from John Muilenburg, his secretary. Dr. [Wynand] Wichers, the president of Hope College, had offered me a scholarship. That was the graceful way out. Imhof even gave me ten dollars on the way. I think some of the others did a little more, but on the whole I had less when I arrived in Holland than when I had arrived in Cleveland with $100.

There were, of course, many pleasant experiences to look back on. I had learned a good deal, though not as much as I should have. I had done a lot of public speaking of the type which made me highly acceptable in Holland later. I had made friends—Lida, the Kramers, Florence, Hulda, and Charles; all kept writing for quite a number of years, and even Mrs. Stephens sent me some money the first Christmas. But I was really glad to leave and not so sure that I meant what I had said, that I wanted to return to missionary work after further training.

The following letter written by Paul much later dealt with this period in his life:

To Dr. Randy Miller, 1967 Hope graduate teaching at St. Joseph's College, Philadelphia, 25 September 1979:

You write very well in your book, *Germans in America*, and I find myself in agreement with just about everything you say. On a personal level, I am inclined to question your statement (page 11) concerning the "almost universal rejection of Nazism after 1938." When I arrived in the United States in December 1939 as a refugee from Nazi Germany, I was under the sponsorship of a church group in Cleveland run by an elderly German American Independent Baptist pastor who had come to the United States some fifty years earlier. While he and his family all spoke English (though he had a terrible accent) and considered themselves 100 percent patriotic Americans, there was a great deal of feeling that Hitler was doing not only a good thing for Germany but also for Western Christian civilization by standing against communism and the racial corruption of the good white Aryan race. This may have been only an isolated case. I suspect, however, that until Pearl Harbor, this type of feeling—which was partly anti-British, partly anti-Soviet and anti-Semitic, and generally wishful thinking and isolationist—was fairly widespread.

To Matt Nickel, Vienna Summer School participant and 2003 Hope graduate, in an oral interview, 12 March 2003:

I am a refugee. My father was a writer, my mother a medical doctor. They were intellectuals. There was some Jewish heritage somewhere, but I was brought up in the Protestant church. I was Lutheran. I was fortunate. I came to the United States through the church I was attending in Cleveland. I was the sole survivor of my family. I thought I was going to be a missionary.

CHAPTER 4

Hope College Pre-War Studies (1940–42)

This excerpt from "Summary of Background and Experience," written by Paul during his first year teaching at Hope College in 1953-54, summarizes his early semesters there as a student: "In September 1940, I entered Hope College on a tuition scholarship. During my first two years at Hope, I majored in modern languages, with the intention of later teaching German in a college."

"Paul G. Fried at School"

The *Trumpeter for Israel* published the following anonymous piece entitled "Paul G. Fried at School" (no date, but probably October 1940, page 22).

Many of our readers will be interested to know that a scholarship was granted to our Hebrew Christian refugee brother, Paul G. Fried. On account of anti-Semitic activities in Germany and Austria, his regular schooling was interrupted since his fifteenth year. Now that the Lord has laid upon him a clear call to gospel work among his own people, he realizes an education is essential to meeting them on their own ground. Through influential friends in New York City, a four-year scholarship was obtained at Hope College, Holland, Michigan, where about September 15, he took up his studies.

In a letter just received from him, he gives a bit of news which we are passing on, believing it will be of interest particularly to our friends who know him personally.

"In the few weeks I have been here, since leaving Cleveland, I have had opportunity again and again to prove my favorite verse, Romans 8:28. When I reached Holland, I hadn't the least idea where I would stay or where I could find work. In less than three days, upon application at an employment agency, I was recommended to a furniture factory for a part-time job. After speaking with the manager a few moments, he suddenly asked, 'Are you by chance a refugee?' I answered that I was, and that I was a Jewish Christian. He wanted to know what I meant by a Jewish Christian. My answer was, 'I know that I am saved.' The job was mine! Now I am working in that factory every afternoon. Needless to say the Lord also undertook for a place to stay. The pleasant and surprising part about that is that among the first fellows whom I met at the school was a refugee [Paul Gottwald]. He had arrived just a few hours before and was feeling about as strange as I was. After exchanging a few words, I found he had come from Vienna, Austria, and lived a short distance from where I had stayed when there, and as conversation went on, we even located mutual friends. This fellow is now my roommate.

"The pastor of Immanuel Church, Rev. [C. M.] Beerthuis, welcomed us to his church and home the very first Sunday. We appreciated their solicitation and hospitality and shall make this our church home.

"Yesterday I received my green cap and tie, which all freshmen must wear till Thanksgiving. It also includes a deep bow for every upper classman or girl, and some other gestures, but it is much fun anyway."

Our prayers will follow Paul, and we trust he will be remembered by the many friends he has already made through the work here to the end that he might "be prepared unto every good work."

Early days at Hope College

On 22 January 1950, Paul expanded section three of his autobiographical notes with observations on his life at Hope College.

When I arrived in Holland, about a week before school began, I had fifteen dollars in cash, and still fifty dollars in cheques which Mr. Parry had given me when I left England. I also had a four-year scholarship for the tuition and a promise that the college would help me find a job. One of the first people I met was Millie Schuppert; later I met Paul Brouwer and

With first Hope roommate, Paul Gottwald,
also a refugee from Vienna, 1940

Prof. Lampen. The first couple of days I lived as a guest in the Emersonian House, where I also met Paul Gottwald, Bill Moerdyke, and others. My first reaction to Paul was, "I hope we won't be thrown together," but then that was the obvious thing, and we ended up finding a room at Mrs. Dyke's on 14th Street, for which we paid three dollars a week—together. While I was still at the Emersonian House, a reporter from the *Grand Rapids Herald*, Clyde Geerlings, came and interviewed us and took our picture. I think I dominated the scene since I had an idea what would look good in the GR papers. In the center of the picture was a Bible.

Lampen turned out to be very nice but totally unprepared to find anything like a job to pay my way. I had more luck down at the employment agency, where, on the basis of my brief experience as a painter in Prague, I got a job at the Herman Miller furniture factory in Zeeland. The pay was 30 cents an hour. To start with, I went out by bicycle, but later I arranged to ride with Paul Van Eenenaam and come back with one of the workers. After a couple of months, I got a raise to 31½ cents an hour. My average income was $7.00, and I think I generally managed quite well on that. Room was $1.50, and for 25 cents you could get a good lunch at the Tulip; rusk biscuits for breakfast were 30 cents a pound, and milk and eggs were cheap.

My courses were not hard since I was taking five hours of German. English with Paul Brouwer was the best I had that term. History with [Milton] Hinga was dull, and Bible with [Henry] Bast was repetition of *Religionsunterricht* [religious instruction]. Before long Bruce Raymond asked me if I would speak for the Rotary Club. That paid $10.00, and I met

Larry Lamb, who then was president of the Rotary. Also, it got my name in the paper for a change, and soon I had quite a number of speaking engagements. The Lions in Zeeland, a church in Fennville, Wayland Trinity Church, and open houses at the high school, where I spoke three times—and every time Bob Cavanaugh had to sing "Ballad for Americans." I think I earned something like eighty or one hundred dollars that term, just speaking.

The greatest triumph, socially, was to be asked to speak at Hope Church to the adult group just before Christmas. Rev. [Marion] de Velder was very nice and wanted to know what he could do for my family. I wish he had not asked; anyway, nothing came of it, except a very unpleasant feeling for me and that I did not try to find another sponsor. During this period, I also met Michelson, who offered me a job; [Joseph] Hoffman Cohn, who offered to help with my family, maybe; and Kendal, who thought I might do as a part-time missionary in Grand Rapids. Good thing nothing came of that. Oh yes, I remember a trip to GR with the Hope trombone quartet (Johnny Kleis, Gordon Van Wyk, etc.). Kendal's offer gave me a chance to go to Detroit over New Year's with expenses paid (about $13.00, I think).

Christmas Day the Lambs had invited Paul Gottwald and me out to their home—and what a place it was. We went to her parents' [home] for dinner and later to his parents' [home] to bring presents, but the nicest thing was the home on the lake.

Before Christmas, I had given up my job at Herman Miller, and then I found a new one as part-time baker at the Dutch Kitchen. It started out with just a few hours in the afternoon, but soon the shifts changed, and I worked six to eight hours at night. Still, the pay was good, and while I didn't do much studying, I got good marks from Jim Mearns in English and Doc Warner and also from Dr. Schrier in discussion, which I very thoroughly enjoyed. I even considered entering the oratory contest with something on the "Second Mile." We went to a discussion meeting in Ann Arbor and some other place, too. About this time, through Paul [Gottwald], I met Art Barnhart, went sleigh riding one night and to church a few times.

Towards spring, work at the bakery got heavier. Kramer and Lida came up one time while I was working there. Paul and I were thinking of buying a car and going east for vacation. I almost got a big Buick for thirty dollars but nearly wrecked it one night coming back from Saugatuck. Eventually, after Tulip Week, when I had worked some sixty-four hours (besides attending classes), I quit the bakery. The pageant was going on, and I played Leif Ericksen [in *The Pilgrim*, a play written by Dr. Edward

Dimnent to celebrate the 75th anniversary of Hope College]. Clint Harrison as the watchman was great; Dolly Camp and Nola Nies were prettiest. At Easter I had been in Cleveland (had ridden with Jim Mearns and Carolyn Kramer), and Mr. Milner had signed an affidavit for me. So now I was hoping that Sen. [Arthur] Vandenberg might help. Dr. [Wynand] Wichers gave me a letter of introduction, but by the time I got to New York, the war between Russia and Germany had started, and the four hundred dollars I had for transportation was no longer enough. During the two weeks of vacation with Paul in New York, I met his sister Inge and also Gerhart Honig, and the Forells and Deutsches were fun. I tried to hitchhike, but no luck. I went back and spent some time in Cleveland.

When school started again, I got a job working as night clerk at the Netherlands Hotel after a few days with Padnos. But the trouble was, I didn't get much studying done at night, and worse still, I always fell asleep in Prof. Thompson's biology class. Eventually I quit, and Blaise Levai and I took the exam over again. By this time, Art [Barnhart] had married, and the Gaudeamus Club had been initiated with Dvorak's 5th and toasted ham and cheese sandwiches. During the summer, Art and I had played tennis now and then, or batted the ball around, and one time he took me down to Albion to a student conference at which Angus Dunn was speaking. I spent Thanksgiving with Prof. [Thomas] Welmers. Then I started working as a dishwasher at the Mary Jane restaurant, first for two meals a day, later for longer. I think at Christmas, I went to Cleveland again and probably divided my time between the Kramers and Imhofs.

Jim had gone into the Army, and the draft was getting closer. I kept on working at the Mary Jane, as a waiter now, and piled on nineteen hours my second term. At New Year's, Paul and I went out to Peter Hamel's home, and he tried to get me drunk without much success. I worked all summer at Mary Jane, waiting for the draft call. I stayed at the Cosmo house with Paul [Gottwald] and Irv Hellenga and went swimming almost every afternoon. Jimmy Muddle at the restaurant and the girls there were good company. I went swimming with Howard Zandbergen a couple of times. Jeff Wiersum always smiled and passed the time of the day at Penney's corner. On the whole, it was a very pleasant summer. Finally, the draft call came, and Jimmy and Paul and I went down to Kalamazoo, but only Jimmy and I were accepted.

Tom Sanger gave us a fine sendoff with T-bone steaks, etc. I had taken my things to Cleveland and left them with the Kramers, whom I thereafter claimed as my family to notify in case of emergency. During this period, two things ought to be mentioned. In October 1941, I started to get my own letters back from Prague and thus lost hope for getting my family out; the letter with the affidavit came back, and in December came Pearl Harbor. Certainly, when I left Hope, I knew very little of what was ahead and did not even care to look very far. But I was a lot better off than when I had left Cleveland two years before. I could claim two years of college education, and I could read, and I had had all sorts of jobs which had shown me that I could work at anything without degrading myself and could earn as much money as I needed to live on. Also, with the Lambs and the Schriers and the Mullers, I had found myself more or less accepted on an equal social basis in Holland, which in many ways had more or less become my home. Paul Gottwald's graduation was quite an affair and Princess Juliana's visit likewise.

Included in the archival boxes are several examples of Paul's work at Hope College during these years. Paul's handwritten English 313 paper (22 January 1940) was a "Review of Philip Massinger's *A New Way to Pay Old Debts*" [a play published in 1633.] The only comment from his professor on the B+ paper was: "A sane piece of writing—watch your sentence structure." There is a copy of Paul's book report in German on Franz Grillparzer's "*Der Traum, ein Leben*" for his German 305 class (20 January 1941). There are also newspaper reports of Paul's speeches to the YMCA (November 1939) and to the Holland Rotary Club (1940). Paul also kept a journal of expenses (including the price of almost every meal) from 17 September 1940 to 20 August 1941.

CHAPTER 5

Futile Attempts to Rescue Family

For several years, Paul struggled to rescue his parents and brothers, to get them to friendly nations, to locate them after they had disappeared, and to save them from the deaths which they eventually suffered at the hands of the Nazis. Although many of his letters to family members are not preserved, hundreds of Paul's letters to and from organizations and individuals who might be of help (as well as their letters in response) have been saved. What follows is a sampling to reveal the labyrinthine ways in which young Paul struggled to extricate his parents and brothers. These much-abbreviated excerpts indicate not only his efforts from England, Cleveland, Holland (Michigan), and other places, but also the endeavors of others to assist him. A few samples of letters from his parents (translated from the German) and from his brothers (writing to him in English) are also included. On 26 April 1938, Paul's father wrote to Princess Juliana and Prince Bernhard of the Netherlands seeking help, but nothing materialized. The archive folders also contain passport photos for Paul's mom, dad, and younger brother Felix.

Letters on behalf of family (1939)

To Rev. Robert Smith, B.D., Scottish Christian Council for Refugees, Edinburgh, 19 April 1939:

I have been in touch with the Czech Committee this morning, and to my surprise I have learned that visas have been granted for my family a day or so ago. I sincerely hope this news is true. There are one or two points on which I am not quite clear. First of all, has your society given the guarantee for my family? Secondly, will your society be responsible for their traveling expenses? I should also like to know whether you have been able to find a home for them and if they will be living together. My father wrote me a few days ago that he is now entirely without any money or income. He says that you have kindly helped him in Prague, and I am wondering if you could continue this help while he is there. I am most grateful for your efforts on behalf of my family.

To Rev. Robert Smith, 26 April 1939:

I am so sorry to trouble you again, but I am getting rather anxious about my family—now in desperate need of help before they can obtain passports, visas, and permission to leave Germany. As far as I know, it is necessary for them to get their tickets first in order to get permission to leave the country. I want my family to leave Czechoslovakia before the situation worsens, and as you have their case in hand, I should be very glad if you could let me know at your earliest convenience regarding your intentions in the matter.

To Rev. Robert Smith, 11 May 1939:

I am really sorry to trouble you yet again, but I had a letter from my father last night in which he says that he wrote to Miss Wellington, only to hear from her that she has had no information from you concerning the case of Dr. Fried. My family members have gotten their passports and visas, and I think it is only a matter of their having the necessary money for their tickets and for the permission to leave. Could you kindly let me know if you have sent the money?

From Rev. Jacob Peltz, International Hebrew Christian Alliance, 7 June 1939:

I placed your request on behalf of your parents before our committee some time ago, [but] we are not doing anything just now in respect to refugees in Czechoslovakia. I am sorry that we cannot help.

To Rev. Robert Smith, 19 July 1939:

I am sorry to trouble you again, but it is still impossible for Jews or non-Aryans to get permission from the Gestapo to leave Czechoslovakia. In spite of all their efforts, my parents and brothers are still waiting for permission to leave. My younger brother, who will be fourteen in November, had to leave school some time ago; therefore my parents and I are most anxious to get him to England soon, even if it is necessary for him to come alone. My parents have been in touch with the British children's committee in Prague to arrange for the boy to come here with a children's transport. They were told that the committee in Prague is not able to do this without an order from Bloomsbury House. I went there and saw Mr. Winton of the Czech children's committee, who told me that he would be able to put my brother on the list for the next transport, but he has to have a special guarantee. Could you kindly write a letter to Bloomsbury House that your committee has guaranteed for my whole family? I should [also] like to know if you have a home in view for my brother. If not, I would very much like him to be in London until the rest of my family is able to come here. I think I could find a place for him for that period and wondered if you could help cover the cost of his school fees in London.

From Rev. Robert Smith, 24 July 1939:

We have no home in view for your brother, and it is very difficult to make arrangements at this time of year since our hostel is closed and all available homes are taken up. I have already given the guarantee to the Czech committee, but we must consider what plans can be made for your brother's future. At the beginning of September, there might be an opening for him as an agricultural trainee, and he could be brought over by the Society of Friends. We cannot make any arrangements in London, as our council only has authority to place refugees in Scotland. We cannot pay school fees.

To dearly beloved parents, dear brothers, in a letter from Upper Holloway (London), 23 August 1939:

I am in a great hurry; therefore, I ask you to excuse the brevity and form of this letter. Here is my urgent request as an answer to your questions. Please come together, all of you, and by no means via Belgium but rather via the Netherlands. I hope that the matter of the train tickets has been solved favorably and thus merely the various permits are still missing. I hope that you will receive these soon and urge you to plan everything so that you can leave together a few hours after having taken care of the most urgent matters. Get the tickets to Edinburgh since I doubt that my plans concerning Felix and Julius can be put into action at the present time. I will probably be able to arrange that you can stay here a day or two; longer would not be advisable. It will be much nicer when I can visit you later. In any case, I urge you again: Come as soon as possible. Please refrain from any kind of alternate combination. Meanwhile, I will get my second interview with the American consulate on September 2nd, your wedding anniversary, and it looks promising that I will get the visa. If that is the case, I might leave in October. I would be extremely happy if we could celebrate your anniversary here together. I am waiting for you. I am looking forward so much to seeing you, but I am constantly worried that something might happen to prevent it. [trans. Hope Prof. Emerita Gisela Strand]

From Phyllis Binns, British Society for the Propagation of the Gospel among the Jews, 31 July 1939:

Mr. Winton says he will include your brother in the next transport due here at the end of August or beginning of September. We have a note (two lines!) from Mr. Smith saying he will pay the £5, so that is all right.

To Miss Dougan, Czech Committee, Windsor Forest, 19 October 1939:

I am writing to ask for your kind help in the case of my parents and two brothers who are at present in Prague. They may be able to get to Sweden with a transit visa if a proof can be given to the Swedish Home Office that they will leave the country again. Now comes the point where you may be able to help. They already have the visa for the United Kingdom. Rev. Robert Smith has given the guarantee for them on behalf of the Church of Scotland Christian Council. As you may know, it was not possible for anybody to leave Czechoslovakia during the last few months. Now, it seems that the Gestapo is again giving permission to leave for neutral countries. A friend in Stockholm would be willing to apply for my family and to receive them temporarily.

To Rev. Robert Smith, 27 October 1939:

I am very sorry to trouble you again and again, but I am sure you will understand my anxiety about my family, still in danger in Prague. There is some hope that my parents and brothers might be able to get out of Czechoslovakia and find temporary refuge in Sweden. I had several letters from Mr. Neumann, the former secretary (and my boss) of the Swedish Mission in Vienna. He is now working in Stockholm among the refugees. He would be willing to apply and guarantee a transit visa for my people, if sufficient proof can be given that they will be able to re-emigrate, i.e., to get to England. I have obtained my visa for the United States and hope to leave for America in a month or two. Naturally, it would make me very happy if I could see my people before I go, or if I could at least know that they were safe in Sweden.

From Rev. Robert Smith, 30 October 1939:

It would be a different matter if your father lived in a neutral country, but we cannot give any guarantee which would be of any use in obtaining a transit visa. For the duration of the war, this country will be out of the question as a permanent place of refuge, and your father would only be admitted if he had definite emigration prospects.

To Rev. Robert Smith, 1 November 1939:

I quite agree with your suggestion in regard to the United States, but you will perhaps know that at the present time, it seems almost impossible to find someone to give affidavits. Maybe once I am over there, I can get affidavits for my people, but even then it would take more than a year before they could get the visas.

From Rev. Robert Smith, 2 November 1939:

I am enclosing a copy of a letter we have received from the home office. From it you will understand that only in very exceptional circumstances are refugees now admitted to Great Britain. I feel sure that, in the case of your family, the circumstances would not be considered really exceptional, although I fully appreciate your anxiety on your family's behalf.

To Miss Dougan, 6 November 1939:

I have had two letters from Rev. Smith of the Scottish Christian Council for Refugees during the last week. While he doubts whether my efforts to bring my people here will have any success, I understand that in case they are able to get here, he would undertake to maintain them until further immigration is possible. I wonder if you could let me have a letter (addressed to Israelsmissionen, Stockholm 6) stating that the case of Dr. Fried and his family is in your hands and that you have applied to the home office for visas. I am not sure whether that will be enough for the Swedish authorities to grant the transit visa, but it is certainly worthwhile trying.

From Immigration Department, 8 November 1939:

Miss Dougan has passed me your correspondence about your family. I regret that it is not possible in the present circumstances to apply to the home office for permission for your people to come to this country. Immigration into this country during wartime is reduced to an absolute minimum.

From Han W. Hünd, 10 November 1939:

I am now in correspondence with your family in Prague. They tell me their regular British permits are no longer valid on account of the war and ask me to help them. I have been to all the offices over here, and the Dutch authorities are willing to let your father and mother and two brothers into this country if they have: (a) a renewed permit for a stay in England, or (b) an invitation from the British passport office of The Hague to come here and give information. I will go to the passport office again tomorrow with the photos of the old permits [just mailed by Paul's father], and I will write you so that you know how matters stand. I am writing now to set your mind at ease. I know the English well and feel sure that such learned people as your mother and father would be welcomed if only we could bring them to English soil. I am a born Dutchman. I also speak English, French, German, and Swedish. So write in any language you like.

From Han W. Hünd, 12 November 1939:

I have gone to the British passport office at The Hague yesterday and have spoken to the officials there. They regret that they cannot at present be of any help. [Hünd narrated difficulties with the permits and Paul's need to visit the home office in London.] Please explain to the authorities in London that the case is urgent, especially for your brother Julius, whose German exit permit is of shorter duration than those of your father, mother, and younger brother. I also enclose an important document: a letter from the British passport control office at Prague with a recommendation of "Please Admit."

To Han W. Hünd, 14 November 1939:

It is very good news for me to hear from you about the possibility of Dutch transit visas for my people. I do hope that the British home office in Prague will issue the invitation for an interview. I do hope that once we have this invitation, the Dutch authorities would see their way in granting the transit visa immediately. As soon as my family is in Holland, I would apply again for the renewal of the permits, and I feel sure this would be granted. Thank you for the enclosed letters. It is now forbidden for us in Great Britain to write direct letters to enemy countries, even if these letters are going through a neutral country. Since I cannot let you have a letter for my parents, I can only ask you to write to them about me. It will be of great interest to them that it has become necessary for me to leave for America early in December. There is little hope that they will be here by that time, but if they have reached Holland before my boat sails, I might be able to come over and see them for a day or two. May God give His blessing on you and on the steps you are taking.

To Han W. Hünd, 22 November 1939:

I have been doing everything I could to get the permits renewed. I even went to the home office myself. They told me most emphatically that there was no possible hope to get the visas. They could not consider any application for people who are still in enemy territory. I am afraid that, unless you can get the Dutch authorities to grant the visas without the promise of the British home office to take them in, there is nothing else we can do. When you write to my parents, please assure them that I will keep on making every possible effort to help them, but that there is not much hope of early emigration. I have definite hope of sending some money to them soon.

From Han W. Hünd to the British passport control office, in which he explained in detail the Fried family situation, 9 December 1939:

Their stay in Scotland has been paid in advance a full year, and they will not take employment. These people have been working for several years at various hospitals and universities, making a very important study of painless childbirth; they have written a book on this subject which will be published shortly by a London publishing house of importance; it is hoped that they will be able to correct the proofs of their book themselves, and also that they will be given consent by the authorities to lecture upon painless childbirth for the medical societies in England (without payment, of course). I believe these people, if allowed to come to England [with their two student sons] will shortly leave again for the United States, where very soon their other son will arrive to take matters up with the US authorities.

Letters on behalf of family (1940)

From Julius Fried, a letter written in English from Prague to Paul in Cleveland, 5 February 1940:

My dear brother, you can't imagine how very sorry we are to have no news at all from you, except your Christmas wire, which we were awfully pleased to receive. Certainly you have written meanwhile, but unfortunately not a single letter reached us up to now. Every day we are waiting for the postman and for greetings from you, and every time we have to comfort each other for the next day. We wrote twice to you, on January 2nd and 16th, both times registered and by airmail, but we are also not sure whether you got our letters or not. Most communications are going enormously slowly now. Only a few days ago, acquaintances of mine got letters from the United States dated October 27th.

We are getting on quite well; the main thing is that all of us are healthy and satisfied and happy, as far as it is possible in the present situation. Surely, you will be glad to hear that mother is looking very well lately; she got some work, but certainly she will write about that herself. I have still the same occupation, and I can just manage with my earnings. The most important question at present is to find some possibility to emigrate. I wrote very detailed about that in my last letter, and I do hope it reached you. I am sure you can completely understand my present situation, and you will try hard to do everything in your power for us. I am willing to immigrate to any place you suggest, and therefore I am adding three photos in case you want to fill out some forms or an application on my behalf. I also inform you about the number of my new passport: *Fremdenpass* Nr. 5911, issued by the *Oberlandrat/Passstelle* in Prague, on Dec. 14th, 1939, and good until Dec. 13th, 1940. I hope you remember all the other details about my person.

We enclose another photograph, which surely you will be much pleased to see. It was a birthday present for mother. Mr. Schneider, your friend, was very ill and operated on—something wrong with his kidneys. Now he is in one of the best Prague sanatoriums to brace up. There is nothing else I could tell you today, apart from every good wish for all your future in your new home. I would like very much to learn how you are living now. Please be sure of my deepest and sincerest feelings for you. Kindest regards.

From Julius Fried, an Easter and birthday post card also signed by "friend Walter" and "your loving mother," 14 March 1940:

Once more I am writing to you without knowing whether you'll get these lines or not. It is such a nuisance being without any news from you, and it would be a very great joy for all of us getting a letter from Cleveland. So please excuse if this is only a very short card. We are quite healthy and hope you are as well as we are. Today I do not want anything but to wish you a merry Easter time and many happy returns on your birthday.

To Helen Kirkwood, Centre Quaker International de Paris, 18 March 1940:

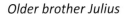

Older brother Julius

Another thing, which naturally is much more important to me, is the emigration of my parents and brothers, who are still in Prague. I have had a number of letters since I arrived here in Cleveland, and every one took almost forty days! Sent by air mail! All their thoughts and desires are to get out as soon as possible. The best thing would be if they could come to the United States. I was wondering whether you had any connection to the American Quakers and if they could in some way assist me or rather my people to secure an affidavit and the visas. Do you have a representative in Prague? If my people could get into Switzerland, Holland, Belgium, or some other neutral territory, they would be free to apply to the British Home Office again.

To Han W. Hünd, 18 March 1940:

Up to now, although I have received several letters from Prague, I have no idea whether my letters have reached Prague. I have not had any answer, and my people ask me every time to write to them. Would you write to them and give what little news you have about me and the assurance that I am doing everything in my power to secure affidavits for them?

From Rev. Dr. F. Neumann, postcard from Haifa, Palestine, 20 March 1940:

We are happy to learn that you have already crossed the Atlantic and are now at your place of work. May God bless you personally and your work. I often remember you. Have you been with my relatives? How are your parents and brothers? Are there any prospects for them? We are here for the Easter Hebrew Christian Conference.

To Helen Kirkwood, 15 May 1940:

I have had two letters from Prague in the last few weeks. Can you remember my older brother? He has been arrested and put in prison. Although my parents naturally cannot write very clearly, it seems that my brother was trying to escape over the Hungarian border and was arrested there on Easter Monday. I have finally received the promise from friends to sign the affidavits for my whole family. My plan—if Sweden should remain neutral—is to get them to England via Sweden.

To Tatiana Schaufuss, The American Committee for Christian Refugees Inc., 8 July 1940:

I am writing to ask you for your kind advice and help in the case of my father, mother, and two brothers who are at present in Bohemia. Their position in Prague is truly a very desperate one. They have already fled twice from Hitler—in 1933 from Germany (our original home) to Austria and later from Austria, too. My older brother has been in prison since Easter and has now been moved into a concentration camp. My younger brother has no possibility of any training or even work. My father is a writer and journalist, probably not unknown to Dr. Thomas Mann, the honorary chairman of your committee. My mother is a lady doctor with more than twenty-five years of experience. My mother (and possibly with her, my younger brother) needs only an affidavit as she is of Russian birth and has an open quota. After receipt of the papers, she would be able to leave Prague and travel by way of Russia. My father and older brother would fall under the German quota and might have to wait some time since they registered only in 1939. As you may imagine, my concern for them is just the same as for the others. My father has been told that if my brother would have a visa and a place to go, he might be released. Once my parents reach this country, they would be able to earn whatever they need for their living and would not depend on any help from your committee.

From Estelle Rank, The American Committee for Christian Refugees Inc., in acknowledgment of Paul's 8 July 1940 letter to Tatiana Schaufuss, 10 July 1940:

Your mother having been born in Russia would come under the Russian quota, which would mean a waiting period of one year. Your father, as well as your brothers, having been born in Germany, would come under the German quota, which means a very long waiting period.

Their only chance would be to wait their time in another country. China requires a landing fee of $400 per person plus transportation if they have no one there to support them. Ecuador requires a landing fee of $1000 per person with $200 additional for each successive year. We are enclosing four affidavit blanks plus an instruction sheet for your convenience; we shall be glad to forward these for you through safe channels once you have found someone to sign [them]. Please be assured of our interest in your case, and do not hesitate to call on us if there is anything else we can do for you.

To Estelle Rank, 15 July 1940:

My parents, and naturally my brothers, too, are Protestant, though of Jewish extraction. Therefore, the Jewish organizations have excluded them from their relief and emigration actions. My mother would fall under the non-quota regulations because she was a member of the medical faculty at the Moscow State University for three years. Do you think that my younger brother, who is included on my mother's passport, could come with her? Regarding my older brother, I was wondering if it would be possible to get a student visa for him.

From Felix Fried, 22 July 1940:

Dear brother! We were very glad to receive your letter of June 23. You asked for an English letter from me? Well, have it. I hope there will not be too many mistakes, and you will be satisfied. I have now finished my chemical course and now am helping a bit. To attend a school, I am sorry, is impossible now. But I hope that, if we were with you, I should be able to make it up. Julius is not with us, and we are sorry about that. Father tries to do all that is possible to get Julius here, and maybe it will be soon. Now it is very hot here, but there's no possibility to visit watering places, and you know that especially I'm not liking to swim. Bathing establishments we often visit, too. The portrait you sent was very nice and delighted us very much. We, too, wished to send you some pictures, but it's now not allowed. Therefore, you don't get any photographs. But you may know that we are still the same, and there's nothing changed. If you have a photograph of your bicycle, send it please. Next time, I shall, to be sure, write you much more. Many kisses from your brother.

From Amalia I. Atkinson, The American Committee for Christian Refugees Inc., 24 July 1940:

Mrs. Rank has referred me to your letter of July 15, in which you kindly give us the information which she requested. With regard to the affidavits of support, we wish to assure you of our willingness to assist if possible. It is, however, becoming increasingly difficult to obtain affidavits from strangers, and at the moment we have no possibility. We have hundreds of requests for the same kind of help, which is, alas, not forthcoming. Your mother could immigrate on the Russian quota in about a year. Your younger brother could accompany her if she obtained a visa. In order to immigrate on a non-quota visa, it would be necessary for her to obtain a professorship in a recognized college or university in the United States, with an adequate stipend for her support. Your father and older brother would be required to wait several years before they could obtain an immigration visa under the German quota. Student visas are no longer being issued, except in extraordinary circumstances. It would seem advisable that they go to Ecuador, Shanghai, or some Central American republic to wait until their quota number is due. There is not much we can do under the present restrictions.

Margaret Sanger letters (1940-41)

To Margaret Sanger, American birth control activist, 29 July 1940:

I am writing to you on behalf of my mother, Dr. Emilie Grünhaut-Fried, formerly of Wiesbaden, Germany, to ask your kind advice and—if at all possible—your help for her. I trust you will remember hosting her on different occasions, as in our home in Wiesbaden, at Congress meetings in Vienna, Zurich, London, and other places. At least, I am under the impression that there was a professional and personal friendship between my mother and you.

Now to my problem. I am the only one of our family who has succeeded in getting to this country. My father, Dr. Paul Fried, my mother, and my two brothers are still in Prague, Bohemia, under German rule, after first fleeing into Austria and then into Czechoslovakia. During the few months I have been in the United States now, I have made every possible effort to help my people out of their desperate condition and to make it possible for them to come to this country.

Unfortunately, I have not been able to find anyone willing to take the responsibility of signing affidavits for my family or at least for my mother and younger brother. You may remember that my mother is of Russian birth and as she registered more than a year ago with the American consul in Prague, she would not have to wait through for her quota number. At present, there would still be the way open for her to reach this country by way of Russia and China.

Another way to come to America as a non-quota immigrant would be open for my mother, a member of the medical faculty at the Moscow

University for three years (1935 to 1938). For her to be admitted under a non-quota visa, it would be necessary for her to obtain professorship in a recognized college or university here, with an adequate stipend for her support.

I do realize that it is quite an extraordinary request I am bringing before you, but I know, too, that you will quite understand my anxiety about my family, especially my mother and my younger brother. I am not enclosing any specified dates about them, as I do not want to burden you with material before I know whether you would be able and willing to help in some way. I would indeed be grateful if that were the case.

From Florence Rose, secretary to Mrs. Sanger, 6 August 1940:

She informed Paul that his letter had arrived when Mrs. Sanger was out of the city for a few weeks. She told him that Mrs. Sanger had already given so many affidavits that it was doubtful that she could provide another, even though she would want to be of assistance, because immigration officials were scrutinizing requests more carefully. She indicated that Paul's letter would await Mrs. Sanger's return, that he had sympathy from both of them, and that she regretted her inability to be more encouraging.

From Margaret Sanger, 15 August 1940:

She told Paul how difficult it would be for her to give any more affidavits. She was now obliged to send in tax receipts and a list of securities to show that there was enough income to guarantee each affidavit. She outlined problems with two recent affidavits sent to Genoa and lamented that she had probably exceeded her quota despite her willingness to save lives. If the Genoa affidavits were accepted, she promised to try to help Paul's mother, but she would not know until late September or early October if that was even remotely possible. She invited Paul to write her again at that time if he had not found someone else able to take the responsibility.

To Margaret Sanger, 29 September 1940:

Making use of your kind permission, I am writing again, hoping that you have had favorable news from your friends in Genoa. In the meantime, I am very grateful for your willingness to help my mother. I don't think I need to assure you that I have done everything in my power to secure help for my mother and brother, but so far with practically no result.

I myself have moved from Cleveland and am now attending Hope College in Holland, where I have been given a scholarship. Naturally it will be even more difficult for me to find someone who will sign affidavits here in Holland, as I am a complete stranger in the city.

My concern for my loved ones is now greater than ever, as you may imagine. What a joy it would be for me to see at least my mother again. I do hope you will be able to help her, even if you should not be able to make out the affidavit yourself.

From Florence Rose, 15 October 1940:

She acknowledged that Mrs. Sanger had read Paul's letter just before leaving on a lecture tour of Massachusetts. Because of an emergency involving a friend abroad, Mrs. Sanger indicated that it was impossible for her to sign another affidavit. Both women promised to be on the outlook for someone else to supply an affidavit, but this letter offered little hope of success.

To Margaret Sanger, 15 May 1941:

You may remember our correspondence concerning an affidavit for my mother, during the fall last year. In the meantime, I have succeeded in securing the necessary guarantee and hope to send the papers to Prague shortly.

After the interest and willingness you have shown in helping my mother, I am wondering if I may ask you to write a letter, addressed to the American consul in Prague, assuring him that—in your opinion—my mother is worthy of his consideration and that she will be an asset to the medical profession in this country (provided, of course, that you are of that opinion).

For the sake of correctness, let me repeat that my mother, Dr. Emilie Grünhaut-Fried, was a delegate to the Congress of the World League for Sexual Reform in London as well as guest at congresses in Paris, Zurich, and Vienna. The book *Liebes und Eheleben*—published by both my parents—received considerable attention in Germany and outside.

I would be grateful if you could write such a letter and am certain that it will be of help to her in securing the affidavit at the earliest possible moment. Will you send the letter, in duplicate, to me so I can enclose it with the other documents? Thanking you heartily in anticipation. [Ultimately, Mrs. Sanger was unable to help.]

Letters connected with Hope Church (1940-41)

To Dr. Joseph Hoffman Cohn, American Board of Missions to the Jews Inc., Brooklyn, 2 December 1940:

On your visit here in Holland, you advised me to find someone to guarantee for my mother and brother and that your organization would take over all responsibility for expenses which might arise. One of my friends here has shown some willingness to help if he had such a guarantee. It would speed up matters if you could write me, stating just this point. I am sure that you understand my anxiety for my loved ones and will do all you can to help me save them.

From Dr. Joseph Hoffman Cohn, 4 December 1940:

Yes, we will be glad to furnish a guarantee to the one who will sign the affidavit of support for your mother. We will assume responsibility for the financial support of your mother after she gets here and will agree with the signer of the affidavit that he will in no way be troubled in the matter in the future.

To Rev. Marion de Velder, Hope Church, Holland, Michigan, from John Muilenburg, Board of Domestic Missions of the Reformed Church in America, 4 December 1940:

This morning I received a letter from Paul Brouwer inquiring about Paul Fried. It seems there has been a bit of suspicion of him [Fried] due to several things which from his [Brouwer's] point of view are quite inexplicable. Enclosed is a statement from Dr. Conrad Hoffmann, whose personal and professional integrity is unimpeachable. Paul is still trying to make satisfactory adjustment. Perhaps there are things about him which are not readily understandable, but the boy is under pressure. His family is still in Europe. He is on the spot in trying to make his way. Many people will judge all refugees by the impression they get of him. He knows this. I do hope that someone can be found who is willing to help the boy and his mother. It will be a fine service to render. I think that you may rely upon the word of Dr. Hoffmann in presenting this to your consistory.

To Prof. Paul J. Brouwer from Dr. Conrad Hoffmann Jr., 4 December 1940:

The Rev. John Muilenburg has referred me to your letter of December 2 regarding Paul Fried. I first met Paul in 1936 in Vienna, and in connection with our important International Missionary Council's Conference in Jewish Missions held in Vienna, July 1937. Paul acted as my office boy and did a really fine piece of work for us in multi-graphing reports, etc., for the conference.

Actually, Paul Fried is citizen-less. His parents are a mixed international couple and in Germany lost their citizenship. In the spring of 1938, when Hitler took possession of Austria, Paul, along with other non-

Aryan refugees who were citizen-less, was rounded up and thrown into prison. There were two counts against Paul: (a) that he was non-Aryan, and (b) that he was citizen-less.

Our local colleague in Vienna learned through the guards of the prison, where Paul was interned, that he and others were to be taken to the Czecho-Austrian frontier and there dumped (literally). We were able to get a suit of clothes to Paul, in the pocket of which we had put two railway tickets from two frontier stations in Prague. By means of this, after various vicissitudes, Paul managed to get to Prague to live there for almost a year, if my figures are right, and then through the help of one of our British missionary societies, we were able to get him to England on the promise that sooner or later we would get him to the States. While in Prague, he was compelled to move every two weeks because a longer stay in any one place would have necessitated his reporting to the police and, as he was illegally in Czechoslovakia, not due to any subterfuge on his part, he would have been penalized on registration with six months in prison at hard labor.

I am a bit surprised that Paul Fried seems unwilling to speak about his experiences in public, though this may be prompted by his fear of espionage and the possible report back to Germany with serious consequences for his parents who are still in the hands of the Nazis. I know many refugees from Germany who refuse absolutely to speak about their experiences for exactly the same reason.

We finally got Paul to the States through the offer of a missionary post with the Jewish Missionary Society in Cleveland from which he then went to Hope College. There is no question about Paul Fried being a refugee from the Nazis, and, in this respect, he is not trying, as you have been led to conclude, to sail under false colors.

I am surprised to hear that there is any question about his German, for in the years in Vienna my recollection is that he spoke German most fluently. It is true that he was almost a year or even more than a year in England before he came to the States, but he could not have gotten to England unless he had some prospect of an ultimate permanent migration elsewhere.

I hope this will satisfy you with regard to the authenticity of Paul Fried, but should you have any other questions or suspicions, I trust you will communicate with me.

From Amalia I. Atkinson, 6 December 1940:

We are happy to hear that you have been able to secure the interest of friends in Holland who are willing to sign affidavits for the members of your family. Please let us know what arrangements you can make regarding the necessary funds for their steamship tickets.

To Dr. Joseph Hoffman Cohn, 17 December 1940:

I feel really sorry for not answering your kind letter of December 4th before. For the last two weeks, I have been going through the usual college examinations and working till late in the evening in the factory. I had asked the minister of Hope Church, Rev. de Velder, about signing the affidavit, and he seemed willing. Since then he told me that his lawyer had advised him not to do it, and he has now brought it up before his church board. Just a few days ago, I had a letter from home after not having heard from my parents for more than three months. They are naturally afraid it may become more difficult as the war goes on. They don't seem to have much to live on.

To American Board of Missions to the Jews, from Henry Winter, 19 December 1940:

[Hope] Church cannot execute such a bond, but perhaps some individual connected with it might be persuaded upon satisfactory evidence that he would be protected or held harmless in the case.

To Mr. Henry Winter from Dr. Joseph Hoffman Cohn, 24 December 1940:

Yes, we will be glad to give you our guarantee that in the event of the mother of Paul Fried coming to America as a result of an affidavit of support having been secured through your efforts there in Holland, Michigan, we will assume responsibility for the care of the said mother of Paul Fried. You will have nothing further to do with the case once she arrives in Michigan. It will be Paul's job to find occupation for her, but we will stand behind him and help him look after his mother until reasonable time shall have elapsed. You need have no fears about being called upon to make good financially in any way whatsoever. We are handling these cases all the time, and we know from experience what to do and how to do it. I hope you will succeed in getting an affidavit of support signed because Paul is considerably worried about the present circumstances surrounding his mother's unfortunate situation.

To Amalia I. Atkinson, 31 December 1940:

Thank you so much for your kind letter of December 6th. Unfortunately, the matter has not been going as well and as quickly as I had expected, and I am still waiting for the papers to be signed.

From Fred G. Kendal, Hebrew Christian Mission, Detroit, 23 January 1941:

I am concerned about your mother. I believe I could secure an affidavit for her. Will you write giving me details about her? Once we have the affidavit, I do not believe it will be difficult to secure passage.

To Paul Fried from Henry Winter, 5 February 1941:

The consistory of Hope Church again discussed the execution of a bond for you at its meeting last Monday. There was considerable hesitancy on the part of the members signing in their individual capacity. Inasmuch as Mr. J. Hoffman Cohn so readily guaranteed support, our members felt that there could be no objection to his assuming the burden direct, instead of through some local person.

To Dr. J. Hoffman Cohn, 18 February 1941:

Unfortunately, after having considered the matter for some two months, Hope Church has decided not to undertake the signing of the affidavit. At present, I see no way in which I could obtain an affidavit here. You may imagine that my anxiety for my people has not changed but rather increased. I wonder if I may hope for your direct help for my mother and brother. I know that you are deeply interested in saving human beings and that you can understand how much it would mean to me to have my mother and brother here.

From J. Hoffman Cohn, 28 February 1941:

It is with much disappointment that I read the news that your own local church refused to give you the affidavit of support for your mother. We ourselves as a missionary society are not eligible to sign such affidavits, and I personally cannot do so. It is, therefore, rather tragic that the friends there in Holland have declined to come to your help in your hour of need. Especially is this incomprehensible since we were willing to guarantee (indeed had) to indemnify them against all responsibility. As to getting for you some other affidavits, it is painful to have to report that our own request to the readers of The Chosen People brought in scarcely a handful of responses, and these were used up by us just as fast as they came in. You can keep on trying in Holland to find someone who will be willing to sign the affidavit with the stipulation that we shall guarantee him against responsibility. If and when you do find such a person, we will cooperate immediately.

Letters on behalf of family (1941)

From Felix Fried, 20 February 1941:

Dear brother, many thanks for your nice letter which we enjoyed very much. I am sorry, but I am not yet studying, but I hope it soon will

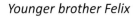

Younger brother Felix

be so. There is not any more news, except a letter from our brother [incarcerated at Mauthausen-Gusen camp in Austria]. He's greeting you very much. The weather is very fine and warm so we hope soon to make some outings on the Easter holidays with our bicycles. This may be only for a short time, but father has brought home two of them, and so we have now three. The sun shines now nearly all the day, and because we live near the park and the river, we are enjoying the good weather. The food is not very cheap but enough for our modest means. We hope that you soon will write again. Is your radio a good one? Do you use it often, and how far do you get with the apparatus? An electric cooler we have, but we don't use it because it would be too dear. Also I have learned to photograph with an apparatus which I got from my brother. But now I must end.

In April 1941, J. Arthur Milner, Milner Electric Company, Cleveland, wrote a petition to the American consul in Prague to have Dr. Emilie Fried and her son Felix come to the USA for permanent residence.

To Dr. J. Hoffman Cohn, 3 April 1941:

Last weekend I visited Cleveland and through the kind assistance of Rev. Kramer, director of the Hebrew Christian Society there, I was able to interest a Cleveland friend in helping my mother by signing the affidavit. I told him of your offer to guarantee him against any responsibility. I would be grateful if you could write Mr. J. A. Milner, Milner Electric Company, 1320 St. Clair Avenue, Cleveland, Ohio, giving this guarantee. Thank you again for your willingness to aid me in getting my people out of the danger zone.

To J. A. Milner, 3 April 1941:

This is just a short note to thank you again for your interest in the welfare of my mother and brother. I am sincerely grateful and pray that the Lord will bless your effort and will work out all things to His honor and to a happy reunion of our family.

Yesterday, Rev. Kendal, the superintendent of the Detroit Hebrew Mission, assured me that I need have no fear concerning the passage money for my mother and brother. I have written to Dr. Cohn in New York and trust that you will receive his letter of guarantee within a few days. I hope that there will be no obstacles and that soon I may be able to embrace my mother and brother.

To Dr. J. Hoffman Cohn, 28 April 1941:

Thank you very much for the guarantee which you signed for Mr. Milner. I am finally in possession of an affidavit for my mother and brother. I owe you a great share of the thanks for this. A few weeks ago, I stopped at Detroit's American Express office and found out that the Pacific passage for third class costs about $200 per person.

To Rev. Fred G. Kendal, 29 April 1941:

You may remember that we were talking about the question of an affidavit and that I had not heard from Cleveland since I had been there in the beginning of April. Well, the Lord has answered my prayer, and yesterday I received a registered letter containing an affidavit for my mother and brother. Before the visa will be granted, the fare and passage have to be guaranteed. I am over the mountain but have a long way to go. The minimum cost is $400. I don't know how to secure the money but know that the Lord has helped so far and will continue. Dr. Cohn has promised a modest contribution, but I don't have any idea what a modest contribution means. Please pray for the matter and see what you can do.

To Amalia I. Atkinson, 29 April 1941:

Only yesterday, I received an affidavit giving guarantee for my mother and brother. I am happy to have these papers and anxious to get them completed and sent to Prague as soon as possible. My mother's quota number has been reached some time ago, and I understand that she would be able to leave Czechoslovakia, together with my brother, without any difficulties. She will be able to travel by way of Russia and can pay for her journey as far as China. The passage money for the Pacific crossing will be provided by friends here.

From J. Hoffman Cohn, 1 May 1941:

We are unable to meet the need of money for passage. We have been carrying such a heavy load with our refugee work that we cannot undertake further obligations.

From Amalia I. Atkinson, 13 May 1941:

Thank you so much for your letter of April 29th with the copy of the affidavit with statement of income executed by Mr. Milner. The affidavit submitted in favor of your mother and brother seems to be in order. The friendship letter should be written by Mr. Milner to the consul, informing him of what plans are made for your mother and brother upon their arrival, as to where they will live and how they will be provided for until they are able to support themselves. I note that you have the passage money for the Pacific crossing, which will be provided by friends, so that they can travel by way of Russia. Our latest information does not support the possibility of their traveling by way of Russia as the Japanese are not issuing any travel visas at this time. Visas are not issued by the American consulates unless it is certain that passage is obtainable.

To Amalia I. Atkinson, 14 May 1941:

On April 29, I mailed a registered letter to you that contained a copy of an affidavit in support for my mother as well as a statement of the treasury department and an application for verification of my entry into the United States. Do you still have the possibility of sending papers to Prague by diplomatic pouch, and do they go only to the American consul there, or can they also be addressed to people in the city? As I am registered for the Selective Service, there is a possibility that I will be called after the college year ends, which adds to my desire to complete all the necessary arrangements in the shortest possible time.

To Rev. Fred Kendal, 15 May 1941:

This morning I received a letter from the American Committee for Christian Refugees telling me that the affidavit and other papers are in good order. They again emphasize the importance of a statement from the travel agency or steamship officials that the passage is paid for or guaranteed and that reservations are made. I have been able to secure fifty dollars, only the eighth part of what I need. I do hope to find people who will help me raise the necessary amount. Meanwhile, I am writing again to Brother Kramer and a few other friends. I am looking forward to the day when I will be able to welcome my dear ones here.

From Fred Kendal, 17 May 1941:

I expect to be going east next week and may be able to see my brother in Philadelphia. Through his good graces, I was able to procure money for another refugee's passage two years ago. I am praying that God will lead me to the right contact so that I may be able to help your mother. God has a way.

To Fred Kendal, 29 May 1941:

I had another nice letter from Dr. Cohn in which he promises to give the last $50 as soon as I have $350. Together with what I personally have been able to save up during the last few months, I have the first and last $50 which, although not much, is a start.

From Dr. Emilie Fried, 12 June 1941:

My dear Paulili! The intense study period at the college has most likely ended. Even though it was probably difficult at times, you most likely were quite happy to be privileged to engage in abstract concepts and psychological problems. We probably don't have to tell you how happy we were to see you on the same path which always gave your parents satisfaction, despite all our worldly worries and pains. How did you spend Pentecost? Your descriptions of Easter pleasures caused us to rejoice with you. One grain of salt is that our good Julius has to miss all of this, and we miss him. We acknowledge with gratitude that you have spent your Easter vacation trying to help us. Now you should concentrate your thoughts and efforts on Julius's joining you after he gets his visa. Until his departure, he will be able to come here to take care of business matters. His closest friend, with whom he shared living quarters last year, has received all the necessary papers from America. How bitter it would be for Julius, our good Julius, if he would have to stay behind. That would leave inconsolable pain in his already deeply wounded heart. It is the most sacred duty for all of us to do everything possible to keep despair and pain away from his noble heart. Whatever can be done here, we are doing. Papa is pursuing any endeavor which offers the faintest glimpse of hope. Julius will be able to catch up with his studies, and we hope that Felix can accomplish the same. Felix is very affectionate but completely out of practice concerning study habits. Well, everything is in God's hands; we want to rely on him, to leave everything up to him. A Russian proverb expresses this very beautifully: "Trust in God, but don't leave anything to chance." This I wish you and your dear good brothers. With the sincerest wishes for happiness and joy of life, Your Mutti who loves you from her whole heart. Also, greetings from the heart from Felix. [trans. Gisela Strand]

From Dr. Paul Markus Fried, 12 June 1941:

Dearest Pauli! It is quite understandable that we did not get your answer to our letter which we sent in May. Nevertheless, we have a great desire to get in touch with you. Unfortunately, for the time being, it can be accomplished only by mail. It is high time that we could do this in person, mostly for the sake of your brother whose golden period of youth goes by without any growth of body and spirit. This hurts our hearts as parents a lot. Felix is a good person by nature, but he is going down fast. He has no interest in learning, and our dear Julius writes that we would not recognize him. All of you deserve to be happy together and thereby infuse your good mother with new life. As far as I am concerned, I have come to terms with my life and will probably not stay behind in despair since I have been able to enjoy enough happiness in my life. I fear for Julius because nobody knows the dangers which surround him constantly as well as I do. For his sake, you have to do everything possible. I enclose a copy of his high school graduation report card which could help you get him enrolled in Hope College. You should also try to get Felix enrolled in a college. Your mother could get preferred status because instructors who have been employed for at least two years at a university prior to applying for a position get preference. Students enrolled at a university who are at least fifteen years old also have preferred enrollment status. Concerning the affidavit, please get in touch with Viktor Ridder at the *Nationale Sozialistische Zeitung* [National Socialistic newspaper]. Either he or the publisher will give it to you. A few persons or organizations could guarantee the affidavit collectively. Would that be so difficult with my past association with the press and your mother's name as an author and counselor? A married couple who has published a best-seller and who is working on another one, dealing with one of the most difficult problems, and who can produce the best references? Try as hard as you can, and may the Lord assist you.

Most sincere greetings and kisses also from our dear Julius! Your old Daddy. Also don't forget to mention that your father is president of a prestigious organization and your mother is docent at a university. [trans. Gisela Strand]

To Fred Kendal, 24 June 1941:

In view of the latest developments, it will naturally be impossible to travel the Pacific way. I am not giving up hope and will try to secure, at least for my mother, the Atlantic passage or the Clipper [airplane]. I need some $570 for the single passage.

Father Paul Markus

From Rev. Paul L. Berman, corresponding secretary, Friends of Israel Refugee Relief Committee, 3 July 1941:

I am glad that you have $250; the balance should not be difficult to secure. I presume that you are a Hebrew Christian. I am wondering if your church could give you a small loan that you could pay back, or perhaps the Hebrew Christian Alliance could give you a loan of $75 and a gift of $75. I shall be happy to give you $150 for passage. Is your mother a Jewess, Jewish Christian, or Gentile Christian? Give me the name and address of your pastor.

From Rev. Paul L. Berman, 14 July 1941:

Had I known all about you and your family, so much time and energy could be saved. You belong to the Hebrew Christians; now it is up to us to stand by and help Hebrew Christians. You can tell Dr. Reich, the president, that I approve giving you aid—the balance from $170 to $200.

To Dr. Max I. Reich, undated but probably July 1941:

I am writing to ask for the Alliance's assistance with the balance yet necessary for my mother's passage on the trans-Atlantic Clipper. The money will be used only for that designated purpose and would be returned in case my mother should unexpectedly be unable to come to the United States.

To Dr. J. Hoffman Cohn, 14 July 1941:

Your contribution would be the last money needed for this purpose. Thank you for your effort in helping my mother. It may interest you to know that I have been placed in class 1-A by the draft board and am due for induction in August. Once I am in the army, it will be much more difficult for me to pursue my mother's interests.

From Rev. Paul L. Berman, 21 July 1941:

Tell Dr. Hoffmann to let me know when he needs the money, and I shall do it right away. Get busy, young man, because Dr. Hoffmann leaves on his vacation for the whole month of August.

To Amalia I. Atkinson, 23 July 1941:

The money for the passage, even by Clipper, has been put up for my mother and can be used without delay. I realize that in the meantime the American consulates in Germany have been closed and understand that visas are now given only in Washington. I hope you will be able to give me some information concerning the new regulations. I have spent so much time and energy in preparing for my mother's immigration that it would be a great disappointment to me and my parents if we had to drop it now.

From Amalia I. Atkinson, 25 July 1941:

I was glad to know from your letter of July 23 that you were able to collect the amount necessary for your mother's transportation by the Clipper. When you have received a reply from Washington, I shall be glad to assist you further in your efforts to bring your mother to this country. I hope that will be prior to your induction into the army.

To Rev. Fred Kendal, 18 August 1941:

I am planning to visit New York and, if necessary, Washington, to complete arrangements for my mother. I will leave Holland this Saturday, the 23rd, and spend the night in Detroit [at the YMCA]. I would like to have a personal chat with you and hope that you will be in Detroit on the 24th and can spare me a few minutes.

From A. M. Warren, Chief, Visa Division, Department of State, Washington, 26 August 1941:

In reply to your communication of 28 July 1941, regarding the visa case of Mrs. Emilie Fried, now residing in Prague, I have to inform you that no action may be taken in this case at present because there are no American consular offices operating in the district under reference.

*Autographed photo of older
brother Julius*

Letters around the time of the death of Julius (1941)

From Dr. Emilie Fried, 3 September 1941:

May God grant you his blessing and strength in your new life and the strength to accept the news of the death of our eternally beloved Julius! There is nothing more that you can now do for his crystal-pure, noble soul than to pray and pray. The small prayer gathering that we were able to hold at home not until ten days after his death offered his parents' blessing in place of a church blessing. Oh, how good he was to all people, in particular to his parents and brothers. He gave his best not only with every word that he wrote to us from his last location but also with every single letter, and he responded in gratitude, although we were able to do so terribly little for him. He always thought of you lovingly. You can no longer do anything to help him, but think of your old grief-stricken father and your younger brother. I will help you to the best strength which the dear Lord has left me and which I endeavor to increase. When the right living conditions come, I hope to assuage the heavy loss little by little through my work. The shining example of your older brother will serve as a guidepost and a guiding star to all of us on all our paths. Remain healthy. With deep love, Mama.

God bless you, dear Paul, and let us hope for a reunion with each other. We will first cry it all out in your arms and then begin our new life. [trans. Brian (1984 Hope graduate) and Barbara Gibbs]

This portion of the same letter had a postscript from both parents.

Dearest Paul, we do not yet know the particular details under which our dear deceased breathed his last breath on 21 August at about 2:45 in the afternoon; we do not yet have the death certificate, as we received the delayed official notification just yesterday. How terrible the moment of this disclosure was, as you, dear Paul, can surely feel. With love and faithfulness, your parents kiss you countless times. Your dear loving parents, overcome by deep grief. [trans. Brian and Barbara Gibbs]

Paul wrote the following letter to his parents and two brothers before knowing that his older brother Julius had already been shot to death in a concentration camp.

To dearly beloved parents, dearest brothers, 10 September 1941:

Most of all I have to beg your pardon for my long silence, but I hope that you will understand the reason. Many thanks for your letters, dated July 20th and August 8th. I am very sorry to hear about Mama's accident, and I hope that in the meantime everything healed up well without leaving any permanent damage. Was it a simple break? How I would have liked to visit Mama or at least to send her flowers.

In my last letter, I mentioned the possibility of interrupting my studies to start a new position. For the time being, the starting date for this position has been moved up to February, and I have decided that I will stay in Holland for at least another six months and continue my studies. As a consequence of this change of my plans, I was able to take a trip to New York (900 miles away from here) in order to try to find ways to help Mama and the rest of the family. I had even intended to travel to Washington from there in order to speed up the matter.

I deeply regret to have to disappoint your hopes as well as mine. In the last two months, travels to the United States have become so restricted that it is almost impossible to obtain a visa. First requirement is that a visa will be issued only if the applicant is in a neutral country (Switzerland, Portugal, Spain). Second: a visa can be obtained only if the applicant has no blood relatives in a country which is conducting a war or lives in an occupied country. Third: each individual applicant has to obtain an affidavit from two persons with high incomes residing here. Finally, a visa will be issued only after the applicant has ordered and paid for his ship ticket.

I believe that these rules will show you that at least for the time being it is useless to hope for immigration (to America) in the near future. I would much prefer to have better news for you. Concerning Julius, I don't think that it is impossible for him to obtain a visa for South America, but that will also take a long time, a lot of work and patience, and possibly in the end will not materialize. Nevertheless, I want to do everything I can. Harry's parents are now in Brazil (I received the address from Harry only yesterday), and I will get in touch with them immediately. I will also try to get in touch with the Bolivian Embassy, but that might possibly be easier for you.

In my opinion, a visit with Uncle Fritz might be promising. I will write him a letter in the next few days, and I suggest that you do the same. To be sure he does not have much money, but he has good connections and quite a lot of influence; if he would invite Julius, then I could possibly send the money for Julius's expenses, but only in an emergency.

Aside from the unpleasant news concerning your immigration, I had a nice, entertaining, and adventurous trip. I don't know if I wrote you what a hitchhiker is. It means somebody is standing on a road holding up his thumb in the direction he wants to travel and waiting for a car to offer him a ride. Of course, this kind of transportation is the cheapest, and for this reason very popular among students, who use it a lot. I also tried my luck a bit and had the desired success.

My roommate, whose mother and sister are living in New York (and by the way his name is also Paul, and he was born in Vienna), and I started our trip at noon on a Saturday. Two cars took us all the way to Detroit. There we spent the night, and on Sunday we took a ship on which we spent the [next] night in a very beautiful and comfortable cabin. Monday morning, we landed in Cleveland where I had to get additional papers for the affidavit. That same evening, we boarded a bus which took us without stops to New York on Tuesday evening. There I stayed for a week with Paul and his mother. During that time, I visited various committees as well as a number of friends who had promised to help Mama.

It had been my intention to travel to Washington after obtaining all the necessary papers; I had several excellent recommendations, even one from a senator. Unfortunately, the papers in my possession were absolutely worthless according to the newest regulations. I left New York the following Tuesday and spent Wednesday in Philadelphia and got to Cleveland by noon the following Thursday. There I had an invitation to spend a few days with friends, which I gladly accepted. On Sunday afternoon, I left again and hitchhiked almost the entire way from Cleveland to Holland where I arrived in good shape on Monday evening.

In a few days, the new college year is starting, and I am really looking forward to spending at least another six months here. You must believe me that nothing would make me happier than to have my loved ones here with me and maybe seeing my brother in the same school.

Felix's English is already quite good, but he still has to learn a lot before he can be admitted to a college. I would really be very happy if I would get a few lines from Julius.

I can only repeat that I did everything in my powers to facilitate Mama's and possibly Felix's immigration, but for the time being it is absolutely impossible. Now I want to concentrate all my strength on Julius, but I also cannot promise any success in this respect. For this time, I close again with my most hearty greetings and most tender kisses, Your son and brother who is always thinking of you. [trans. Gisela Strand]

After finally learning of Julius's death, Paul wrote the following letter to his parents and younger brother Felix.

To dearly beloved, treasured parents, dear brother, 28 September 1941:

Your letter has shaken me up deeply, and I still cannot grasp that our dear Julius is no longer with us. I have always looked forward to welcoming him here to talk about our experiences. From the time when all of us lived in Vienna, we have always been closer to each other than most other brothers. I share your pain completely, but what is that compared with Julius's lonesomeness in his last hours.

Despite this, we are not allowed to stop living and look back into the past but must move courageously on into the future. Maybe it is better this way. I have often asked myself if and how Julius would have gotten used to a new life here and forgotten everything that had happened. I prefer seeing him rest in peace than to live with a broken body or, worse, a broken spirit. Perhaps this is his last sacrifice and last token of love for his parents and brothers. Be that as it may, we want to commemorate him with love and loyalty—but without pain—hoping to meet again in the future. God has given; God has taken. Praised be the name of God. Everything will turn out well.

I hope that you have received my last letter, dated the 10th of this month, and that you have understood the newest regulations. When I wrote the letter, it seemed impossible to do anything from here since I could not expect that all of you would be able to get to Switzerland, and there would not have been any purpose in trying to get there without Julius. Maybe it could now be possible. That is why this might have been Julius's last sacrifice for all of us. You should try with all your strength to get to Switzerland so that his last sacrifice will not be in vain. I can't help you much with the first step. Maybe Mama's friends from the past can be useful. I have five hundred dollars ready for your travels and could get more. The affidavit for Mama and Felix is still valid and in my possession, and even though I need one for Papa, I don't think that is impossible. A trip to the capital is still a possibility. If necessary, I could try to get in touch with the Swiss Embassy here, but I don't have great hopes for success. It seems more promising if you would try. Please, Papa, apply all your strength to this. I can't do anything until you are in Switzerland. All other plans are much more difficult to execute; thus this plan of action would be the best.

I am still curious to know how Mama's accident happened and if the injury and break have healed completely. Please write about your daily lives. If Felix were to come here, it would be helpful if he knew what kind of profession he might want to pursue. Is he still interested in medicine? As far as I am concerned, one of my greatest difficulties is to decide on a profession. I would be very happy if I could save Felix from this agony.

My life has changed a bit since the beginning of the academic year. I quit my job at the bakery and am working in a hotel as a night clerk. All night long I have nothing else to do except accept some money from a guest and show him to his room. I can spend the rest of the night studying, reading, or writing. Here it is now 2 a.m.; for you, it is time to get up. How I long to be reunited with you again! That's why I repeat that what has happened [to Julius] is very, very sad, but we who continue with life must not look back but stride forward with courage and determination.

With my deepest kisses and hopes that we can be together soon, with love and mourning, always loving you. [trans. Gisela Strand]

The following three letters, enclosed in the same envelope, from his father, mother, and younger brother may be the last pieces of correspondence that Paul received from these family members.

From Dr. Paul Markus Fried, 4 October 1941:

Dearest Pauli! God bless you and preserve your courage to face life and your strength for your work and for living. The letter from you today is witness to this. We resolved to write to you each month, and just today we received your dear letter. Today we also received, as a sign from heaven of your brotherly bond beyond the here and now, in eternal memory of our dear Julius, a short account of his last hours. It was reportedly over swiftly. That is a comfort amid the incomprehensible suffering since it would be dreadfully depressing to think that during his last days and weeks he was longing and pining for us. He was so endlessly dear and tender in his devotion to all of us and to everything, even in the painstaking meticulousness and care he took of his things. I still can't get a hold of myself and wish nothing more than to see my dear ones in this life to be united with each other than to be united soon with those in the hereafter. Unfortunately, the former is more difficult than ever before; the entry requirements for the United States have been made more difficult here, too.

Won't there be an appointment to an academic institution for someone who has written as much as Mama has and who has been successful at three university clinics in such a sought-after specialization as surgical gynecology? For the past three years, she has devoted herself to the globally significant problem of low-pain birth and pain-free birth. Wouldn't influential advocates be of help? And if Felix is not able to be admitted to a college, then being taken in by Uncle Fritz remains the most desirable option. I will inform him today of your brotherly willingness to provide the necessary financial support. That will be good, less for Fritz himself, but for the authorities, since he would be pleased to take in Felix. Please also write, dear Paul, the same as quickly as possible. Unfortunately, hope is not too great since one year ago he was unable to fulfill this same request for Julius. Perhaps now, following the passing of our dear, blessed Julius, he will make greater efforts. Felix is in desperate need of mercy since he is suffering terribly, not only emotionally due to our grief, which, despite our efforts to control our feelings, we are unable to hide, but also physically, as he has barely received the minimum nourishment in the midst of his growth spurt. I urge you not to make any financial arrangements. Even by any stretch of the imagination you would be unable to accomplish much since, even if you undertook great efforts, 100 dollars are just 400 marks, and with that he would not be able to manage to put on the 20 kilos that he is deficient. At a height of 165 cm [5'5"], he weighs 42 kg [93 pounds]. The fact that he has no employment naturally makes him unfavorably conspicuous. Efforts to help Felix must not fail. We love you very much, but you should not become our only son.

In addition to your and our appeals to Fritz, we also ask that you focus your efforts on other possibilities to enter, perhaps to Havana or another intermediate country, as a way to gain entry to the United States. Do you not have the address for Miss Littleton, who was so sympathetic towards you? Perhaps she would take in Felix; he would certainly brighten her life. Perhaps Mama would also be able to stay there? There is no Bolivian consulate here, and no other visa-granting representations; everything must be attempted from abroad. The committees know this well. We were very interested in your journey, Paul. To the extent our sorrow permits, it even amused us. May the Lord grant you, according to your wishes, professional success and contentment in life. May you be as happy as your father and your own namesake was until Julius's departure, and be dearly greeted, kissed and hugged in spirit by your old, unhappy father, Paul. [trans. Brian and Barbara Gibbs]

From Dr. Emilie Fried, 4 October 1941:

Our good Paul! It was a month ago that we had to share with you our unspeakably heavy sorrow over the hardly bearable burden of Julius's death. As inconceivable it is to our hearts and minds never again to encounter our precious son on earth, we have now become accustomed to focusing our sights on the hereafter. Don't believe that my courage to live is failing me; I will continue to work and will always be willing to help others in every way possible up to the last minute that may be granted me. Now we must help our youngest above all; then, aside from our spiritual desire to be reunited in the hereafter, we parents have the duty to care for him who has not had much in life and is very pessimistic anyway. The cry from your father's wounded heart is understandable; at present as far as physical well-being is concerned, we are dealing more with fears than facts. Every day can present changes to our presently somewhat bearable existence since our low income can fall below subsistence level and the ability to feed ourselves.

Even though a positive outcome to the efforts on behalf of Felix can't be expected soon, we must ask you to act as though we were no longer there and to get Uncle Fritz to take interest in him. He is a slender, very intelligent, quiet youth, who in reality has no youthful wishes and faces life with resignation. When a purpose in life presents itself, we would hope for a chance, since he is practical and upstanding. He loves us beyond measure, and you have been such a friend to this child in such a great and noble way beyond how you were with your blessed brother. Your intimate, warm mutual relationship gave Julius the beauty of youth. We remember this by keeping in mind every little picture that shows the two of you together. Did you receive the pretty postcard photo that shows Julius together with me? We will enlarge it to life-size, and you will receive one of these when we see each other, if the Lord so permits. If not, you know that our parental blessing and thanks for the care of your younger brother reach beyond the grave. In eternal faithfulness and love, and with kisses to you, Mama. [trans. Brian and Barbara Gibbs]

From Felix Fried, 4 October 1941:

Dear brother, We are constantly thinking of our dear, unforgettable Julius, whose deeds and being will always live on. Of course, we don't forget about you for a moment, and we thank you for your love and the efforts you have undertaken to secure our reunion. Somehow and

Mother Emilie with Julius

somewhere we will see each other again. Mama's leg is almost healed. Countless kisses, Felix. [trans. Brian and Barbara Gibbs]

The following two letters, enclosed in the same envelope, were addressed to Paul's parents' Prague address and dated 23 October 1941, but they were returned to him since his parents and brother Felix had already been deported to Lodz, Poland, on 16 October 1941. In these letters, Paul tried to move forward despite the death of his brother Julius.

To my dearly beloved parents, 23 October 1941:

When I sit down to write to you, it is still very difficult, almost impossible, to imagine that our dearly beloved Julius is no longer with you. Friends here who knew him express their deepest sympathy. Pastor Forell and Mr. Deutsch have promised to write to you; both of them are mourning over Julius. Nevertheless, life has to take its orderly course again. I hope that you received my letters dated September 10 and 28.

At the moment, hardly anything can be done from here about your departure. Only after you succeed in getting a visa for a neutral country can I make a petition for you. I would like to help you financially, but my inquiry at the local bank showed that it is not very easy to transfer money to Prague.

Now I will attempt again to give you a true picture of my life here but not without asking you to do the same by extensively describing your life. This semester I am enrolled in an English poetry course and two courses in German literature ("Romantic Literature from Novalis to

Nietzsche" and "Schiller's Works"). In general, Holland is a very small town, and the only thing one can do is see a movie on Saturdays and go to church on Sundays. On Sundays, all the movie houses and stores are closed. I lasted only about four weeks in my job as a hotel clerk since I had so few opportunities to sleep that mostly I slept during my college lectures, which is not exactly the right place. A week ago I returned to my old job at the bakery as a substitute.

I enclose a separate letter to Felix and hope that he can read and understand it. I would love to send him something for his birthday, but unfortunately that's not possible. So far I have always talked about him as my "little" brother, but it is quite possible that he is already taller than I am; in any case, he is no longer little. You can hardly imagine how happy I would be to have you and him here with me. With deep love and most ardent kisses, I remain your grateful son, Pauli.

To Felix Fried, 23 October 1941:

Beloved brother, First of all, I want to wish you a very happy and successful new year in your life. And a very, very happy birthday, too, of course. I wish I could at least present you with one of those big, nice birthday cakes which I have to make so often. I am sure you would enjoy it. Well, perhaps next year. We will hope for it anyhow.

I am glad to see that you are getting on so well with your English and hope you will not have any trouble reading this letter. I wish you would write to me in English, and not just for a few lines. Surely this would be very good practice for you. Too bad dear old Mr. Bradley is not in Prague any more. He really helped me more than anybody else as far as my English is concerned.

Are you still taking English lessons? What about your schooling? Have you given that up altogether, or are you doing some studying? Please don't give up; I know how hard it is to get started after a long pause. Try not to forget the languages you have learned; they may be of great value to you in the future. Have you learned to speak Czech yet, or don't you have to, now?

I still have my bicycle, and every once in a while I take it out and give it some exercise, not enough though. I am afraid you will hardly know me when you see me; I am getting real fat, with a double chin, you know! I also bought a tennis racket this summer and have played a few times. Once in a while, I also went swimming in Lake Michigan (look that up on a map). That is about all the sports I had this summer—not counting, of course, the football games I watched.

Are you taking part in any sport? Do you have a bicycle of your own now? I often wonder if you are still as much afraid of going into the

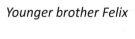

Younger brother Felix

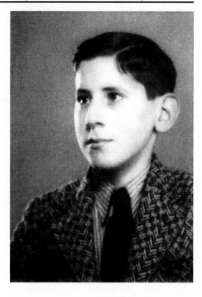

water as you used to be—remember? Or can you swim now? I often wish I could play some kind of musical instrument, and I always hoped you would at least take piano lessons. Now I am taking a college course in music appreciation, but that's not the same as being able to play yourself.

I am going to close now, as I have quite a lot of homework. Please write to me a little more than before. You are soon going to be a young man and not a boy any more. I remember how I hated to write letters, even when I was long past your age, but now I get a great deal of joy out of writing and receiving letters. Again wishing you every good and perfect thing for you birthday, I remain, in love, your affectionate brother.

To Rev. Fred Kendal, 17 November 1941:

Regarding my mother's immigration, nothing can be done at present, and I suppose I had better get used to the idea of waiting to see my family until after the war. My parents seem to be fairly well, except for their grief over the loss of my elder brother, who died late this summer in a German concentration camp.

From J. Hoffman Cohn to Brother Pernov, 26 November 1941:

Paul Fried will write you about his parents, last heard from in Prague. Please do all you can to locate them and bring them to Stockholm. We will refund you all expenses.

Paul's communication by mail with his parents and younger brother probably ceased after their deportation and the return of his 23

October 1941 letters. He simply did not know where to write to them or how to intervene to locate them. Paul focused his energies on classes at Hope College and on enlistment in the army in 1942. In the years immediately after the end of the war, Paul had only the slightest hope that his parents and brother Felix might have survived, but he did do some ultimately futile searching as revealed in the following letters.

Post-war searches for family

To Lida Imhof, 14 September 1945:

At the moment, it is difficult to get into Czechoslovakia. Even if I could get to Prague, there is little I can do there since I don't speak the language and have no idea who the friends of my parents were or how to find them. We'll just have to continue to hope and pray for them. Actually, there is only a very small remnant of survivors of the Nazi terror. If any trace of my family should appear, I would certainly stay here in Europe, but if not, I think I will just have to return to the United States.

In response to a 17 October 1945 inquiry from Paul, a "Report from American Red Cross" indicated that the "stateless and Protestant" Paul, Emilie, and Felix Fried were deported from Prague on 16 August 1941 "with transport 'A' (numbers 710, 711, 712) to Lodz (Poland). Did not return." Paul knew that this date was incorrect since he had received mail dated as late as 4 October 1941 from Prague from his parents and brother. The Central Tracing Bureau for Holocaust victims later listed the deportation date from Prague as 22 October 1941.

From Col. J. R. Bowring, director, Central Tracing Bureau, United Nations Relief and Rehabilitation Administration, 30 January 1946:

Reference is made to your enquiry of 1 July 1945 concerning Paul Markus, Emilie, and Felix Alexander FRIED. Enquiries based on the information supplied were made, but it is very much regretted that a report has now been received stating that no trace can be found.

To Director, Central Tracing Bureau, United Nations Relief and Rehabilitation Administration, 12 March 1946:

Private inquiry in Prague was made by a native, and he reported that only Dr. Paul Fried was listed as having been deported on 22 October 1941. Your report indicates that all three members of the family were on the transport. I would appreciate a further check on this matter. My mother, Emilie Fried, was said to have been in a hospital with a fractured leg or hip.

To Margaret Mills, 15 December 1946:

I went to a forum sponsored by the International Student Council and heard a very witty and brilliant speech by the Czech foreign minister, Dr. Jan Masaryk. His English is much better than that of most Harvard or Hope lecturers. [Paul then told Margaret that he had asked Masaryk about DPs and that Masaryk had invited him to write to him about family details.]

To Dr. Jan Masaryk, son of the first president of Czechoslovakia, 15 December 1946:

In accordance with your suggestion made a few days ago after your most interesting lecture here at Harvard, I am writing to you in regard to my family. My father was an Austrian journalist who came to Czechoslovakia in 1937 after having been forced to leave Germany and Austria. For a time he taught at the Masaryk *Volkshochschule* [folk high school] in Bratislava; later he moved to Prague. My mother, who worked in Russia for three years, came to Prague to join my father in the summer of 1938. My two brothers were with them when I left Czechoslovakia in January 1939. The last letter I had from my parents was written in October 1941; after that, my own letters were returned unopened. The Red Cross report came back with information that my parents had been deported in August 1941, which is hardly possible, as I was still getting mail from them [from Prague] at that time. The other answer was that my father had been deported from Prague on 22 October 1941 with police transport N. 318781/41. No indication was found whether or not my mother and my younger brother had been included on this transport. I am still hoping that sooner or later a trace of at least my mother and younger brother will be found. It seems that my mother had an accident with her bicycle and was sent to a hospital. She may have been left in Prague when my father was deported. My older brother died in a German labor camp in August 1941, but there is no indication of what has happened to my younger brother. Enclosed are the details regarding my family and passport photos. I am anxious to find any member of my family or to know what has become of them. I will be most grateful for your aid in this matter.

To Margaret Mills, 8 January 1947:

Yesterday I had a very nice note from the office of Dr. Jan Masaryk saying that he would take my letter with him to Prague and have his office try to trace my family.

To Fred Bradley, 27 February 1947:

I wish it were possible to turn back the clock on the war. As you may have gathered by now, my family has apparently been wiped out completely. I have had three different investigations made in Prague, but there is no trace. As a last resort, I spoke to Dr. Jan Masaryk, when he lectured here in December, and he promised to have his office check the information I have. I am afraid there is little hope of anything but a negative report.

To Han Hünd, 20 July 1947:

I am wondering if you are still in Holland and if you have been contacted by any member of my family. I have not had any word from my parents or brother since October 1941 when they were arrested in Prague and sent to a camp in Poland.

From Han Hünd, 7 August 1947:

I was deeply touched to learn from your letter of 20th July that evidently your dear parents and brothers have not escaped their tragic fate. Shortly before the war in this country, I have made every effort and done all that was humanly possible—even approaching the royal family of the Netherlands—to help them. All was in vain. I never knew your parents personally, but a Dutch clergyman I met had known them rather well, and he spoke very highly of them as people of great learning and culture. Maybe I can still find the little package of letters, passport photos, etc., that I collected re: the Fried case. Even though there is little hope, I am confident that you will not give up your fight to trace their whereabouts. They may still be alive, and you are the only one who can do something about it. So, do your best.

To Harriet Cook, on stationery labeled Office of Chief of Counsel for War Crimes, 18 August, 1947:

This past weekend I was at long last able to make a short trip to Prague. My family was there until 1941. Unfortunately, stores were closed on Friday, and I could not do anything to pick up the trail of events of 1941. I met one friend who is the son of the people with whom I used to stay. He is now twenty-four and had fought in the Czech underground against the Germans. Later he worked against the Communists and ended up with two years in a concentration camp.

To Han Hünd, 27 August 1947:

No, I have not given up the search for my family, although I really have little hope of finding any of them alive. I have even sent a couple of inquiries into Russia. Last week I was in Prague and spoke to one of the people who will do a lot of looking in the next few weeks. I hope I may find some of their personal effects. Please let me know if there is something you would like to get from the States.

To Rev. Goete Hedenquist, 10 November 1947:

Unfortunately, there is no trace left of my family. As far as I can determine, they were sent to a concentration camp in 1941 and must be presumed dead. Thus far I have not made any attempt to start a family of my own.

From Han Hünd, 11 November 1947:

I have searched in vain for that little package of correspondence. I must still have it, but where it is, I simply can't say. When my house was bombed, we collected some of the things from the ruins, and I distinctly remember finding and saving that particular package. There's such a mess of damaged, unrecognizable things piled up in our attic now that it is impossible to pick out any given thing. Trust me to continue the search.

To Ike Auerbach, 18 January 1948:

In the matter of my family, I have had to decide that there is no point in looking any farther. On my last visit to Prague, at Thanksgiving, I finally located the former landlady of my parents. She remembered everything quite well, although she herself had been in a concentration camp for over two years. She told me that my parents and my brother (all together—the point I had always questioned) had been sent to Poland with the very first transport from Prague in October 1941. I am afraid practically nobody could survive that long in a camp. I sometimes wonder if I am right in trying to forget this as much as I can.

From Han Hünd, 15 March 1948:

On the 11th of November last year, I promised you to continue my search for the little package of correspondence from your family. At long last it has been found, and though I am not sure that it can be of any help to you, I believe that you will want to have it as a remembrance in case you must consider them lost, a possibility which I am still reluctant to accept.

To Fritz Neumann, 9 February 1949:

In Prague, I found the woman with whom my parents had roomed in 1941, and she is quite sure that they, together with Felix, were on the first transport to Poland which left Prague in October 1941. I am afraid that is the end of the line as far as my investigation is concerned. I looked through the list of survivors from the concentration camps as early as July 1945, when they were first made up in Paris.

To Margaret Mills, 22 January 1950:

One letter [that gave me much pleasure] was from the publisher in Germany who had published the book my parents wrote. This past year he had put out a third edition without asking anyone, and just by chance I had come across it in a bookstall shortly before I left Germany. I first thought of getting a lawyer to write to him and find out about royalties but then decided to write myself and ask for information on the arrangements which had been made between him and my father. He wrote back a long letter, and believe it or not, after all these years, this is the first real letter of tribute to my parents or sympathy for their passing which I have received from anyone. Though I am fully aware that he has definite financial interest in making a good impression, the tribute sounded so sincere and heartfelt that it is worth a good deal more to me than a few thousand marks would be. The man, by the way, spent about six months in prison after the Gestapo found the plates of the book and other correspondence in his basement, though that was probably only one of the charges against him. He is considering the possibility of an American edition, which I think would not be easy to produce or sell, in which case I would get half the proceeds. [Interestingly, this book by Paul's parents seems to have appeared in a 27th printing in 1963.]

To Mary Herz, 31 July 1972:

You are right about each age having its compensations. I am not sure that life gets nicer each year, but it does get more comfortable in some ways, as long as we have a good income and no major upheavals strike. I am only now starting to realize what Hitler must have meant to our parents—or fathers, at least. Not the concentration camps and terror, but simply in terms of having established some sort of life and family and then, at the age when they thought they were "set," to find that everything about them collapsed, and they had to start a new life, perhaps in a country with a different language. I am sure I would be much less critical of my father's failure to see ahead or to decide to move the family abroad when there was still time.

It would be decades before Holocaust records that confirmed the deaths of Paul's parents and brother Felix in Poland in 1942 came to his attention. Chris Spencer reported that it was too painful for Paul, then residing in the Warm Friend Resthaven Care Community in Holland, even to look at these documents. Paul felt that reading them would solve nothing.

CHAPTER 6

Army Training (1942-43)

Early days from Michigan to Colorado

The following paragraphs from section three of Paul's autobiographical notes were written on 26 January 1950.

I started my Army career at the induction center at Camp Custer, Michigan. All the things which happened to Private Hargrove [a reference to *See Here, Private Hargrove*, a book (and a 1944 film) chronicling Marion Hargrove's experiences in becoming a soldier in the US Army in World War II] did happen, in some way or other. You found yourself walking through a long narrow warehouse with nothing on, finding shoes here and a shirt there until you had a heavy bag full. At the end, there was a large table and a big Negro who checked my things to see if I had what I was supposed to get. He asked with a grin if I wanted to take them along or pay later. I wished I could have had the presence of mind to tell him to send the bill to my uncle. I just stood there and said, "Huh?"

From Custer, after three or four days, I traveled by troop train, I don't quite know how, to Camp Robinson, Arkansas, and basic training. Jimmy Muddle stayed behind at Custer to wait for some clothes to be made for him since he was too short and fat to fit into anything they had there.

At Camp Robinson, Little Rock, Arkansas, 1942 (Hogue Photos)

The huts had room for only four, and I shared mine with two tall Dutch fellows from Grand Rapids and a boy from the Pennsylvania coal mines. Time passed very rapidly, and there was little to spare except for letters now and then and one or two visits to Little Rock, where there was nothing I wanted to see except the Capitol, somewhat like Denver's. In camp, there was more and more training with bayonets, assault nets, a rifle range in red mud, outdoor bivouac, and then a final inspection parade, during which I almost got caught. I had worked very hard to clean my rifle, and with all the dust, had put in a patch which I wanted to take out just before the inspection. Well, in the excitement, I forgot. When we got out on the parade ground, I looked and saw the patch. I tried to get it out with a pencil but only pushed it in deeper. Finally, the sergeant saw my frantic appeal for help and came over while the general was already inspecting the other company. But he could do nothing either. So I just stood there waiting for the worst. But only our platoon lieutenant came. He put out his hand, and with perfect timing, I dropped the gun. Mechanically, he flung it up, and there it stopped. He turned it around and tried to look in on the other side—once more. When he asked, I told him: "A patch, sir," and for once I had the right answer, for when he wanted to know the reason why, I said, "No excuse, sir." Much to my surprise, I was not on the gig sheet that night.

And then another train—we didn't know where we were headed. Someone looking out of the cattle car noticed Kansas and Nebraska.

Finally, forty-eight hours later, very, very early in the morning, we came in at Camp Carson, Colorado. There was snow on the ground, it was cold, and the drivers of the trucks wore little wool caps which we had never seen. Soon our whole group was broken up, and I was the only one sent to the headquarters company of the 354th Infantry. Without much ado, the captain shook hands and took me over to the barracks to find me a bunk. For two days, I didn't know where I would go. Finally, I was assigned to the Intelligence and Reconnaissance platoon and sent over to the school held by Lieutenant Brochu, a young redheaded art student from New York. School was fun, and even the field training, on the snow, in the warm winter sun was enjoyable. I had trouble getting used to the high altitude. Soon Christmas came with lots of packages from many friends: the Schriers, Mullers, Lambs, a big one from the Kramers, and from Lida Imhof, and even Mrs. Dyke and the Bergmanns and Mrs. Stephens, and lots of cards. Still, at that time people always got lonely.

Oh, yes, I think I went to the Episcopal church once where there was something of the Christmas spirit. I also thought of going skiing—I think with Richard [Yee], or first alone—and went into a local ski shop. The boy there, Bob Lucas, I think, asked me if I would like to come along on Sunday, and we went up to Glen Cove, which was a lot of fun, in an old open Ford coupe with six people, six pairs of skis, and lots of food. Bob drove like mad up that mountain on a snowy road. The lodge was wonderful, but I am afraid my skiing was not; nor was I too much of a success with the college girls there—like the fifth wheel. I guess there were not enough girls anyway.

A little later I first took advantage of the invitation to go to the Shaws on Saturday evening. The home was beautiful, the records very good, and the people really charming. Dr. Lloyd Shaw was principal of Cheyenne Mountain High School, known for its wonderful folk dancing, and had written a book on cowboy music, the proceeds of which had gone into his Capehart [phonograph] and the records. Mrs. Shaw was a poet and made wonderful cookies and chocolate with brandy for refreshments. The home was really unique and consisted of two interconnected cottages. There was a room with a big hand loom on which all the carpets had been made. The pictures, too, had been painted by Dr. Shaw.

Later came the Division Intelligence School. I still had only a faint idea what it was all about but managed to get an excellent grade in the course. Lieutenants Kennedy and Cutler and a few other enlisted men were there. When I got back, I was sent to driver's school. During those long afternoons in the barracks with someone endlessly going on about motors, I fell asleep and didn't understand a thing. I had to cheat on the visual test and reaction time. Then we took the road test. Once I almost smashed into the jeep in front of me; the lieutenant thought I was just showing off! Little did he know. Frank Simon was on the trip, and I think Gene Mabbut, too. Anyway, I did get the license but no vehicle. Soon after that I started to work in the office, in regimental headquarters. This was really a very nice bunch, except for the executive. Brochu was hardly ever there, so I learned a lot and wrote a lot of long letters, too.

Just before Easter, Mrs. Schrier wrote that she had a friend in town and would I go to see Mrs. Mills, or Margaret. Well, I did, and after that I spent almost every Sunday there; I think my first visit was on my birthday. Soon Richard Yee accepted my invitation and came along, too. We went to the Garden of the Gods and many other places, on picnics, etc., or just stayed home and listened to the radio, or debated almost anything that came along. Spring passed, and we went out on maneuvers in the mountains. I remember especially the one at Lake George—was it ever cold. I almost spoiled the convoy on another trip. Later in the summer, we went out in the desert; I was prepared with a gallon jug of lemonade, oranges and limes, cookies, and a pair of tennis shoes. Somewhere along the line, Brochu became ill, and Hartley, our platoon lieutenant, knew nothing about the S-2 job, so I, as a private first class, was acting regimental intelligence officer. I was proud of it. During the Lake George maneuvers, my citizenship hearing came, and one day Gene Mabbut and Tom Conway and I zoomed down in a jeep. Did it ever feel good to take a shower and get clean clothes on. Afterwards we went over to Margaret's but could only have hot chocolate on the porch because her son Keith had just caught the measles.

During one of the maneuvers, we had received a few replacements, and since Brochu did not want me to drive—for his own safety and convenience—and since I was supposed to be at the S-2 command post all the time and could not spend time digging ditches and camouflaging the jeep, we got a driver, and then, a little later, an assistant clerk. I guess subconsciously I was being very much a bureaucrat to get more people working for me. Anyway, Chet Schultz was sent to us, and before long we were very good friends. I still remember that first day, trying to eat a can of C-rations in the back seat of a bouncing amphib, going cross country.

Well, after this, weekends in town became more interesting. Richard Yee had gone with me a number of times. We went to concerts, and I remember the impression of democracy I had when we found that General [Thomas] Finley, the division commander, was sitting five rows behind us. Then there were those wonderful concerts under the stars out at the Broadmoor [Hotel], and swimming in the Broadmoor pool or at the

Photo on Paul's Certificate of Naturalization, 1 June 1950

YMCA, or going up on Mount Manitou to ride the mules. We tried tennis and bicycles and horses. One day six of us went up on Pikes Peak: Gene Mabbut, Frank Simon, Richard Yee, Peter Gjerde, Chet Schultz, and I. We even had a snowball fight—in August. Margaret Mills somehow did not care very much for Chet, probably because I tried very hard to make her like him. I think this is about as close as I ever came to having a real friend, or buddy, in my whole army career. We spent most of our time together, probably because we were so very different. We even gambled together and always came out even.

Somewhere along the line I had seen something about the interrogator school, so with Brochu's permission, I applied. Before I was transferred, I even got to the point where I had to keep the secret CS files for the regiment—knowing who the agents were and that ridiculous system of reports. But I was gratified to be trusted with it.

On the whole, my stay in Colorado was a very happy one. I had met Margaret Mills and Richard Yee and Chet Schultz, friends for life; I had seen a lot of the country, enjoyed the freedom of weekend passes, learned something about the army, and knew at least what went on. I felt bad when I did not get into the platoon but knew that I was not the man for it—nor did I really want to change. It was fun going to the Hotel Pikes Peak for Singapore Slings and to the Broadmoor for supper, or staying in town, or going up into the mountains, to concerts, etc. When my orders did come, I was almost sorry; of course, I rather thought I might get back. But the division was going to change, we had a new CO, and a lot of my friends had left. Chet was still there, but later went to the paratroop school and then to the 104th. Gene Mabbut left, owing me twenty dollars.

One episode will always stand out in my mind—a minor sort of rebellion which worked.

Paul with army buddies at Pikes Peak, summer 1943

Heading downhill with army pals in Colorado, 24 July 1943

We had come in late one Thursday evening from two weeks in the desert sun, dirty, tired, and eager for passes into town. The CO had announced that there would be an inspection on Saturday morning, so everyone was scrubbing the barracks, the belts and leggings, the guns, etc. Only a few had time to stand in line for a haircut at the PX. When Saturday came, most of us were restricted because we didn't have haircuts. There was a smoldering resentment, especially when the 1st Sergeant announced at 1:00 p.m. that there would not be any passes—except for the NCOs. I got out my typewriter, and within a short time everyone was gone. So when Monday came, I asked Brochu if I could go to get a haircut in the morning; he said yes, and I almost had a shave. When I came back, the whole office laughed—which is what I had planned. Smiling Jack (Major Fowler, the colonel's son-in-law) came over and had a look and wanted to know what had gotten into me, so I told him. He told the old man, and before long (perhaps I flatter myself), we had a new company commander. But I really didn't care anymore since I was waiting for my transfer to Camp Ritchie, Maryland. [In July 1942, Camp Ritchie opened a World War II intelligence school with training in psychological warfare. Most of the soldiers there were Jewish refugees who had fled from Nazi Germany and Austria before the war. They were drafted because their fluency in German would make them effective interrogators of POWs.] When it did come, I had to rush; Margaret got me a Pullman reservation and saw me off at the station.

Interrogation training in Maryland

The following paragraphs from section three of Paul's autobiographical notes were written on 24 February 1950.

The trip to Camp Ritchie was something novel. I traveled all by myself. If I had only known, I could and would have stopped off on the way in Chicago and Cleveland. As it was, I had only a brief look in at the wonderful service center in Chicago before getting on the Senator, which left me off at Cumberland very early in the morning. When I finally got to Camp Ritchie, no one knew I was coming, and for the next few weeks, I found myself busy building the service club. There was a rather good introductory show by some of the other MIS [Military Intelligence Service] characters at the movie house and a talk by General Banfield and Colonel Shipley Thomas, whom I had admired from the distance in Colorado after reading his *S-2 in Action*.

When classes finally got under way, the whole thing was much like a college campus. Again I was impressed with the democracy. There were all grades of officers and enlisted men together in the classes. Only the work was harder than in any college I have ever heard of. Eight hours of classes: map reading, organization of the different armies, Morse code, and many other topics. Impressive were the mid-morning and mid-afternoon visits at the PX. Sitting at the counter, or a crowded table, one could hear almost any language—Russian, Polish, French, Spanish, Italian, or German—only English was the exception. People of considerable background slept forty in a barracks; there was Hans Habe [Hungarian-Austrian writer and newspaper publisher who became an instructor in psychological warfare and later created many newspapers in the American occupied zone], a fellow who had been [Polish tenor and actor] Jan Kiepura's manager, and many others. The only two I remember well are Max Flatow, a flaxen-haired boy with a broad Berlin accent, and Fred Praeger [later a famous publisher], who kept encouraging me in my studies. But just before the eight weeks were up, I got a cold and decided a few days of rest in a hospital would do me good. I felt much better after that and finally got through the course.

Too bad the end of the course did not mean what we had been promised: either return to the unit or shipment overseas. I did KP at the officers' mess, which was not bad, and then went out to the "Russian

Front" at Camp Sharpe, Gettysburg, Pennsylvania, for a couple of weeks, and then came back, took an exam for OCS, but did not pass the drill. Then I had a three-day pass just before Christmas, so I went to New York, visited the Forells, went to see a number of shows—*The Merry Widow*, the opera, Radio City Music Hall, etc.—and even a concert in Carnegie Hall. When I got back, I found that I could get a seven-day leave, so I went to Cleveland to stay with the Kramers; then, when I got back, I was on overseas alert, and about a week later, I was back in Cleveland again on leave. I stopped by to see my former Hope roommate Paul Gottwald at Columbus and met Sally, too. From Camp Ritchie, I went to Fort Slocum, a nice and pretty permanent post, in New Rochelle, New York. I had no duties but also no fun waiting.

Letters relevant to army training days

To Margaret Mills, 9 May 1950:

I have to think of the one charming English woman who traveled across the States stopping off to see her many wartime boys. But you have gone so much farther than just to offer us a pleasant resting place in wartime in your home.

To Arthur Frederix, 21 April 1970:

A very old friend, Lothar Sudekum, who had been at Camp Ritchie and in MIS and in France with me, came to visit. [With five others], we finished four bottles of *Gumpoldskirchner* [Austrian wine] before moving on to the Point West restaurant for dinner.

To Albert Lee, 16 February 1974:

I have been reading a couple of chapters in a most enjoyable book by Joseph Wechsberg, *The First Time Around*. A number of his experiences, particularly in the army at Camp Ritchie (where I was stationed at the same time) run very much parallel to mine. I only wish I could write as well as he does.

To Chet and Louise Schultz, 20 June 1983:

More importantly, on June 1, I celebrated the 40th anniversary of an event which Chet probably can remember. We were on a field exercise in the Colorado mountains when I got word that I had to be in the district court to be naturalized. One way of getting a hot shower, clean clothes, and a change from the rough life on maneuvers! Anyway, since the date happened to come at the same time as the completion of my new deck, I decided this was a good reason for a party. Sorry you could not have been here, but if you come to visit, that will be another good reason to have a party.

To Margaret Mills, 20 June 1983:

I have been meaning to write to you since June 1, that day I celebrated the 40th anniversary of becoming a US citizen—and also the completion of the new deck on my house. It was a cool night to be out on the deck but a warm and very pleasant occasion, particularly as I related the way you helped me celebrate the occasion in 1943—having to hide the jeep in your garage, etc. I may have written to you that just a few months ago, I was asked to speak to some sixty or seventy new citizens as they went through the formal ceremony at the federal court in Grand Rapids.

To Chet and Louise Schultz, 20 March 1993:

The particular date I have in mind is June 1, 1943, when the 89th was on maneuvers in the mountains. It so happened that I was permitted to go back to camp for clean clothes, etc. In any case, you might recall hearing about the trip and the short celebration—hot chocolate and cake at the home of Mr. and Mrs. Mills—when Sgt. Conway was concerned about having someone see our jeep on the street, and we had to hide it in the Mills garage. Not only were division vehicles not supposed to be in town, but we also exposed ourselves to the possible infection of measles since Keith [their son] was home with them. So we had the refreshments on the front porch, watching for MPs.

To Goran Satler, 21 March 1993:

Sincere congratulations on becoming a US citizen in December. I hope you will feel as much at home in the United States as I do after nearly fifty years. I expect to celebrate the 50th anniversary of becoming a citizen on June 1. At the time, I was already wearing an American uniform and was stationed in Colorado Springs. A few months later, I was on a troop transport to Europe. I hope that your parents will be safe [in Yugoslavia] and that you will be able to see them again once all this is over. My father had the same reluctance to leave familiar environment when he could have, so none of my family survived the war.

To David and Betty Dethmers, 22 January 1995:

The fact that I did my infantry basic training at Camp Carson in Colorado in 1942-43, I fell in love with the area and have gone back a number of times during the past five decades.

CHAPTER 7

World War II Experiences in Europe (1943–45)

Martin Baierl, in several interviews with Dr. Fried, reported that Paul trained in England for several months and served with the 35th infantry in combat until the end of the war. Paul interrogated natives and POWs and "line-crossers" about information concerning landscape, minefields, patrolling habits, population, etc. Most of the time, he was behind the front lines. Sometimes quarrels erupted about who might interrogate an important informant. Paul's team included John Elmendorf (a warm-hearted language leader), Barnaby Keeney (a PhD in history ["Sometimes I could have kicked him in the ass happily," Paul recounted.]), Lothar Sudekum (a German immigrant and insurance agent, who kind of adopted Paul), Karl Bock (a cook of German origin, who was later wounded), and Henry (called Junior) Salm.

Return to England: black hole and old friends

The following paragraphs from section three of Paul's autobiographical notes were written on 24 February 1950.

Finally, off on a British freighter which took us up to Halifax, and then, in slow convoy in sixteen days to Bristol, England. The only recreation in the black hole where we lived was chess and poker. I signed up for KP so I could stay inside in the damp weather and have good company. Fritz Fisher and a couple of others were about a good bit of the time.

At Bristol, we were split up according to branches, and only three of us—Barone, John Royce, and I—were sent up to Yeovil. What a place that was. The 18th Infantry cadre, veterans of a couple of years of demoralizing non-combat duty in Iceland, ran the place like a prison. It was not much better than what Litchfield was reported to be. KP one day, guard the next, training during the day, no pass, KP, no mail, guard, and KP again, and no appeal against it, and no idea what would happen and when.

Now and then I got into Yeovil. I met the Buffords through Mrs. Lambotte, but it was rather strained, and the time was so very limited. I tried to get to London—no dice. Then Mr. Parry was going to pass through, and we arranged to meet in town for lunch, but I had not counted on the troubles. Volunteered for KP, but that didn't help; went to see the chaplain, and that made things worse. I had myself put on latrine duty, put on my ODs and helmet and belt, and then went through the gate as if I were a guard off duty. In the very rigid but stupid censorship, which insisted that we could not write to anyone in England where we were, no one considered the phone. There was a public booth in the camp. Anyway, Mr. Parry and Ken came out to the YMCA hut, and we visited for about an hour, but it was not much fun.

Finally, the rest of the MIS fellows showed up. We tried to get transferred to their company so we could train with them. Surprising how quickly they organized the camp to run on their schedule. Baietto with his cadenza nearly drove the cadre nuts; so did the others, who would start talking in Italian or French among themselves when some of our stupid guards of the 18th were about. The transfer was messed up, perhaps intentionally by someone, and Barone and I were shipped out to some place in the middle of nowhere—a windy hill, not too far from Taunton and right next to a British airport, so that regular air-raid alarms got us out of our tin huts at night. Once I was on KP and had to get out four times in one night, nearly catching cold. D-Day came and went, but our training went on. Barone left, and I was now all alone—not happy, but perhaps not too unhappy to be no longer typed as MIS. Frank Young, a fellow from Knoxville, Kentucky, was good company.

We played chess and even passed the time going over the obstacle course in the evening—strange thing for me to do—but there just was not anything. Then, one day, the theater came to town. Sure enough, here was the old MIS crew, having talked some colonel into letting them go around giving security instruction. It was great. Royce, the actor, and many of the rest of the gang were there. The play was so familiar that I nearly went backstage before it was over to try to find out if I could be rescued. Royce and, I think, Baietto promised to see what they could do, and sure enough, before long I found myself transferred to the cadre of company GG on Windwhistle Hill, Lord Nelson's estate, not far from Chard. There was nothing there to start with. We had to unpack the tents and set them up, and our first sergeant, Puza, did not think very much of fellows who couldn't swing a large sledge hammer. He took a special dislike to Angulo, of the Harvard Law School, and me because we wore glasses. But finally we got all set up and settled down to a sort of comfortable, if uneventful, life. We got passes now and then to Taunton, a visit to Winsam or Chard, and walks in the country.

I started a fad by building furniture for my tent—Club 31, I called it; it even had a deck chair and a few bottles of rather poor wine. Still, it was not too bad after the six months which had gone before. George Scott used to pass through now and then and leave with an orange or some candy. Later his mother did my laundry, and I spent a few evenings at their home. One Sunday, George and his brother Bernard and I cycled all the way down to the sea; it was very nice. In Taunton, I also met some nice people. Mrs. Stott was at the Red Cross and took care of the records there. She asked if I would like to come out to their home sometime. I went there a few times, and also to Max Putzel's, whom I had met on the truck coming back from Taunton one evening. Through Mrs. Stott, I later also met a couple of nice people at the Avon Hotel in Amesbury.

On the whole, Company GG was quite a pleasant change, even though we did have to go out one day to cut grass with mess-kit knives on a large meadow. After a couple of months, we moved to Tidworth and once more were close to the rest of the MIS people. One of the fellows had in the meantime set up a "Museum of German Weapons" (he was a private first class but seemed to know how to get colonels to give him trucks and how to get 88s shipped from North Africa). In GG, in addition to Baietto, Angulo, and Puza (the stupid first sergeant), there were more Italian boys like Camerion and Celuci, as well as Ralph Horowitz and Harold Fritz. The only one I got to know reasonably well was Fritz, our mail clerk. He went to London with me once or twice and even stayed at St. John's Villas. At least, from Tidworth I managed a few passes to London, twenty-four hours as a rule. Oh, yes, from Chard I had made one trip to Exeter, why I don't really know. Another trip was up into Monmouth, Wales, to visit Stanley Dover. We had also met once at Taunton, where he had told me a lot about his job as director of entertainment at this hostel. But from Tidworth, I usually went to London, although one or two visits at

Amesbury were very nice, and Salisbury was interesting. Tidworth House, the Red Cross Club, was probably one of the very nice clubs in England. At least it seemed so to us, after the long isolation on windy hills.

Finally, GG was dissolved and most of us shipped, after almost ten months, back to the MIS group which had come over with us. A few days later, alert orders were ready, and all of a sudden the army was in a desperate hurry to get us into the war. I went up to London but stayed only a few days, with a number of pleasant visits to Mrs. Lambotte and a weekend at Mr. Parry's. But only too soon the few days I had in London were up, and I had my orders to fly to Paris. Curiously enough, I as a private first class was given a group of four to take over, including Fritz Fisher, Fred Feiner (whom I had also known at Ritchie), and Fromm. For three days in a row, we went out to the air field. On the first day Feiner and Fisher left, and then the weather closed in, so Fromm and I stayed. I went back to St. John's Villas and said goodbye again. When Sunday, the third day, came, the weather was really bad. Fromm and I met at the air transport command at noon. There was nothing, so we went to a Polish restaurant on Oxford Street and had a really good meal and then to Tom Curry's long bar and had some *Kümmel* [liqueur]. When 2:30 p.m. came, we were pleasantly full and warm and not at all expecting the long drive out to the airport again. But somehow we did get on the plane, loaded down with our stuff and mentally not prepared for the trip.

From the time of the takeoff, the plane kept bumping about, and my Polish dinner kept moving about instead of resting peacefully and allowing itself to be digested. Every once in a while the green and damp English countryside would start rushing at us sidewise—and I was turning more and more the color of the countryside—and damp, too. A nice and fatherly looking major from the engineers noticed my predicament and told me to put my fingers out the little air hole; he had had his there until then. All went fairly well, and I tried to ignore even the angry waves of the channel until we hit the coast of France. And I do mean hit—or at least it felt that way when we dropped down some fifty or one hundred feet in an air pocket. My stomach did not go down all the way, and my Polish dinner departed. I was really airsick, so sick that all I could think of was that I hoped the plane would crash or at least have to make an emergency landing.

Dark days: from France to Germany

One of the most ambitious sections of Paul's autobiographical notes is section four (November 1944 to October 1945). He divided the text into thirteen parts with no dates of composition listed. Each part received an individual title reprinted here in bold; the first twelve parts now appear in this long chapter on Paul's World War II experiences. Remarks in a few of Paul's letters indicate that he may have intended to use these autobiographical notes as the basis for a novel about World War II.

Into the War Zone

These orders came out on a grey November afternoon. "You will proceed on or about 29 November 1944, by military aircraft, to Paris, France, reporting upon arrival to the Commanding General, European Theater of Operations, for duty with Military Intelligence Service."

I had been in England for nearly a year, doing kitchen police and guard duty, so I was actually eager to get into the war zone at long last. The orders sounded impressive and mysterious, particularly to a private first class. Together with my orders, I had been given a Paris telephone number, which I was to call upon arrival there. The sergeant warned me not to write the number down but to memorize it. The whole thing surely looked like exciting cloak-and-dagger stuff.

London weather in November is rarely nice, but this time it seemed worse than ever. Almost as soon as we left the airfield, the plane began to bounce up and down, and sometimes the whole English countryside seemed to come sliding up to us sideways. I felt miserable but valiantly fought to keep my dinner down. When we finally reached the coast of France, I thought my battle had been won, but just then the plane seemed to drop about one hundred feet. My stomach dropped only ninety-nine feet. This was my first experience with airsickness, and I hoped it would be the last. My only thought was: "I wish we would have engine trouble so the plane would have make an immediate emergency landing." But the plane continued on schedule, and in less than an hour, we were in Paris.

Paris on a Sunday afternoon. I called the carefully memorized secret telephone number. The sergeant who answered the telephone did not seem the least bit impressed with the importance or urgency of my mission and told me that I would have to stay in the city until the following afternoon when a truck would pick me up.

Thousands, perhaps millions, of soldiers have dreamed of a free night in Paris. "The first time I saw Paris," love, excitement, gay night life. I saw none of these. I did not even know in what part of the city the bus had dropped me. My school French proved inadequate to even the simplest conversation, and so I ended up eating in a GI mess and getting a bed in a drafty department store which had been converted into a temporary billet for American soldiers. I did not even get a glass of wine. Here the war seemed much closer than in London.

In the week which followed, I found out that I had indeed come closer to getting into action. Within two days after my arrival in Paris, I had been assigned to an intelligence team consisting of one officer and two other men. We drew two jeeps, a trailer, a tent, maps, and all sorts of other equipment, and by Saturday morning we were on our way. We had been assigned to an infantry division which was then fighting in the Saar. Two days later, near Saargemünd, I set foot on German soil for the first time. My war had begun.

On the evening of our arrival, a volunteer was needed for a dangerous mission to interrogate a group of people who had sought refuge in a shelter outside the city. The Germans had the entrance to the place covered by artillery. Our captain wanted to go. "You are not expendable," said the colonel; "send one of your men." For the next week or ten days, we made our home in the basement of a china store. What beautiful hand-painted plates we had for our C-ration meals.

Working with us, at that time, was a French liaison officer. He was a very pleasant Paris lawyer, who unfortunately thought he could speak English. Our own captain, for some reason, was convinced that having passed his language exam at Harvard meant that he could speak French. Fortunately, the French officer had an Alsatian driver who spoke German. Thus all conversations between the American and French officer were actually carried on through two interpreters in German. This solved the problem but was quite complicated.

We had been in Saargemünd for about a week. Christmas was approaching, and I had secured a duck and other items for the occasion. I had even found a pleasantly plump midwife who was happy to cook for us, when orders came to move. We were told that the division was going to Metz for an extended period of rest. We had the duck anyway on the 20th, and five days later we had Army turkey in a garrison mess hall in Metz.

Early the next morning, our rest period was ended, and we started to roll in the direction of Bastogne. The Battle of the Bulge was on, and we were going to be in it. Even with the sound of shells dropping near and around us in Saargemünd, the war had not seemed real to me. Now, suddenly, we were in the midst of it. One moment we were driving through the lovely snow-covered countryside of Luxembourg and Belgium. The sun shining on the peaceful-looking villages painted scenes like those on Currier and Ives Christmas cards. The next moment we discovered a burned-out American tank with the lifeless bodies of its crew next to it. Now there was a constant rumble of guns and tanks and the smell of burnt powder and decaying bodies.

Most of the villages proved to be completely deserted. Only here and there a lone cow or some other animal wandered, lost in the ruins. Once we found an old woman who had barricaded herself in the back of her partly destroyed cottage. We offered to take her back behind the lines, to safety. "This is my home. Here I have lived for over seventy years and through three wars, and here I want to die," was her answer. We had to leave her there and go on.

New Year's Day 1945. Bastogne was ours again. In our little Luxembourg village, just back of the line, the mayor and other local dignitaries toasted the New Year and prayed for an American victory. The immediate danger of a German breakthrough was gone, but so were thousands of our best men. From our little team one man was missing, and two of us had frozen toes.

A few weeks later, we found ourselves in position along the Dutch-German border. The whole area seemed to have been drenched in rain and mud. When we moved into one of the small towns not far from Maastricht, we found that it was completely deserted. The Canadians who had been there before us had taken off all the doors and window frames of the houses to line their fox holes in the fields outside. Since we wanted to set up our headquarters in a house, I had to devise some way of replacing the windows. I finally found a large piece of plate glass in one of the store windows which just suited the purpose. Blankets had to provide the door. Just after I had the little house all fixed up, with straw on the second floor for our sleeping comfort, we found that the roof had begun to leak. So we moved next door. As usual, though, we had no sooner settled down to enjoy these newly acquired comforts when the order came to move again.

One morning, just before we left this area, our security patrol brought in two young Germans. They told us that they had been on the way to visit relatives nearby. But after a long and exhausting interrogation, first one and then the other confessed that they had been sent as spies by the German army unit which was facing us. The older boy was seventeen, the other one about sixteen. Both looked like nice clean kids who should have been out playing football or baseball. Caught in the whirlpool of war, they had been drafted into the German army, and to prove themselves they had volunteered to go on a dangerous mission behind the American lines. Both signed confessions and were convicted as spies but later pardoned.

Finally, the long-awaited spring offensive came. Within a few days, we had almost reached the Rhine when we were stopped. While still waiting for the buildup of our forces, we received an urgent call. One of our companies had apparently been cut off, and the colonel wanted us to find out what had happened to them. After a careful look at the intelligence map, we decided to get into our jeep and drive at top speed to the spot where the company had last been reported. Fully expecting to roll out of the jeep if necessary, we bounced along the dirt path at sixty miles an hour. Nothing happened until we came up to a large farmhouse which looked somewhat like a medieval castle with an archway and large wooden gates. Cautiously, we parked under a tree and went up to the gate, machine gun ready to fire and one hand on a grenade. All seemed quiet. We entered the farmyard with still no sound. Two deserted jeeps at the far end of the building made us fear that our troops had been wiped out. But what had happened to the Germans?

We did not have to wait long for the answer. An old man appeared in a doorway and beckoned us to follow him into the cellar. We did, ready to shoot if he made a wrong move. But then we began to hear American voices singing college songs and others. The old farmer turned out to be a schnapps manufacturer, and his two daughters were making the rounds pouring drinks for the boys from five-gallon jugs.

Gradually, the full story emerged from a very sober and unhappy young officer—the only one who had survived the battle of the previous day. Knowing that his men were too drunk to go out, and that if they did get into battle they would easily be killed, he had reported his company as cut off, so he would not be ordered to advance. Before going back, one of the girls wanted to put a five-gallon jug into our jeep. Reluctantly, we declined since it might get spilled.

[This handwritten note interrupted the narrative.]

P.S. Be sure to listen to tomorrow's exciting adventure. Do I drink the five gallons of schnapps before leaving, or do I take one of the two daughters along to carry the loot?

Returning from this brief interlude, we found that one of our battalions was getting ready to attack, using tanks and infantry. Their intelligence officer asked, "Would you like to come along? We could use you." Lothar [Sudekum] and I decided to go along, asking only that a message be sent to our headquarters. That night, just outside the town of Rheinberg, we passed dozens of burning tanks and other evidences of heavy fighting of the previous week before we reached a little farmhouse, where we settled down to a steady stream of interrogations. Finally, shortly after midnight, we had a fairly good picture of the situation and made our report to the colonel. He was pleased and told us to go get some rest. A few minutes later, a message came that a German officer had been captured, so we got up again and waited. As it turned out, the officer had been wounded, and the soldiers who had shot him down in the dark had just dragged him into a doorway. They were much too busy to evacuate him, and we were told to go get him if we wanted to talk to him. So, with two medics who were just as foolish as we were, we took off into the town in a jeep, put the man on a stretcher, and brought him back to the aid station. Only the next day we found out that the road we had used had not been cleared of mines.

For the next five hours, Lothar and I took turns talking to our prisoner. He had been very badly wounded, both by the machine gun which had cut him down and by the motorcycle which he had been riding. The medics gave him several transfusions and bandaged him as well as they could, but it was quite doubtful if any of this would help save him. He was a young fellow, not more than twenty-one years old, who had been on an unauthorized trip to see his girlfriend when our patrol had spotted him. Even though he was weak from loss of blood and occasionally lost consciousness, this German officer was able to give us a great deal of valuable information since he had been the division liaison officer. Sometimes he did not seem to know that he was talking to American soldiers, but then again there were times when he was quite clearly aware not only that he had been captured but also that he was dying. "Why did you have to fight against us?" he asked. "We only wanted peace."

As this young German lay dying in my arms, I wondered, "Was he right? Did we both want the same thing? Was this war altogether pointless, the result of propaganda which had taught us that 'the only good German is a dead German'? Was this for us the war for survival? Were we really fighting for democracy?" Perhaps the German was also right, and we were all just caught up in a whirlpool which drew all of us down. But what about all the atrocity stories? How about all my friends who had been killed in cold blood in the Battle of the Bulge?

But there is no time for reflection in war. The next day Lothar, who had been with me, was changing a tire on our jeep when a German mortar shell exploded near him. He was luckier than the boy whom we had interrogated the previous night. He has finally come home, and he limps only a little.

Into the Heart of Germany

Finally, we were ready to cross the Rhine. The moon was bright on the pontoon bridge, and the night was alive with the zing, zing, zing of the riflemen who sat along the bridge and fired at everything that floated towards them. Just after we had crossed the river, moving in a slow steady column, a German plane appeared. "Take cover!" The foot soldiers dove for the ditches alongside the road. John and I jumped out of our jeep and crouched beneath the remains of a bombed-out house. A minute later, when the plane had passed and we emerged, our jeep was no longer where we had left it. We were relieved to see it peacefully ambling down the road at two miles an hour and ran to catch it.

Although it was night, the destruction was visible everywhere. Hardly a house was standing. We were glad when we had left the river road. Too many houses were in flames and showed our positions. But we were rapidly advancing into the heart of Germany, and we knew that the end was near. Here and there white flags appeared. Three days later we were in the Ruhr. Only a few fanatical party leaders wanted to resist; the rest of the people were sick of war and wanted to surrender. We learned of one party boss who, by sheer force of his personality and submachine gun, had prevented the surrender of a whole city. So we dispatched an agent to assassinate him. Other towns and mayors were more cooperative; some surrendered by telephone. Most of the people wanted us to move on as quickly as we could. Not that they wanted us to win—or Hitler to lose—they just didn't want any fighting near their own homes, mines, and factories. Soon we were ready to oblige them and were rolling down the autobahn.

One place we stopped for a few days was the home of a chocolate manufacturer. The house was beautifully furnished, and in the cellar we discovered vast quantities of chocolate, canned goods, suiting, cleaning material, and every other conceivable item which was short in the wartime economy of Germany. Obviously, the man had stocked up for a long war. When he heard that the Americans were approaching, he loaded his daughter and valuables into a car and fled. Since he helped us replenish our depleted supplies, we felt very kindly toward him and always referred to him as Uncle Gus. Although we never met Uncle Gus, we had many pictures of him. He was a tall and enormously fat man, somewhat similar to [Hermann] Göring in structure, with a large shining bald head. It seems that he was an ardent nudist; at least there were a lot of pictures about the house showing him with nothing on. If I ever have to meet him, I hope he will be dressed.

Apparently Gus's well-stocked basement was no secret and was the envy of all the poor people living in the town. Several times a day, people came to the door and asked if they could go down to the basement to get something which Mr. Brenner had permitted them to store there. We always refused to let people come in since there was still danger of sabotage. But when I knew we were leaving on the next day, I told several people that they could come the next afternoon at 2 p.m., and I would let them in. We left at 1 p.m. and forgot to lock the door.

The day before, our troops had liberated a German camp in which some 650 Americans had been interned. Most of them had been captured during the Battle of the Bulge and had been made to walk halfway across Germany. Many of them were in very poor physical condition, and all of them were starved for something besides bread and water. That night, the chaplain had made the rounds among our division troops and asked for small donations of cigarettes, candy, or other sweets or extras. He came to us with the same request. The good man was completely speechless when, with the compliments of Uncle Gus, we presented him with 650 large candy bars for his collection. He came back the next day to tell us that Gus's candy had done more for the morale of the liberated PWs than almost anything else.

As the American armies advanced deeper into Germany, more and more of the prisoner-of-war camps and slave labor camps were liberated. Whole streams of liberated Dutch and French slave workers passed us as they went home in vehicles of every type and description. Their trucks were garlanded and decorated, and they cheered and sang as they passed us. At the same time, tens of thousands of Polish and Ukrainian workers began to move in the other direction. They also wanted to go home. Not so happy were the inmates we liberated in the various concentration camps which we had passed on our way to the Elbe. In most cases, these men and women had lost everything and had no homes or families to which they could return. We soon learned that Hitler had brought more than five million slaves to Germany to work in the war effort.

As we came closer to the Elbe, we began to notice that while many of these former slave workers were trying to return to their homes in the East, another large-scale movement of people was going on. We began to meet groups of Germans from East Prussia and other areas recently conquered by the Russians. They told terrible tales of Russian terror, plunder, rape, and murder; they hoped to find refuge in the West. Mixed in with them was a stream of deserters, spies, and people of every age and description. When we reached the Elbe, it was my mission to comb a large wooded area to determine if there were any large enemy units hidden in the rear. With half-a-dozen jeeps and two light reconnaissance cars, we covered miles of deserted forest paths. Within one hour, I picked up some sixteen German deserters ranging in age from fifteen to sixty-five. The fifteen-year-old boy was from Leipzig and had only been in the German Air Force for six weeks. He had bright blue eyes, beautiful blond hair, and a flashing smile. To him the whole thing was one grand adventure, and nothing pleased him as much as when I permitted him to ride in our jeep. He was glad it was all over, though, and he was eager to get home. The old man of sixty-five had also been drafted during the last days of the war and had been forced to dig trenches and walk for hundreds of miles. He said, "I am too old for all this. Just let me go home."

More arrogant were two young SS men who had stolen some civilian clothes from a farmer. The one wore a short black jacket with silk revers [part of a garment that is reversed to display the lining or facing outside], just a tailcoat made to fit the emergency and to hide the uniform he wore underneath. The war was almost over, but not quite, and many of the more fanatical troops were trying to reach the mountain hideouts or infiltrate behind our lines to commit sabotage. We suddenly discovered a whole SS division behind us but were fortunate in capturing their commanding officer before they could do any damage.

However, we found not only deserters and saboteurs behind our lines. One of the strangest groups we encountered during the last days of the war came from Hungary. One evening, while on my way to headquarters, I suddenly saw a tall young man approaching on a path through the woods. He wore a perfectly beautiful uniform, light green with red, white, and gold trimmings. On his chest was a colorful array of medals. He looked as if he had stepped out of a technicolor production of a Sigmund Romberg or Johann Strauss operetta. By the time I had determined that he could not understand German, French, or English, another young man, not as splendidly attired, had appeared. He turned out to be the interpreter. The officer introduced himself as a baron and a lieutenant of the Royal Hungarian Guards; he was attached to the commandant of the Royal Hungarian Artillery School at Magdeburg as adjutant. It turned out that he had been put in charge of a detail of ten men with orders to take the wives and families of the Hungarian staff officers across the Elbe, and to hide with them in the woods until the American armies had passed the area. He then was to surrender and request asylum for the civilians under his care. I went back with him to the hiding place in the woods where the little group had spent the past ten days. There were a large number of trucks, loaded with household goods, silver, linen, and other personal belongings. There were about twenty to twenty-five women and a dozen children. All seemed to belong to the upper strata of society in Hungary. The commandant's wife, in particular, was a handsome woman of almost royal bearing, tempered with a great deal of Viennese charm.

We had no idea what should be done with these people, but after some hurried consultations, we were able to requisition a schoolhouse and help them set up temporary housekeeping there. For the next three or four days, it became my pleasant duty to act as liaison agent for this small group. All were most grateful for every small service performed for them. What made this all the more enjoyable was the fact that Edith, the colonel's daughter, was there. She was about twenty, small, dark, and very attractive. She had studied voice in Budapest and Vienna and had joined her parents only a short time before when the Russians were approaching her home. She hoped to become a famous singer, and her great ambition for the future was to sing in the Met in New York and to see the United States. She kept asking me many questions, and I was all too willing to go into great detail in my answers. But it was spring, and you can't talk about cities and music all the time, so there were a few times when her mother permitted her to accompany me on short errands. I all but forgot that there was a war on. After all, we had stopped fighting some days before and were just waiting for the arrival of the Russians, who were to join us at the Elbe.

But the war was not quite over after all. One night we received a message that a German general had asked for a meeting under a flag of truce. When he came, he offered to surrender his division, but only on the condition that his men could stay together when they joined our army to fight the Russians! He was shocked to find that the offer was refused. Perhaps we should have been grateful for his willingness to help our cause. But at the time, we did not think quite that far. Two days later our orders came. We were to go back to Hannover for occupation duty. Reluctantly, I said goodbye to my friends in the schoolhouse.

Paul inserted a note at this point in his text about other information on the war that he could provide from various published authors: "Here could follow a description of the last days of Berlin based on Trevor-Roper, [Michael] Musmanno, and Rolf."

Visit to a Salt Mine

Just a few days before we went to Hannover, an informant came in with an exciting story. Not far from our headquarters was the entrance to a large salt mine. We had been told that it was shut down. Now our

Paul in army uniform, 1945

visitor explained that down in that mine were six levels in which all sorts of arms and other things were stored and that there might even be an SS regiment hidden some three hundred feet below the earth's surface. While this last possibility did not sound very inviting, we felt that we ought to go down and investigate.

We looked up the manager of the mine, who, however, told us that all the machinery needed to work the lifts was out of order and that there was no other way of getting down. Having first talked to one of the older workers who was looking forward to the end of the war, I knew that this was not true. Of course, the manager's unwillingness to help us get into the mine made us all the more suspicious and eager to go and find out what was down there. We suggested that he go over with us anyway and that we pick up a couple more of his people on the way. He willingly agreed, after I had prominently shifted the submachine gun which always dangled from my shoulder so that it more or less pointed in his direction.

When we got to the mine, I asked the old man to get the machines started. He simply replaced a couple of fuses and one or two small cogs, and the large wheels which powered the lifts began to move. According to the people who worked there, it was necessary for a striker to go down into the shaft before we could go in. By this time, we were wondering if we really wanted to go down. Suppose that SS regiment really was down there? The striker could alert them—if indeed they had not been already informed—and they could murder us in cold blood when we got down there. Perhaps we should have pretended to believe the manager when he insisted that we could not go, but we could not back down now. So we asked for four more men and sent two down with the striker. They had strict orders to shoot the man if he made a wrong move. After that we had to wait for what seemed hours before the signal that "all is ready" finally came.

We left two men guarding the machinist who operated the lift, and together with the still reluctant manager and one other official, we got into the lift basket. Of course, we still had no idea how all this would end. We had no way of knowing if our two GIs had safely reached the level to which we wanted to go, or if they had been killed before the signal had been given. As the lift slowly started to move, I lifted the flap on my gun and kept my finger close to the trigger. If there was any foul play, we were going to make sure that we would not be the only ones to go. Barney had taken along two hand grenades and was now holding one in his right hand, ready to pull the pin if necessary.

We reached the sixth level—about four hundred feet below the surface—without any mishap. Here was the striker, and our two boys were trying to converse with him in German. On the way down, the manager finally admitted that his mine had been used to store valuable books and other records so that they would not be lost during air raids. Arriving at this level, we found that it was well-equipped with electric lights, leading deep into white tunnels. We walked and walked; I am sure the distance was more than a mile until we finally came to a room of gigantic proportions.

There was no SS regiment, but there seemed to be several people of indefinable age who were shuffling about among what turned out to be endless rows of card files. These men were obviously quite surprised to see us, but they seemed quite harmless. They sort of gave the impression of gophers or field mice. I had the feeling that they had lived underground most of their lives. Further questioning and examination revealed that the files were those of the German government Social Security system and that here were cards on some thirty or forty million German people, with information regarding their age, work, etc. If these cards were lost or destroyed, none who had paid into the social security or pension funds would ever get back anything. The concern of these little grey men was genuine enough, and we allowed them to go back to their work, although it still is a mystery to me just what they were doing at that point. But bureaucracy is hard to explain even in the most normal of circumstances.

We went on deeper into the large room and discovered row after row of wooded crates stored in one corner and marked "Library of the University of Hamburg." Just to be sure, we opened one of the boxes. It really contained books. But then, a little further on, we came to a section marked "Ministry of Propaganda." A casual examination showed that here was material which would reveal much about the Nazi period. But we did not have the time to do more than just glance through some of the stacks of documents neatly piled up here. In one section were hundreds of pictures of Hitler, Goebbels, Göring, and all the other Nazi "greats," and next to them were shelves of records with their speeches. I would have liked to stay, but we had to get back up. We had left word that, if we were not back at the end of two hours, the guards were to give the alarm, so the division could be ready for a possible surprise attack [on or by?] whomever was down in the mine. Now our time was getting short. After another long walk, we got back to the lift and were relieved to find our two faithful GIs still improving their German vocabulary. We breathed much easier both mentally and physically when we reached the top again and found that nothing unusual had happened. But we only made it back with a few minutes to spare before the expiration of the two-hour time limit. Both the guards and the old German breathed a sigh of relief when they saw us again. But their relief was nothing compared to ours. Of course, we still had scratched only the surface of the mystery of the salt mine. There were five other levels, and there were large portions of the sixth level which we had not even seen, but at least we were reasonably sure that whatever was in the mine did not represent an immediate danger to the safety of our troops. Of course, we sent in a full report on the mine and sent it forward. I am sure that a few days later, a team of experts came to examine all the contents of the hidden treasure we had located. I would have enjoyed staying on for this treasure hunt.

The Strange Case of Herr von S.

Our main objective in the first few weeks after the end of the war was to locate and arrest all those Germans who, by virtue of military rank or former high position in the Nazi party, might be dangerous to us. We felt that they could become the centers of resistance against the occupation and lead something like the French *Maquis* [resistance fighters] movement. Of course, a lumbering army directive cannot take into account individual cases, and so it frequently happened that men who were not at all dangerous had to be arrested, simply because they belonged to a certain category designated as automatic arrests.

Most of the people we did find were just small fry, but once or twice we also found a bigger fish in our net. Perhaps one of the most interesting men, however, was one whom we did not arrest, although we should have done so according to our printed instructions. On a very pleasant afternoon, I stopped in one of the villages assigned to us, and, in lengthy talk with the mayor and a few other people, my curiosity was aroused concerning one Baron von S. [Paul's handwritten notes later identified him as Baron von Schell.], who was supposed to be living just outside the village on the estate of his sister. He had only very recently come from Berlin and was supposed to be an estate manager by profession. However, according to several of the local farmers, he could just barely tell the front end of a pig from the rear.

We drove out to the estate to meet this peculiar farmer. On arrival, we were ushered into a very comfortable drawing room, and soon Herr von S. appeared. He was a tall, good-looking man of about forty-five and appeared very much at ease in talking to two members of the occupation army. In reply to my question about his occupation, he stated that he was an agricultural expert and had charge of his sister's estate. He then started to elaborate on the importance of the potato in the German diet and significance of his contribution to the food supply for Hannover. I interrupted to ask if he had not been in the army. "Yes, as a soldier," said Herr von S. He did not look like an ordinary soldier, so I continued to press the point: "Were you a solider or an officer?" Continuing in a pleasant conversational tone, Herr von S. admitted that he had been an officer. But when I said, "What was your last grade?" his manner changed. Sitting very erect, he announced in the short clipped voice of the Prussian officer: "I retired as lieutenant general of the infantry." The answer impressed me but not quite the way he had hoped it would. I did not click my heels and say, "Excuse me, sir, for bothering you with questions." I was now fully convinced that the man could well be considered a risk to the security of our troops, especially after he told me that he had been deputy chief of staff on Hitler's personal staff.

The thing that puzzled me was that, although he must have fully known what my mission was, he kept on smiling and seemed not a bit perturbed by the questions or our presence. The explanation for his behavior came soon enough. When I informed him that we would be obliged to take him back to our division for questioning, he said, "Oh, I understand that, but I have already been interrogated by your counterintelligence corps people and have been cleared by them." At the same time, he produced a piece of paper, signed by a CIC officer of our corps headquarters, to support his statement.

This was confusing. The man definitely fell into the automatic arrest category. Why had he been released? Herr von S. started talking about the importance of the food supply for the city of Hannover again, but he soon admitted that his release had not been based on that. When he saw that this explanation did not satisfy us, he finally told us the whole story. Back in 1931 when he was a young major in the German army, he had been sent as an exchange officer to the American command and general staff school at Fort Leavenworth, Kansas. During his year at this school, he had roomed together with a young American major. They had become good friends, and Herr von S. had followed the career of his American friend with great interest. Promotions had come to both men over the years, and by 1945, Herr von S. was high up on Hitler's staff. The American had also become a general and was in command of the corps to which our division was attached. Early in April, when General von S. knew that he had to get out of Berlin if he wanted to stay alive, he had a young German medical officer prepare a medical discharge, which one of his own subordinates then signed. Leaving his impressive general's uniform behind, Herr von S. made his way to the area already occupied by our troops and surrendered himself to the corps commanded by his friend. Claiming the right of a general officer, he demanded to be taken to the corps commander. The German general and the American general spent a very pleasant, long afternoon exchanging memories and talking about the world at large. After a good many hours, the American general instructed one of his junior officers to write a release for Herr von S., who was urgently needed to put German agriculture back on its feet and prevent starvation in the area.

We left, with the half-hearted warning that we would check the story and that we would be back. He smiled as we departed. He had been in the army a long time and knew more about it than we did. Our division intelligence officer was shocked and went to the division commander with the story. But our general had also spent a great many years in the army. He simply decided that, if the corps commander wanted Herr von S. to raise potatoes, who was a mere division commander to interfere? And there the story ends.

An Unscheduled Trip to Hamburg

Karl [probably Bock], who had joined our team a few months before, was eager to go to Hamburg. His home had been there, but he had left Germany some twenty years before and had settled in the United States. During all these years, he had corresponded with his parents and planned to come back for a visit but never quite made it. Now he was back in Germany as an American GI. Of course, with all the bombardments and fighting in the north of Germany, Karl was very concerned about the safety of his aged parents and other relatives.

When we received word that the British army was about to enter the city, Karl asked for permission to go up to look out for his family.

Since we were only doing occupation duty then, the captain gave his permission, if we could work out a good official reason for the trip. One of our informants had brought in a report that Himmler had fled from Berlin to the north. Our mission was clear: we were going to Hamburg on a tip to capture Himmler. It must be admitted that we had little hope of finding Himmler and that Karl's main concern was to find his family.

The one-hundred-mile trip from Hannover to Hamburg was not as simple as we had imagined. Everywhere bridges were out, roads blocked, and army units on the move. On several occasions, we were stopped by the British-line troops, but when we told them we were going after Himmler, they became most cooperative. In one place, mistaking me for a high-ranking officer—perhaps because I looked so well fed—all the engineers working on a temporary bridge put in an extra bit of effort so that we could pass hours before the bridge was opened to regular traffic.

I have been in Hamburg many times since, but I have never been able to discover just how we got into the city that day. Everywhere there seemed a great deal of confusion. It turned out that the British report of the capture of the city a few days before had been premature and that the Germans had surrendered only a few hours before our arrival. At times, I was not so sure that we had unknowingly passed the front line. There were seemingly endless stretches of ruins when we came to the section in which Karl's former home had been. Nowhere was there any evidence of any Allied troops, but then, suddenly, a fully-armed German battalion, marching in perfect order down the middle of the road, came toward us. There was a moment when we thought of turning our jeep and getting away, but we had come too far. The Germans marched right up to us and passed us, without any British escort, but apparently on their way to surrender. In any case, while the major looked at us, he made no move in our direction, so we continued on our way.

A few minutes later we came close to Karl's former home. Still we could see nothing but wide expanses of rubble where once houses had been. I could feel Karl getting more and more agitated and afraid that his home would be gone with his parents buried under it. At a bend in the road, we saw some trees and, behind them standing like a finger against the sky, a single building. American and British bombers had left nothing but ruins for miles around, but Karl's old home still stood as he had left it twenty years before.

By this time it was early afternoon. Since there was no one outside the house, Karl went inside. I can only imagine the scene which took place when his parents and other relatives, all assembled in the house, recognized Karl. Soon he came out again to invite me to share in the hurried feast that was being put on for the lost son who had returned with the conquering armies. Only too soon it was time for us to leave; we had to get back to Hannover again that night.

It was getting dark, and we still had some thirty miles of difficult driving to do when we noticed ahead of us a slowly moving convoy of German army trucks. There were about eight large vehicles with several dozen soldiers packed into each one. As we proceeded to pass, we noticed that there were no escorts of any sort. In fact, there was only one officer in the whole group, a young German who rode in the cab of the first truck. Again ready to shoot, we flagged down the lead vehicle and asked the lieutenant where he was going. "I don't know," he said. "We were just told by our commander to drive until we hit Allied troops and then surrender to them."

He was very happy to accept our invitation to follow us. We promised that we would get them safely to a place where he and his men would get food and shelter. A couple of hours later, our provost was surprised to find that the division had just added another three hundred prisoners to its list of captives. The trip to Hamburg had started out with the announced plan to capture one man. We did not get him, but we brought back enough other prisoners to add to the prestige of our little team. Of course, we did not hesitate to explain with what great courage and difficulty we had obtained this surrender!

Behind the Factory Wall

A few days later we received a hot tip. Our informant said that a high-ranking SS officer, whose home was in a small town not far from Hannover, had just returned from the East, and, putting on civilian clothes, had assumed personal control of his airplane fuselage plant there. We had not even known that such a plant existed in our area, so we quickly got into our jeep to check the story. To our surprise, the factory seemed to be humming with activity when we arrived. Having to wait a while to see the manager, who was out on a visit, I spent a very profitable hour or two, talking to several of the older workers there. The plant was producing wooden chairs, tables, and other consumer goods, but I was told that it had switched to civilian production about three weeks before. Then I asked one old man, who claimed to have been an anti-Nazi all his life, what had happened to the tools. "Oh," he whispered, "they have been hidden." After further questioning, he told me that he did not know exactly, but one of his friends who was a mason had been there when the equipment connected with the war production had been brought into the cellar. After a little search, we found the other man and quickly persuaded him that he ought to tell us what had happened. He seemed very much afraid that someone would overhear us, so we went into a hallway where he drew a quick sketch of the cellar. Pointing out one section of his sketch, he related how, a few days before, he and a couple of other masons had put up a new brick wall in this part of the basement, and that, if we wanted to knock down the wall, we would find what we were looking for. But he was not a bit eager to go with us.

In the meantime, the manager had returned and welcomed us most cordially. Yes, he had been in the SS, but only as a private first class, and then it had not been his choice at all. "You know how these things are; in war the government has not the least respect for private enterprise," he said, claiming that he had been drafted against his will. Now he was happy to be home and able once again to do his share as a member of society. "Wasn't it terrible, all that destruction?" But then, he really could not complain since his factory had not suffered much and with all the homes and furniture destroyed, there was much demand for his product. Yes, he was happy to be working again and doing something constructive. The conversation, on his part at least, flowed like a stream. After a while, we asked if we could see his plant.

Oh, yes, he would be delighted: "Of course, you understand, everything is very primitive, not like in the United States, but with hard work, the output is fine." We asked what the plant had produced during the war. Of course, he had not been there, but as far as he knew mostly the same thing, with much of it going to the army. "Some other things, too, but nothing important," he asserted. We went along with him, politely listening to his conversation, until we came to the building marked by my old informant, and we asked to see the basement.

"Oh, but it is an awful mess, not cleaned up at all; besides, you will get all dirty, and there is nothing down there," he said. Well, we went anyhow. We passed the new wall and stopped after I had run my finger over some of the still wet cement. "What is behind the wall?" we asked the manager. "Why nothing; what could there be?" he said. We wanted to know and sent one man for a sledge hammer. When it came, Barney asked the manager if he would be good enough to swing it against the wall a few times. He gave a bittersweet smile to these crazy Americans! He took a few gentle swings until Barney pulled out his pistol and barked, "Hit it hard!" Still he tried to keep up the front of an innocent man wrongfully manhandled by bullying Americans just because they have the guns. Then the wall began to crumble. First, there was a small hole, and then the whole section came down. Our manager was still swinging, but by now the veins on his forehead were purple, and for a moment I was sure he was going to swing the hammer around and hit Barney. So I, too, pointed my gun at him, and that quieted him down a bit. Finally, the whole large section behind the wall lay exposed, and here, in neat and orderly arrangement, was everything needed to reconvert the furniture plant into an aircraft plant in a couple of days.

The flow of chatter stopped. He was no longer the amiable businessman, eager for American approval, but a sullen German SS major whose greatest regret was that he had not been able to shoot a few more American GIs when he was still in uniform. He understood that he would have to be arrested and was almost eager to have everyone see that we were taking him away. Perhaps he thought of himself as a martyr for Germany. I have often wondered how many such plants we did not find, and if he and his friends were just waiting for the day when they could reassert Germany's greatness and help her regain "her rightful place in the sun."

Cleaning Up

During the weeks in Hannover, we worked an average of from twelve to thirteen hours a day, driving from one village to the next in efforts to locate and put under arrest all those people who, like our general and the factory manager, might spell some danger to our occupation troops. Frequently, people named in our directives had no idea that we knew of their previous activities for Hitler's party. As a result, they would be most cordial in their reception and assure us again and again that they were at our service, willing to cooperate with the Allies. Of course, they were somewhat offended if we put them under arrest after pumping them dry on other party officials in the area.

Sometimes this willingness to help us really made our task much easier. One such instance occurred in a county seat not far from Hannover. I had, more or less by accident, located the chief propaganda official of the old party organization. He was a small-town publisher, with a greatly exaggerated idea of his own significance. After he had gone on for some time about his eagerness to work with us, and that most of the people had only been in the party because they had been forced to join, I suggested that it would be a good thing to get all the important party leaders in the county together for a meeting. We made up a list of the people who should be invited—based on my "wanted list"—and he agreed that they would be at the city hall the next afternoon for a meeting when I would talk to them.

I was not sure that the device would work but requested a large truck in any case. Apparently, my friend had persuaded all his old associates to participate in the meeting. When I got there, all I had to do was call the roll and then request the assembled dignitaries to climb into the back of our MP truck, which took them to a temporary internment camp. Surprised at the ease with which the device had worked, we used it in several more cases, but never with such complete success.

As time went on, and I sent more and more people to our internment camp, I began to wonder just what would happen to them there. It seemed to me that in most cases, the people we arrested were not particularly dangerous and that whatever information of intelligence value they had would be lost if they were put into a stockade with many others who would quickly convince them that they should not give any help to the invaders.

Since two fellows who had been stationed in the United States with me were working in one of the camps, I was eager to go there sometime. The opportunity for a trip came soon enough. We had located a very important and very obstinate SS colonel who was wanted for immediate interrogation, so we decided to deliver him ourselves and combine the trip with a visit to the camp.

My friends were most cordial. We had briefly met in the darkest hours of the Battle of the Bulge when both of them had been with the armored division in our sector, and we had passed each other just after the Rhine crossing without being able to stop, so there was much to talk about, adventures to relate, decorations to show off, and a lot of bragging to do. Their hut was very pleasant and the food better than anything we had tasted in our division mess since Christmas.

When we had caught up with the past, I asked about their work in the camp and said that I would like to see something of their interrogation methods. So we went over to the building in which the prisoners were received. As we approached, I saw a long line of people, of all ages, standing at attention outside the interrogation hut. Once in a while, a sergeant would bark in German: "Next." There would be a slight movement, but then the line would again freeze into rigid attention. I marveled at the apparent discipline.

Once inside the hut, I began to understand the reasons for it. What I saw there made me think of all the horror stories I had read about the Nazi concentration camps. It made me shudder to realize that this was an American camp and that these were good, average American GIs, and not the inhuman SS guards of the Nazi dictatorship. The room was completely dark, except for one very bright spotlight fixed so that it would blind the prisoner the minute he entered. As soon as the door closed behind him, someone would yell, "Take off your hat," snatch it from his head, and toss it into a far corner; then someone else shouted, "Pick up your hat," and as the man bent forward to do so, he received a vicious kick in his rear, which sent him stumbling clear across the room. At the same moment, some other nice American barked, "Name, address, age."

I did not stay for the interrogation because I felt that if I remained in the room much longer, I would be forced to throw up. As I left the camp, I wondered if our soldiers were not becoming infected by the vicious disease which had thrown back the country of Bach and Beethoven, Goethe and Schiller, Kant and Hegel into the darkness of barbarism. After that day, my enthusiasm for making arrests and the pride I had felt in apprehending as many suspects as possible was greatly reduced.

The Beautiful Rhine

Early in June, we left Hannover for our new assignment along the Rhine. There was quite a difference in the trip back to the West. When we had come through the Ruhr and over the Rhine before, it had been cold, and there had been war. Now, warm spring days and green countryside made the trip a pleasure. Instead of being faced by guns and tanks when we came to a German town, we now had to fight off only the groups of German youngsters who begged for chewing gum or chocolate or a cigarette for papa. Somewhere along our travels, one of the fellows had picked up an old-fashioned hunting horn which produced the most beautiful and loud tri-colored tone. So now, as we passed through a village, one of the fellows in the front jeep would sound the horn, and the captain in the second jeep would sit very erect in the middle of the back seat, trying hard to look like Göring or Hitler, about to receive the ovation of his people. It was a lot of fun watching the Germans stare, but we soon got tired of the game and gave the horn away.

At long last, we reached the Rhine. Our small five-man team was assigned to do counterintelligence work in one of the most beautiful areas in Germany, just a few miles away from the famous Lorelei Mountains. The people living in this region seemed to be affected by the soft climate and pleasant country, and most seemed willing to cooperate with us and even to enter into friendly relations with our boys. All along the road, as we approached, the cherry trees were heavy with fruit; near every town, the children lined the streets, holding up bunches of cherries, arranged like grape clusters over a small green twig, which they swapped for gum or candy.

Of course, not only the small children were eager to trade with us. After we had moved into our new quarters in Boppard, in a very nice old house facing the Rhine, we discovered that only a few yards upstream a river barge was anchored. Like many European river barges, this one was equipped with fairly nice living quarters, occupied by the skipper, his wife, and two rather good-looking daughters. Of course, we were not supposed to fraternize with the Germans, but we always could say we were investigating subversive activities or calling on one of our sub-agents. Besides, the skipper claimed to be Dutch, though he was probably thinking of the Pennsylvania Dutch. In any case, Junior [Henry Salm] and Karl became quite friendly with the family, and although the captain had said something to them, they frequently disappeared for long walks.

Not far from our house lived a very jovial German wine-grower who had asked me if I could not help him get transportation for his wine. It seems that he had some forty thousand bottles of very good Mosel wine stored in his vineyard and that he was willing to let our division—or me—have ten thousand of them, if we would only help him get the rest to the market in Koblenz. Although I had to turn him down, we parted on the best of terms, and he invited all of us to his place to taste his product. Of course, we could not accept. But a few nights later Junior and Karl were there with their friends from the barge. The party lasted into the early morning hours and grew fairly noisy. Suddenly there was a heavy knock on the door, and an authoritarian American voice demanded admission. Karl and Junior, expecting an MP check, quickly hid in the bedroom. They left the door slightly ajar so that they would be able to keep informed on developments and would be ready to take off through the window if necessary. The American entered, but they could not see him. They only noticed that he was greeted with some familiarity by the host and willingly accepted the glass of wine and easy chair offered him. He then proceeded to make himself comfortable. Karl and Junior became restless. Their girlfriends were in the other room, and so were the still half-filled glasses. Soon the group began to sing, and then, as the American turned his head, the boys suddenly discovered that the late intruder was none other than our own captain who had warned them not to fraternize. They quietly waited until his glass had been emptied and refilled. Then they casually strolled out of the bedroom and greeted their commander with a cheerful "How nice to see you here, sir," as they joined the party.

But of course, not all was play. In fact, we again worked almost from dawn to dusk. There were sixty-seven towns and villages in the county assigned to us, and we had to contact each of the mayors at frequent intervals. When we arrived, we had been warned by the departing American intelligence officer that there was a lot of sabotage in the area and that we would have to be very careful. Soon an incident in the hills of the Hunsrück Mountains confirmed that report. An American truck, loaded with supplies and food, had been stopped by a roadblock, the driver killed, and the truck first robbed, then burned. In the same area, we also found a number of places where strong wire had been strung across wooded roads at shoulder level. Since most jeeps then drove with the windshield turned down, this device could be used to detach the head of any jeep driver who happened to pass at a fair speed and had failed to spot the wire in time. We quickly had a wire-cutting arrangement welded to our front bumpers to protect our own necks.

Naturally, we made every effort to track down the criminals. Our search led us to one small village as the most likely place of residence for the men we were seeking. While the mayor professed to be eager to help us, he insisted that he had not the faintest idea of what would be helpful. Convinced that he had more information than he was willing to give, we went back several times. The answer was always the same, and since the war was over, we could not compel him to talk. However, just as we were about to give him up as a lost cause, he came to our office late one afternoon. He looked as if he had received a heavy beating. His clothes were dirty and torn, and his face showed scratches and bruises. Before I could ask him what had happened, he burst out, "Those dirty scoundrels; I'll show them that they can't do that to me." It appeared that a short time before, as he was returning on his motorcycle to the village, he had suddenly come upon one of the ingenious wires strung across the road. Luckily, he had spotted it at the very last moment, or it would have snapped his head off. But since he could not stop in time, he had been forced to throw himself down and had landed in the ditch with the motorcycle on top of him. It was not necessary to urge him to turn over to us the list of a half dozen fanatical Hitler youth in his village who were involved in the affair. I suppose he felt that, while it was all right to harass the occupation troops, so recently portrayed as Germany's greatest enemy, it was quite another thing to endanger the lives of peaceful German citizens, and particularly that of the *Herr Bürgermeister* [mayor].

In another town, the mayor was more eager to create a good impression. After he had talked for perhaps half an hour during my first visit to his town, he casually mentioned that there was a champagne factory close by, and that, in fact, he owned it, and would I not like to take back a few bottles for my mess or my comrades. Although I protested, I later found that twenty bottles had been placed in the back of my jeep.

While we did not find any major war criminals or other people of great importance hiding in our area, we did run into some interesting people and situations. Once, on a tip from an agent, we went to pick up an official of the former French Fascist Party, who was wanted by the

Luxembourg government. Since we knew that he was in his house, but there had been no answer to our repeated knocking, we broke in, only to find our suspect, a man of fairly advanced years, in the bedroom with his young blonde secretary. Both were in an embarrassing state of undress and confusion. I think that he resented his arrest less than the fact that he had been caught in an undignified situation.

We thought we would run into somewhat the same situation a few days later when we went to arrest another man. He had been described to us as very dangerous by many people, but when we first came to the area, he was not to be found. We later learned that during the last days of the war, he had joined the SS unit fighting in Berlin. After the fighting had ended, he slowly made his way back to his home. Within one hour after his return, we had received a call. The poor man was shocked. He nearly wept, said that he had spent weeks on the road trying to get home, and had not even had time to take off his dirty clothes. Would we not have pity? He had not seen his wife in many months, and surely we could not deny him the request to spend one night with her. Junior, with romantic understanding, was almost persuaded. Then he happened to ask, "Where is your wife?" thinking that she might have gone to get something special to celebrate her husband's return. "Oh," he admitted, "my wife is staying with her parents in the country." When pressed for the address, he said they lived near Munich.

Summer Days

Despite many long hours and frequent incidents, the weeks we spent along the Rhine in June and July of 1945 will always stand out in my memory as the most pleasant period of my entire army career. Our house was right on the Rhine, the windows of my bedroom looked out on a small chapel across the river, and in the evenings—with double summer time—we could sit out on the porch until almost eleven and read or watch the people pass. Frequently, we would spend a good share of the evening swimming. There was a half-sunken pleasure boat some one hundred yards from the shore, with its top deck slightly above water and tilted just right for sunbathing and relaxing. Out of nowhere, Junior produced a German army rubber boat, so that we even could get out without having to swim, if we were really lazy.

Another pleasant break in the routine came when I was asked to act as tour guide again, as in Metz during the winter. Again the troop did not have much to do, and the colonel felt that the men would be interested. I don't know how interested they were in our tours, except perhaps the one which took visitors through the champagne plant and offered samples of the product. That always drew a great crowd, so that it had to be limited to officers. My own assignment was Stolzenfels Castle, a romantic spot which Frederick William IV of Prussia had reconstructed along medieval lines before he became king in the middle of the 19th century. Since there were no English notes, I had to go through the place with a German guide and his very charming daughter to become familiar with the interior. Later the girl and I worked out a complete tour in English, which, I think, was even better than the German text her father had.

She was very eager to learn English and a good pupil. Later, when we left, I typed and bound the notes and the historic sketch I had prepared, and I presented them to her as a parting gift. I would not be surprised if she were still using them, unless her improved ability to communicate with the American visitors has since helped her meet the right man, and she now conducts guided tours of friends through a modern Texas bungalow.

The condition of the castle and the furniture was still quite perfect. In fact, the curator was so worried lest the many visitors scratch the beautiful floors that everyone was given a pair of felt overshoes before he was permitted to enter the main state rooms. The reaction of most of the GIs was the same as that of the average tourist. They admired the beautiful old furniture and then asked, "Where is the bathroom?" Of course, I asked the same question and found that when the queen wanted to take a bath, a large metal tub was carried up to her bedroom and then taken out again. I suspect that the difficulty of that procedure led her to limit such luxuries as soaking in warm soft water to the proverbial Saturday night scrubbing.

Another place we visited was a group of caves in the hills in which the whole *Nibelungen* saga had been reproduced, but since very few of the boys had ever heard of Siegfried of Hagen, we decided against taking larger groups there.

The tours, however, were not limited to the immediate vicinity in which we lived. On one occasion, we went to Brussels, but that meant getting up at three thirty in the morning and getting back about the same time—with only eight hours in the city. Another time we took our jeep to Liege, but the radiator developed a leak on the way, so that we had to stop every few miles and try to get some water from Belgian farmers. Not all of them were sure that water was all we wanted, so they locked their doors as soon as they saw us approaching their houses.

While we were down along the Rhine, our division headquarters was located in the hills, not far from Bonn, in a very lovely old monastery. The place was still in use, and since the monks could not be evacuated, they just stayed and went about their daily duties as if the American troops and officers were no more than a group of visitors from some other religious order. It seemed odd to walk out of a briefing room in which the war was still very evident and pass the chapel with praying monks or their schoolhouse in which they had again started to give instructions. Of course, since the Catholic Church had suffered a great deal of persecution under Hitler, the monks regarded us perhaps with less hostility than the majority of the German population did. After a while an order came out permitting us to attend services in German churches, but since we were still required to carry arms whenever we went outside, this meant that some of the boys had to go to church carrying a submachine gun—a strange sight indeed.

Then, just when we had decided that we could stay on in our Rhine villa forever, the news came that the area would be turned over to the French occupation troops and that our team would have to report back to our headquarters located in a little town near Wiesbaden. The fighting in the Pacific was still going on, and the rest of our division was scheduled to go there after a short rest in the United States. We felt sorry for them, but as things turned out, they came home long before we did, and since the war soon ended, most of them were discharged without much delay.

Bad Schwalbach

With great reluctance, we parted from our friends of the division with which we had served throughout the last months of the war. We had an idea that at the headquarters where we were going, no one would have much to do, and as a result there would be the usual amount of army details to make life uncomfortable. We were right on the first count. On the other hand, most of the officers in the MIS did not belong to the regular army and were civilians at heart. The result was that life in Bad Schwalbach turned out to be something the average soldier dreams about.

The town itself is a small but famous health resort which boasts a number of mineral springs which were known even to the Romans when they occupied the same area nearly two thousand years before we got there. Because the springs had always attracted a great many visitors, the town was full of fine hotels which were now requisitioned to house the occupation troops. On arrival we were assigned rooms, just as if we were checking in at the Conrad Hilton in Chicago; of course, the rooms were not as comfortable, but then, they were not as expensive either.

Looking for the mess hall, we found that our mess sergeant had taken over part of the municipal recreation building, which was constructed with a view to making the stay of tourists as comfortable as possible. Instead of going through a chow line with mess kit in hand, having some C-rations and bad coffee thrown at us, and later having to wash the gear, we found ourselves in a comfortable dining room with white table cloths, cooks who asked how we would like our eggs or steaks, and waitresses who came to fill our coffee cups at the table and cleared the table for us.

The same shock came to us when we looked for the movie and recreation room. Instead of being in some dingy hall, the recreation center was located in the casino building, which in peace time must have seen the glitter of many a royal party. Here we found a wonderful library; rooms for bridge, chess, billiards, ping-pong, and movies; and a lounge where wine was served for ten cents a glass by discreet waiters. All of this was rather startling to the GIs—especially if one had come from a farm in Arkansas—but somehow the atmosphere impressed them enough so that most soon acted as if they had always been members of the German upper class or the smart international set which used to congregate there.

We were wrong also in regard to being assigned dreary duties. There were none, and we were free to swim, read, or write letters so long as we did not get into anyone's way. A most pleasant way to be treated in the army! We knew it would not last, but we did enjoy the change a great deal. Occasionally, we were called in for some special details. One such gave me a chance to visit the SHAEF (Supreme Headquarters Allied Expeditionary Force) headquarters in Frankfurt.

I had been given some papers to deliver to the supreme headquarters, and since I had never been to Frankfurt, I enjoyed the trip through the summer countryside very much. It was shocking to see how completely a large section of the town had been destroyed. We were even more amazed to find that the giant IG Farben building, where the headquarters was located, had escaped completely unharmed—but perhaps that was the result of a plan. Approaching the enclosure, we had to stop to show our passes and trip tickets. After checking our papers, the MP informed us that we could not go into the enclosure since we were not wearing ties. However, they offered to lend us two ties for the trip, provided we gave them back upon leaving.

My errand was more quickly finished than I had expected, so I had to wait for a while before the driver returned. While standing in front of the building, I noticed an extremely large army limousine (I think it was a custom-built Cadillac) standing near the ramp. Looking more closely,

*Paul's surprise snapshot of
Gen. Dwight Eisenhower,
1945*

I discovered that it was marked with five stars on its hood. That could only mean that General Eisenhower was inside the building. Thinking that this would probably be as close as I would ever come to the great man, I took out my camera—a souvenir from a friend in Boppard—to take a snapshot of the front of the car. Just as I snapped the picture, the big car began to move towards me. I quickly turned and saw MPs coming to rigid attention. Rewinding the film as fast as I could, I quickly followed the car and managed to get a picture of General Eisenhower as he came striding out the door.

Instead of getting in at once, Eisenhower stood waiting at the car until his WAC aide had gotten in. In the meantime, two officers at the far side of the ramp had spotted him and asked, "How about a picture, General?" He smiled his broad grin and posed. Since I had been behind the car when he came out, I had now come along the side of the driver and could snap a picture just over the hood. I was so excited that it did not turn out too well, but it certainly made an occasion out of a routine courier trip. What impressed me most was the ease and the natural friendliness with which "Ike" had responded to the request and the fact that he was not surrounded by a dozen guards or Secret Service men, as one of the German generals would have been.

Furlough to France and England

Since we had no work to do, it was easy to get a furlough, and I had over sixty days accumulated. So, together with our captain and several others, I got into the back of a truck which took us to our headquarters in Paris (where we had been outfitted in December when we went off into battle). The weather was perfect (about the end of July), and by the time we had passed through France, all of us had nice suntans. Along the way, we saw the many stations set up by the transportation and supply corps—the once vital "Red Ball Highway," now known as General Lee's hot dog stands. We were glad to have these resting places along the way since there was nothing to be bought in the French villages.

Thanks to our captain's very careful calculation of leave-train departures for England, we arrived in Paris Wednesday evening, just a little too late to get on the transport the next day. The WAC sergeant was most apologetic when she told us that we would have to wait until Tuesday for the next army train to London. Of course, we were absolutely heartbroken but finally accepted four-day passes to stay in Paris. Since Paris was overcrowded with American troops at that time, it would have been impossible to get either a furlough or a pass to stay in the city if we had not been compelled, through no fault of our own, of course, to wait there for the next train.

Paris had changed a lot since those dreary December days. Now the boulevard cafés were crowded and the nightclubs filled; the beautiful women had come out of hiding and were showing off their model dresses on the Champs Élysées. I spent four days seeing as much as I could of this old Paris but found that an American soldier was not too well regarded everywhere. I spent a whole afternoon in Versailles, where the furniture was just being put into place again. In the evening, I visited Montmartre, the Folies Bergère, and other places. The next day I took a tour through the city to Napoleon's Tomb, the Arch of Triumph, and Notre Dame. That evening I saw *Coppélia* in the Opera House. Just to see the glitter of the well-dressed people there and the lights and beauty of both the theater and the performance was enough to forget that there had been a war just a few weeks or months before and that the war was still being fought in Japan. Sunday morning, I went to the American church in Paris, and later I saw Bernard Shaw's *Saint Joan*, performed by an English company in one of the theaters.

By the time I was ready to leave, I had walked so much that my shoes needed resoling when I got back. The days in Paris were most enjoyable, but at the same time, I felt that many of our French allies looked at us with the question: "Why don't you go home?" Although we paid exorbitant prices for every little thing that we bought, most of the French seemed to think that we were living at their expense. I guess what bothered us most was their attitude that they had won the war. The feeling of antagonism was even stronger when we reached Le Havre a couple of days later. We stayed there for two days waiting for the boat to England and were warned not to go into town after dark. Finally, on Saturday morning, ten days after leaving Germany, I reached London. Now my furlough started.

I had a full seven days for London. I visited a number of friends I had made while I was stationed in England before, so I did not have to stay in a hotel. One afternoon I took a train to a small country town where one of my friends was then manager of a hostel. I nearly got lost on the way since the train was divided, and only the front half went to my destination. I was in the second half and did not discover the error until two stations after we had passed the junction. Fortunately, a Canadian soldier in my compartment had made the same mistake. After some searching we located a taxi, which took us cross country on deserted roads, and before long we were standing on a platform and waiting for the half of the train which had escaped us before. Since this was shortly after the elections, I was most interested in the reaction of my English friend. He had been a Labor supporter all his life but felt that the Labor victory at that time was a tragedy. "The country faces many problems today which cannot be solved in any easy fashion," he said, "and whatever the new government does, no matter how good, will fall short of what people want. They will then blame the Labor government. It would have been better to let Churchill do the work of cleaning up the post-war mess instead of letting him retire as a war hero."

I did not spend much time talking about politics since I wanted to enjoy the feeling of being a free citizen in a free world not dominated by guns and uniforms and commands. One day I went to Bexhill on the south shore of England; another day I went to Cambridge with a lovely redheaded girl I had met when I was in England before. She had studied at the university and proved a most satisfactory guide. The day we went to Cambridge happened to be the day on which the 8th US Air Force was given the "Freedom of the City." There were many generals, both British and American, and many distinguished civilians in frock coats and striped trousers with gold chains about their necks. It was quite an experience to see some of these representatives of the old nobility and one of the oldest universities of Europe buying beer (warm, of course) for some unsophisticated American Air Force boys from farms in Ohio and Kentucky. There could have been no better evidence of the fact that Britain acknowledged the importance of our contribution to the winning of the war.

Time passed all too quickly, and soon I was on my way back to Southampton and then Paris again. This time we had to wait only two days for our truck. One afternoon, while on my way to the Eiffel Tower, I passed a line of American soldiers and nearly bumped into a friend from Holland, Michigan. Of course, he left the line, and we went to the Eiffel Tower and a few other places together, refreshing our memories of mutual friends. The last time I had seen Bob had been on the day before he was wounded, early in March. He had been out of the hospital only a short time and was waiting to go home.

Our truck left Paris on the day before V-J Day was announced, so we missed the celebration there, but there was one going on when we arrived back at our casino club in Germany. It seemed hard to imagine that the war and all the bloodshed were over so suddenly. I don't think we grasped the full implications of the way it ended then. All that the boys talked about now was going home, getting out of the army, and settling down to the peaceful life we had known before.

Peaceful Heidelberg

Of course we had fully expected that our pleasant days in Bad Schwalbach would not last too long. By the end of August, our old team was split up. Junior transferred to the paratroops and went to Berlin, the captain went home, and so did Karl. John went to Paris, where his wife was working with the Friends Service committee, and Henry transferred to military government. I was sent to Heidelberg, to work with the mobile field interrogation unit there. (The only thing is that the unit was not mobile, and we did not work or interrogate.) This unit had been instrumental in the capture of Göring and many other important figures of the late Nazi regime.

When I came to Heidelberg there were some four hundred general officers and high-ranking civil service and foreign service officers interned in our camp. We were supposed to interrogate them. Actually, it is hard to imagine a sergeant interrogating a field marshal or a secretary of state. What happened in most cases was that these men wrote their memoirs in our camp and from time to time submitted parts of what they had written for study. We would then make out preliminary reports on what information could be obtained from the particular man.

Perhaps one of the most interesting reports I read while I was there was the one by General [Karl] Koller of the German Air Force, who described in great detail the last few days of the war and life in the Berlin bunker in which Hitler died. (Trevor-Roper's book must at least in part be based on this account; also, I think Koller has written a new book.) My own assignment was to get information from a Munich insurance executive who had been one of the first members of the Nazi party and who had personally participated in the abortive Putsch of November 1923. He had been wounded at the time and still suffered from stomach trouble, or so he said, so he asked for a doctor's certificate which would permit him to have food brought in for him.

Of course, this group of intelligence men also consisted largely of graduates from our alma mater, Camp Ritchie. So I found a number of friends who had gone to school with me in the United States. One shared my room. He had spent a lot of his time taking notes during the interrogation of Hermann Göring. He told how, after Göring had surrendered, the American major in command of the unit had offered Göring a house, a servant, etc. The house had then been wired for sound, and the major had spent several very pleasant evenings talking to Hermann and using a great number of wine bottles in the process. The resulting records were fascinating, to say the least.

Interesting, too, was the story of how these former Nazi leaders, cabinet members, and masters over whole countries, quarreled like little children over a pair of trousers or an extra ration of some luxury item. One thing soon was apparent in talking to these men. Few if any of them had any sense of guilt or thought they had in any way done anything inhuman when they ordered the deaths of thousands of Poles, Russians, and Jews. It had never occurred to them that the concentration camps were an outrage against the moral sense of man in the 20th century. Since the state had ordered those things and assumed responsibility, why should they question the order of things?

Actually, there were not too many occasions when we talked freely to the prisoners. Most were handled with kid gloves most of the time, though I remember one time when word came that some weapons had been found, and we had to search all the rooms. A corporal called attention, and three field marshals and three four-star generals jumped up, so that a second lieutenant could inspect their bunks. Perhaps I would have enjoyed talking to some of these people under different circumstances. I am sure it would have been both interesting and profitable.

Heidelberg in the summer is lovely. It was one of the few old German towns which had not been hit by Allied bombing and had thus preserved some of its old charm. The old university, temporarily closed, but soon opened again, served as a reading room for our troops. The beautiful old castle, partly demolished after the Napoleonic wars, furnished the setting for some very fine Sunday evening concerts of Bach, Beethoven, and Mozart. The Red Cross Club was located in a very fine old patrician home. Everywhere there was the atmosphere of refinement, learning, interest in art and classics—a strange transition from the concentration camps, bombings, and atrocities committed only a few months before. Was it only in Heidelberg, or was there a general change in the country?

We often talked of the incongruity of how the Germans had produced such great musicians as Bach and Beethoven and such great poets as Goethe and Schiller and Heine, and of how this cultured country had also produced people like Himmler and Streicher and Göring and placed them in positions of leadership. Which was the true Germany, or was there such a thing? As I talked to the people around us, it seemed as if they were shrugging off what had just passed as a bad dream. No one admitted to having been a member of the party, and the resistance movement, which culminated in the 20 July 1944 attempt on Hitler's life, must have had some ten million members if we were to count all those who claimed in 1945 to have been connected with it!

Most people, however, talked little about politics. They were more concerned with the problem of finding something to eat, locating their relatives, or rebuilding their homes and lives. All seemed to suffer a great deal, and almost all of them were ready to blame their distress on some outside causes. Few would admit that Germany had to a large extent caused the suffering they were now enduring. Yes, it was a sad thing to have lost the war.

By comparison with the people around us, we lived like kings. Our barracks were comfortable, and our mess really the last thing in luxury. Somewhere in its travels, our outfit had captured a Hungarian field kitchen, so all the cooks and all their spices changed sides. The big old Hungarian who ran our dining room always looked hurt if we did not come back for seconds. I think if I had stayed long, I would have put on fifty pounds. On a few occasions we went out, but the non-fraternization ban was still in force.

Early in September we all started counting discharge points and wondering when we would get home. The war in the Pacific had ended, and everywhere units were being disbanded. My notice came, almost unexpectedly, toward the middle of the month. In a few days, I was on my way. First came a brief stop at the old headquarters in Bad Schwalbach, then an even briefer stop over at Frankfurt. I went to the Palm Garden service club there and passed a few pleasant hours before reporting to the train. Once, when a soldier and his girl passed on the dance floor, I thought I recognized the young daughter of the Hungarian colonel whom we had captured just before the end of the war. But then they were gone, and I had to leave for the RR station.

Soon we were being packed into French box cars, marked with

the encouraging words: "40 Men or 8 Horses." We were glad that there were no horses. Even though the train was crowded and just seemed to crawl along, no one minded very much since we were on our way home.

The first lap of our journey took us to a camp not far from the French-German border where we had to wait for some ten days. We were paid in French francs, and I was surprised that the exchange was still fifty francs to the dollar, when fifty francs would buy almost nothing. Then it turned out that the French government also paid us something to make up for the difference, so we had to sign two payrolls. It hardly seemed worth the trouble, but then we were on our way again to Marseilles. The train stopped again and again, perhaps to change engines or to let other trains by. Every time we stopped, the train would no sooner have come to a halt when French women and children would come scrambling up the embankments with onions, tomatoes, and tea kettles full of hot water, which they wanted to swap for candy and cigarettes. We wondered if the trains always stopped at these places. The hot water was useful for making coffee or tea in our box cars.

At one place we landed on a siding next to a French troop train. It was also going to Marseilles and was filled with soldiers and tanks and other equipment going to Indochina. The equipment was American, but we were happy to see that the men were not.

Another few days—this time at the staging area in the red dust just outside of Marseilles—we were sad to find that we could not go and explore the famous, or infamous, French port city. But our ship was waiting, and on the 10th of October some six thousand of us marched up the gangplank on the last leg of the journey home.

Bronze Star Medal

On 3 April 1945, Technician Fourth Grade Paul G. Fried, 36400117, Infantry, US Army, received the award of Bronze Star Medal "for meritorious service in connection with military operations against an enemy of the US in Germany on 5 and 6 March 1945."

The official report from Capt. Barnaby C. Keeney, CAC, OIC, from Headquarters 35th Infantry Division, APO 35, US Army, MII Team 427-G, 17 May 1945, described activities from 20 January to 9 May 1945 in ALSACE (20-29 January), preparation for the ROER crossing (6-24 February), and from the ROER to the RHINE (25 February-10 March). Here are a few excerpts from the report: "While working with Task Force Murray in the capture of RHEINBERG, Sgts. Fried and Sudekum distinguished themselves by advancing beyond our forward outposts at night to procure a wounded German officer, whom they carried back and interrogated until he lapsed into a coma. Since the man was a liaison officer, he furnished information of great interest and value. At the conclusion of this campaign, the OIC was gratified to hear his team publicly described by an officer of the 137th Infantry as responsible for more dead Germans than any other Intelligence agency." In another section, the report stated: "Two members of this team, M/Sgt. Elmendorf and Sgt. Fried, were among the first division personnel to cross the RHINE."

In this undated piece ("Item # 17: Military Experience") written at 25 Conant Hall, Harvard University, Paul reviewed his World War II experiences.

MII Team 427-G was attached for operations to the Intelligence Section of the 35th Infantry Division, A.P.O. 35. The team consisted of one officer and from three to five intelligence interpreters. At times, I was the only German interpreter. The work of the team was divided into two periods:

(1) During combat I served as intelligence interrogator. My work consisted of questioning German civilian and military personnel for tactical information about enemy strength and dispositions, defenses, communications, supply, morale, reserves, and condition of roads and bridges under enemy control. The information obtained had to be evaluated and disseminated on the spot since the work was often done at the front and under fire. I also assisted in the counterintelligence and security work of the division. This included the interrogation of suspects and the investigation of civilians working for the division.

(2) Following the end of hostilities in Germany, the team was directed to assist in the accomplishment of the counterintelligence occupation mission. As special agent, my duties included the interrogation and arrest of German political leaders, party officials, and the search for personnel wanted by higher headquarters. I was also engaged in supervision of local security arrangements and in the gathering of material and evidence for use against criminals. On two occasions, I was assigned to work in collaboration with local military government units. I had to screen German officials, teachers, and others who wanted positions with MG, investigate complaints and denunciations, take part in raids, interrogate civilians suspected of subversive activities, and maintain an effective system of German civilian agents and informants.

The team was detached when the 35th Division left the European Theater. During my service with the unit, I had traveled through France, Holland, Belgium, Luxembourg, and Germany. I was promoted three times and recommended for a direct commission toward the end of the war. During the first phase of operations, I was awarded the Bronze Star; later I received a certificate of merit. The commanding officer of MII 427-G was Captain Barnaby C. Keeney, now residing at 37 Creighton Street, Providence, Rhode Island.

In August 1945, I was assigned for temporary duty to the Seventh Army Interrogation Center at Heidelberg, A.P.O. 758. At this center, some four or five hundred German general officers and civilians connected either with the German foreign service or espionage were held for detailed interrogation. Each interrogator was assigned a few new cases for which he had to prepare by doing research, writing briefs, and investigating the background of the individual. I was engaged in interrogation, research, and in the writing of preliminary and final interrogation reports. I remained at this station until alerted for my return to the United States.

Letters about World War II experiences with Army of Occupation

To Margaret Mills, 26 July 1945:

As soldiers, we are offended by the attitude of most French people that the French won the war, and what are all these American troops doing here? American civilians on official business have to be fed by the Red Cross to keep from starving. Many French claim we are to blame for the food shortage. Just before we left the division, we had to turn our territory over to the French troops. They requested to the mayor of "my" town to send in thirty girls. Well, that's their business, but they could have waited until we had left.

To Lida Imhof, 30 July 1945:

I have just been going through a whole stack of old letters which I left here when I went to France, and I must say I very much enjoyed reading over some of your earlier epistles. I might as well confess that during the time we were in the field, I burned all of my letters as soon as they were answered—for security reasons.

To Margaret Mills, 25 August 1945:

Your letters have certainly made these two years seem much shorter. I have a general idea what my job will be, but I can't see any point to it. A good share of the German general staff are down here (that's not for repetition in public) writing their memoirs, answering questions, and (some think) making plans for the next war. I am not saying that this might not prove a very interesting assignment. I would like to have been here when they had Göring, von Ribbentrop, and a lot of the war criminals!

Certainly the SS and the concentration camps are outrages against all moral sense in man. It is also true that many people knew about them, yet many did not. Even if they had heard about them, it did not interfere with their moral sense because the state did those things. I give up! I will have to see if I can find a professor of philosophy to interrogate on the matter. If I do, I will send you a copy of the report—through channels.

To Lida Imhof, 29 August 1945:

No doubt, you have heard about the famous university town of Heidelberg. It is one of the few of its size that has not been bombed. There are many beautiful old buildings, and the Red Cross has been located in one of the best. In the evening, the small band plays on a balcony—all this to coffee and doughnuts. Sunday morning I went to a German church service. I can't say that I felt too much of the spirit of worship listening to the Protestant preacher. In the evening, I went to the *Schloss* [palace] where the civic symphony gave a very good outdoor concert of Viennese music. Here we busy ourselves with questioning high German general staff officers on the historical questions of the war. I never thought I could sit quietly opposite an SS lieutenant general and ask him questions in a polite manner.

To Margaret Mills, 4 September 1945:

We have Hungarians cooking for us, Czechs firing the hot-water furnaces, and German gardeners looking after the grounds. The amount of interrogating done here is rather negligible. [Paul, very uncharacteristically, then confided to Margaret that he may decide to go into a business career to make lots of money!]

To Lida Imhof, 9 September 1945:

After three years in the army and nearly two overseas, this is almost too much of a shock! How can the US Army expect to get along without me? Of course, there is some comfort in seeing colonels getting discharged, too.

To Margaret Mills, 11 September 1945:

If I ever buy or build a house, I am sure it won't be in a large town. Think of the destruction wrought in the towns over here. The only thing I miss at the moment is a good mattress, but I guess a soldier can't be too fussy. On the other hand, I can't help but feel that some of our prisoners are more comfortable in their rooms than we are.

To Lida Imhof, 14 September 1945:

My job is such that I sit in the office five-and-a-half days a week.

When a desk is available, I put my feet on it; otherwise I just sit quietly in a corner and read or write.

To Richard Yee, 20 September 1945:

Another advantage of being stationed here is that it is the headquarters of the Seventh Army. We have three movies, a theater, and a Red Cross club. There are a large number of good concerts given by local German musicians. While the weather was good, the concerts were given in the courtyard of the old castle, a truly beautiful spot. I know your watercolors would make a good picture of the Schloss.

I can imagine how you must have felt when the Japanese finally surrendered without a struggle. I hope you won't get into the Army of Occupation but get back to the United States soon. At the moment, German-speaking personnel here are frozen, but we don't think it will be for long. Of course, I want to return to the States. I have found no trace of my family thus far and have little hope in that respect, so I may as well go back. I am going to look for an interesting meeting when we both get back and become civilians. Perhaps we will meet in Colorado Springs. It should be an interesting "bull" session with intelligence work in both theaters. My idea is that you were in some sort of monitor service listening to broadcasts or else deciphering codes? I may be way off.

To Lida Imhof, 30 September 1945:

We returned to the station to board one of the cattle trains. That would have been fine if the locomotive had stayed with us, but since they changed it almost every station, we got bumped around a bit. It still seems like a dream to most of us that we are on our way back. I won't believe it until I see the Statue of Liberty and the little white paper with my discharge.

To Margaret Mills, 21 October 1945:

We left Marseilles on the tenth and for nearly two days basked on the decks in the Mediterranean sun.

To Margaret Mills, in a letter that Paul typed in the Pentagon just after being discharged from the army and becoming a civilian again, 25 October 1945:

On the bus, I sat next to a very nice lady who told me some of the spots to see in Washington. She turned out to be the wife of an Iowa congressman.

Later letters with World War II reminiscences

To Margaret Mills, 1 March 1947:

In the mail this week was a brief letter from a family in Chard, England, a place where I had been stationed for some time when I was in GG company. The mother used to wash for me, and I would bring things from the mess hall in return. Her girl, who is writing on behalf of the family, tells me that the old army huts are still standing on the estate of Lord Nelson, but that British civilians have moved into them now. It was bad enough there in the summer; now with eight inches of snow, I certainly wouldn't like to live there.

To Margaret Mills, 3 April 1948:

I believe I once described to you how I observed our troops going through a town, looting the houses, or told you the story of Junior and the diamond ring. Anyway, when the Russian soldier, who never in his life had seen these things, took something or went about the town wearing five wristwatches on his arm, it was at least understandable. It was less so when an American did the same thing purely for private enterprise or profit.

To Lothar Sudekum, in a thank-you letter for sending a second batch of seeds for his gardener, 27 July 1948:

On the way back from England, I stopped at Boppard where the team had been stationed in June and July 1945, and the man we had thrown out of the house came to the door, looked at me, said, *"Ach, der Amerikaner,"* and invited me in for a bottle of good Rhine wine.

To Harriet Cook, 19 August 1948:

In July I spent a week in England seeing a lot of old friends. The last time I was there was in 1945 just before V-J Day [15 August 1945].

To Willard De Pree, 7 December 1954:

I remember the *General Patch* but with more comfort since I went cabin class in 1949. We played bridge for nine days and threw the cards into New York harbor on the tenth. That, however, was the exception. I can well put myself into your shoes when I think of the *Admiral Capps* on which we came back in October 1945 with from five to six thousand men.

To Elwood A. Rickless, 18 July 1955:

The story of your assignment to Metz sounded delightful, and I congratulate you on having learned the army way of doing things. Ah, yes, I remember Metz well, but there was a time when I hated to leave there:

Christmas 1944. We were going to have our nice turkey, and then, the day before the dinner, we had to help some other outfits who had gotten into trouble at Bastogne. I froze my little toe, but, unlike my brilliant captain, failed to get the Purple Heart (he froze his big toe). What I remember best about Metz is the cathedral since it was my job to conduct "culture-seeking GIs" (a contradiction in terms) through the place.

To John Dryfhout, 23 January 1965:

Yesterday afternoon, I commented to a young man that I had never been in the Netherlands at this time of year. Only then did I remember that I had actually been there exactly twenty years earlier in the early part of 1945. At that time, our 35th Infantry Division had been taken out of the 3rd Army after the Battle of the Bulge and placed into the 9th which was then in the Netherlands. We drove into Maastricht in utter darkness, and my jeep lost contact with the one ahead while we were going over the Wilhelmina Bridge. We guessed at the street to take and obviously made a mistake, for after ten minutes of driving, we were on our way out of town again. We turned about along some canal and found that there were some forty vehicles behind us whose drivers had assumed that we knew where we were going!

To Alan and June Metcalf, 24 November 1968:

About a month ago, I was awarded a very lovely gold medal by the Austrian government in recognition of my "service to the Republic of Austria," so now the citation hangs below the one for my Bronze Star. And that brings up the question of whatever happened to the original medal. I really have forgotten. I know it was in your deposit box at one time. You were going to give it back to me, but I can't find it, even though I now have a deposit box of my own!

To David Havinga, 26 November 1970:

Your activities in the army bureaucracy sound familiar. I was one of the "flagged" GIs once, having been taken out of the infantry for MIS training and sent back to the infantry for reassignment via the great replacement pool in England prior to the invasion, only to find out that there was a "flag" on my form 20 that said I could not be assigned. So, for six months or more, some five hundred of us ended up as permanent KPs and guards in various replacement depots in England until we were discovered and flown with top priority to Paris.

Final notes on war experiences

This anonymous article summarizing Paul's military experience appeared in the Hope College *Anchor* on 19 December 1945.

Paul Fried enlisted in the army in the fall of 1942. He went to Camp Carson, Colorado, and from there was transferred to Camp Ritchie, Maryland, where he was a student at the Military Intelligence Training Center. In January of 1943, he landed at Bristol, England, and spent the following ten months in southern England. He then went to Paris for two days, and two days later, he was at the front in the Saar Valley. He was with the Third Army attached to the 35th Infantry Division as an Intelligence Specialist. Christmas Day, 1944, he was alerted to the Bulge, and New Year's Day he spent visiting Bastogne. In the middle of January 1945, the 35th Division was sent to the 7th Army for two weeks and then to Maastricht, Holland, the 9th Army, and on across the Roer and Rhine Rivers.

Paul worked in a team with four other men, and in a two-week period these five accumulated nine decorations. Their officer received the Silver Star and Captaincy; three got Bronze Stars and two the Purple Heart.

After V-E Day, Paul went to Hannover and then to the Rhineland for the occupation. The division was now in the 15th Army. Paul remembers this as the most enjoyable period overseas. Teams composed of two men each were assigned to a county as counterintelligence agents. Their job was to clear the county of Nazi big-wigs and to look for saboteurs, etc. The Germans referred to them as the "American Gestapo." Paul said that out of the three or four thousand people asked if they were convinced party members, only one woman answered affirmatively. Paul met Jeff Wiersum about this time.

In June his division was sent home, but Paul stayed in Germany. He was reassigned to the Detail Interrogation Center near Heidelberg where 250 general staff officers were interned. Paul stated that the interrogation of these men will be the basis for textbooks on World War II. About ten of the major criminals went through this center, Göring included. Paul himself interrogated Kessler.

"Everybody in Germany squeals on someone else due to his Nazi training." This is, of course, a help to the occupational forces. Paul said that the biggest problem in the occupation organization is the German campaign to spread distrust among the Allies. Paul is a senior this year, and even though he won't be with us long, we are glad to have him back at Hope.

Paul received several form letters (although they were very sincerely worded) from officials in the White House and the Defense Department thanking him and other military personnel for their sacrifices and achievements in World War II.

In an oral interview with Matt Nickel, 9 April 2003, Paul remarked: "I spent a little more than three years in World War II as a GI. I even have some decoration for it—no particular consequence because lots of people got them."

CHAPTER 8

Hope College Post-War Studies (1945–46)

An excerpt from "Summary of Background and Experience," written by Paul during his first year teaching at Hope College in 1953-54, summarized his return to civilian life: "During the war, I became seriously interested in history, and when I returned to Hope after the war, I shifted the emphasis of my studies to the field of social sciences. I graduated from Hope, cum laude, in June 1946 and was accepted for graduate study at Harvard."

Paul provided no date of composition for the following paragraphs from "Return to Civilian Life," the final part in section four of his autobiographical notes.

Return to Civilian Life

The discharge formalities took only a few days and then, less than a month after I had left Germany, I was free once again and on my way back to school. The familiar Hope College campus seemed undisturbed, just about the way I had left it. The only difference was that there now were about seven times as many girls and almost no fellows. But soon, in a couple of months, many of my old friends also came back to school.

I think there was a great difference in our school work before and after the war. Most of us were a great deal more interested in our work than we had ever been before. In my case, the chance to work with "intelligence men" who forever had to probe and ask questions had left its mark. Whenever I began to write a paper, I could visualize my former captain asking, "How do you know? Where did you get that information? How reliable is the man who told you? Did you try to find out what is behind this?"

Before I had entered the army, my major field had been German language and literature. I had been taught to admire the works of Goethe and Schiller, the humanism of Alexander von Humboldt, and the greatness of a score of other German inventors and scientists. There seemed to be no field of cultural enterprise in which the Germans had not produced some outstanding leaders. But when I had come in contact with the Germans, it had not been with the type of Germans my college books had led me to expect. The first people had been soldiers and spies. But then there was a war raging, and one could not fight to the tune of Beethoven's 9th Symphony. When the war was over, however, I began to wonder what had happened to the great people I had always admired. I met only little men who claimed to have been the tools of the Nazi leaders, who had been led astray as if they had no intelligence at all. Had they suddenly changed, or had I been misinformed by my teachers? I determined to try to find some of the answers which my captain would undoubtedly have demanded of me.

Soon I was concentrating on history instead of German. I wanted to find out what had happened to the Germans and how it had been possible for Hitler to gain that hold over the people. John [probably Elmendorf], who was still in Germany, tried to answer my questions by sending me a whole set of high school texts used in the Nazi school system and saying, "Look at them; find out for yourself."

I suppose that to some extent every nation tries to describe its own role in history as favorably as possible. But what I found here was a complete perversion of the truth, a blending of every fact to fit the ideology of the Nazi party—the ideology of the master race which was destined to rule the world. It was not until several years later, when I read George Orwell's *1984*, that I realized that the Germans had only copied the well-tried system of the Russians.

But here was the question I tried to answer: Which Germany was the real thing, and which the illusion? Was the Germany of Goethe and Schiller, Beethoven and Bach, gone forever—replaced by the Germany of Hindenburg and Himmler, SS men and Gestapo? How could this throwback to the dark ages be explained? The more I read, the less certain I became about the answer. However, the more I tried to fit the German question into the overall question of the new world order, the more important it seemed to know just what we could expect of Germany. She seemed to be the key to Europe. I read Nietzsche and listened to Wagner. But then I read Max Weber and listened to Hindemith and Strauss. I began to study the writings of Alfred Haushofer, but in the process I came across the sonnets his son had written in jail. I followed the godless trail of Mathilde Ludendorff and other neo-pagans, but I discovered the confessional church and the revivalist group around von Kleist.

The more I studied, the less I seemed to know. Then I wondered if I could really judge Germany and the Germans by what I had seen in 1944-45. I had met only soldiers, former Nazis and officials, and a few of the people who worked for the Americans or made their money from them. Perhaps I had just mingled with the wrong class; I realized that I would not feel comfortable in the company of similar people here at home. What I needed was a chance to meet young people, who, like me, were students, who were interested in many things, in books and music, in politics and sociology.

Suddenly, it became quite clear to me that I would have to go back to Germany, not as an enemy soldier or a member of the occupation army, but that I would have to live there as a student, among other students, if I wanted to find out what the young German thought and what role Germany would play in the years to come. Soon the necessary arrangements had been made, and only about three years after I had left there, I was on my way back to Germany.

Early work on return to Hope

Paul provided only an outline for part one, "Return to Hope," from section five (October 1945 to June 1947) of his autobiographical notes. He referred to various Hope professors, young and old friends, work as a clerk at Montgomery Ward in Holland from winter 1945 to May 1946, graduation from Hope, summer in Colorado, and admission to Harvard University. No date of composition was indicated.

Included in this section of Hope's archival holdings is an intriguing paper on "The United States as German Travelers Saw Them during the First Half of the Nineteenth Century." Paul submitted this as an assignment for his American history course on 9 January 1946. His instructor gave him an A grade with only a brief comment: "A very scholarly paper; very interesting." On page two, in a footnote, Paul said:

"When quoting from German sources, I have translated primarily the views and opinions expressed. Considering the stilted language of the early 19th-century German writers, a literal translation would often lengthen and complicate the paper unnecessarily."

In a book report submitted in May 1946 on C. S. Lewis's *The Screwtape Letters* for his senior Bible class, Paul wrote: "In war there is a chance for self-pity, but it is also a time when no man can ignore that death may come at any time." Also included in this section is a newspaper report about Paul's address to the DAR (Daughters of the American Revolution) in April 1946.

"The Price of Peace"—Paul's award-winning oratorical essay

Paul's oratorical essay, "The Price of Peace" (January 1946), won him first prize in the local Hope College competition and allowed him to enter Michigan's state competition later that semester. The essay was distributed to all those who attended Paul's memorial service in 2006. It is reprinted here in its entirety.

On March 5, 1945, I knelt in the dimly-lit basement room of a German farmhouse. It served as our battalion aid-station. On a stretcher lay a dying German officer. While a medic gave him plasma, I questioned him in German about the disposition of his troops. He tried to answer, but all I could hear was: "Why did they shoot me? . . . Why did you Americans come here? . . . We wanted peace!"

Could it be that the supermen who had attacked Poland, ravished Norway, and plundered the Netherlands and all of Western Europe had become "peace-loving"? I didn't think so! But I am sure that in his last moments, this young German suddenly realized what an awful price he and his country had to pay for the war. And as I watched him die, he ceased to be the enemy to me, and I, too, saw for the first time the ghastly results of war.

The sacrifice humanity made at the altar of Mars can never be fully imagined. From the shores of North Africa to the mountains of Italy, from the beaches of Normandy to the banks of the Elbe, and from the gates of Moscow to the suburbs of Berlin, the soil is saturated and made sacred by the commingled blood of the "United Nations."

Today the world is confronted with the crucial questions: Can we prevent a third world war? What are the chances for "peace in our time"?

We hope for permanent peace, but there are dark clouds on the horizon. Soon after the war was won, Americans began, all too quickly, to press for a return to normal, peacetime living. America ceased to be

Delivering "The Price of Peace," his prize-winning oration, 1946

seriously concerned about the problems of her war-time allies. Without warning, we stopped lend-lease, and UNRRA [United Nations Relief and Rehabilitation Administration] had to fight and beg for the money we had already pledged. At the same time, we discontinued rationing. At Thanksgiving and Christmas, our tables were loaded with more food than any of us could eat, while half a world away women and children froze, starved, and died for lack of the things we threw into our garbage cans.

As after the last war, civilians and veterans alike prefer to forget all about the war and its causes. Once more we are about ready to withdraw into the shell of isolationism. Unwilling to face our commitments abroad, we urge the armed forces to send home all of our loved ones, while we hesitate to continue the drafting of replacements for them. Too many of us indulge in the luxurious delusion that we can have peace and security by ignoring the rest of the world.

I have been back in the United States only a few months. In that time, I have heard almost daily casual comments about the next war. Can we keep the atomic secret?

How fast will other nations develop atom bombs? We suspect Russia! We dislike the French! We are afraid of British imperialism! Americans can't even agree among themselves on what to do with Germany and Italy!

Truly, as we listen to these dire predictions, another war does seem inevitable.

And yet we do want peace! But are we prepared to pay the price of peace?

If we want to prevent another war, we must first realize that peace is not just the absence of war. Real peace is order, based on law and justice, not only among individuals but also among nations. I believe the price of peace will be the all-out support of a world government, a federation of the nations, the union of all people. This will mean the sacrifice of a portion of each nation's national sovereignty, specifically that portion that involves the power to make war.

Until nations give up some of their sovereignty, the way our thirteen colonies did, we can never hope for permanent peace. Think of the founders of our nation who toiled to mold these discordant states into one harmonious union! Under it America has prospered and grown. The constitution they wrote should serve us as the inspiration and the model for the union of the world.

I am not proposing a new structure, nor even a revolutionary change in the existing United Nations Organization. President Truman, in his annual message to Congress, calls it a "minimum essential beginning, which must develop rapidly and steadily." We must transform that loosely knit advisory body into a strong world government. If we want permanent peace, we the people of the United States of America, must take the lead in the formation of the United States of the World.

This we owe to those who sacrificed their lives to win the war. Now it's up to us to make the necessary sacrifices to win the peace. Let's face it—a world government will require sacrifices. We will have to change some of our tariff laws. We will have to give up the right to make war on other nations. We will have to submit our disputes to a world court on which there will be other judges besides Americans. Most of all, we will have to discard our imperialistic ideas about inferior races. We will have to accept all other nations as our equals. This will be the test of the democracy we profess.

Other sacrifices will be necessary. We will have to share some of our wealth with others. At first this will cost us money, labor, materials, and some of our other resources. Our living standard might even drop a few points. But it will certainly never cost us the two hundred billion we just spent to win the war. And in the long run, all of humanity, as well as America, will be the richer. Therein lies the test of the Christianity we profess.

America developed the atomic bomb. American aviators dropped it on populated cities. We fought this war without mercy. Have we the right to expect mercy from the aggressor in the next war? No, America will not survive another war. Our future and the future of the whole human race will depend on our willingness to pay the price of peace before it is too late.

Which of these would you choose? To contribute some of our food surpluses to starving Europe, or to suffer again the privation, fear, and anguish of war? To allow tariffs to be lowered and to admit some foreign goods, or to experience again the loss of loved ones and the sacrifice of the youth of our country? To sit at a conference table with black, brown, and yellow men and to submit to a world court, or to see our great country devastated by atomic bombs, our cities leveled to the ground, and to live like moles in underground shelters?

We, the people of the United States, you and I, must choose now, between one world or none, between survival and extinction, between life and death! Perhaps my oration should end here! But I could not close without telling you why I chose this subject. I was born in Germany. My father was a journalist. In 1933 he was sent to a concentration camp. I was in Austria when Hitler occupied that country, and I landed in prison at that time. Later I escaped to Czechoslovakia. My family was still there when the war broke out. Where they are now, I don't know.

Christmas 1939, I landed in the United States. For the first time in years, I enjoyed peace and freedom from fear. For a while Ohio was my home, later Michigan. It occurred to me that neither of these two states, each about the size of an average European country, had any intention of attacking the other. Then I wondered how long it would take the world to learn from America that Poles and Czechs, Swedes and Germans, Italians and Russians could live together peacefully. I wanted to speak then but didn't because, after all, I was only a stranger, enjoying the hospitality of a generous nation.

Six years have passed. Over half of that time, I wore an American uniform and carried a gun to help to protect the freedom I had found here. Today I no longer feel a stranger here: America has become my home. As an American, I hope I may soon find an opportunity to work with one of the social agencies of the United Nations organization. I am proud to be an American because my faith in our country and in the American people is unlimited.

The first month I was in America, this sign caught my eye: "The difficult we do at once, the impossible may take a little longer." To me this has always exemplified the true spirit of our country. Is permanent peace a dream? Is the world government impossible? It may seem so to other nations. But if we, the American people, are prepared to pay the price of peace, all we have to do is to roll up our sleeves and go to work . . . to accomplish the impossible.

We can do it!!

Letters and writings about final months as Hope College student

To Lida Imhof, 12 January 1946:

My trip was terribly tiring from Detroit to Holland, over twelve hours. I made up my mind to hitchhike next time. I went to work on my paper and finished the first copy. Then Dr. Schrier started bothering me about my oration. Finally, I finished the draft and then spent the afternoon at his house watching him tear it apart.

To Lida Imhof, 7 February 1946:

If you ever find yourself in the mood for light entertainment and have an escort, I can warmly recommend a picture called *Kiss and Tell* with Shirley Temple. I am not leading you astray, am I?

To Alan and June Metcalf, 7 February 1946:

The same day I finished my finals, Montgomery Ward found out they couldn't take the inventory without me, so I worked about thirty hours last week. In addition, my oration is going to take a good deal of time. What I feared has happened. I won the local contest and now will have to go to Detroit for the state contest. I have no illusions about getting anywhere near the top there, but I am supposed to work as if I had.

To Rev. Arthur and Martha Kate Barnhart, 14 February 1946:

About 120 new students entered Hope with the second semester; most of them are veterans. The boys are not the same as when they left. I think there is a growing demand for better teachers and more collegiate courses.

To Lida Imhof, 18 February 1946:

It is rather exciting to be in the last semester. All at once the teachers seem to treat you as their equals, and you wish you had another year to go.

Paul helped edit a series of *Anchor* "Ambassador" articles written by ex-GIs for the Hope College newspaper in the spring of 1946. Paul worked with Renze Hoeksema in gathering these reminiscences from veterans Allen Valleau, John Buursma, Jack de Kruif, Fred Wight, Preston Stegenga, Robert Snow, Eugene Rothi, and Donald Scholten.

Paul's own *Anchor* Ambassador article appeared in the 7 March 1946 edition:

"Wenn jemand eine Reise tut, dann kenn er was erzaehlen." I couldn't help remembering this old German saying, "When someone

takes a journey, he has something to report," as I listened to a group of my old schoolmates as they talked about places they had visited. I enjoyed their stories about many countries I had never seen. In recent months, we have heard much about the UNO, international cooperation, and "one world." I think that one of the primary prerequisites for peace is the understanding of the other nations on the globe. We might go to the library and pick out a book on Belgium or about the customs of the Chinese, but we have too many books to read already.

A much better way to learn something about the nations with which we have to share this world would be to let those who have been there tell us about their personal experiences. Today over a hundred veterans are attending Hope. More than half of them have been overseas, in Europe or the Pacific. Their acquaintance with the people and the customs of many nations was intimate. The *Anchor* could do much to educate Hope students for peace and good will among the nations by publishing articles by our own classmates who have experienced something of the comradeship of the United Nations during the last few years.

To Lida Imhof, 12 March 1946:

It's a good thing you didn't bet any money on me. I placed fourth [in the state oratory contest]. All the same, I am not the least bit disappointed. I am quite sure the others were a lot better than I was. I am quite proud that I could represent Hope College in a state contest. After all, the other contestants all spoke English since childhood.

To Lida Imhof, 31 March 1946:

Thinking about Easter and your upcoming birthday, I happened to notice some nylons in the safe of the store [probably Montgomery Ward]. Unfortunately, they are all very small, but I thought I might put a bid in for some when they come in again. If you let me know the size, I can try. No promises made, though.

To Lida Imhof, 10 April 1946:

I really appreciate the thought and care with which you selected a birthday gift for me, but I must make a confession. My neck got fatter, and I now wear a 15½, 32 and am afraid this shirt will not fit me. Perhaps you can call that store by phone, and I can send the shirt back. Otherwise, I will have no trouble finding a boy here who can wear it.

To Margaret Mills, 10 April 1946:

I am materialistic enough to ask why he [Archduke Felix] is doing it, and the only answer I can think of is that he, or rather his brother Otto and his mother Zita, want to get back the lost throne of Austria. I know that Otto, the oldest brother and pretender to the throne, made a very definite attempt to establish an Austrian government in exile here in the United States (like the Dutch and Polish governments in London) with himself as the head. The State Department must have given him some encouragement at first because he attempted to raise an Austrian army to fight with the US forces. The plan remained just that, except that one Austrian battalion was set up. It was a mess and soon discontinued. While I was at Carson, I was asked if I wanted to join it. I said NO, and that was all. A friend of mine was not as lucky and just transferred into the outfit. His comments wouldn't make pleasant reading.

To Paul Gottwald, 28 April 1946:

In January, I entered and won the oratory contest at Hope ($30 prize). Later I went to Wayne State University with it and placed fourth in the state contest. I also found myself appointed to the student council and went to work on the *Anchor*, where I now edit a full page of travel accounts of veterans. For this semester I chose, among other things, a play production course and a course in modern drama. For the drama course, I promised to try to get material on the Burgtheater in Vienna— enough for a report. Of course, there is nothing in the library here, so I could use your help. You might give me some ideas about your own impressions, experiences, and recollections of the place. If you can find a book or some articles relating to the history, directors, first performances, and stage experiments, I should most certainly appreciate these things very much.

To Margaret Mills, 23 May 1946:

Another event I better report was a meeting with my first American friend (I met him in Vienna in 1937) in Grand Rapids. He was actually instrumental in bringing me to the United States and later getting the scholarship at Hope for me. He felt very strongly that I should not go back to Europe but settle down here in the United States. I think I agree with him, and unless I get a very good offer from the War Department, I shall not go. I was offered a position as teacher of social studies and Bible at a mission school in North Carolina. After very serious consideration, I decided against accepting. Instead I have made up my mind to attend graduate school. I am going to apply to Harvard.

Paul wrote "Education in Nazi Germany" for the Hope College *Anchor* 58, no. 16 (29 May 1946), shortly before his graduation. Here are a few passages from that article.

During the latter part of the nineteenth century and in the beginning of this century, German schools and German scholarship were highly respected throughout the world. To this day the biographies of Emil Ludwig, the discoveries of Albert Einstein, and the literary achievements of Thomas Mann remain unchallenged contributions to the progress of human knowledge.

But the same country which produced these men and boasted of its fine schools was also the scene of uncounted murders, of concentration camps, and was the breeding place of fanatical racial hatreds. It has been claimed that Hitler and his party ruled the country by terrorism, that Himmler and the Gestapo were responsible for most of the atrocities committed by the Third Reich and that the majority of the Germans were not aware of these things.

To accept this view would be to assume that the nation which had produced many outstanding scholars and the universities which had enjoyed international fame had suddenly been stricken by blindness. Rather than to subscribe to this improbability, we must search elsewhere for the facts which made it possible for Hitler to replace the cultural achievements of Germany with medieval superstition, blind nationalism, and warped morality.

The answer can only be found in the fact that under Hitler all schools became the instruments of the party. To be sure, there were a number of teachers and university professors who refused to surrender the right to teach the truth, but they were soon dismissed or sent to concentration camps. The great majority of the German teachers found it impossible to resist the pressure of the party for any length of time. They soon resigned themselves to the inevitable and taught what they were told.

The results were obvious. German schools ceased to be concerned with the development of character, the search for truth, or the preparation of the students for peaceful occupation. The support of the Nazi ideology was now the primary function of the teacher. In order to prove the theories of the racial superiority of the German race, the myth of the divine calling of Germany to rule the world, the fanatic hatred of the Jews and other minorities, and the evils of democratic ideas, it became necessary to provide textbooks which would serve this end.

Paul's essay then examined translations of passages from grade school and high school textbooks used in Germany since 1933. These books denounced Christianity and democracy and advocated German racial superiority. His essay concluded with these two paragraphs.

We must realize that the soldiers who faced us in battle, the SS troops who committed atrocities in concentration camps, and the young women who prostrate themselves before their conquerors today are all the product of this education. Even the innocent boys and girls, who eagerly accept the candy offered to them by American soldiers, have been exposed to these teachings.

Whether we treat the youth of Germany kindly, fraternize with him, and consider him our equal, or whether we treat him as the defeated enemy, will in the long run make little difference if we do not succeed in re-educating him. We can only hope for a peaceful Germany and a peaceful Europe if we can help the German youth to recover mentally and spiritually, if we can impart to him the love for freedom, democracy, and Christianity which is the foundation of our way of life.

To Lida Imhof, 3 June 1946:

Today I wore my gown for the first time. Quite unexpectedly, and rather undeservedly, I was chosen as one of seven seniors for faculty honors. We had to sit up on the platform while the president made a speech referring to our scholarship, love of learning, integrity of character—and so on, and on, and on. One good point: we were invited to a luncheon by the faculty at the Warm Friend.

To Walter A. Scholten Jr., 5 December 1946:

Hope is crowded. Some nine or ten barracks have gone up on campus during the summer. The college has also taken over the junior high school on Graves Place as a girls' dorm, a house on 9th Street, and the Temple Building. Dr. Schrier was quite downcast; I don't think he forgave me for having my tonsils out three weeks before the state oratorical contest.

To Don Vandenberg, from Nürnberg, 7 January 1948:

No doubt Harvard is a better school [than Hope] in matters academic. But what matters here with this German boy [applying for admission to Hope] who should catch a glimpse of the workings of democracy is not how important the professors are, how many buildings the campus has, or even how big the endowment is. What does matter is the evidence that there is Christian fellowship, a classless mingling of those whose fathers are laborers and farmers and those whose fathers might own half a town, a free and easy mingling of boys and girls, and a relation between student and teacher which is friendly and not authoritarian. All those things are better observed on a smaller campus like Hope.

To Margaret Mills, 14 June 1955:

Thank you for the clipping about Rev. Bob Schuller [founder of the Crystal Cathedral mega-church in southern California]. Did you know that Bob and I competed in the 1945-46 oratory contest? He placed second, but only because he probably had less to say. I am sure he is a better speaker.

CHAPTER 9

Harvard University Studies (1946-47; 1949-51)

Harvard 1946-47

An excerpt from "Summary of Background and Experience," written by Paul during his first year teaching at Hope College in 1953-54, highlighted Paul's first year at Harvard University.

Professor Harry Rudin of Yale was my advisor. My major research project concerned "German Imperialism in the Marshall Islands." This study was based on the unpublished archives of the American Board of Missions. Copies of the paper are in the Harvard Library and in the library of the American Board of Commissioners for Foreign Missions in Boston. I took courses under Professors Brinton, Owen, McKay, Gilmore, and Karpovich in various fields of history, and under Professor Wild in government. In June 1947, I received the MA in Modern European History.

Paul provided only an outline of part two, "Harvard Graduate School," from section five of his autobiographical notes that cover September 1946 to June 1947. He briefly mentioned names of friends and professors, problems of preparation and adjustment, a Christmas reunion in New York City of M11 427 G, his research project on imperialism in the Marshall Islands, job offers from Hope College and the US War Department, and his last-minute appointment to Nürnberg.

To Harriet Cook, Paul's landlady at 36 Graves Place in Holland [She kept almost every letter from Paul in its original envelope; Paul put little crimson Harvard pennant stickers on many envelopes to her.], 23 September 1946:

I spent Saturday afternoon and Sunday in Providence, Rhode Island, with my former commanding officer. Never thought I would enjoy his company so much when we were in battle together. He used to teach here at Harvard, so he was able to give me quite a bit of valuable information.

To Harriet Cook, 2 October 1946:

I am so glad you have such a nice bunch of boys. I bet you are glad I am not there anymore. I never made my own bed. I wonder if you would do me a favor. My big blue trunk is standing in the attic. If you open it, right on top should be a pink blanket. Not very far from there is my little green album with all the pictures I took in Germany. I would very much like the blanket. The album is not so important; I just want it so that [Mary] the wife of Dr. Keeney can look at the pictures.

To June Metcalf, 3 October 1946:

I am enrolled in four courses, all of which are very interesting. One course, "The United States in World Politics," is attended by over five hundred students. Two others run about one hundred each. Fortunately, there are only twelve members in my seminar. For that I will have to write a short paper, some sixty or seventy pages. The reading lists are endless, and I have yet to settle down to serious work. I am fascinated by the library, which holds some four million books.

To Harriet Cook, 22 October 1946:

Have you read Walter Lippmann's *American Foreign Policy*? You can get it in the twenty-five-cents edition; I'm sure you will enjoy it.

To Lida Imhof, 22 October 1946:

I have a roommate [Robert Friend] now. He has taught at the University of Panama for a number of years; his field is English.

To Lida Imhof, 3 November 1946:

Oddly enough, my present work has a good deal to do with missionary reports regarding the German occupation of the Marshall Islands. I have gone through three volumes of missionary letters, 1857-70, looking for occasional references to the other white settlers. My findings have been few, but I enjoy the letters just for their own sake.

To Lida Imhof, 17 November 1946:

A few days ago, I happened to run into a fellow who had been with me through most of the rough spots in England; he is now in the law school. Another fellow who went overseas with me in the same boat is in two of my classes. There are always interesting lectures. I heard one by Dr. Karl Gruber, the young Austrian foreign minister who is in the country trying to stir up sympathy for Austria. They have chosen a good man for it.

To Margaret Mills, 2 December 1946:

I can tell that I have still not overcome this intellectual snobbery in that I feel a certain envy towards those who did their undergraduate studies at Harvard and not at Hope!

To Metta Ross, Hope history and English professor, 3 December 1946:

The more I see of the workings of a large university like Harvard, the more I feel grateful for the advantages of a smaller college like Hope. The only thing I really admire at Harvard is the library. I am constantly surprised when I find books mentioned in an obscure reference of some German writing in the 1880s.

To Rev. Arthur and Martha Kate Barnhart, 10 December 1946:

My courses are interesting but too crowded. The topic of one seminar is 19th-century imperialism. I picked the Marshall Islands for my study of German activities, mostly because I had found that the American Board of Missions had some missionaries out there and that their archives are stored here.

To Richard Yee, 23 December 1946:

It might be well for you to have a year or two in a small liberal arts college—yes, like Hope. You do need something more than a big place like Harvard can offer. I shall be happy to introduce you to a number of my friends on the faculty.

To Paul Gottwald, 31 December 1946:

So far, I must say that I have not found many of the compensations of graduate work, only the disadvantages. Basically, I was never cut out to be a scholar, and in history you find too many people who worry about the beard of the emperor.

To Margaret Mills, 8 January 1947:

Tonight at supper, the fellows who sat with me got on the subject of when their ancestors had arrived in the United States. One fellow said his came in 1636 and so on down. When I told them that I had come to America in 1939, nobody would believe me, which was rather gratifying to me.

To Margaret Mills, 29 January 1947:

I certainly think that there is something wrong with our whole educational system which puts a premium on cramming ideas into the student's head; if properly reproduced, such ideas will lead to a good grade. If, however, he should respond to those ideas with thinking of his own, chances are the tests would find him a poor student.

To Richard Yee, 29 January 1947:

I was very much surprised by your reference to a possible visit to China, a complicated and most expensive venture. I am well aware of the feelings that you have for your father and mother. I certainly would be only too happy to find my parents alive and well and would even consider going to Europe to see them, if they were found. But I would be aware that my trip would take money they could well use for a better purpose.

To John De Vries, 31 January 1947:

I think there is something unhealthy, like a hothouse, about this place. Too much artificial scholarship—quite well wasted because it doesn't mean anything.

To Hilda Cook, 3 February 1947:

I have a nice sitting room here in Cambridge, and since my roommate moved out a few days ago, the walls are quite bare. If you can find an inexpensive and colorful picture of England for me, I should be very happy to look at it when I get home from lectures. In case you are wondering about my taste, I don't have any. But I remember several scenes which seemed to express England very well: the Backs of Cambridge, the old inns or cottages, and then the many points of interest in London. [On 27 April 1947, she sent him a lovely etching of King's College.]

To Max Putzel, 9 February 1947:

The walls of my study are quite bare, so now I am trying to get some pictures to hang up. I certainly would like a print or etching of some typical Berlin scene. I don't mean one with a woman leaning against a lamppost.

To Robert Friend, 17 February 1947:

I am afraid my record here is very poor: three Bs and one B+. On the Marshall Islands paper, the only comment below the B was: "Very ordinary language, jerky sentences." You may well imagine that I was p.o.'d at first, but on second thought, he could not have paid me a greater compliment. Ordinary English is exactly what I have been striving for in the last five years.

To Robert Friend, 6 March 1947:

I was glad to hear about all the work you and the friends at the mission are doing to aid in the feeding of Europe. Here at Harvard, we have a drive for $25,000 to help in the reconstruction of four universities: Vienna, Athens, Warsaw, and Peiping.

To Don Vandenberg, Hope student who had worked with Paul at Cliff House in Colorado, 5 April 1947:

In my part-time job with the *Boston Herald-Traveler*, I am doing some investigative work into graft in the city administration. Regarding the value of training here, I am changing my mind. Slowly, out of the maze of new impressions and assignments, there crystallizes the idea that I am under the instruction of some of the best men in the field and that what they say and teach is new, that it goes deeper and beyond the information obtained in college courses.

To Metta Ross, 6 April 1947:

The burden of your work sounds almost too heavy. At Harvard, all professors in history have readers who correct all tests and read most term papers. Professors are said to do all the correcting of graduate papers, but in some cases there is reason for doubt.

To Richard Yee, 30 May 1947:

Today I went to my first baseball game and found out something on how the game is played.

To Helen Hathaway, 13 November 1947:

I am not too much of a Harvard fan, so I am rather amused when people think I ought to be downcast when Harvard loses.

Included in the Harvard memorabilia are an ungraded paper that Paul submitted (6 May 1947) on "Lord Runciman and the Sudeten Problem 1938" for History 42 and many one-cent postcards mailed by Harvard professors with notification of the grades that Paul earned in their courses.

Paul spent the next two years working as a translator at the US Military Tribunals in Nürnberg, Germany, and earning a PhD from the University of Erlangen, but he returned to Harvard University for three semesters from September 1949 to January 1951.

Harvard 1949-51

An excerpt from "Summary of Background and Experience," written by Paul during his first year teaching at Hope College in 1953-54, declared:

I returned to Harvard in September 1949 in order to continue study and research in history and international law, with the thought of better preparing myself for a teaching career and eventually obtaining a Harvard PhD as well. Major research projects which I completed during this period dealt with: "Friedrich Flick and Hitler's Rise to Power" (a study of the role of German industrialists in the political developments until 1933); "The National Socialist Concept of International Law"; and "Rumania's Entry into the Second World War." My principal advisor was Professor H. Stuart Hughes. I also took seminars, lecture courses, and reading courses under Professors Fay, Langer, Friedrich, and Goodrich."

Paul's tuition and maintenance at Harvard were financed by the GI bill. He was in Cambridge from 1949 to 1951. Paul met the mathematics major, musician, and satirist/songwriter Tom Lehrer, who lived in the same hall (Dunster House). On many evenings, the piano was pushed into the hallway, and Lehrer composed and later recorded songs.

To Jane Bender, colleague in Nürnberg, 24 September 1949:

I am back at school again trying to get a PhD in history. Can't you just see me sitting in a classroom listening to a prof?

From Jane Bender, 30 November 1949:

Jane's response to "Dear Paulie boy" teased him about "sitting in all those dull classes with that quizzical yet cherubic little expression on your face," and then she asked him when and where he had acquired such a wonderful disposition.

To Frank Buster, in a letter that recommended the detective-novel style of Hugh Trevor-Roper's *Last Days of Hitler*, 31 December 1949:

I had to work like the dickens to get that paper done on "The Degeneration of Law in the Third Reich." It dealt with the effort Hitler and his gang made to eliminate all legal codes and to dictate to the judges how they must do their jobs. For example, if a German Nazi owed money—

for a legitimate purchase of a house or anything else—to a non-German (a Jew or Pole or Frenchman), the judge was not supposed to find the German guilty (he was a member of the master race and the others were inferior, so how could they be right and a German wrong?). This is not something I just made up in my head; that's about what the minister of justice said in a circular to the German circuit courts in 1942.

Included in the Harvard files are Paul's paper (plus a retyped version) on "The Degeneration of Law in the Third Reich" for government 170 at Harvard on 11 January 1950. The professor made a few comments within the paper but provided no final evaluation with the grade.

To Richard Yee, 21 January 1950:

Competition is very keen here, and the attention given to students is at a minimum. This is one of my weaknesses, but I would rather be a big frog in a little pond than a little frog in a big pond. This pond, Harvard, is very big. For the first year, they drop you into it, just to see if you can swim, and if you can't, no one cares; they let you sink.

To Annabelle Werley, 12 February 1950:

Life here at Cambridge is quite interesting. Pandit [Jawaharlal] Nehru and his sister were here. I am invited to hear the prime minister of Pakistan (had to look it up on the map) this week.

To Margaret Mills, 26 February 1950:

Friedrich Flick is an industrialist [who controlled much of Germany's coal and steel production]; he was tried in Nürnberg and convicted to seven years of imprisonment for crimes against humanity— use of slave labor, etc. My primary purpose will be to determine what political role he played in 1928-33 to bring the Nazis to power. I am really excited about this project.

To Margaret Mills, 18 March 1950:

I hope to get some more material for my paper on Friedrich Flick. Just this morning, I had a very cordial letter from Prof. [Robert] Kempner, who was deputy chief of counsel in Nürnberg. After I have seen him and perhaps General [Telford] Taylor, I will know a little more whether I can use this topic for a thesis.

To Margaret Mills, 27 March 1950:

I have now collected most of the material on Flick but still have to write the paper. General Taylor wrote that he would be glad to see me. Last night I was able to make an appointment to see Dr. Heinrich

Bruening, one of the last chancellors of Democratic Germany from 1930 to 1932. He has served at Harvard as professor of government.

To Margaret Mills, 15 April 1950:

I had a very nice conversation with General Taylor. He put me on the trail of Charles Lyon, one of his young men who handled the Flick case. I spent about two hours with Lyon on Thursday and almost as much on Monday getting a great deal of valuable material.

To Max Putzel, 15 April 1950:

Part of the reason for my trip was to gather material for a paper on "Friedrich Flick and Hitler's Rise to Power." If you are familiar with the name, you will know that he is hardly ever mentioned anywhere (except by Franz Neumann) and that material is not easy to find. Of course, the larger question of industrialist support for Hitler has been discussed quite a bit and is very interesting. I am using quite a bit of the trial material from Nürnberg.

To Larry Wells, 8 July 1950:

I just wanted to wish you all the very best on your trip through Europe. If there is any way I can help you with introductions or (in Germany) with money [let me know]. In Germany, I have an annual income of three hundred marks from a small investment I made there. Friends of mine are located in Rome, Paris, London, Liege, Stockholm, Vienna, Salzburg, Munich, Starnberg, Augsburg, Nürnberg, Erlangen, Marburg, and Bad Nauheim. Just let me know if there is some place where you will want contacts.

To Jane Bender, 15 July 1950:

I have a large kitchen, so I can get some of my lunches. This summer I am not working too hard—just taking one intensive course in French. The class meets for two hours every day, and we are supposed to spend five hours preparing for it. I never do.

To Manzar Bashir, 22 August 1950:

Life here during the summer has really been a lot of fun. I did not do too much work on my French course but spent a good deal of time on social activities. Early in the term I found a very nice roommate, and I don't think more than five meals have passed since when we have not had guests for lunch or dinner. We do most of our own cooking and have turned up with a really amazing variety of dishes.

To Manzar Bashir, 10 September 1950:

The longer I stay here at Harvard, the more I find that I would really not be too happy in the type of life for which I am preparing (college teaching). As a matter of fact, I had thought of this profession only as a means to help me get into public service later since, as a naturalized citizen, my chances to get in on the regular lists were not very good. Somehow I got much more involved in the academic field than I had at first thought I would and almost lost sight of my goal. Now, I have come to the conclusion that if I can get a decent position with the Department of State, I shall take it on the theory that the present state of emergency will continue for some time and that I will be more apt to have a career in that work than in teaching, even if we should get into a shooting war.

To Fred Bradley in Prague YMCA, 10 September 1950:

Thanks for your comments on marriage. The question is thus far academic with me. Still, my father was forty when he married, and I think he enjoyed having a family.

January 1951: Paul received an A- for a long paper at Harvard on "German Diplomacy in Rumania, July 1940 to February 1941."

From Bob Bernen, 9 March 9 1951:

Bob told Paul that memories of him remained "warmly alive, I might almost say glowingly alive (with a sort of California sherry glow) in Cambridge. Scarcely a day passes that I do not hear some inquiry about you. The whole town perceives, now that the bright warmth of your personality no longer illuminates our streets, the slightly harsh grey tint of steel girders on every side. But like Odysseus, your fame reaches the heavens, and like pious Aeneas, your name is spread on the tongues of men even beyond the sky."

To H. Stuart Hughes, 27 February 1953:

Naturally, the question of whether or not to proceed with plans for a Harvard PhD before embarking on a teaching career arose in my mind. Much as I would like to finish my work at Harvard before starting to teach, I decided that since I would prefer a job in a small or medium-sized college to one at a big university, my European degree would probably serve as well.

CHAPTER 10

Translation Supervision at Nürnberg Trials (1947–49)

Paul offered a brief synopsis of his work at the Nürnberg trials in "Summary of Background and Experience," written during his first year teaching at Hope College in 1953-54.

At this point, I interrupted my studies for financial reasons and accepted a position with the office of the Chief Counsel for War Crimes, in Nürnberg, Germany. After working as a translator and reviewer for about two months, I was appointed chief of the section for German Foreign Office translations. In this position I planned, directed, and reviewed the translation of nearly all material and documents submitted in the Ministries Case (approx. 50,000 pages). Documents and briefs used in this trial dealt with political, economic, racial, and diplomatic problems, and their correct translation frequently necessitated considerable research in these fields. I therefore prepared a special glossary of these terms for the tribunal.

When I accepted the position at Nürnberg, I had done so partly in the hope of locating material for a thesis while in Germany. With this thought in mind, I established contact with Professor Anton Ernstberger of the University of Erlangen. Under his supervision, I began research in German diplomatic history, particularly in the field of German-Czech diplomatic relations during the Nazi period. After I had made some progress on the subject, Dr. Ernstberger urged me to complete my thesis while still in Germany and submit it at the University of Erlangen. I accordingly enrolled there and submitted my doctoral dissertation: "Die tschechische Frage in den Akten des Auswaertigen Amtes" [The Czech question in the files of the German Foreign Office]. I passed the required oral examinations under Professors Ernstberger, Weipert, Schoeps, and Baron Guttenberg. In August 1949, I was awarded the degree of doctor of philosophy, magna cum laude, from the University of Erlangen.

Martin Baierl's interviews (1999 and 2003) with Paul provided a few more details about Nürnberg days. Paul worked hard to create a good atmosphere as a civilian employee of the United States government: "I did not care how often colleagues stayed away (getting food or whatever) as long as they got work done." He lived in Schloss Stein with about fifty other Americans but would have preferred living downtown. In a *Stars and Stripes* lottery, he won the right to buy a Volkswagen.

Paul was involved in the preparation and publication of the sixty-five-page *English-German Glossary of Legal Terms* (prepared for the office of the United States Chief of Counsel). It began with *abandonment* (*Preisgabe, Aufgabe, Verzichtleistung*) and ended with *writ* (*Gerichtsbefehl, Vorladung, Rescript*). Paul also helped with the preparation and publication of the 129-page *Glossary for the War Crimes Office and Judge Advocate General's Office*. It began with *Aberkennung der bürgerlichen Ehrenrechte* (forfeiture of civil rights) and ended with *Zwangskartell* (compulsory cartel formed by an order of the government).

Letters relevant to Nürnberg Trials (1947)

To Margaret Mills, 15 March 1947:

At the main office of the Civil Service Commission, the list of jobs offered in Germany proved very interesting, the salaries even more astounding, and the temptation to fill out applications for a couple of the positions offered too strong to resist. The job I filled as a PFC—that of interrogator—when I first came to France should pay $4,700 to $5,100. Enough to say that I invested two afternoons to fill out applications.

To Don Vandenberg, 7 May 1947:

Suddenly, last Saturday, I got a wire from the War Department saying: YOU HAVE BEEN SELECTED FOR POSITION OF TRANSLATOR IN NUREMBERG, GERMANY. ANNUAL PAY $3,776.25. PROCESSING INITIATED. YOU MAY EXPECT TO LEAVE FOR GERMANY BY AIR ON MAY 12 FROM NEW

YORK. Well, much as I might have wanted to accept, it would have meant the loss of a whole semester and not getting the MA (of course, if I flunk out of my courses, which is not impossible, I won't get it either). Anyway, I wrote, "No, thank you," saying I should be glad to go after June 5.

To Margaret Mills, 12 June 1947:

I walked into the War Department office in New York at 10 a.m., and at 11 a.m., I walked out with a $3,775 job in Nürnberg.

To Margaret Mills, 3 July 1947:

On Friday evening, June 27, the C54 which took me to Europe was not equipped with seats but had litters in their place. The first day was rather uncomfortable, but after we left off passengers in Newfoundland and in the Azores, things became more comfortable, and I could even go to sleep. The group on the plane was well-mixed: a number of army hostesses and librarians, a lieutenant colonel, a naval officer going to Morocco, a lady of "leisure," and a group of GIs. Arriving at Nürnberg at 4 a.m. on Monday, I put up at the Grand Hotel and rested until noon.

To Alan and June Metcalf and the Kramer family, 8 July 1947:

I left Westover Field on Friday, June 27, and on Saturday evening I was in Paris. Sunday morning I went on from Paris to Frankfurt by plane and from there by train to Nürnberg. The processing here went very quickly, so that by Wednesday I was ready to start work. While I came over as a translator, I was assigned as translator-reviewer, probably because my Harvard MA impressed them.

To Isaac L. (Ike) Auerbach, 9 July 1947:

My head keeps spinning about with complicated legal German; we are trying some of the top judges of the Reich.

To Tom Bennett: 12 July 1947:

Just now the German doctors who conducted experiments on human beings are on trial.

To Alvin D. Coox, Harvard friend, 15 July 1947:

I wish you could drop in for a visit. I have a very nice office on the first floor of the Palace of Justice. Here in this building the big international tribunals were held. It gave me quite a thrill to sit in the courtroom we have seen so many times in the newsreels. Now the American Military Tribunals are being held here. Right now the German judges and some of the German doctors are on trial.

Schloss Stein: Christmas card from Paul's palace in Nürnberg, 1947

Schloß Stein
bei Nürnberg

1947

My job is not translation but reviewing of translations, which sounds better but is actually harder. I work with a nice group of people. There are two very nice English girls in the office, so I may come back with a British accent instead of a German one. If you come over for a weekend, you are very welcome to stay with me at Schloss Stein where I am billeted. The castle is some five miles out of town in the midst of a beautiful park. We have our own dining rooms, bars, band, library, tennis court, barbershop, and tailor. I have a large double room, but for the present the other bed is not occupied. I keep giving the manager cigarettes to make sure it won't be in the future. The cigarette is the standard means of exchange; you leave one on the dinner table for the waiter, you give it to the taxi driver, or you may use two or three to get into a German movie. Just to keep in training, I have signed up for a course in basic Russian and beginning shorthand.

To Rev. Arthur and Martha Kate Barnhart, 19 July 1947:

Quite by chance, I decided to drop in the office of the secretary of war to see about a job, and here was one waiting for me at a fair rate of pay. I work in the Palace of Justice in Nürnberg, but I live some five miles from town in a lovely palace that belongs to the brother of Eberhard Faber (pencils). We have our own large park, dining rooms, ballrooms, bars, libraries, band, etc., so it is possible to be quite comfortable. The

Reviewing trial translations in Nürnberg

Germans seem to be waking up out of the stupor of defeat at long last and have made a few slow steps in the direction of recovery. They have a great deal more freedom now, and conversely the Americans, outside of their own clubs and compounds, have a lot less.

To Eugene (Gene) Burgstaller, 20 July 1947:

I work in the Nürnberg Palace of Justice, translating sometimes dull and sometimes interesting documents brought in by the defense, whose main ambition seems to be to bore the judges to sleep and prolong the trials.

To Don Vandenberg, 29 July 1947:

Now I am doing translations. Boy, is that dull!

To John De Vries, 29 July 1947:

At long last, we came to Wagner's house and visited his grave. The house was almost completely destroyed by an American bomb, but right next to it is a lovely new building in perfect condition. We found out that it is the Führerhaus. Hitler was very fond of Wagner's music and also of the family, so he had this place built right on the estate. It is now an American officers club.

To Margaret Mills, 29 July 1947:

Aside from a good amount of work in the office [last week], I did some swimming, played badminton and ping-pong, walked a good deal, continued my Russian and shorthand, and took a trip to the University of Erlangen on Saturday and a trip to Bayreuth on Sunday. In the Führerhaus, now an American officers club, with considerable pleasure, I plumped down into one of Hitler's comfortable chairs to sip an iced Coca Cola.

To Dr. William and Mrs. Ada Schrier, 30 July 1947:

I went out to the Zeplinfeld. Where Hitler once ranted before his followers, there is now an American baseball field.

To M. Eugene Osterhaven, chaplain and professor at Hope,1 August 1947:

It would be very nice if you could stop by here on your way to Sarospatak, and I could put you up with all the style becoming a VIP. My office is in the Nürnberg Palace of Justice, but I live some five miles outside of town in a very nice castle. I am sure you would like it. I have met only a few Germans thus far, though I will admit that it will take me quite a long time before I can have the feeling of confidence in the German people as a group. Of course, with individuals, it is different.

To Howard Zandbergen, 7 August 1947:

You would be very interested in the trial of the doctors here. Most are under indictment for having performed experiments on involuntary human beings. The whole thing is very sordid, but when you read the defense speeches and the character witnesses, which is what I do (translate them), you would think they had all been angels.

To Harriet Cook, 18 August 1947:

I made a mistake not to take my uniform with me. For every day, I prefer civilian suits, but when you have to go on the train or hitchhiking, the uniform right away is the identification of the American. So I wonder if I may again trouble you for a favor. My uniform is on the bottom of the blue trunk. There are a cap, a coat, trousers, two tan shirts, and one wool shirt. If you could have these things packed and mailed for me, I should be very grateful. I have one smaller request. I bought a very nice candlestick, but here it is impossible to get any colored candles, so if you could include a few red, green, or yellow candles, I could use them to decorate my room.

To Lothar Sudekum, 19 August 1947:

It is hard to gain an adequate picture of what goes on here in Germany. There is still a terrible disorder in the economic life. The mark is inflated so that it has practically no purchasing power, or rather there is nothing to buy. People will not sell but barter. The German police carry guns again, but the Americans may not have arms.

With Harriet Cook,
Holland landlady

To Dr. Barnaby C. Keeney, 19 August 1947:

The work at the trials has been little more than routine translation of documents for the doctors, judges, and Flick trials. Things certainly have changed since we left here two years ago. The Germans have a great deal more freedom, and the Americans have a lot less. Nürnberg is centrally located. Weekend tours are offered to Austria, Switzerland, and Czechoslovakia. I made the trip to Prague this past week. I managed to see two people whom I had known before but found no further information regarding my family.

From Stuttgart, I decided to hitchhike back to Nürnberg instead of waiting almost twenty-four hours to go back on the Orient Express. Had a number of interesting rides and conversations with the *Oberbürgermeister* of Ahlen, a German banker, a Russian worker who had come to Germany in 1929 and stayed, and [a GI who had charge of German Youth activities].

To Huntington (Hunt or Terry) Terrell, later a philosophy professor at Colgate University, 20 August 1947:

We walked into the Hotel Paris, one of the better hotels in Prague, and managed to get a very nice room with twin beds, tile bath, etc. Everyone at the hotel was very nice, and it did not cost much. For two nights, we paid a little over four hundred crowns, which, depending on where you change money, is from $3½ to $9. On the advice of our driver, we went to a small Czech restaurant for dinner. You should have seen the steaks! They cost less, even with a bottle of wine, than our lunch at the hotel.

To the Metcalf and Kramer families, 20 August 1947:

I wanted to tell you about my trip to Prague. I met Otto Just, the son of the people with whom I had been living in 1938. He is now twenty-four and a giant. During the occupation, he worked in the underground against the Germans and was arrested for sabotage. Later, he spent two years in a Czech concentration camp because he worked against the Communists. We went to a real Bohemian restaurant on Saturday evening and had some delicious steaks and a bottle of Slovak wine. Later we went down to the Moldau to watch the fireworks which were set off to celebrate the International Democratic (Communist?) youth festival.

To Al Coox, 20 August 1947:

Many thanks for the interesting letter from the Bronx. I am sure I would like to go to a couple of those ball games with you and meet some of your friends. In return, I might even give you enough German lessons so you can buy hamburger—only now you won't get hamburger in Germany, or anything else for that matter.

That we will not be rooming together at Harvard in the coming year is a matter of considerable regret to me. My contract reads for two years, but I rather expect I could terminate it by the end of next summer. In any case, I am planning to return to Harvard in either one or two years to get (sounds simple, that word) a PhD. In the meantime, if I see a stray one over here, I shall pick it up for purposes of decorating my walls.

That is one reason why I want to keep up on history and on new publications. I should very much like it if you could get me a copy of William Langer's *Liberalism, Nationalism and Socialism*, as well as his *Diplomacy of Imperialism* (either new or used), and mail them to me. I would further offer to pay the whole cost of the Sunday *Times* for you, if you were to send the book section to me. Any of the books you listed would be welcome additions to my library, if you can get them in good second-hand condition.

Now I shall try to answer some of your questions. By the way, don't be afraid to ask them; I can always say I don't know. The attitude of the Germans toward us can be divided into two general classes: (1) the larger number of Germans who, directly or indirectly, work for us—secretaries, waiters, drivers, officials, etc., and (2) the rest of the Germans. The first group reaps material benefit from their contact with us—food, clothes, shelter, special favors, smokes, soap, etc. As long as they get these things, they are as nice as can be. I think most of them are quite well aware that our presence here is not a drain on the German economy, but a boon to them personally.

It is quite different with the other group. All they see is that we have food aplenty, big houses and castles to live in, one hundred servants for 150 people, taxis and buses, more clothes than we can wear, and that we don't do much. If they judge us by their own behavior, and it is natural that they should, they must conclude that since we have these things and they don't, we have taken them away from them and live in royal style at the expense of the average German. That is what they did in Czechoslovakia, France, Holland, and everywhere else.

Here is the answer to your question of Nazism. For a young person, boy or girl, the simplest criterion is the then-and-now method. During the first part of the war, after the plunder of the occupied countries, the Germans lived in very good circumstances; they had perfumes, silk, furs, etc. Now they have nothing. The first part of the war was under Hitler, the present under democracy; it was good then, it is bad now; ergo, Hitler was good for the Germans (too bad he lost the war; that was wrong), and democracy is bad for the Germans (especially if administered by someone else). This, of course, does not mean that we deal with an active revival of Nazism.

Rather, the whole thing ties in with our own attitude. Since the end of the war, 1945, we have given the Germans more and more freedom, while restricting the rights and contacts of our own personnel here to their own circle. That is, we have made no attempt to bring about friendly relations, which would have been all right had we remained the conquerors, but since we have not done that either, the Germans go their own way. Does that sound too confused? For example, German policemen now carry guns again, but Americans are not allowed to own firearms, except for very specific duties, such as guarding mail.

Well, before I close, I want to tell you about my visit this past weekend to Prague. I started on Thursday noon, and by the Orient Express, got there by 10:30 p.m. It was a relief to see all the lights, whole houses, stores with things to sell, and crowds of people. One boy, Otto Just, is the son of the people with whom I roomed. Now his only desire is to get out as quickly as possible. Perhaps I can help him in some way.

I hope you realize just how much it costs the government when I write such a long letter to you in the office. Of course, I would not be writing if there was work to be done. For the present, I am working as translator, but in the next few days I expect to move up as chief of a subsection which will handle all translations of foreign office materials. That was my idea to establish such a section. I hope to get something to go on for my thesis.

To Gene Burgstaller, 25 August 1947:

I have found a few very interesting items, such as a letter from [Karl] Haushofer to [Rudolf] Hess and a report from Haushofer to Hitler—two days after Hess's flight. If you are going to take a seminar with Langer this year, I might be able to get you some firsthand poop.

To Tom Bennett, 26 August 1947:

Work can be quite dull, but now I am working on material which is of considerable interest to me. Since we work only five days a week, the long weekends are sort of a compensation. I should very much like to send you something from here. How about some chocolates or soap? You don't have to worry too much about my spending money since I am getting quite a fair salary here. In fact, I am thinking of buying a car.

To Ike Auerbach, 11 September 1947:

I can well understand your personal feelings about the Palestinian problem, but I can tell you that a good many Jews here have told me that they consider the Irgun [a Zionist paramilitary group in Mandate Palestine from 1931-48] to be worse criminals than Hitler. One man, a well-educated German Jew from Berlin who worked with me for some time, thought of [Avraham] Stern and his gang as the same type of political opportunists and criminals as any other dictator. Certainly, they are wasting the sympathy of the non-Jewish world. Once you kill, you can no longer ask the outside world for consideration as a religious group. Well, I am not competent to pass any judgment on this matter, but I know that I do not believe in meeting evil with evil.

I wanted to ask you a favor. The few bright and gaudy ties I have cause a considerable stir among the younger members of our staff out at the castle who just love them. I would like to get about half a dozen of the loudest possible—or impossible—ties to distribute as the occasion arises. If you should find yourself in a bargain basement, I should like to get some, but I don't want to spend much. You might have liked to attend the party we had last night to raise funds for the Jewish DP [displaced persons] children. Since you couldn't come, I am sending you the ticket anyway.

To Howard Zandbergen, 10 November 1947:

I now supervise the work of a section, which is a lot more work than plain and ordinary translations. I have some twelve expert and high-strung American and Allied translators and almost as many not-so-expert German secretaries and typists to take care of. I allowed myself the luxury of buying a small dog. One thing leads to another: the car, the job, the dog did not fail to impress the female of the species; hence, I now have a half-and-half girlfriend. I don't think we will get along too well for very long because we are too different in temperament. I am grateful for this friendship all the same.

To Lothar Sudekum, 10 November 1947:

You asked if there is something I wanted. A gardener at Stein has done a number of favors for me. I have flowers in my room and greens in the office. Since he can't get any seeds, he asked if I could get some from the United States. He wants "Asparagus Sprengeri," the green plant used between flowers. He would like about five or six pounds. I looked through a number of magazines for ads of seed houses but couldn't find them. If you could order this stuff for me and have it shipped to my address, I should be very pleased. I wouldn't like to spend more than ten dollars. If it is more expensive, he will have to take a smaller amount.

To Huntington Terrell, 12 November 1947:

I promised to say something about the tribunals. After the great trial (Göring, et al.), each of the Allies set up their own tribunals to deal with the "lesser" war criminals. The first one was against the doctors who used concentration camp inmates as human experimental subjects. Next came the judges who bent the law to fit Nazi theories. Also running: the hostages case (Field Marshals [Maximilian] List and [Wilhelm] Weichs, who had about a million hostages killed in the fighting in the Balkans), the Flick case (Flick was the super-industrialist who profited most by Nazi aggression and occupation of conquered countries; he had even more holdings than the Hermann Göring A.G.), the *Einsatzgruppen* case (the special SS units created to run the gas and other extermination camps in the East; they are charged, on the basis of their own daily reports, with a million murders), the IG Farben case (which may prove a considerable embarrassment to American industry and which is charged with the use of millions of slave laborers as well as the deliberate planning of war), the Pohl case (the SS commandant of a camp who has just been sentenced to death). Also going are two cases against Nazi offices: the RHSA (*Reichssicherheitshauptamt*, which is the agency of Himmler, a part of which was the Gestapo and the Secret Service, spy system, etc.) and the RSuRHA (*Reichssiedlungs und Rassehauptamt*). This agency, under the cover of soil reform, etc., deliberately caused the extermination of native populations in areas considered valuable as future German *Lebensraum* [habitation]. They also ran the *Lebensborn*, a legalized breeding place for good German girls and SS men, etc. None of this is pretty.

The case which interests me most has not started. It will indict the principal officials of the German foreign service for planning a war and preparing for it. I asked to be assigned the translations for this case. That's how I happened to get this section. I expect it will open about Christmas. Perhaps I will find some material in this trial for the PhD thesis.

To Ike Auerbach, 14 November 1947:

Since the last writing, I have had seven typists added to my staff. We handle a weekly average of 350 to 400 pages of translation (a good-sized book). I also put out a special glossary (dictionary) to be used in translating foreign office documents.

To Al Coox, 19 November 1947:

First, a tip to the absent-minded professor. An APO address, such as mine, is considered to be within the American postal zones; therefore, it is quite enough to use ordinary American postage, three cents or five cents for a letter, depending on whether you want to send a regular letter or to hasten delivery by sending it airmail.

Now, I can properly thank you for your air letter of October 18th. If you think you have been busy, you should spend a couple of days in my office. Since last writing, I have moved about three or four times and have been promoted once. Since the raise is somewhat over a thousand per annum, I have no reason to complain.

To answer your question about my work, I was translating and reviewing. I still do some of that, but primarily function as Der Führer of a translating section which includes some ten or twelve American and British translators and about eight German secretaries. Four of my translators have doctoral degrees of some sort or other; you may imagine how that makes me feel.

The interesting part about my present assignment is that it is the more-or-less direct outcome of my interest in European diplomatic history. I asked to be assigned translations of the documents to be used in the foreign office case, which is to open here in about a month. Now I have a whole section working on these documents. I just get time to read some of them. Anyway, I am sitting at the fountain. I only wish I had enough containers to preserve some of the flow.

One way of doing just that has opened in the meantime. I made several trips to the University of Erlangen, and it now seems that I will be able to get a PhD there by writing a thesis and taking an examination. Yesterday I had my first meeting with Professor Ernstberger, under whom I will work, and we agreed on the subject—broadly. It will be something on the diplomatic preparation for the occupation of Czechoslovakia. Just how far back I will go, I will have to see later. He was very nice and said he would not mind taking the thesis in English. He wants about 250 to 300 pages.

Of course, if I get a PhD here, that will not mean the cancellation of my plans to return to Harvard for the same purpose. But it may help me later on. I think this paper might later be expanded into something which may be acceptable at Harvard. In any case, a European degree still has a certain amount of snob appeal, at least at Hope.

Your work at Harvard also sounds quite hard but interesting. Let me know if you run across any good papers on the Czech problem. I think you had a couple in Rudin's course. Wonder how the old boy is. I have not written to him as yet but shall do so in the very near future.

Well, my office seems to need my attention, so I better close and do some work. As a rule I don't even get this much time for a letter in the office. I still think it is nice to have a letter to answer when I write, so I would like to see one of yours when I write again. Hope you passed your German exam. I will have to think about my French, but I rather forget it for the present.

To Preston J. Stegenga, 17 December 1947:

One of the chief reasons why I took this job (apart from a small consideration of about $5,000 a year) was the fact that it would bring me into firsthand contact with documents dealing with recent history and especially diplomatic history of Europe. You probably know that after the international Military Tribunal closed, the "minor" war criminals were to be tried by the respective occupying powers. Well, here in Nürnberg, there have up to now been eleven cases before American Military Tribunals. The one which interests me most is the case which will open this week against the foreign office. My section has been making most of the translations. On the side, I have interested myself in the possibility of picking up a stray PhD here.

I am afraid it would be too long to get onto the problem of the Germans and their present attitude. I have the distinct impression that they would like nothing better than a war between the United States and Russia. They think they have suffered enough for Hitler's errors (not theirs) and that the Americans are criminals for not feeding them.

To Max Putzel, 17 December 1947:

With the exception of the ten German girls who work for me, and who are neither good looking nor interesting, though they may be good typists, I have no contact with Germans of any sort. The Americans build a self-appointed upper class where the Cabots speak only to the Lodges.

Winter revelry in Nürnberg days

Letters relevant to Nürnberg Trials (1948)

To Don Vandenberg, 7 January 1948:

My work here is terribly interesting, though I sometimes get too much of it.

To Harriet Cook, 15 January 1948:

I spent Christmas in Geneva and met one of my oldest friends, Dr. Hoffmann, and went to the American Church in Geneva with him on Christmas Day.

To Chet and Louise Schultz, 31 January 1948:

I work on the case against the Nazi foreign office, and since I get a very high salary (twice the amount I would have had as instructor at Hope), I can't complain. I like to get around the country and see some of Europe in peace time. I have been to Prague a number of times, also to Switzerland, France, and Austria. At Christmas, I spent a very pleasant two weeks traveling down to Nice.

To Margaret Mills, 16 February 1948:

We are so isolated here from all important news that Berlin could go up in flames, and you in Colorado would know about it long before the news got to Nürnberg. I have only the faintest idea of the Marshall Plan and have had no means of following the United Nations or anything else. I wanted to tell you about the final plea of Gen. [Otto] Ohlendorf, the former chief of the *Einsatzgruppen*, those units which were formed for the specific purpose of running extermination camps. He and his fellow defendants are accused of something like one million murders. His final plea was that we were substituting democracy for the lost ideal of Christianity, whereas he and the Germans had substituted another ideal (blood and race). In his plea, he indicated that the two were about the same—substitutes for Christianity. In a way, I am prepared to agree, but there is a fundamental difference. In the problem of Russia, you might be even more justified in comparing Nazism and Communism as being substitutes for the faith which was lost in the age of materialism. Both democracy and Communism at least claim Christianity as their basis and maintain some of the ethical principles of the religion. Violence and lawlessness exist in both countries (political trials and labor camps in the USSR and race riots and the Ku Klux Klan in the US), but in neither case have they been covered by an elaborate set of decrees and a great deal of teaching which make them both legal and apparently right and moral actions. The point is that one million people were deliberately murdered—cleanly, orderly, with less confusion than in a Chicago slaughterhouse—and the man who was in charge of the killing calmly stands up and speaks of his deep religious feeling and his faith in God. Since the man is not insane, there is something terribly disturbing about that. It is all the more terrible if others listen to his plea (or Göring's plea that he was not doing anything someone else had not done) and think that the man is not to blame for what he has done.

To Huntington Terrell, 3 March 1948:

Here at the tribunal, we are trying Germans who committed aggression against other nations and crimes against humanity. It is, naturally enough, the aim of the defense to show that our former allies committed those same crimes and to draw the conclusion that they are on trial not for crimes committed against peace and humanity but because they have lost the war. I am not prepared to admit the similarity of the violations.

To Hilda Kloucek, 5 March 1948:

My work here at the tribunal continues to be quite interesting. Yesterday we had Admiral [Miklos] Horthy, the former regent of Hungary, on the witness stand. He is nearly eighty but carries himself extremely well and answers questions with such humor and speed that I was reminded a bit of a comic opera—especially since he spoke German with a very funny Hungarian accent.

To Hilda Cook, 6 March 1948:

Over the Easter holidays, I hope to go to Vienna for a few days. This will be my first visit there in ten years. I expect to celebrate the tenth anniversary of my release from jail in Vienna. At the time, I had to sign a piece of paper stating that I would never return and would not make any claims against the government. Well, times change. My job here is very interesting. I have been able to work primarily on material used against the "gentlemen of the Wilhelmstrasse," i.e., the trial of the foreign office. Since modern European history is my special interest, I have been collecting material for a thesis on the subject of Nazi diplomacy.

To Mary and Bernhard Herz, 20 April 1948:

Life in Germany is pleasant for members of the occupation, especially for civil servants like me. Regarding the things left to Bernhard by his mother, I would certainly like to help. I know these mean a lot to you, but I see not much hope of getting them to you. I think you have a mistaken idea about their value. Two thousand marks today are two cartons of cigarettes (which I get for $1.60). For the same amount, or a little more, I could buy a typewriter. For forty thousand marks ($40 to me), I could buy a good German car, but none of these transactions is legal, and I have no interest in risking a very good position. I am just trying to show you the conditions here. I do hope that you are not too much attached to these things. I have learned that it is not worthwhile to worry about the past. I did not even bother to put in a claim for our house in Wiesbaden because it is damaged, and the trouble involved would hardly be worth it. I would rather concentrate on building a home of my own in America.

To John and Mary Elmendorf, 25 May 1948:

For a good many months, I have been chief of a translation section, which has given me considerable experience in the handling of minor problems and personnel troubles. At the same time, it has kept me quite busy.

To Robert Friend, 13 June 1948:

Baron von Weizsäcker, the former German secretary of state, is now on the witness stand. This morning Bishop [Eivind] Berggrav of Norway was here to testify on his behalf. Weizsäcker even introduced an affidavit by General Marshall and other affidavits by people like Bruening and Butler (British), so we shall have quite an interesting time when they get here to testify. Of course, in Weizsäcker's case, the question before the tribunal really boils down to whether or not a civil servant or other individuals should continue in their posts or quit if the orders they have to sign are contrary to their better judgment.

To Dr. Barnaby Keeney, 30 August 1948:

Now the Czechs will let Americans in again, but the army has threatened to punish anyone who is caught going there contrary to present regulations. Baron von Weizsäcker now claims to have been one of the leaders of the German underground and is bringing such a mass of evidence that he may be able to convince the tribunal that he really was a resistance leader.

To Max Putzel, 19 September 1948:

You would be surprised if you could visit Germany now, after the currency reform. All the stores have beautiful luxury goods; there is food, there are clothes, the rubble is being cleared away, and new constructions are begun—as if a magic hand had suddenly awakened the sleeping powers of reconstruction. All this is pleasant to see, but I can't help but feel that it would be fairer if we were to help some of Germany's victims a little more instead of feeling sorry for the poor Germans.

To Preston Stegenga, 4 October 1948:

The chief defendant is Baron von Weizsäcker, who now claims to have been a member of the anti-Hitler resistance movement. Life over here in the occupation and work for the government is somewhat demoralizing. There is an atmosphere of intellectual stagnation which sooner or later engulfs you. Because of the currency reform and the improvement of general conditions, Germans are more apt to resent our presence here. The most dangerous thing is that one is apt to become cynical and lose faith in humanity. I have discovered with something of a shock that I have become quite pessimistic about ideals which meant a great deal to me not so very long ago. Perhaps that is just a passing phase marking the transition from the student to the man in contact with the outside world?

To Henry Krieger, 20 October 1948:

I often think back with pleasure to our work on the Rhine. I am afraid that our policy of helping Germany back on her feet is not doing anything to re-educate the Germans towards democracy. There is no reason to think that the Germans will not take whatever we offer them, only to decide to side with the Russians if there should be a conflict and the Russian Army is nearer than our troops.

Playing tourist in Nürnberg days, most likely on the Pegnitz River

To Preston Stegenga, 3 November 1948:

You ask about a possible underground here. I don't believe there is much of that now. However, you might find the resistance movement under Hitler of considerable interest. A lot has been said about it, even to the point of claiming that the whole foreign office was involved in it. That, of course, is bunk! I just managed to get a copy of General Halder's diary (he was chief of staff from 1938 to 1941), and it is most interesting, especially in regard to the Russian campaigns. The last of the cases, the one I am interested in, will close in a couple of weeks, and all we have to translate now are the briefs and pleas of the defense, all claiming that the men charged with crimes are saints, that they never had any authority, never hurt a fly, never were in the party, and only wanted the best for everyone! The stuff is routine, but the perverted logic gets on your nerves after a while.

To Huntington Terrell, 4 November 1948:

Would you do something for me? I lost my discharge button some time ago and feel very much in need of wearing it. Especially now that the place is flooded with all sorts of newcomers who think they can play the part of veterans. If you could buy one for me, I would be most grateful.

Letters relevant to Nürnberg Trials (1949)

To Max Putzel, 22 January 1949:

There is not too much *Gemütlichkeit* [cordiality] here. The US attitude toward Germany is getting more disgusting as more former Nazis

On vacation from the Nürnberg Trials, probably in the Bavarian Alps

return to high places. Still, there are some compensations. One of them is that we are able to help others once in a while. I just had the pleasure of seeing a young man off to the United States; he will spend a year at Hope.

To Hilda Cook, 10 February 1949:

My job here keeps getting postponed. Apparently, the judges cannot reach a verdict in regard to Baron von Weizsäcker and the others. They were supposed to be ready in December, then in January, and now they have promised to be finished in March. After that, we have to translate the judgment into German so the defendants can understand it. Following the conclusion of the case, we will have to translate appeals for some six or eight weeks. It looks as if it will be May before I am quite finished.

To Bob Ruggles, 16 February 1949:

If you want to do something for me, you could buy a wool scarf (either brown or yellow) for me since I only have that green army one which is three yards long. If you see some Noxzema cream, please get a couple of jars for me.

To Huntington Terrell, 20 February 1949:

We have really put Germany back on her feet, not only in outward appearances but also from the point of international trade. Here in the West, we have, in fear of Communism, had to take back many of the old nationalist and even National Socialist leaders, offending the liberals and the working classes. The result is that the loyalty of this part of Germany is assured only for as long as we have enough troops here to defend them.

To Bob Ruggles, 2 March 1949:

Clay has now given strict orders to us to stay out of German restaurants and bars, in part to cut down the rate of "incidents."

To Metta Ross, 21 March 1949:

The enclosed survey will give you an idea about the type and amount of material involved. I realize that something like four hundred thousand pages (German and English) may present something of a problem for the [Hope College] library. However, they will be packed and crated and shipped free of charge and are assembled in paperback volumes. The potential value of the documents cannot be overestimated. The history of the origins of the Second World War and of the diplomatic relations in Europe during the war is for the most part contained in the material used in connection with the Ministries Case. The documents might encourage some of your advanced students to do research in this particular field. If you want the material, please let me know as soon as possible.

To Kathleen (Kay) Stout, a translator and reviewer in war crimes cases who received orchids from Paul in February 1949 for her send-off, 8 April 1949:

About an hour ago, I delivered the last of the 822-page judgment to Mr. Rehberg. It will be read beginning Monday, and you will hear about it in the papers. It is about what was to be expected—quite weak. On top of that, Judge Powers is writing a dissenting opinion.

To Prof. David Owen, chair of the History Department at Harvard, 29 April 1949:

I am very glad that I took your advice. The work on the war crimes cases, especially on the case against the foreign office, has been most interesting.

To Kay Stout, 19 May 1949:

I have been working, not like a horse, but like one of those heavy-duty Indian elephants. Have translated about one hundred pages for Weizsäcker and another thirty for [Ernst] Woermann (horrible German and twisted logic). My brain is drying out.

The trip back was quite pleasant. About thirty miles out of Paris, there were two GIs hitchhiking. They looked frozen stiff and had a little fire by the side of the road. They had been robbed the night before and

Enjoying the company of bathing beauties, again during
a break from the Nürnberg trials

had no tickets home to Bamberg. We decided to take them along, even though it crowded us a little. Five hundred miles a day is about the record for hitchhiking.

To Howard Zandbergen, 24 September 1949:

I achieved all I set out to do in Germany and Europe: save some money, gather some material for a thesis (I wrote the thesis and submitted it at the University of Erlangen, where I got the PhD just before I left), and have a great deal of fun and some very interesting experiences meeting a lot of people—even cousins.

To Kay Stout, 28 September 1949:

After some delay, I left Bremerhaven on August 14th in the company of far too many German war brides. Still, a young American couple from Berlin and an Air Force officer and I got together and played bridge—interrupting only for meals and a few hours of sleep. Incidentally, I think I learned quite a bit about the game. On the other hand, we got so sick of the game by the time we reached New York that we threw the cards overboard. The next day, when we had to wait four hours for the customs official, we got a new deck.

From Jane Bender, 30 November 1949:

Judging from the prolific correspondence you carry on with the femmes de Nürnberg, I would say that you, like the Navy boys, must surely boast a girl in every port.

Later letters relevant to Nürnberg Trials

To Henry Krieger, who is about to take a position in Germany, 15 February 1950:

The attitude of the Germans will rub you the wrong way. More than that, it will make you boil to see American administrators in high places swallow the German nationalistic line "hook, line, and sinker" and try to out-Nazi the Nazis and impose Prussian social order on their staffs and in the army. I honestly was glad to get out of it all.

To Margaret Mills, 18 February 1950:

I have a tendency to lapse into long, involved sentences. The funny thing is that, although this habit has its origin in the German style, I have always vigorously objected to long sentences in German. My pet aversion was the way my father wrote (with considerable success). He used very long sentences, sometimes covering a whole page. His letters, written in a very small, neat hand, were works of art from that point of view. The degeneration of this style was very much in evidence at Nürnberg where defense lawyers used endless sentences in order to cloud the meaning of what they were saying. That seemed to impress some of the judges and partly served to string out the proceedings. In the case of Baron von Weizsäcker, the advantage of the method was clearly demonstrated. The verdict rendered in April 1949 certainly was much less severe than it would have been had it been rendered in 1947.

To Dr. Randall Miller, 6 June 1972:

I am delighted to hear that you and Linda will visit Nürnberg. If you need a haircut, or Linda needs a good hairdresser, I hope you will call on my old friend, Herr Joseph Schoell, Friseursalon Schoell, Lessingstrasse 4, in one of the best hotels—Deutscher Hof—and directly opposite the stage door of the opera, which is why all the stars go there. Please give him my warmest greetings. Many years ago, he used to give me a shave every morning when he was our resident barber at Schloss Faber, and later I lent him the money to start his present shop, which for a few years made me part owner of a barbershop in Germany. He has long since paid me back, but I have a residual income in the form of a shave or haircut whenever I pass through the city. If you tell him you are one of my friends, you can be the beneficiary.

To Jo Reischer, 30 July 1972:

Did I tell you that I published a brief essay on Weizsäcker in a book which [Rolf] Italiaander edited last year? It's not great, but there is the pragmatic matter of getting printed; it is in German, so my dean and president will never know how superficial it is.

To Willard De Pree, whose daughter did research on German General Franz Halder under Paul's guidance, 14 December 1989:

We talked about the Halder diary which was translated in my section. My copy is one of one hundred mimeographed in Nürnberg for use in the trial in Case Eleven (Weizsäcker, et al.). I thought you would enjoy the enclosed "Foreword" and the general introduction which was also prepared in my section. The copy I have was bound for me as a personal memento, along with some other materials. There are five volumes, about 11 inches high, taking 11+ inches of shelf space [now in Hope College's Van Wylen Library].

To Ed and Ina Fogels, 11 December 1995:

The other event on my tentative schedule for the early part of 1996 is a visit to Washington celebrating or discussing the 50th anniversary of the opening of the war crimes trials in Nürnberg.

To Lothar Sudekum, 11 October 1995:

Contacts with the college continue on several levels. One is through a new history faculty member who is now giving a course on the Nürnberg Trials (on which he wrote his PhD thesis). I am supposed to give a guest lecture in his a class and plan to focus on the "climate" of the place rather than on the legal questions since I am not too certain he does not know more than I do in that field. But I know he was born several years after the trials had become history!

To Jan Evert, 3 November 1996:

The question is what I could or should do with the pile of material I have on Nürnberg. I gave the forty-two-volume set and the earlier ten-volume set to the Hope library, and it seems that it has had fairly good use over the years (spines of four volumes were replaced, and a couple have received completely new bindings). Had a long conversation this evening with the librarian about perhaps putting some of the documents into the archives.

Paul kept extensive files on issues and people related to the Nürnberg War Crimes Trials, including ones on Albert Speer (labeled confidential), Krupp, Ribbentrop, and Obersalzberg; a *Der Spiegel* cover article on Flick (5 June 1963); a few Nazi-era photographs; a "Courtroom Program for International Military Tribunal, Nürnberg, Germany, 1945-1946 (Prepared by Public Relations, HQ CMD, IMT)"; a final brief for Weizsäcker (about 600 pages); his Harvard paper on "Friedrich Flick and Hitler's Rise to Power"; and a note on his 27 March 1991 "WWII Remembered Seminar" to the Hope Academy of Senior Professionals. On 19 November 1996, Paul spoke on the "Nürnberg Trials (50 Years Later)" for the Holland Area Historical Society.

Paul also left a folder with this description of his History 295 course at Hope: Brief survey of pre-war period, including the rise of German and Italian Fascism, the policy of appeasements, and the diplomatic prelude to World War II. The major portion of lectures, readings, and reports will be devoted to the European phase of the war as seen, experienced, and reported by Axis and Allied sources. The course will try to examine the Holocaust, anti-Nazi resistance movements, diplomatic efforts to end the war, and the decision to hold the war crimes trials.

Essay on "The Case of Baron Ernst von Weizsäcker"

Paul composed an undated essay entitled "The Case of Baron Ernst von Weizsäcker" to pull together his conclusions on this important trial. A German version of this essay was published in 1971 in *Diktaturen im Nacken*, edited by Rolf Italiaander. Here are Paul's words in English:

I must admit that, when I arrived in Nürnberg in July of 1947 to become a member of the translation staff for the American Military Tribunal, the name and career of Baron von Weizsäcker did not mean much to me. Soon, however, I found myself assigned to the translation of documents which were to be used in the so-called Wilhelmstrasse case. A few weeks later, I was appointed chief of the translation section which was to deal almost exclusively with materials for this trial. In the next year and a half, I think I must have translated or read translations made by members of my staff of more than thirty thousand pages of documents.

Our translation services were available to both prosecution and defense. Before the trial opened, however, we worked mostly on the translation of documents from the foreign office's files that were selected by the prosecution in the preparation of the case again Baron von Weizsäcker. The picture they painted was quite clear and incriminating. Weizsäcker's position as state secretary in the German Foreign Office seemingly placed him in direct control over German diplomatic missions around the world and made him the essential link between the foreign policy plans conceived by Hitler and Ribbentrop and their actual execution. Weizsäcker's name appeared on hundreds of documents which seemed to support the prosecution's charge that he was guilty of having taken part in crimes against peace, war crimes, and crimes against humanity.

The indictment listed Weizsäcker's positions, including his membership in the Nazi party and his rank as SS Brigadeführer, and summarized the charges against him and his fellow defendants as follows: "These crimes included planning, preparing, initiating and waging wars of aggression and invasions of other countries, as a result of which incalculable destruction was wrought throughout the world, millions of people were killed, and many millions more suffered and are still suffering; deportation to slave labor of members of the civilian population of the invaded countries and the enslavement, mistreatment, torture and murder of millions of persons, including German nationals as well as foreign nationals; plunder and spoliation of public and private property in the invaded countries pursuant to deliberate plans and policies intended not only to strengthen Germany in launching its invasions and its aggressive wars but also to secure the permanent domination by Germany of the continent of Europe."

On the other hand, as Weizsäcker's trial progressed, the defense submitted an increasing amount of impressive evidence intended to show that Weizsäcker had not really shared Hitler's aggressive and criminal aims and that, quite to the contrary, he had on many different occasions used his high office to try to prevent war from breaking out and to protect individual victims of Nazi excesses wherever he could. In time I came to know as much about Weizsäcker's defense as I had about his indictment, and when his attorney started to prepare his closing brief in Weizsäcker's defense, I gladly agreed to work with him on the language of this document in order to make it as effective as possible.

The question of Weizsäcker's innocence or guilt, which the tribunal attempted to answer, is one which can hardly be discussed here in a few lines since the final judgment against Weizsäcker ran to more than eight hundred pages reviewing tens of thousands of pages of documents and testimony. After reading this, as well as the dissenting opinion of Judge Powers, I am still not certain what the answer is to this question. Probably because there is no simple way of deciding what a man should do when he has to choose between loyalty to his government and his nation and the dictates of his moral, ethical, and religious convictions.

In many ways, the case of Baron von Weizsäcker illustrates the dilemma we all face a good deal of the time in various situations. Weizsäcker was a gentleman; his father was a Protestant minister; he had first served in the Imperial Navy and had then become a civil servant during the Weimar Republic. He was intelligent, cultured, efficient, and respected. He moved up in the foreign office until, in 1938, Ribbentrop chose him to be his chief administrative officer in the foreign office. Weizsäcker, during his trial and in his memoirs, stated time and again that he accepted the appointment and remained in office, though he fundamentally disagreed with the aims and methods of the Nazis. He summarized his reasoning as follows: "What does a sailor do when the weather and the captain have brought the ship into danger? Does he go below deck in order not to have any responsibility? Or does he set to and do all he can to help, with all his strength and all the means at his disposal? I did not attempt to leave the danger spot but tried to stick it out and fight. Such was my decision. My goal was peace—peace for my country and for the world I lived in" (Weizsäcker, *Memoirs*, 310-11).

There is little doubt that Weizsäcker did indeed do his best in a number of instances to help people from the excesses of Nazi policy. He helped some Jews as well as political and religious victims of Hitler's system. He also was in contact with some members of the German underground who hoped one day to overthrow Hitler. But all the time, he was caught in the rather hopeless conflict of being a German nationalist and patriot as well. He did not really object to the aim of building a "greater Germany" and overcoming the "shame of Versailles." He simply hoped that it could be achieved without war.

And once war began, could a patriotic German really hope for the defeat of his country? Henri Bernard in *Lá Resistance allemande contre Hitler* (quoted from 20 July 1944 in an anthology edited by Hans-Adolf Jacobsen, Bonn 1969, page 15) makes this comment: "In the course of hostilities the German resistance was confronted by a frightful dilemma: how to combat its own government, how to put an end to the abominable Nazi regime without detaching itself from the mass of fighters? Dare one risk encouraging civil war while a war is going on against other countries? Has one the right to hope for the defeat of one's own country? . . . One cannot expect all the resisters to think as the theologian Dietrich Bonhoeffer: 'It is only through defeat that we shall atone for our terrible crimes against Europe and the world.'"

Weizsäcker, though in sympathy with the resistance, was not really part of it. He simply meant well. He meant to preserve some order, dignity, and respectability in the foreign office; he wanted to keep the ship from sinking. So he stayed on. Perhaps this took more courage than to resign and go below deck. But did this save the ship? Unfortunately, it did not. On the contrary, it has been argued that Weizsäcker and other "decent Germans," by staying in office "to prevent the worst," helped make the Nazi regime appear respectable to the outside world. At a time when refugees from Hitler's terror tried to warn the free world of the new German danger, diplomats and respectable people in Paris, London, and elsewhere could look at Berlin, see Weizsäcker installed as number two man in the foreign office, and feel: "It can't be as bad as all that; I know Weizsäcker, and he is an honorable man. He would never stand for it if these stories were true." As the court said in Nürnberg: "One cannot give consent to or implement the commission of murder because by so doing he hopes to eventually rid society of the chief murderer."

Of course, the dilemma of Baron von Weizsäcker is not new, nor is it a problem of the past only. All through history, men have had to decide the question what to do in the face of governments which were unjust or oppressive. There have always been those who became exiles — voluntarily or otherwise—and those who remained at home supporting the regime, passively accepting it, or collaborating with it to a greater or lesser extent. A fascinating study by Werner Warmbrunn dealing with *The Dutch Under German Occupation* (Stanford University, 1963) shows that even the Jewish community leaders in the Netherlands were faced with the same dilemma: "Thus, Secretary-General Frederiks argued that it was important to remain in office as long as possible in order to protect individuals and to prevent the execution of worse measures by persons who would be willing henchmen of the occupying power" (273). Unlike Weizsäcker, Warmbrunn concludes, however, that "any collaboration with the absolute evil represented by National Socialist principles, politics, and institutions, backed up by the police power of the totalitarian state, was bound to corrode the good intentions of all collaborating individuals or groups. . . . In this perspective, the collaboration of Secretaries-General Frederiks, Verwey, and Hirschfeld cannot be justified" (274-75).

What of the present? Are the questions which face Weizsäcker and Frederiks in any way similar to those which American citizens and soldiers may have to consider in regard to the war in Vietnam? Do they relate to the decisions to stay or to flee which young Czechs had to make in the summer of 1968 or to the dilemma which has faced many Germans in the DDR who have relatives in the West? The answer should be obvious: there is a relationship, but the response cannot be the same in all cases.

The basic democratic process which exists in the United States makes it possible for citizens, even soldiers, to voice protest against government policies—even though the protesters may not be popular. In the present situation, there is, however, a strong indication that

Surrounded and soothed by natural and architectural wonders,
away from the intensity of the Nürnberg trials

opposition to the war is growing even in Congress and among political leaders and that the government is forced to respond to this protest by a change in policy.

The situation in a country in which the political police plays a major role is entirely different. Here the question may well be: "Does it take more courage to stay at home or to emigrate?" Before the wall went up in Berlin, West Germans seemed to take great delight in reporting the ever-increasing stream of refugees coming from the DDR. Here was obvious proof that the one system was superior to the other. Obviously, the refugees from the East had "voted with their feet." All the same, one cannot help but wonder then what chances for improvement or change there would be in the East if all the people with spirit, youth, ambition, and imagination emigrated to the West. The answer depends on the individual and on the degree to which he is willing to make a real stand for the ideals in which he believes.

Here perhaps may be the resolution of Weizsäcker's dilemma— and our own. If, as A. J. P. Taylor comments about Weizsäcker, "his opposition to Hitler was conducted so discreetly that no one noticed it, Hitler, least of all," our objections are too feeble; it might be better to go below deck or to get off the ship. Taylor, reviewing Weizsäcker's *Memoirs for the New Statesman*, goes on to say: "There is something rather nauseating in this champion of peace who began the war comfortably and ended it comfortably as German minister at the Vatican." Ultimately, it will take the spirit of individuals like Bonhoeffer who are willing to accept national defeat and risk their own lives to succeed in making resistance to evil meaningful.

CHAPTER 11

Air Force Intelligence Work (1951–53)

The following two paragraphs from "Summary of Background and Experience," written by Paul during his first year teaching at Hope College in 1953-54, described his assignment when he returned to Germany for two years to work for the Air Force.

In January 1951, I was offered a position with the Department of the Air Force which I accepted partly for financial reasons and partly with the thought of entering government service on a permanent basis. I was assigned as civilian advisor to an Air Force intelligence unit in Germany. The exact nature of the work I performed in Germany is classified. Much of it related to historical research and therefore coincided with my interest in recent European history.

This assignment in Germany also brought me into contact with the European program of the University of Maryland. With the help of Dr. A. E. Zucker, then director of the program, I was able to establish a branch of the university in Hof, Germany. I acted as educational advisor for my unit and was also able to conduct two evening courses during my spare time. The first during the summer of 1951 was "European Diplomatic History from 1870 to 1914," and the second course, given during the winter of 1951-52, was "The World in the 20th Century." This brief experience in teaching, together with the general lack of stimulation in the government position I occupied, convinced me that I would prefer to enter the teaching profession. I resigned from my position in Germany in the summer of 1953.

In his interviews with Martin Baierl, Paul elaborated on his role as a civilian employee from 1951 to 1953 for the United States Air Force Historical Research Division in Germany. In the WRINGER Project (a debriefing program), he set up interrogation centers in German towns under the cover of historical research. He would ask German POWs repatriated from the Soviet Union and other Eastern European countries for information on food, industry, transportation, the military, and so on, in the Eastern Bloc. Informants were paid, sometimes with PX goods (especially cigarettes and coffee).

To Manzar Bashir, 10 September 1950:

This past week I was asked by the State Department if I wanted to go back to Germany to work on the publication of a German anti-communist magazine. Since the development of the Korean crisis, and more so since Truman's last two speeches, I have come more and more to the conclusion that we are in for a long period (ten years or more) when all thought of a "normal" life and peacetime occupation is pretty pointless.

To Gene Burgstaller, 1 October 1950:

Next came the offer of a job as interrogator for the Air Force in Germany under General Millard Lewis who is in Wiesbaden, I guess. I thought that you could probably tell me something of the man and also of the work, or rather, to what extent it conflicts or coincides with the CIA projects in Europe. I am still eager to hear something of your impressions of post-war Germany and your life in the occupation.

To Dorothy Kramer, 12 January 1951:

The Air Force has discovered that it needs me in intelligence work in Germany (as a civilian) to interrogate former German prisoners who have been in Russia. Sounds like an interesting job.

Paul penned the following handwritten document on 27 February 1951 and called it "Sailing Day: F. Hamilton 0715."

This bright morning everything seems possible and within reach. Today I think I have ambition enough to attain all the various goals I set myself: advance in the military service, publications, and translations.

The study of Russian seems a little more remote. Perhaps I shall someday discover a talent for writing historical fiction and make money that way.

The question of saving and settling down somewhere, or at least acquiring some "home," is also very present these days: a cabin in the Alps or on Lake Michigan or in the Rockies—or a castle. Perhaps when I find the girl I want to settle with, the whole thing may become easier. I am still thinking of _____ _____ as a definite possibility, if only she were not so heavy. This is something I, too, have to fight against. At the PX yesterday, I weighed 175 pounds. Eating is in many respects a way of passing the time and covering up boredom and frustration. To sit down to write or read would be the best way of overcoming both of these.

I must work on style. Letters to Bob Bernen should help, if he proves an interesting correspondent. At the moment, I am looking forward to his letters with as much anticipation as to those from Margaret Mills. The temptation to spend time, money, and energy on travel is going to be greater than ever this time. I do want to see new places, but I can get interested enough in the assigned and extracurricular work to travel only for travel's sake and not from boredom. I should try to work for what I want rather than to hope to drift into the desirable thing.

Paul continued the handwritten document on 28 February 1951 and called it "On the *General Patch*."

Is it dangerous to underestimate one's fellow workers? I suppose so, yet I can't see much that would give any of the other three ascendancy over me. I should like to start a curriculum vitae for Bob or Margaret. As for entertainment, I hope something comes to the idea of a classical hour for the troops. Not only would I like to hear the records, but the idea of playing them for GIs appeals to me very much.

How different this trip is from the previous ones. On the *Veendam*, I was in a hole with no knowledge of what lay ahead on that little British steamer—off to war and not caring too much. The return trip on the *Admiral Capps*—again faced with uncertainty—to finish college or what? The *Henry Gibbons* in 1949—to return to Harvard, teaching, and normalcy only to be met by *1984* and political change? This time I seem to have a clearer idea of what I want to achieve. Perhaps that is merely a sign of growing up. Of course, I have never traveled so comfortably—with private shower, etc.

To Sam De Merit, 7 April 1951:

Hof an der Saale was founded as a village at a river crossing point about 1230 and went through some eventful episodes in the six hundred years which followed, but never managed to get much above the status

Ready to party in ribbon tie and fez near Hof an der Salle

of a border village. Only after 1840, when the Bavarian King Ludwig I, who liked to play with railroads, made it the northeast terminal of his new railroad net, did Hof come to play a role as a new industrial town. There are ten to twelve beer breweries and almost as many textile factories. Of cultural life there is little.

To Fred Bradley, 11 April 1951:

The news of MacArthur's dismissal is still red hot, and I am wondering what view you and others in Britain make of it. I rather hope, like the retirement of Clay, it may be a sort of peace offering on our part.

To Margaret Mills, 17 April 1951:

The soldiers here [Wiesbaden] are about the same type as they were at Camp Ritchie. Most of them are bilingual, having either been born in the United States and then taken back to Germany by their parents, or having gained American citizenship some other way. Conversation is usually carried on in two languages at the same time, which is quite funny.

To Manzar Bashir, 14 May 1951:

The most startling fact about Germany is the absolutely incredible recovery of the economy. The shops are bulging with food, clothes, and luxury items of every description. The tragic thing is that people in England are still living on a few ounces of meat a week. Say the Germans: "Well, who asked them to win the war? Serves them right." We have long been aware of the revival of German nationalist sentiment, but it seems by now the whole past has been completely forgotten. Even if it is politically

Merriment galore in nightclub near Hof (WRINGER Project days)

convenient to be friendly with Germans, and I certainly have friends among them whom I respect, I cannot feel that the change in the political constellation should make us overlook or excuse the dreadful crimes of mass murder and total disrespect for human dignity and life shown by many of our present friends.

To Margaret Mills, 30 May 1951:

I have a very special feeling for your own untiring and unselfish activities during the war. I have long felt that this element of recognizing our responsibility toward our own boys has been lacking among the privileged classes (officers and civilians) here in Europe. In Nürnberg, there were over a dozen judges, top men in the field, elected or appointed representatives of the people, who had big homes, servants, cars, etc., and made no effort to exert social and moral influence. None of them ever invited any soldier or anyone except their own "set" or ever spoke to them outside of an office or bar. With this in mind, I have begun a campaign, quite locally and without saying much, to make our very elaborate and pleasant facilities available to enlisted men in our own outfit. The first step was a birthday party I gave for our commanding officer, a captain who doesn't particularly like the men. He was overwhelmed, commented on how well the men had behaved, and invited all of them to a party which he will give on return from leave. He also granted blanket permission for them to use the swimming pool here (the only one in Hof). I feel I am making some progress.

To Gene Burgstaller, 28 December 1951:

When I arrived in Germany in March and looked around in Wiesbaden, I had the strong impression that I had been hired on false pretenses, and when I got to Hof, that impression turned to certainty. My supervisor was a twenty-year-old sergeant who had no idea of what was going on but would not admit it. The same held true for almost everyone all the way up the line. I spent almost six months working myself up into the type of job for which I thought I had been hired, only to find that the colonel did not want any civilians in key positions. I was replaced again by a recently arrived PFC with a high school education.

I began to look for outside interests, and with the end of the GI bill in view, I found one in the University of Maryland, which was trying to get as many people in under the wire as possible. I offered to help them set up a branch office in Hof and to teach history courses here. My first course, "Diplomatic History of Europe from 1870 to 1914," proved interesting and provided me with an outlet for my unused energies. I hate to tell you how little time I spent preparing the lectures. The course seems to have gone over fairly well, so I have just begun a second one, "The World in the 20th Century." I have seven officers (including my CO and adjutant) and seven enlisted men in the course. I hope that the enlisted men will put the officers to shame.

To Dr. Barnaby C. Keeney, Paul's former CO, 28 December 1951:

The psychological climate among these ex-pilots is not very pleasant.

To Ike Auerbach, 12 January 1952:

Coming back to Europe, the third time since I left here in 1939, has been quite an experience. The [German] recovery has been amazing. There does not seem to be a shortage of anything, and all the horrors of war (at least those inflicted on others) are long forgotten. Not that Germans don't still feel sorry for themselves for having lost the war. What gripes me is that they are much better off than any of our friends in England or France. Anti-Semitism is as strong as ever, or perhaps would be as strong if there were any Jews left here.

To Margaret Mills, 25 January 1952:

It horrifies me to see the Nazi movement or period exonerated as something that was not bad and should perhaps have been permitted to go on. Is it possible to ignore the openly pronounced policy of murder of 30 million Poles and Russians in order to create space for Germans, or to condone the running of breeding areas where their "finest stock" of young men and women could meet for a few days in order to lay the foundation for a larger population?

To Huntington Terrell, 5 February 1952:

The second University of Maryland course, "The World in the 20th Century," turned out to be a good deal more interesting than I had expected, and I am actually enjoying teaching this time, which is more than I could say in the past summer.

To Walter Recknagel, 12 February 1952:

Last night was the last of my University of Maryland lectures. Yesterday, I think I actually reached a certain level of professional achievement, but then that was the last lecture and best prepared. Just recently I met a very nice young lady in Nürnberg; she is a graduate of Hope College and is doing post-graduate work at Erlangen, and we have a lot of mutual friends. Spent one weekend in Nürnberg taking her to dinner at the Grand and the movies and out to Stein Castle.

To Helen Hathaway, 10 May 1952:

Kiel is still very much destroyed (it was one of Germany's major naval bases). However, the location on the Baltic Sea is very nice and within half an hour's drive are several nice beaches—nothing like those in the States, much more rugged. Denmark and Holland are but a few hours away, so I can't complain.

To O. A. (Junior) Buchmann, 13 May 1952:

Congratulations on attaining that distinguished rank of PFC (poor f—g civilian). The Kiel Detachment, of which I am CHIEF, consists of [Arthur] Frederix and me. I let him be CHIEF every other day and assume the even more impressive title of DEPUTY DIRECTOR! Kiel is still very much in ruins and uninteresting in every respect.

To Helen Hathaway, 14 August 1952:

As you know, I have the same desire to have a place which I can call my own and am getting tired of living in hotels and clubs. This new apartment is not quite ideal since there should be a woman around, but I guess one can't have everything all at once. I have never been too much at ease in the company of women my own age or younger; you are a notable exception. I hope you are keeping in mind my question, put early this year, and will let me know how your thoughts on the matter progress. Please don't think I have changed my mind if I don't bring it up every time. I am sure we can be good friends regardless. I have had one contact with the CIA and if I am offered a good job with them, I may stay in Europe.

To O. A. Buchmann, 27 August 1952:

In the meantime, the operation in the British Zone has grown considerably, and it appears that a full-sized squadron will eventually be operating here in Essen. For the past three or four weeks, I have been helping set up the basis for this by screening and hiring personnel, training them, and dealing with contractors who remodel our building.

To Bob Bernen, 21 September 1952:

I was in charge of a small Air Force detachment in Kiel. Since then I have moved and am now in the heart of the Ruhr area in Essen. I looked for a place and was fortunate to find a small, well-furnished apartment, 1½ rooms, bath, and kitchen. Since I have been living in rooms all the time that I was in Hof, Kiel, Wiesbaden, and Cologne, I really enjoy the privacy and the chance to mess about in the kitchen. The place is not quite as big as 3 Athens Terrace, but I have been doing quite a bit of entertaining in it all the same.

To Margaret Mills, 17 October 1952:

The weather was glorious with all the many colors of fall along the Autobahn, and I even found pleasant company from Nürnberg to Hof. I noticed an elderly couple trying to get a ride. I usually do not pick up more than one person if I am alone, but this couple looked nice and seemed desperate for a ride. It was nice and warm in the car, thanks to an excellent heater, but very cold outside. He was a violinist from the Hof Symphony Orchestra, and his violin (which he carried tenderly under his arm) had needed repair in Stuttgart. He and his wife had not enough money for the return trip and were delighted that I was going to Hof. They had gotten up quite early to go to church in Nürnberg, and she had said a prayer that they would get home safely that day. He gave himself up to the utter enjoyment of listening to a very fine broadcast of Schubert's *Unfinished Symphony* and later some violin music. I never appreciated my car, its heater, or its good radio as much as that morning.

To Walter Recknagel, 27 October 1952:

Things in Essen keep moving along, so we can't get bored. Up to this point, I have been doing just about everything the operations officer should have been doing, along with my own work.

To Margaret Mills, 19 November 1952:

I consider it a very dangerous thing to help the Germans rebuild their industries to the extent to which we have been doing it without at least doing the same amount for the French and British.

To Ike Auerbach, 15 January 1953:

Here in the Ruhr area, I have seen a repetition of the 1920-30 development in industry and politics. Krupp, only a few years a convicted war criminal, is fully back in business and owns about half of this town. I get my gas at his station; park my car in a garage owned by him; buy butter, meat, bread, and potatoes in his store; walk through his park to work; and burn his coal to keep from freezing.

To Larry Wells, 15 January 1953:

I finally decided that I am really guilty of criminal stupidity if I stay here much longer and shall try to get a passage home about June or July. My contract is up in March, but it takes several months before one can get a boat. Besides, the spring is nice here.

To Peter V. Pohlenz, 6 February 1953:

The desire to settle down is one of the paramount reasons for giving up my present position. I think I would like to get married but am not sure that the girl I have in mind will buy the idea—at least she has not thus far!

To Hilda Cook, 13 February 1953:

I wonder if you have been following the recent reports on neo-Fascism in Germany. I actually was very pleased with the uproar caused by the arrest of the seven former Nazi leaders. I think this action may point out, more clearly than any report, the danger we face in Germany. Perhaps you noticed that just two days ago a new paramilitary organization was uncovered and dissolved in Hamburg and Bremen. I am getting rather tired of the whole business over here, and I am definitely planning to return to the States this summer.

To Dr. Paul and Sally Gottwald, 17 February 1953:

For the past year, I have moved about a great deal, which certainly was more interesting than staying in one place like Hof. I first was sent to Wiesbaden and from there to the British headquarters near Cologne. Then I spent 2½ months in Kiel as chief of a US Air Force detachment. After that, I was assigned to Essen for six months, and recently I have come to Hamburg. This all may seem mighty adventurous to a schoolmaster, but by now I find it rather tiring and, if you want, we can exchange jobs! Too bad our fields are not the same because I am really serious about it, although I am now in GS 10, and my salary (with various increments) comes up to something around $7,500. I feel that I have had quite enough of life in occupied Germany. After serious consideration, I turned in my resignation and asked for transportation home for June or July of this year. There is the possibility that I may find the type of job I want with the Department of the Air Force in the Pentagon, but frankly I am not sure that I would accept an appointment there since most of my training has been in preparation for teaching, and I definitely would like to try that on a full-time basis.

To John Anderson, 19 February 1953:

The one thing my job does not give me is intellectual stimulation and a feeling of accomplishing something worthwhile; that is probably one of the principal reasons why I decided to quit now instead of staying on indefinitely here. I realize that the grass is always greener on the other side of the fence, and probably when I am located in some small college, I will long to be traveling in Europe and doing "cloak-and-dagger" work.

To Chet and Louise Schultz, 20 February 1953:

Germany is rebuilding at a tremendous rate, and in many cases, industries have returned to their pre-war level and, in some cases, have even exceeded that. Unfortunately, the strong German nationalism which was submerged for a few years after the war seems to have returned together with this apparent prosperity and, at the moment, it looks as if the followers of Hitler—neo-Fascists or whatever else they may call themselves—are one of the most influential groups in Germany.

If there should be any doubt concerning the future of a country under Soviet control, the situation in Berlin and the stream of thousands of refugees who pour across the zonal borders every day should answer the question. I had one very interesting talk along this line last year when I was stationed near the Czechoslovakian border. Perhaps you will remember the spectacular story of the "freedom train" which came across the Czechoslovakian border close to Hof. I was among the first Americans to talk to members of that group, and what impressed me most was that the people who fled from Czechoslovakia were not government officials or people who had incurred the political enmity of the government in power, but rather ordinary, everyday people: small-business people, a small-town doctor, a train conductor, a farmer with his wife and children—all the people you would expect to be the least ones to engage in such a hazardous and adventurous enterprise. To me this emigration is quite different from those we are accustomed to reading about in history books, even in the history of the last war. This flight of the mass of little people may forecast the early collapse of governments east of the Iron Curtain; at least we can hope so.

To Mary Herz, 25 February 1953:

It is hard to realize that you have actually been in Australia all these years. I still hope that I will be able to visit that continent before I get too old or too fat to enjoy traveling. At the moment, I have decided to take your advice and settle down in the States. Perhaps I shall also act upon the second half of that advice and raise a family, if I can meet a girl who answers my ideal and if she will have me! But first, I will have to find a job on which I can support a family. The last two years I have been stationed almost everywhere in this country. My holiday trips usually took me down to Salzburg or other parts of Austria, except that in November and December 1951, I also went to Sicily and North Africa.

To Max Putzel, 6 March 1953:

Have you been following the political developments in East Germany? Recently, I have had occasion to talk to a number of people who have escaped, and it certainly appears as if the whole government there were in a state of disintegration. It may be that the Russians are deliberately permitting the escape of tens of thousands of intellectual leaders in the hope of creating a vacuum which can be filled up by loyal Communists. I wonder if our encouragement of this flight and the granting of political asylum may not have detrimental effects for us [in the future]. These are people who value freedom and who would very likely be our most valuable assets east of the Iron Curtain in case of war or as the nucleus of a resistance movement. Naturally, I am glad for every individual who manages to escape from oppression and finds a new existence elsewhere. There is, however, another side to this problem. The great increase in the number of political refugees who have no economic basis in the West will tend to create a point of political instability, which may well help push us along the road towards war.

To Larry Wells, 16 March 1953:

Your letters wake me up in the morning when I am in danger of oversleeping! The special-delivery messenger usually comes about twenty minutes after seven. I shall send this letter—special delivery—to see if it will speed up the censorship process.

To Margaret Mills, 7 April 1953:

The more I see of the situation, the more convinced I am that government service is not the right thing for me. One never knows when they will come up with the restriction that only native-born citizens can be considered loyal Americans.

To Bob Bernen, 9 April 1953:

Perhaps I am wrong in giving up a well-paying job here in favor of the uncertain prospect of a teaching position in the States, but I am not happy here, and it seems a shame to spend one's days doing something useless or uninteresting. Here in Hamburg, the whole world situation seems very remote. This is a beautiful city which I like better than any place in Germany that I have seen in recent years. There are half-a-dozen theaters and concerts at all times, not to mention all sorts of other entertainment. Also, for the first time in four years in Germany, I have found a small group of congenial Germans more or less of my own group, so that I am not quite confined to the company of people with whom I have to work all the time.

To Walter Recknagel, 5 June 1953:

I guess all parting is difficult, and I am quite attached to this city by now, so that I am continuously disturbed by doubts if I should not stay on—especially when the question is put to me by the CO. Nevertheless, I have remained firm, although I still have no job prospects in the States. The new Mercedes 300 can be seen everywhere. I am told that few of these cars are privately owned, that they belong to the big industrial concerns and run on "business expenses" and are paid out of tax money. The large concerns pay practically no tax at all, and only the wage earner and salaried employee have to pay. I took a group of some twenty people through two of the Krupp plants, and without knowing who we were or anything else, they invited us for a very elaborate lunch with wine, etc.

To Larry Wells, 12 August 1953:

Left Hamburg on the 28th of June, hung around Bremerhaven for a few days, and left there on the *General Stewart* on July 1st. 2500 GIs, 300 officers, 40 civilians—all men. No space to sit or sleep on deck. Four tables in the lounge where I played bridge a good deal of the time. Most of the officers were very young and nice. The trip took ten days, and everyone was happy when it was over.

To Arthur Frederix, 15 May 1955:

The tragedy is that ten years after the end of the war, it is as if Buchenwald and Belsen had never existed, as if Hitler had never menaced the world, and we have fallen almost victim to the Nazi propaganda slogan that we made a mistake when we did not join the Germans in their crusade against the East.

To Don Jansen, 12 June 1984:

I hope you will write once you have settled down in Germany. I am interested in your comments on changes you note in Europe and in the kind of US soldiers you encounter today. One thing which always troubled me about the US military establishment overseas (and I had over four years of this, not counting wartime service) is the tendency to live in enclaves and to avoid all unnecessary contacts with the "natives." I hope that is changing.

The file of letters to Dr. Debby Klomparens Bock contains the draft of a paper written by her seventeen-year-old son Patrick for the International School in Vienna, Austria, on "What Was the True Liberation of Austria after World War II?" Patrick had interviewed Paul on 10 August 1995 to learn about his involvement as a member of the US Air Force WRINGER Project for which he had set up interrogation centers for former war criminals.

CHAPTER 12

Fascination with Automobiles

Paul Fried loved automobiles. He longed to take lengthy drives crisscrossing the United States and Western Europe. He loathed driving alone and often invited army and air force buddies, current and former students, and random hitchhikers to share his car and company. Paul's letters have literally thousands of references to his cars, from the Old Nash that he and Bob Bernen purchased when they were at Harvard to the many Mercedes vehicles that he drove around Europe and shipped back to sell to American friends. Paul often named these vehicles: Dusty III, Scarlet Lady, Nelly, Black Beauty. This section focuses on a few cars and on a few individuals to whom Paul wrote lots of letters about his cars. Perhaps most intriguing was the car that Paul won the right to purchase through a *Stars and Stripes* lottery when he was serving as a translator at the Nürnberg War Crimes Trials. Paul chose a 1947 Volkswagen.

1947 Volkswagen bought in Würzburg

To June Metcalf, 23 September 1947:

I can get just about everything I need here, even a car. Of course, cars are hard to get, so the army runs a lottery for the few cars which come over and the ones made here. I put my name in and, presto, came up a winner. I could buy a small German car, a Volkswagen, so I think that's what I will get.

To Helen Hathaway, 23 September 1947:

I like the name you picked out for the new car—Nelly Junior. I don't have it yet, but I hope to have a Volkswagen by the end of this week. It's a small, new German car, cost only $645—instead of a Ford which would cost $1,770. Anyway, the thing is said to have four wheels and even runs on occasion. So, if you are not afraid, I shall be glad to let you ride in it when you come over.

To Lothar Sudekum, 10 November 1947:

I am now the proud half-owner of a Volkswagen; I could just afford half. The other half belongs to a good friend, a T/4 who works at the message center. We have taken quite a few trips with Nelly (the VW), and if you treat her like a lady, she behaves that way.

To Ike Auerbach, 14 November 1947:

A car, too, is a responsibility. I had the right to buy any make—including a new Buick for about $2,500—but settled for a 1947 Volkswagen. It is a really small car, something like that Austin we used to see on the way to the cafeteria on the corner. You may remember I was about broke when I left Cambridge. I bought the car on a half-and-half basis with a friend still in the army. I have by far the better deal since the car is put up at Stein, and I have it to go to work in the morning and most evenings, too.

To Alvin Coox, 19 November 1947:

I ought to tell you about Nelly, a dandy little thing, even though she is German. It takes a great deal of attention to keep her, but she is not too expensive and seems willing to go almost anywhere. Nelly's family name is Volkswagen, which is the people's car Hitler promised to the Germans but failed to deliver. I had to hire a mechanic named Franz, who always seems to have something to do for her.

Martin Baierl's interview notes with Paul also mentioned the mechanic Franz. Paul said that young men hoping for jobs and tips were always hanging around the courthouse in Nürnberg. Paul often had trouble getting his car started, and men helped by pushing. One day Franz approached Paul to ask if he would like a chauffeur. Franz wanted no money, only goods (milk for his baby, etc.) from the PX. Employees often borrowed Paul's car and chauffeur to transfer goods. They tipped Franz well, and Paul found an "enhanced working atmosphere."

To Preston J. Stegenga, 17 December 1947:

Just so you don't think I spend all my time working, I might tell you that I got a small car—a Volkswagen, but not the wartime one—and have been going about our zone quite a bit. Drove to Prague twice and hope to drive to Switzerland, France, and Italy over the Christmas holidays.

To Harriet Cook, 15 January 1948:

I have two requests: some simonizer for Nelly, my car, and two or three dozen tulip bulbs from Nelis Tulip Farm for the Schloss garden.

To Margaret Mills, 29 January 1948:

Paul talked about pulling his car out of the mud on a visit to Pastor Teufel.

To Richard Yee, 15 February 1948:

If you come to Marseilles, I could probably meet you there with my car. On the other hand, it might be possible to buy a good car in the United States without having to pay the excessive prices demanded here, and you might bring one over for me. I could sell my Volkswagen. At any rate, you might try to find out what the prices on the better used cars are now in your part of the country, or even if it is possible to get a new car, like a Nash or Pontiac, without having to pay extra. I can have a car shipped over free if I stay here.

To Frank and Charlotte Buster, 31 December 1994:

I just came back from four weeks in Europe, mostly Germany and Austria. Driving with an old friend through areas I knew well—including Nürnberg, Bamberg, Munich, and Würzburg—I was reminded of when Frank and I went to pick up the new VW in Würzburg and found that it was out of gas before we got to the top of the hill outside the city. With Frank at the wheel, we safely made it back down into town. I related the complicated arrangement we had to make so we could actually share the use of the car—with Franz driving Frank back at night and picking me up some six or ten miles the other side of the city the next morning. I also recalled the time we drove to visit a German pastor and his family. Only ten-year-old Klaus was at home, but he had the treat of letting Frank help him drive the car down the hill and chasing some cows from the middle of the road.

1941 Olds (Dusty I) bought in Nürnberg

To Hilda Kloucek, 5 March 1948:

Having had the use of a car the last six months, I have done quite

Dusty I, 1941 Olds

a bit of driving about. Today I have sold the car, so I may have to stay home a bit during the next few weeks. I hope to buy an American car later on, which will be more satisfactory.

To Margaret Mills, 28 April 1948:

The repairs on the car are progressing at a fair rate. The motor has been completely reconditioned (new pistons, cylinders reground, etc.), the body has been repaired, and today the motor should be back in the car. The chrome parts will be finished on Friday, and in a couple of weeks, the car will be painted. If I can get some good material or leather, I shall also have the seats and the inside refinished. You will get a photo, but I still wish you would come over to Germany and take a ride in it!

To Hilda Kloucek, 1 May 1948:

I sold my Volkswagen and then for a month went about on foot. However, having grown fat, I found it uncomfortable to move about so much and finally decided to buy another car. I think you will have a chance to pass judgment on it and ride in it—if you trust my driving—as I intend to take the car along on holiday.

To Hilda Cook, 1 May 1948:

Yes, I did buy another car. It's an Oldsmobile 1941, and I think you will like it. At present, my plans include taking the car to England with me if at all possible. The question will be how much gas (petrol to you) I will be able to get for use in England.

To Edith Lambotte, 26 May 1948:

My car will be finished (painting) on Friday, and I am really looking forward to have you beside me in it. Have written to the Royal Automobile Club to see what I can get in way of petrol.

To Helen Hathaway, 27 May 1948:

Nelly Junior has been replaced by a new 1941 Olds. The car was in rather bad shape when I got it, but I had it painted, put in red leather upholstery, got the motor overhauled and the wiring replaced. I also re-hired Franz, my former driver.

To Gene Burgstaller, 18 October 1948:

Last fall I bought a small Volkswagen which I kept for six months and then sold with a slight profit. The money was then invested in a larger Oldsmobile which I still have but which keeps me in a state of near bankruptcy by always luring me away from here. I think I was hardly ever in Nürnberg on a weekend throughout the summer.

To Huntington Terrell, 4 November 1948:

Did I tell you that I stopped a tree on the Autobahn (returning from Innsbruck) three weeks ago? I must have gotten a little sleepy. The car is nearly as good as new but will have to be painted.

To Chet Schultz, 2 February 1949:

In April last year, I bought an Oldsmobile for $1,100 and went to Austria, Switzerland, Italy, Belgium, Luxembourg, France, and even across the channel to England. All in all, I drove twenty-five thousand miles between April and December.

To Frank Buster, 9 February 1949:

I sold the Oldsmobile just before Christmas. I got $1,200 for it, which is not too bad since I paid only $1,100 in April. Thea, the girl who bought the car, is giving a masked ball on Saturday to which I have been invited.

1948 Olds (Dusty II) bought in Nürnberg

To Kay Stout, 8 April 1949:

The other news is that I have bought a car again! It's an Oldsmobile 1948! Will bring it to Paris if I can get a couple of passengers to pay for

Dusty II, 1948 Olds

the gas. Actually, I bought it only to keep an old promise made to Dr. Hoffmann, the man who got me to the States, to lend him the car when he comes. He arrived here Wednesday, so I went to Stuttgart to meet him and left the car and a new driver there with him. Next week I expect to go up to the British zone with him for a few days. I am really tickled to be able to do something like that.

To Frank Buster, 11 April 1949:

Last week, I bought a 1948 Olds, four-door, for $1,650. I may decide to take it home with me, unless I can sell it for the same price here before I leave.

To Ike Auerbach, 25 April 1949:

You told me last year that I was getting to be quite a car dealer. What is the situation in the States now on new cars and on the cheaper used ones? What I would very much like to do would be to order a new Chevy coupe now so I could have it on arrival.

To Frank Buster, 31 December 1949:

No, you hadn't said anything about the Ford pickup. What year is it, and what do you need it for? Boy, I really miss a car. Even a Volkswagen would be nice to have, though it is good and cold here now, and I remember that we nearly froze that one time coming back from Prague with Hanna. Remember that little place where we stopped to warm up and had some *Slivovitz* [plum brandy] or benzine and oil or something.

Dusty III, 1947 Chevy convertible

1947 Chevy convertible (Dusty III) bought in 1950

To Kay Stout, 24 April 1950:

I should be working now but have just been out for a short ride in a very nice convertible coupe, which I may buy. Spring fever has really affected me; my old sickness of looking for a car has come back! One of the fellows at the college is selling his 1947 Chevrolet convertible. He wants $1,300, and I offered him $1,100 (more than I should spend), but he will let me know in a couple of days. If I get the car, I will at least be able to show you about in the style to which we both have tried to accustom ourselves—no chauffeur, though.

To Harriet Cook, 9 May 1950:

I thought I ought to send you an announcement of the arrival of Dusty III [photograph in envelope]. It is very nice but needs a rearview mirror, so I am going to use the present you sent me for my birthday to get it.

To Frank Buster, 30 July 1950:

Oh, did I tell you about the arrival of Dusty III? He is a 1947 grey Chevy convertible. I have had a lot of fun the last couple of months, but I guess I will have to sell the car at the end of the summer to finance the rest of my time at Harvard. I will keep it until the end of August, so if you come up before then, we will be able to see the country in our old accustomed style.

1927 Nash bought in Cambridge, Massachusetts, in 1950

To Margaret Mills, 1 September 1950:

Bob Bernen and I started talking about buying a cheap car together. We found a 1927 Nash in almost perfect condition without a single rattle or squeak. The cost: $75. We have driven it some one hundred miles without the slightest difficulty.

To Frank Buster, 14 September 1950:

We have a most remarkable car—a 1927 Nash—but she is a dignified old lady!

To Dorothy Kramer, 12 January 1951:

Our Nash had a leak in the radiator. The result was inevitable: a cracked block. He still runs, but we did not think it worthwhile to register him again (about $40 for insurance), so he just sits in front of the house waiting to be traded off for something better soon.

To Bob Bernen, 29 January 1952:

I am rather busy these days teaching another University of Maryland course and working fairly hard at the office, and I would not be writing to you if I had not just received a bill for automobile tax on the old Nash, and, following that, a warrant for my possible arrest (!!!) for nonpayment of charges. Since I may want to enter the Commonwealth of Massachusetts again some time, I have paid the bill—$6.59. I don't mind the money so much, but I don't mind telling you that my sweet temper was almost lost thinking of the number of times I have requested you to clarify various bills and how unsuccessful I have been in getting any answer from you, even when you finally decided to come down from Mt. Olympus long enough to write. But I don't know if my time is so much less valuable to justify the need for two or three letters from me in order to get one from you. Well, suit yourself.

To Bob Bernen, in reference to mutual experiences at Harvard, 24 April 1997:

Our dignified limousine needed to have either water or oil every few miles. I left to go back to Germany to work for the US Air Force—leaving you with the car, which I gather still reposes in the Charles River.

1940 Mercury

1940 Mercury bought in US and shipped to Europe

To Harriet Cook (from the Atlantic, aboard *Gen. Alexander Patsch*), 1 March 1951:

I managed to buy a nice little car, a 1940 Mercury convertible. Would have liked something newer but couldn't afford it. Had to go to New York a day early so I could arrange for the shipment of the car. Just now the sea is rough, but if it doesn't get any worse, I shall have no trouble. Accommodations are just wonderful. I have a stateroom with private shower on A Deck, which is the best I have ever had.

To Manzar Bashir, 6 April 1951:

I arrived in Germany not quite a month ago. I was able to get the car I had bought just before leaving the States off the boat, so at least I have transportation now, which is a blessing, since I am at the end of the US zone rather in the middle of nowhere.

To Frank Buster, 17 April 1951:

The car I bought is pretty much of a rattletrap, but it gets me about, and last weekend I went down to Garmisch for a couple of days.

1947 Chevy two-door sedan

To Bob Bernen, 14 July 1951:

I sold the convertible—it rattled too much—and bought a 1947 Chevrolet two-door sedan which runs quite well.

To Hunt Terrell, 23 September 1951:

Yes, the 1940 Mercury was replaced by a 1947 Chevy—torpedo body, looking much like Dusty I.

To Frank Buster, 5 February 1952:

I think I told you I now have a 1947 Chevy. But I don't think it's as good as that 1941 Olds with the red seats we used to drive about. Would like to get a new car—preferably a convertible—this spring.

1950 Olds 88 bought in Germany

To Margaret Mills, 10 March 1952:

I just bought a new car again; it seemed irresistible. A sergeant was going home and offered his Olds 88, hydromatic, 4-door sedan, black, 1950, with 18,000 miles and all the trimmings for $1,500. We settled for $1,400, and I am really pleased.

To Helen Hathaway, 20 March 1952:

A couple of weeks ago, I was offered an Olds 88 at a very reasonable price, so I bought it. I am sure you will like it, too. It is still more comfortable than the Chevy. The only trouble is that up to now, I still have not sold my old car, so for the present I am in the capitalistic position of being the owner of two cars—but having no money to spend.

To Preston Stegenga, 27 March 1952:

I still try to get away from here as often as possible. Just splurged and bought an Olds 88, so I am well-equipped to take off. Except I don't dare drive fast since I got two tickets in the last three weeks.

To Helen Hathaway, 3 April 1952:

It certainly is a good thing I happened to get a larger car. Oh yes, it has been named Black Beauty—a portrait enclosed.

1950 Plymouth (red convertible with zebra-striped upholstery) bought in Germany

To Bob Bernen, 21 September 1952:

I am glad you got rid of the car. Since leaving Cambridge, I have had the 1940 Mercury, a 1947 Chevy, a 1950 Olds, and now last week I bought a 1950 Plymouth red convertible. The only trouble is that I will now have to go on vacation to the Riviera or to Italy in order to justify buying it and to see if the automatic top works.

To Lida Imhof, 26 February 1953:

This is a wonderfully warm spring day, and I feel like going out for a drive along the Elbe with the top of my red convertible down for the warm breeze.

Other cars

To Margaret Mills, 25 January 1952:

By the way, for once I did not make a spelling error. I said Mrs. Moore should buy a FIAT, not a flat. A Fiat is a small Italian car, somewhat better than the Crosley. It's not a car to keep for years, but it would certainly be nice for a summer trip.

To Kay Stout, 25 June 1952:

I am going to be in England, mostly London. You could do me one great favor! I am wondering if I could rent a nice British car for the week and how much it would be. I would like to get to the beach or perhaps to the north where I have never been. If the price is less than ten pounds for the period and two hundred miles, I wish you would make a definite appointment for me to get a car on Monday. The nicer the better, but if need be, I'll settle for an Austin.

To Edith Lambotte, 18 November 1953:

I am glad my car finally has a name: Scarlet Lady. I use her about once or twice a week to go to Grand Rapids on Thursdays, when I go the YMCA for a swim, and for some shopping and to get my laundry.

To Arthur Frederix, 3 October 1954:

Your choice of a Chevrolet is probably very good, but you should wait until November or December when the new models will be out. I understand they will be radically different.

To Bob Cook, 25 January 1955:

I have a line on a very good used 1954 Plymouth (8,000 miles) convertible, which I might get on a trade with only about $1,000, plus my car. Does that sound reasonable?

To Lotus Snow, 9 March 1955:

I suggested to your mother that there are other ways of approaching the matter, if you want to buy a new car and are ready to pay cash: (1) You can, through someone in Detroit, get a new car at 10 to 20 percent less than list price. I have such a contact in the person of Bob Cook, who was at Hope last year, and has a father who is VP at General Motors. He has offered to get me a brand new convertible, with everything, listed at $2,975 for about $2,395. The offer tempted me, but, alas, is way beyond my means; (2) You can always find someone who has a used car and wants to sell it to let you have it for trade purposes. Thus, my car, which might be worth about $650, might bring $800 as a trade-in since a dealer is willing to take that much of a loss in order to sell a car. If you want my car for that purpose, you may have it—on the basis of splitting the difference; or (3) You may want to consider buying either a used car—you can get low mileage 1953s for under $1,200—or a new 1954 model, which should not be more than about $1,400 to $1,500, with all the trimmings you get on the 1955.

To Bob Cook, 16 April 1955:

In the meantime, I finally traded cars. Have a 1953 Plymouth (convertible again, but no zebra upholstery), blue, in very good condition, with Hi-Drive. I paid $800 plus my car. This is probably more than it would have been in Detroit, but there is a little more chance for getting adjustments made here if something should turn out wrong. In any case, my car would have needed some $200-250 work on it.

To Margaret Mills, Thanksgiving Day, 1956:

I was interested in Keith's proposal to bring back a Mercedes. Let me add to his sales talk. The cars are wonderful and sell for a great deal more in the United States. He would save not only on the duty (5%) and the sales tax but also on the shipping cost ($300). I imagine he could get the car for $1,500-2,000 less in Europe, and he could sell it in California for a profit if you do not want to keep it in the family.

To Frank Zvonar, 10 February 1959:

While I am in Europe, I am going to pick up a car this year: the new Mercedes 220S. It keeps me broke saving for the thing. I will drive it to Nürnberg, Vienna, etc., and then ship it back in August.

To Ike Auerbach, 13 September 1959:

I tried to get the headrest for your Mercedes but was told that they would have to have number, model, etc., of your car. They would not even sell me one for my car since I had not ordered it beforehand. My Mercedes is now on the water and due to arrive in Chicago in two weeks. I drove 3,500 miles this summer.

To Everett Nienhouse, 10 November 1961:

Yes, I have a Mercedes 220—the 1961 model. I sold the 1959 in 1960 and the 1960 in 1961. Have lined up a customer (I hope) for this one for June 1962 and hope to get a new one then. Nice arrangement since the difference between factory and US cost is something like $1,200, so that I can almost sell the car for what I paid and still give the buyer a real bargain.

To Bob and Inge Boelkins, 16 July 1962:

I am sorry to hear that the car is still in George's shop. I am reluctant, however, to try to sell the new one. If by the time you get the letter, he has not been able to do anything, go ahead and tell George to lower the price. But I most certainly would not want to take less than $3,000 for it. I am really pleased with the new car. There are no significant changes except that I have a power brake, which is a real improvement.

To Margaret Mills, 3 November 1962:

In your last letter, you ask about my addiction to new Mercedeseseses [Paul's sense of humor with "es" repeated four times]—I now have my fourth.

To Alma Scarlett, 24 July 1964:

Could you phone Gezon Motors to find out for what they are billing me $33.36? I suspect that it is the additional cost for having the car delivered in Munich instead of my picking it up in Stuttgart. If that is the case, will you please tell them that I have paid for this charge? If this is a service bill, I shall be glad to pay it next time.

To Arthur Frederix, 6 December 1964:

For the moment, I still have two Mercedes Benz 220s. The new one was quite banged up on the ship, about five hundred dollars worth of repairs, but thus far I have had no word from the insurance company.

To Richard and Hope Brandsma, 28 October 1965:

I wonder if you have purchased your new Porsche? If not, perhaps you ought to hold off until next summer and pick one up in Europe. Or, if you can't go, I shall be glad to do it for you. I would then, for a small consideration, drive it all summer, put five thousand miles and several dents on it, and bring it as far as Grand Rapids. Alternately, I could keep it here until Christmas and drive out to California for a vacation. Does this sound like a good deal? [In a 9 November 1965 letter, Richard accepted Paul's offer.]

To Frank Buster, 5 June 1967:

I'm going to be in Stuttgart in almost three weeks to pick up my new Mercedes 250S—a beautiful car—and if you and Charlotte ever come to visit in Europe, I'll pick you up at the Vienna airport in it.

To Bob Cook, who had inquired in a 30 July 1967 letter about a friend interested in buying Paul's Mercedes, 15 August 1967:

The car is a Mercedes 250S, 1967 model, dark green with tan upholstery, white walls, radio with front and rear speakers, reclining seats, etc. I would be glad to consider a bid on the car as of June 1, 1968. I expect that it will have twelve thousand miles by that time.

To Lothar Sudekum, 15 May 1968:

As of now, I have made no final disposition of my car. The Mercedes dealer in Grand Rapids is prepared to allow me $4,100 if I order the regular 280S and $4,400 if I order the 280SE model. I have not put in my order, partly because there is some question as to his ability to guarantee delivery of a car to me in Munich at the time I want it. If I cannot get a new Mercedes this summer, I may decide to keep this one and rent a Volkswagen or another car for the time I am in Europe.

If you are seriously interested in the car, you certainly have first claim. It is a Mercedes 250S four-door sedan with whitewall tires, Becker Europa radio with a rear speaker, tinted glass all around, a regular floor shift, and power brakes. The car has about sixteen thousand miles on it. If I drive it to New York, this would add about one thousand miles before I could deliver it to you. If you really want the car, I would be quite happy to settle for the lower figure since I really do not think I want to spend the extra money on the SE model. While I have no real obligation to turn the car in to the dealer, it would obviously be best for me to know soon if he can expect the car or not.

To L. Bruce van Voorst, 1954 Hope graduate and later a correspondent for *Newsweek* and *Time*, 21 May 1968:

When I get to Munich, I expect to pick up a new car again, and this time it will be a Mercedes convertible that should give me the proper style, although I am not quite sure that it is not folly for someone my age to buy that young a car. I would love to have you and Marilyn as passengers.

To Arthur Frederix, 3 March 1969:

Bob Moore picked up Easy Gearhart and me to go to dinner with him and Congressman Guy Vander Jagt (from our district) and his wife.

Then we went in the congressman's little VW to Constitution Hall for the concert. Arthur Rubinstein was terrific, even though the [Washington] symphony orchestra is not that great. After that, we went to the State Department where Secretary of State [William] Rogers was giving a reception for the patrons of the orchestra and Mr. Rubinstein. Bob took the four of us as his guests. You would have loved the party in the Adams rooms which are all in early American and antique style with marvelous flower arrangements and rugs. The mayor of Washington was in the receiving line. Later, Hubert Humphrey and his wife came. Needless to say, food and drinks were excellent, free, and plentiful. We saw Rolls Royces and even a Mercedes 600 as we got back into our little VW.

To Arthur Frederix, 4 February 1973:

I am trying to decide if I should get a new car. This one is going to be five years old in June. It still has a very high resale value but will probably start to cost money in another year or two. I put an ad into *Road and Track* to see if I can find a *Liebhaber* (aficionado) who is willing to pay a high price for it.

To Arthur Frederix, 10 March 1974:

Go ahead and trade in your old car for a chic red sports model! Sixty-five is no age at all. [Konrad] Adenauer and Churchill just about began their careers at that age. Instead of my buying you a book or some records, why don't you let me put something into your car which you would like? Fog lights, a tape deck, a radio? Just so you won't be too modest or too extravagant, figure on something between fifty and one hundred dollars. That way I will be able to ride in your car and feel that I have made some small contribution to your continuing pleasure.

To Peter and Beverly Fuhrmann, 5 August 1979:

I sold my 1968 Mercedes convertible (I was offered about $4,000 more than I had paid for it 11 years ago, and it had been driven 111,000 miles). As a result, I have money in the bank, but for the moment, only a VW which belongs to a friend who is off to Germany for three weeks. By then, I hope to be fully motorized again.

To Ingrid Heyden-Walter, 7 August 1979:

For the moment, I am car-less. Yes, I finally sold my old Mercedes and am looking around trying to decide how to replace it.

To Arthur Frederix, 14 August 1979:

I finally decided on a new car—a Japanese Toyota Cressida, silver grey, metallic paint, red crushed-velvet interior, air conditioning, power drive and steering and brakes, automatic windows, etc.

To Bob Bernen, 7 August 1988:

One of my recent "jobs" was serving as grand marshal of Liberty Fest [in Holland, Michigan], which mainly consisted of riding a red Mercedes convertible in the parade and having my picture taken.

To Stephen Hemenway, 27 June 1989:

When you get back, you will be picked up in my new Toyota. It is not a convertible but comes close to rivaling the old Mercedes with air-conditioning and a sun roof.

CHAPTER 13

Hope College Professorial Years (1953–84)

Paul Fried's initial job at Hope in 1953 was very tenuous, but he remained a full-time faculty member in the Department of History until his retirement as professor emeritus in 1984. During that time, he served as chair of the history department, as director of International Education, and as founder and director of the Hope College Vienna Summer School.

Letters about Hope College (1947-60)

To Fred Bradley, 1 June 1947:

I had an offer to teach German at Hope College next year but decided to turn it down since I am really more interested in teaching history.

To Walter Recknagel, 3 February 1953:

One thing I found about life in a college community, and perhaps that is one of the reasons I want to get back to it, is that you hardly ever have a chance to be lonely, and there is always something interesting to do, or someone interesting to talk to.

To Kay Stout, 25 February 1953:

I would like to find a teaching job, preferably along the West Coast. I have also thought quite a bit about the possibility of abandoning the idea of an academic career altogether and trying my hand in business, either hotel or restaurant or perhaps even insurance, but I am really not sure that I am cut out for that.

To Bob and Inge Boelkins, 27 April 1953:

I received notice of a job at a girls' college in Georgia—220 female Baptists. But I would be head of the three-person Department of History.

To Larry Wells, 2 May 1953:

I have only had one job offer—in a girls' college in Georgia, pay $3,900 for nine months. If nothing better comes along, I will probably take it. It does not sound too bad, except that the poor girls can't smoke, drink, or dance on or off the campus. I wonder what that means for the faculty. Do you suppose they would trust me with all those beautiful young Southern belles? Can't you just see me in one of those nice colonial mansions?

To Dr. Irwin J. Lubbers, 29 June 1953:

I am really eager to remain in the United States and to pass on some of the things I have learned during the past ten years. I need not say how pleased I would be, should I have the opportunity to do so at Hope College.

To Larry Wells, 12 August 1953:

The president of Hope College led me on a personally-conducted tour of the place, and if there were a vacancy in the history department, the job would be mine for the asking—but there is no job, so I started on my way west. It was a wonderful feeling to get out of the hot and humid Midwest into the mountains in Wyoming and then on to California. I don't think I want to take advantage of the offer to go back to Germany. Life there is pleasant enough but a dead-end alley all the same.

To Dr. Irwin J. Lubbers, 24 August 1953:

Naturally, I would be very happy to receive an appointment at Redlands University. At the same time, I am very grateful to you for thinking of a part-time position for me at Hope. That might not be a bad thing for me since it would give me an opportunity to work on the book on Germany I started in Hamburg. Actually, I think I should start out with a full-time job and see if I cannot do my writing in my spare time.

To Larry Wells, 1 October 1953:

I ended up here at Hope after all. The vacancy occurred the day before school opened.

To Preston Stegenga, 3 October 1953:

The day school started, on September 21st, I received a telegram from John Hollenbach asking if I were still available and to call him collect. I was in Berkeley, and since I had no definite commitment for a job, I accepted when he asked me to come to Hope. It took me four days to drive the 2,800 miles; I was tired for a week. I still feel a little tense in some of my classes, but I can notice the improvements over the first day.

To Fay and Peter Hamel, 19 October 1953:

There is a very nice "little theater" on the top floor of the science building and a special faculty member to teach drama. In fact, Hope has an art department of sorts, and they teach painting, sculpture, etc. I enjoyed the play very much.

To Captain Harold (Hal) Chase, 24 October 1953:

I teach fourteen hours a week and mostly things for which I was not prepared too well.

To Walter Recknagel, 7 November 1953:

One of the few diversions I permitted myself this past week was going to a meeting of the chess club. I was properly punished for being so unscholarly by being beaten two out of three by a freshman! The shame of it!

To Samuel De Merit, 14 November 1953:

Yes, I am enjoying the chance to teach here, though I don't know if it will be something I want to do the rest of my life. It might be, but for the moment, I still think it's a bit narrow.

To Walter Recknagel, 21 November 1953:

You think that midterms are hard on students? Well, what about the poor profs who have to read them? I stayed up until 2 or 3 a.m. several nights last week and got so mad Sunday night that I could hardly sleep. I had seventy-eight freshman papers and short essays to correct and thirty senior papers in the American Diplomatic History course. I found two papers that were just about the same and then one which proceeded to quote from our textbook without quotation marks for about four pages. I can't say that I felt that this was an insult to my intelligence since even the most stupid individual could spot this if he had read the book. Or did

Endless exams, papers, and new courses, but "I am content."

this student think I had not read the text? Anyway, it's a great life if you don't weaken.

To Rolf Italiaander, 28 November 1953:

I have been very busy preparing lectures since I came here; I have not had any chance to work on my notes. I have delivered about six speeches and written a couple of articles for the school paper, the local newspaper, and one small magazine in Cleveland. Do you think there would be any interest in Germany for articles on college life in the United States? I would like to do something like that.

To Samuel De Merit, 7 March 1954:

On the faculty of a small college, I am definitely learning more than I have ever learned before. I now teach four different courses: Western Civilization, American Diplomatic History, Russian History, and a freshman course, "World News of the Week." That means I have to be up in all four fields, but it has the advantage that I am forced to synthesize in my own mind and develop some sort of correlation between subjects, which I might not do if I were teaching only my specialty. So I am content—for the time being.

To the Honorable Gerald R. Ford Jr., who had sent Paul a congratulatory note (12 October 1953) on being appointed instructor of history and had urged Paul to call upon him if he ever needed assistance, 8 March 1954:

A rather belated thanks for the pleasant note you sent me last fall when I was appointed to the faculty of Hope College. In it you suggested that I might call upon you for assistance. During the current semester, I am teaching a course in "World News of the Week." I try to stimulate discussion on significant topics in domestic and foreign affairs. I am wondering if you have material on issues before Congress which would be of interest to our students. If you should be in Holland sometime during the next few months and have the time and inclination to speak to one or more of my classes, I would be most happy to have you as a guest. In any case, I am looking forward to meeting you at the time of your next visit to Holland.

In a 10 March 1954 letter, Representative Ford offered to mail Paul immediately the "contemplated program" of the House and Senate, copies of the House and Senate bills on the proposed calendar for the next week, and several relevant pages from the *Congressional Record*. Although he did not expect to be in Holland in the spring, he was open to an invitation to speak to Paul's students in the fall.

To John and Mary Elmendorf, 3 June 1954:

I have been reappointed with a slight raise in pay and an advance from instructor to assistant professor. I am most pleased since I really like this college and have a great many friends here. My own plans for the summer center mostly around building up my notes for next year's courses in Western Civilization and American Diplomacy and preparing an outline of German history and a freshman handbook for the Department of History.

To Helen Hathaway, 31 October 1954:

I am trying to make the school UN conscious. I have had four book reviews accepted by a quarterly, *Books Abroad*, which is published by the University of Oklahoma Press. I was elected secretary-treasurer of Phi Alpha Theta, the national honorary history fraternity.

To Larry Wells, 27 November 1954:

Since coming back to Hope, I have been working pretty hard. I started out with seventeen hours of lecturing per week, which is a lot, even though it includes three sections of the same course; that is almost more taxing than different lectures, except that you don't have to prepare so many. I enjoy my work very much. Of course, I don't think I want to be buried in this town; at least, I want to be able to get out for the summers.

Along with a 20 January 1955 letter, Representative Gerald R. Ford Jr., sent Paul a requested copy of the "Hearings before the

Subcommittee on International Organizations and Movements of the Committee on Foreign Affairs" and a booklet entitled "How Foreign Policy Is Made."

To Al Coox, 28 June 1955:

I am a great deal happier since I started teaching.

To Margaret Mills, 13 November 1955:

This weekend I have been indulging in the luxury of doing things I wanted to do. Friday we had an open house at the Cosmopolitan fraternity with Dr. Paul de Kruif, author of *Microbe Hunters*, as guest. He was absolutely brilliant in his comments and remarks. He said he would not make a speech, so questions just poured forth. The current president of the fraternity is distantly related to him, so he just called him up and asked him to come. When de Kruif wanted to know "Why ask me," Jerry just said, "Because you are famous!" What could the poor man do? It was a very stimulating evening and stimulated discussion that lasted until after midnight.

To Dr. Paul and Sally Gottwald, 7 December 1955:

I have three sections of freshman history, and the students' ignorance is monumental. I think some don't even know where Europe is.

To Harriet Cook, in an August 1956 note not mailed until 13 May 1957:

The note included a flyer entitled "Speakers Advisory Series," which said that Paul was available to speak on these topics: Germany Today: Bridge or Battleground between East and West; Soviet Policy in East Germany; Austria Since the Russians Left; Intellectual Renaissance in Germany; Prospects for European Unification; Western Europe and the United Nations; World Leadership Challenges Young Americans. His fee was twenty-five dollars plus travel expenses within Michigan, fifty dollars outside Michigan. Paul indicated that he could speak on the Hungarian Problem when he got back from Europe.

To Larry Wells, 12 October 1956:

This was our homecoming weekend. The weather was glorious, and we won the game 25-7 (our first win of the season)!

To Edith Lambotte, 14 April 1959:

It is a good idea for you and Daisy to stay at the YWCA in London where you will have fewer stairs. To help with this, there is one more enclosure, a check for thirty dollars. I am giving two lectures to women's clubs in the next two weeks, and they will bring in almost twice that amount.

To Dr. Irwin Lubbers, 27 July 1959:

The main reason for this letter is a conversation which I had last Friday with Dr. Bruno Kreisky, the new Austrian foreign minister. As you may recall, Dr. Kreisky received the Hope College group last year when he was state secretary. He was most cordial and spent over an hour answering our questions. When the new Austrian cabinet was announced about ten days ago, he emerged as foreign minister. I then requested another audience for the group and was most pleased that he agreed to receive all of us last Friday. He spoke very informally, without notes, and answered questions in a most interesting and candid fashion. I extended an invitation to him to visit Hope whenever he comes to the United States. In our conversation, he took up the idea and said that he expected to be in the United States for part of the next UN General Assembly session and that he would very much like to see something of the Midwest. To confirm my impression of his interest in a visit to Hope, I asked if we might send him a formal invitation. He said that he would be pleased to consider it. If you think we want him at Hope, you might send the invitation to me, but addressed to him, so that I can deliver it in person.

In a 5 August 1959 letter, Dr. John Hollenbach asked Paul to change the dates settled on for inviting Dr. Kreisky because of a conflict with a "big all-campus religious retreat planned for that weekend at Camp Geneva."

To Dr. Irwin Lubbers, 12 August 1959:

His [Dr. Bruno Kreisky's] presence on our campus would be an item of major interest to American and Austrian papers alike and would reflect favorably on our Vienna Summer School program and on the college as a whole.

To Rolf Italiaander, 6 May 1960:

I am profoundly honored that you are dedicating a book to me. I am not sure I deserve it, but I am very pleased.

"Great Expectations"

On 18 January 1963, Paul delivered a Hope College chapel talk entitled "Great Expectations." Here is a slightly abbreviated version.

The year 1945 is of worldwide historic significance. In Europe, Hitler committed suicide, and the German armies surrendered. In the

Pacific, atomic explosions brought the Second World War to a speedy end. Here at home, Dr. Irwin Lubbers was named president of Hope College.

The Hope College *Anchor* reported all of these events, giving most space to the last item. Its first issue that fall printed the following letter from the new president: "In many ways Hope College is an entirely new institution to me. I share with freshmen and other newcomers the pleasure of novel experiences. The war is over, and we look forward to reaping the blessings of peace. It will take all the intelligence, patience, and determination we possess to make it the year of great opportunity instead of a year of frustration. We welcome you to the task of building the greater Hope on the foundations that have been so well laid throughout the years."

I was a member of the senior class that year. As you know, seniors are used to the ways of the world, and it takes more than impressive prose to convince them. They know that freshmen tend to be green and brash, are eager, and wear bright smiles, but that it is best to adopt a cautious "wait and see attitude" with them. Needless to say, new administrators often are not so very different from freshmen.

The editorial appearing in the same issue of the *Anchor* indicated that we were willing to give the new president a chance to prove himself. Here is what the senior editor wrote: "Dr. Lubbers is assuming his position at a time when Hope has to gear her thinking and curriculum to peacetime living. The transition, coming so suddenly, will undoubtedly present unusual problems. We are therefore taking this opportunity to pledge to Dr. Lubbers the cooperation and wholehearted support of the student body. It is our earnest prayer that our new president and his family will feel themselves valued members of the Hope family." Do you detect a slight note of doubt in these words? Could Dr. Lubbers really turn frustration into opportunity? How would he be able to deal with the many problems which faced the college?

There was, for instance, the matter of enrollment. The prewar high of 1940 had been 570 students. In September 1945, Hope had 364 students: 263 girls and 101 boys. A deplorable situation from the point of view of the women—the more so because most of the boys were either a very green seventeen or 4-F [ineligible for the military draft]. To the delight of the ladies, Dr. Lubbers quickly reversed this unfavorable ratio by adopting a policy of admitting veterans throughout the year as they were discharged from the army. At the end of March 1946, enrollment had passed the 600 mark. The *Anchor*, edited by a young woman, noted with pleasure that men had begun to outnumber the women on campus.

There were other questions raised by the influx of all the new students who had served in every part of the globe. They had discovered the world but needed guidance to understand it. Could Hope College rise above the isolationism and narrow parochialism which marked the whole Middle West and our own community? We soon discovered that, with Dr. Lubbers at the helm, it could indeed and that the college was becoming increasingly conscious of national and international issues. In January 1946, Dr. Lubbers presided over a student council-sponsored, city-wide forum which brought together representatives of labor, industry, the church, and the professions to discuss the topic: "Is Democracy Workable Today?" They found that it was.

The following month students and faculty joined enthusiastically in a drive to send aid to a sister college in Communist-dominated Hungary. By then the *Anchor* had given over a weekly page to detailed firsthand reports on all parts of the world. A new course dealing with contemporary world issues had been added to the curriculum, and the International Relations Club was getting under way.

Of course, some minor problems remained. As it does to the present day, the *Anchor* discussed the new policies regarding class cuts and chapel attendance. There also were editorials about dancing on campus and equal rights for women in the use of tobacco. Worst of all, there was the announcement that tuition would go up from $62.50 to $85 per semester.

Nonetheless, as the year progressed, it became obvious, even to the skeptical seniors, that Dr. Lubbers was exceptionally well prepared to deal with the many problems confronting the college. By the time June came, the class of 1946 knew that even though Dr. Lubbers had only just completed his freshman year, he had started a chain reaction at Hope which would help him guide the college to a future development far greater than we could even imagine at the time. We heard and believed his earnest pledge:

> Our record points the course we take
> to greater records we shall make,
> for hope springs not from what we've done
> but from the work we've just begun.

Letters and essays about Hope College (1964-81)

To Huntington Terrell, 11 April 1964:

I finally made full professor last March, and now there is really nothing left but to become an administrator. This, actually, is going to be the case, at least part time. Our new president, who is a very dynamic

"Yes, they still hear my German accent."

and able young man, is most eager to see us expand the foreign study program, so I will become director of foreign study, along with keeping the chairmanship of the Department of History.

On 22 January 1965, Paul's article on "The Lesson of Winston Churchill" appeared in the Hope College *Anchor* two days before Churchill died. Here are a few excerpts in which Paul praised Churchill as one of the greatest statesmen of any age.

Hope students cramming for finals may find it easy to identify with young Winston Churchill, who was a decidedly poor student and passed his exams at Harrow only with the greatest difficulty. Though Churchill was a poor student, he had courage and integrity, an unquenchable thirst for knowledge, boundless energy, and a lifelong desire to be a doer and not an onlooker.

It was not until Britain faced almost certain total defeat that Churchill emerged as the ablest, most determined and eloquent leader of the Western world during the Second World War. After the war, he again turned from making history to writing it and lived on to become one of the principal architects of the New Europe. Today his life stands as a shining light and constant challenge to all of us, for he taught us that, with the help of God, man can be the master of his fate and mold history; he does not have to be the helpless victim of circumstances.

In the best sense of the word, Winston Churchill's life is that of a Renaissance man who combines an interest in art and music, war and philosophy, history and politics, social reform and loyalty to his king, profound scholarship and good food, and who is capable of lofty idealism and down-to-earth realism. "Mr. Churchill's tastes are simple," said Lord Birkenhead once; "he is easily contented with the best of everything."

In October 1966, Paul's article on "Hope's History and History at Hope" appeared in the Faculty Focus section of the Hope College *Anchor*. Paul examined reasons for the paucity of students pursuing majors in history and other subjects in the humanities as opposed to the many students committed to the sciences. Here are a few remarks from the latter part of his article.

What then caused the difference [so many science majors, so few history majors]? I believe that it must have been primarily a matter of attitude toward the subject of study. Students feel most challenged when they can become partners with the faculty in the actual search for truth, when not all the answers are handed them on a platter, when they can raise questions and search for solutions; when they can conduct experiments and begin to see that there may be not one but several answers and that they might even be able to discover something new.

Since Hope and the Reformed Church were not seriously involved in the controversy over evolution, there seems to have been little objection—even in the early days of the college—to allowing students free range in scientific inquiry. On the other hand, the prevailing social, political, and religious attitudes which provided the climate in which the college operated would have made similar scientific approach to the study of social institutions, political behavior, and religious life highly undesirable and even suspect.

In these fields, the community already knew the right answers. Asking unnecessary questions could only lead students to become critical of the existing order of things, make them rebellious, and threaten to destroy our well-insulated way of life. To be safe, one best stayed with an approved textbook and memorized dates and events rather than to worry about causes and effects or controversial interpretations.

It took the Second World War and the increasing demand for well-trained graduates in these areas to break down the social parochialism that had kept us from following the natural sciences in applying rigorous and objective intellectual standards of inquiry to topics which might bring the student into conflict with the establishment. Today, as Hope College begins its second century, there are strong indications that students have begun to see the challenges offered to the analytical mind in the social sciences. They see that the world has become smaller and that their own opportunities to study other cultures as well as their own have been vastly expanded.

"May history at Hope be truly worthy of Hope's history."

An increasing number of Hope students have, in recent years, gone into law and foreign service and have gained fellowships to study social sciences and humanities in graduate schools. All this makes me hopeful that it may not be too long before history at Hope can be truly worthy of Hope's history.

To Arthur Frederix, 28 July 1969:

I was immediately caught up in preparations for our annual Hope College Village Square, which I have never seen in operation. I had promised Frau Schnee, chair of the Vienna Coffee Shop, that I would help with decorations. This is sort of a *Volksfest* [public festival] combined with a "sale of works" (handmade things by churchwomen) at a garden party. The Vienna Coffee Shop, which was more or less my idea some years ago, involves having women bake and donate Viennese pastries, which they sell with coffee topped with *Schlag* [whipped cream]. We had a very nice outdoor Kaffeehaus with flower boxes, Viennese music, slides of Austria, etc. I invited the Austrian Consul from Detroit to join us.

To Robert Anderson, 2 September 1969:

My own summer was rather unusual in many ways. For one thing, I spent it in Holland, which is something I had not done for the last twenty-seven years. Would you believe that 1942 was my last summer here? Actually, the place is not bad at all. After I bought air-conditioning units for the offices Mrs. Scarlett and I occupy, it became quite comfortable. In the meantime, we had to move. At the beginning of the second semester, there was a small fire in Kollen Hall. The fire marshal determined that the place was not fit for human habitation and hence the girls had to move out. The administration, in a quandary, decided that it was ideal for faculty offices since faculty were, of course, expendable. Also, they are not supposed to be sleeping while working in their offices.

To Arthur Frederix, 24 February 1970:

Wednesday evening we had a very posh buffet supper for [astronaut Colonel Frank] Borman at the home of President Vander Werf. I even sat next to Borman while we were eating. There was a snowstorm that evening, so the man who set the stage for landing on the moon could not land a small plane at the Holland airport and had to go back to Grand Rapids. The convocation was very nice.

To Arthur Frederix, 18 July 1970:

When forty Japanese students arrived at Hope, Paul gave the welcome address at a dinner; later they all attended a steak fry and swimming party at the lake home of Dr. Paul de Kruif.

Do you remember the book *The Microbe Hunters*? It made him a millionaire. I mostly sat and talked with the third Mrs. de Kruif. He is quite ill or "out of it."

To Ike Auerbach, 14 May 1971:

I am interested to hear more about your work in Jerusalem. I have long felt that we needed to counterbalance the vaguely pro-Arab bias of our students by sending some to Israel and also by having some Israeli students enrolling in our [GLCA] schools.

To Arthur Frederix, 9 December 1972:

This week brought a rather impressive and fat book: *Who Is Who in Austria*. With only about five hundred new names included in this eighth edition, I feel very flattered by the amount of space given to my entry—longer than the one for Kreisky or a number of more important people.

To Arthur Frederix, 13 April 1974:

I had a call from one of the Qatar boys (he comes from the royal family in Kuwait) that he had had an accident in Florida and was now back in Holland in the hospital. I took him some flowers arranged in a horse container with the comment that as an Arab, he should perhaps stick to horses instead of bicycles.

To Arthur Frederix, 28 April 1974:

Col. [Saleem] Karachy was visiting family locally. Two of his sons married American girls and live in Holland and Zeeland. Two live in Jordan—one with a high post in the government, the other as director of public relations for security purposes.

To Janice Osterhaven, 2005 Hope graduate, 17 May 1974:

It sounds as if you are making good progress with research for your paper (in Hungarian history). Let me caution you to allow enough time for composition: writing a draft, revising it, getting footnotes checked, getting the thing typed and proofread, etc. No paper, no matter how interesting in content, is likely to be marked with an A unless it is excellent in both form and content. In other words, lack of care in writing, grammar, spelling, and, most importantly, in documentation will detract from the value of the finished report.

To Arthur Frederix, 24 October 1975:

During homecoming weekend, I went to the Cosmopolitan fraternity dinner at a ski lodge and met a number of former students, many now in high places. The party was one of the nicest affairs of this kind I ever attended. I must send a note of congratulations to the fellows who organized it.

To Arthur Frederix, 8 February 1977:

A couple of days later, I had an open house for the boys from Centennial Cottage (German house). Eight of the nine residents came for beer and sandwiches around 9 p.m., and the last went home about 1 a.m. Included were my three young friends from Germany, plus two or three who had lived there for a year and one who hopes to go to Freiburg this fall.

To Provost David Marker, in a letter requesting a significant merit increase for Alma Scarlett, office manager for the International Education office, 17 May 1978:

Since we do not have an assistant director of International Education, Mrs. Scarlett is the only back-up person on the Hope College staff who could carry on the functions assigned to me if it became necessary. There is no doubt that Mrs. Scarlett's involvement in her various roles as manager of the International Education office, as the key administrative figure in the summer program for Japanese students, and in her day-to-day role as counselor and confidante of our foreign student population is considerably greater than might be suggested by any job

Sharing early April birthdays with Alma Scarlett

description we have drawn up for her position in the past. Logic compels me to say that Mrs. Scarlett is virtually irreplaceable, while that may not be the case with me, as long as she remains on our staff.

To Jerry Bevington, 5 May 1981:

I move back to the Department of History and into much smaller quarters in Lubbers. I guess this is a sort of foretaste of the time when I have to give up my apartment to move to Resthaven or some such place. Not too soon, I hope.

Letters about Hope College (1984-96)

To Frederick A. Praeger, 15 January 1984:

It does not seem possible that forty years have gone by since those cold days in Camp Ritchie! I still enjoy teaching my classes; this semester I have some very bright-eyed and bushy-tailed young people in three different classes and a couple of talented young women taking independent studies with a focus on Austrian history at the turn of the century. I could not ask for anything more for my last semester—plus knowing the secret that some of my former students are preparing a festschrift.

In May 1984, Paul received the title of professor emeritus from Hope College.

Posing with Alma Scarlett in front of Vienna poster
(courtesy Tom Renner)

To Charles Lemmen, 27 May 1984:

Your long, kind, and interesting letter was a delight. If I still were using the old dictaphone which I bought in Vienna, I would have been tempted to start my reply to you at once. I probably would not have done it, however, since I never liked to use that mechanical device when sharing thoughts and recollections with really good friends. Anyway, a quiet Sunday afternoon at home is better for writing to friends. Here the

In full academic regalia
(courtesy Tom Renner)

Paul autographing copies of
Into All the World
(courtesy Tom Renner)

phone rang: Bruce van Voorst checking in from Washington, where he is now the *Time* magazine man at the Pentagon. We talked for some time about US foreign policy as well as Hope. Like you, he has helped enrich my life at Hope by staying in contact, making me feel that I have enlarged my family.

To Bob Bernen, 28 May 1984:

Perhaps the most exciting thing that happened in connection with my retirement was the surprise announcement that a number of former students and friends had put together a festschrift in my honor. It has been in the works for more than two years but will not be ready until later this fall. I am, of course, most thrilled and eager to see the finished product since, from the titles and authors, I fully expect that it will be a very readable book.

To Don Jansen, 12 June 1984:

Students still are very nice, but they look so much younger these days. They mumble—so do my colleagues—and even the telephone company does not make decent bells anymore. That's why I have a hearing aid handy.

To Ingrid Heyden-Walter, 19 April 1987:

Last week I finally broke down and bought a computer and word processor which, I was assured, even a fool could learn to operate. The trouble is that I am not a fool.

Paul with Into All the World *editors and essayists: (*back, l-r*) George Arwady, Julie Van Wyk, Elton Bruins, Etta Hesselink, John Hollenbach, Gordon Van Wylen (*front, l-r*) Neal Sobania, John Mulder, Paul Fried, Robert Donia, Irwin Lubbers (courtesy Tom Renner)*

To Dr. Paul and Sally Gottwald, 14 January 1988:

The son of my 1940 employer, Max De Pree, is now chairman of the Hope College Board of Trustees and president of Herman Miller. I guess our work at 30 cents an hour helped to make them millionaires. But they seem willing to share!

To Reinhard Grond, 19 May 1988:

It was most interesting to meet a number of "old timers" [at the University of Minnesota Symposium on "*Anschluss* 1938—50 Years Later"] like Dr. Karl Gruber, who was the young leader of the Austrian resistance in April 1945 in Innsbruck and later became Austrian foreign minister and then ambassador to the United States. I invited him to give a lecture at Hope College in October 1955, and he still remembered the visit to Holland after all this time—particularly because he could not get a drink here. I assured him that he would have no problem now. One reason I decided to attend this conference is that I am scheduled to teach a seminar this summer on "The Munich Crisis of 1938—A Historical View."

To Hilda Kloucek, 9 April 1989:

My birthday was much more exciting than I had planned. One of my former students, Peter Scheer, originally from Hamburg and now a professor at a university in California, called me several weeks ago to

*Celebrating 70ᵗʰ birthday with Peter Scheer (left) and
Stephen Hemenway (right), 4 April 1989*

say that he had to speak at a conference in Chicago on April 3 and would come up to Holland the following day to take me out to celebrate my birthday. He insisted on taking me to the most expensive restaurant on Lake Michigan where I found some forty people waiting for us whom he had invited from New York, Ohio, California, and various cities in Michigan. I could not have been more surprised and touched by seeing so many friends who had come from great distances.

To Bob and Satia Bernen, 20 April 1989:

There was a surprise party for my 70ᵗʰ birthday. It was a delightful and somewhat overwhelming affair. Of course, I am most grateful, but I am not sure I would survive a similar event ten years from now.

To Bob Bernen, 3 May 1989:

Since the festschrift includes a very well-written and fairly accurate biographical essay by one of my "old" teachers, I no longer feel the need to write anything about myself. For whom?

From Dr. Fritz Fellner, Austrian historian from the University of Salzburg who had spoken at Hope in 1960, 14 September 1990:

Dr. Fellner lauded Hope College for establishing the Paul G. Fried International Center "to honor my friend for his long service in promoting international understanding through academic exchange programs. [He] is one of the pioneers of student exchange activities and, as an Austrian,

Plaque for dedication of Fried International Center

I have to be grateful to him for making so many American students understand the historical role of Austria in the past and the problems of my country in the contemporary world."

To Kay Stout, 28 December 1991:

I had a great many visitors from all over, starting with Professor Koljevic, who had just been elected to the presidency of Bosnia. He and his wife and daughter stayed at my home during most of January. They are back in Sarajevo and, as of about a week ago, were still okay.

To Marty Costos, 8 May 1994:

In the meantime, I have become a member of the Hope 50-Year Circle, since I started [in 1939] with the class of 1944 which was "inducted" into that elite body yesterday. Of course, back in 1942, I was "inducted" into the elite US military service which provided a free trip to Europe, so I did not graduate until 1946. I will have an excuse to celebrate again in two years!

To Kevin Kane, 21 February 1996:

Yes, the academic process can be rather depressing, and I am not sure if there is a cure-all: diversion, interruption, discovery of a new possible career. Perhaps World War II came at the right time for me, as did the challenge of being assigned to an incredibly challenging group of people. Teaching at Hope might easily have become dull routine if there had not been contact with international students and the chance to develop a program in Vienna.

*Rev. Marion de Velder (left)
and Pres. John Jacobson
(right) laud Paul at Fried
International Center
dedication,
22 September 1990*

From Bruce Neckers, a few lines from his speech delivered to honor Paul on the dedication of the Fried-Hemenway Auditorium, 15 October 2005:

This auditorium is a fitting culmination to the honors which have been afforded to Paul during his distinguished career. The first thing named after Paul was the Friedburger, a delicacy allegedly invented by him which included a couple of hamburger patties smothered in cheese and placed in a bun at the old Kletz in the bottom of Van Raalte Hall; he is really the inventor of the double-meat cheeseburger.

*Dedication of Fried-Hemenway Auditorium, 15 October 2005
(courtesy Tom Renner)*

Pres. James and Martie Bultman with Paul and Stephen
at auditorium dedication (courtesy Tom Renner)

Of all the useful things that Paul taught me, the most significant was how to make travel an opportunity to explore places out of our comfort zones. He was always teaching, telling rich stories, mentoring a generation of historians to think rather than just learn the rote facts. He was the first to challenge me to develop the skills that come from critical and creative thinking. He was particularly astute in his interpretation of historical events of the first half of the twentieth century. Many a night, I listened with other students and faculty as he challenged us to recognize the complexities of war and the long-term consequences of governmental decisions made during and between the two world wars.

CHAPTER 14

Feelings for Holland, Michigan

Paul had a like/love relationship with Holland, Michigan, but he stayed here forever. His early "like" attitude was a bit lukewarm, but he soon learned to love Holland as his permanent home. These initial excerpts were culled from letters that he wrote after graduating from Hope College and then after teaching there for several years.

Letters about Holland (1946-78)

To June Metcalf, 3 October 1946:

I am very fond of Holland, wouldn't mind settling there.

To Harriet Cook, 24 November 1946:

Many thanks for your letter of last Sunday. I am always glad to get news from my "hometown."

To Margaret Mills, 20 September 1952:

Being with Preston and Martha Stegenga in Essen this weekend revitalized my old dream of settling down in some quiet college town to a sheltered and not too exciting life.

To Walter Recknagel, 6 October 1953:

The matrons of the town are busy trying to get me matched up.

To Frank Buster, 19 October 1953:

I thought you might enjoy looking at the enclosed booklet about Hope College. I went to school here, so I feel very much at home. The first three weeks I stayed in a tourist home, but now I have a nice furnished apartment about one block from school. It looks out onto the city park, so I will get to see the Tulip Time parade right before my window.

To John Anderson, 18 November 1953:

I have to teach fourteen hours a week, which is a lot by any standard and leaves me no time at all to myself. This is a town of fifteen thousand with forty or fifty churches and two perfectly impossible beer parlors. It is impossible to be seen going in there, or even buying a bottle of wine in the A&P, not to mention a visit to the state liquor store. I buy my supplies in Grand Rapids. Of course, dancing is considered highly immoral, not to mention sports or entertainment of the indoor variety. I am looking forward to a visit to Chicago during the Christmas vacation if only to have a few martinis in a respectable hotel and see a couple of shows. If you come back this way, and if the weather remains as it is now, we can put down the top of my red convertible, the scarlet mistress, and go out to Lake Michigan for a swim.

To Edgars Fogels, 4 January 1954:

The second and third week of May is Tulip Time and is really worth seeing. My apartment is right on the parade route, so I shall sell seats, like for the coronation. I shall reserve one for you. I like Holland and Hope College very much. This is the place where I did my undergraduate work, and of all the towns and cities in the United States, I feel most at home here since I spent more time here than anywhere else and have more friends here for that reason.

To Jane Bender, 7 January 1954:

Holland, despite the nice tulips in May, is too cold in winter and too humid in summer to qualify on a long-term basis.

To Edith Kamarasy, 9 February 1954:

Life here in Holland is pleasant, if somewhat less cosmopolitan than I would wish for.

To Arthur Frederix, 16 December 1972:

In a small town like this, it is possible to influence a good many people—like presenting a request for $200 for a student from Ethiopia to the Rotary Club committee and getting it without much question.

To David Havinga, 1969 Hope graduate who settled in Austria, 23 February 1975:

Although retirement is still some time off (nine years, to be exact), I should start making plans soon. Particularly if I do not want to stay in Holland, and I really think I do not. At one time, I thought of a nice place in Austria, but inflation and other factors are against that. I am still attracted to Mexico and may check that out again before long.

To Alvin Coox, 10 February 1977:

I am seriously wondering if I want to retire in Michigan when the time comes (in 1984). California seems an attractive alternative.

To Richard and Ellen Yee, 28 January 1978:

This is my 25th year of teaching at Hope, so life is fairly predictable. I did make one major change in my lifestyle. After renting a very nice apartment for nearly twenty-four years, I finally bought the house. Now I am the landlord, collect rent on two apartments, and pay the bank. Perhaps you have watched the news lately and seen that Michigan has been hit with a blizzard. There are about five feet of snow in front of my garage, which does not matter much since the police will ticket anyone who takes his car out unless he is on an emergency call.

1980 inventories

In January 1980, Paul composed a nine-page "Library and Living Room Inventory," a four-page "Bedroom and Passage to Living Room Inventory," a five-page "Kitchen and Back Room Inventory," a three-page "Entrance Hall and Stairway Inventory," and a two-page "Voorhees 19, 20, 21 [Office] Inventory." For each item, Paul included the date and place purchased, the original cost, and the estimated value. Here are a few colorful examples from each category.

Library: Six inlaid Italian lacquer tables (Gargiulo and Jannuzzi) bought in Sorrento in 1973 for $260 were now worth $450. One black swivel chair bought at Herpolsheimer's in Grand Rapids in 1973 for $40 was now worth $25. One antique Hungarian samovar bought in Budapest in 1974 for $65 was now worth $175.

Bedroom: One royal plum rug bought at Venema Floor Coverings in Grand Rapids in 1973 for $243 was now worth $100. One Claus Moroder wood carving of St. George and the Dragon bought in Salzburg in 1974 for

$150 was now worth $375. One "Dancers with Drum and Spear" etching by Congo artist Zicoma purchased from Rolf Italiaander in 1961 for $20 was now worth $40.

Kitchen: One antique inlaid wooden letter box received as a gift from former landlady Harriet Cook in 1969 was now worth $250. One painted spice board purchased at the Saugatuck Flea Market in 1976 for $1 was now worth $10. One Kelvinator refrigerator purchased at BF Goodrich in Holland, Michigan, in 1967 for $62 was now worth $35.

Entrance Hall: One bronze lamp (in the shape of a stag and tree) purchased at the Dorotheum in Vienna in 1959 for $35 was now worth $125. One used Maytag washer purchased from Beckman and Hulst in Holland, Michigan, in 1979 for $85 was now worth $50.

Voorhees: One Jordanian brass table with inlaid folding legs received as a gift from the Karachy family in 1961 was now worth $150. One Albrecht Dürer colored reproduction of Innsbruck purchased at a Michigan State University bookstore sale in 1976 for $5 was now worth $15.

"The Michigan Experience: They Came and They Stayed"

On 19 January 1987, Paul delivered the sesquicentennial celebration lecture at Muskegon Community College: "The Michigan Experience: They Came and They Stayed: Settlers, Immigrants, Migrants, and Refugees Who Said Yes to Michigan." Here are a few excerpts.

This topic, for a number of reasons, is very close to my heart. As a first generation immigrant, I think I can relate more readily to the problems and concerns of those who have come to Michigan. I do remember some of my early impressions that helped underscore the difference in attitude between Europeans and Americans. I learned quickly that there seemed to be very little distinction between social classes. Working every afternoon in a furniture factory next to a middle-aged man who appeared to be an ordinary laborer, I discovered that this man, who would have been regarded as a member of the proletariat, really was something of a capitalist who thought and acted like a member of the middle class. He not only owned his own home but also had one or two other houses which brought him rental income, and he was sending his children to college. Though he may not have had more than a grade-school education, he clearly did not feel that he was inferior to anyone. Certainly, he was not impressed by the fact that I was a college student or that both my parents had university degrees.

That same fall I received an invitation for a Sunday dinner with a family living in one of the most stately homes along Lake Macatawa.

There were three boys in the family—one of them close to my age. What surprised me was that there were no servants. The mother had done all the cooking, and the boys seemed cheerful about helping set or clear the table and other household tasks. When the youngest boy asked and received permission to visit a friend who lived some miles away, I expected that he would be taken there by one of the two cars that were parked in the driveway. I was surprised when he left, and the cars were still there. When I asked how he would get to his friend's house, the mother answered, "Oh, he will hitchhike. Someone will give him a ride." Surely, this was the home of a capitalist, but there seemed to be no notion of the kind of traditional class distinction that was so familiar to the European.

Last years in Holland

To Richard Wunder, 30 June 1991:

Having spent so many summers away from Holland, I am now discovering that it is actually a very nice place to spend the summer attending lawn parties, the summer theater, and other activities. Quite a few friends and former students come back to Holland [in the summer]. I look forward to meeting twenty Russian students here tomorrow.

To Goran Satler, 21 March 1993:

While I enjoyed visiting Vienna, Prague, Wiesbaden, and Berlin, I would never want to live there on a permanent basis. So I have no difficulty regarding Holland as my home!

To Christine and Rudolf Jocher, 9 December 1993:

Having been a guest in your home, it is my turn to invite you to visit my home. Holland in winter is not the same as Traunkirchen [Austria] in summer, but we have Lake Michigan, and if you are in Chicago, it takes only three hours by train or car. The von Trapp Family, Karl Gruber, Hilde Gueden, and lots of other Austrians were here and seemed to like the place.

To Hilda Cook, 18 January 1998:

Selling my home should not be a serious matter since it is very well located. Of course, the process of downsizing is not going to be very simple.

From Bruce van Voorst, 1 September 2006 email read at Paul's memorial service:

Paul always seemed to operate an open house at his 12th Street home. He had a great circle of friends, and you could always count on good conversation. My wife Barbara, having heard my descriptions of Holland as an extremely conservative Republican stronghold, listened closely to the conversation of some twenty guests the first time she came to Paul's. She then observed, "I don't know what you're talking about; these people all sound like Democrats to me." "Yes," said Randy Vande Water, "all the Holland Democrats are in this room." Paul's eyes twinkled, and his shoulders bounced with that endearing laugh.

Paul Fried made Holland his permanent home from 1953 to 2006. He left almost his entire estate to Hope College in exchange for permanent care while alive, and he moved into the Warm Friend senior living community in downtown Holland in 1998. He remained there until moving to Resthaven's Good Shepherd Center in the last year of his life.

CHAPTER 15

International Relations Club

The Hope College International Relations Club (IRC), of which Paul was a charter member, started under the leadership of Professor Metta Ross in the spring of 1946 and is still active today. Paul brought excellent leadership and vision to this group for many years.

To June Metcalf, 5 May 1946:

Right now we are in the midst of plans to organize a foreign relations club. I spent part of my evening yesterday drawing up a tentative constitution. I have also been asked to join Pi Kappa Delta, a national honor society. I don't know if I will, as it means a $5 initiation fee.

To Margaret Mills, 23 January 1955:

My old friend and teacher Miss Ross recently asked me if I would take over the sponsorship of our International Relations Club, which she has held since its foundation nine years ago. I said I would. I was one of the originators of the organization in my last year here. In fact, I drew up our first constitution and served as chairman of the nominating committee. I hope that the club, which has been fairly inactive recently, will pick up again.

To Dr. Karl Gruber, Austrian ambassador to the United States, 6 October 1955:

We are delighted that you have accepted our invitation to deliver the annual [Ella Amelia] Hawkinson Memorial Lecture on October 24th, and we are looking forward with real pleasure to your visit. Since this date marks the tenth anniversary of the United Nations, the college and community are coordinating plans for a UN Day observance which will be highlighted by your lecture.

United Nations Day chapel talk

On 24 October 1955, Paul delivered a United Nations Day Chapel Talk on behalf of Hope's International Relations Club. Here is almost the entire speech:

Today we join with millions of other Americans and with the peoples of more than sixty nations in the observance of United Nations Day. When I was asked to speak on behalf of the International Relations Club on this tenth anniversary of the United Nations, I was glad to accept but wondered how I could best approach the topic.

First, I thought of reviewing for you the record of the past ten years, which is impressive, and of quoting President Eisenhower, John Foster Dulles, Herbert Hoover, and men the world over who have affirmed their support of the United Nations. But then I decided that you had probably heard most of these things before, and that, since this was to be a chapel talk, it would be more appropriate if I related our celebrations of United Nations Day more directly to our highest ideals: Christianity, democracy, and loyalty to our school.

So I went home and spent a good many hours writing and revising something which I thought would make a very appropriate chapel talk. I tried to show that everything in our Christian faith, in our democratic heritage, and in the tradition of Hope College contains an emphasis on the brotherhood of all mankind, and that there is nothing in any of these ideals which could be called provincial. I illustrated each point with specific examples, such as the sending of missionaries into all parts of the world, the aid we as Americans have given to struggling democracies everywhere, and the number of Hope graduates who have become Hope ambassadors abroad. When I was finished, I thought I had a fairly good draft.

The next morning I showed it to one of my friends with hope for some favorable comment. He read it with care but said: "It's all right, I guess." I suppose what he meant was that, while everything I had written was true, it contained nothing that had not been said before and would probably not disturb the sleep of anyone who was tired from the activities of homecoming weekend. Finally, it occurred to me that what might interest you most would be an account of the personal experiences which have made me a violent opponent of racial and religious prejudices, of narrow nationalism, and of totalitarian dictatorships that have been founded on these concepts.

I became acquainted with the effects of one of these dictatorships in 1933, when Hitler came to power in Germany. My father, who had been editor of a democratic Berlin paper, was thrown into a concentration camp and lost everything but his life. Only the fact that he was an Austrian citizen made it possible for us to escape from Germany.

Five years later, in 1938, Hitler invaded Austria. This time, when the Gestapo came, they did not find my father, so, since I have the same first name, they took me instead. Of course, my fate, or that of my family, was not unique. More than ten thousand people were arrested in Vienna alone during the first week of Hitler's rule. In the same prison with me were the mayor of Vienna and nearly all the leaders of the former government; I actually felt it was quite a distinction to be included in this group.

Because I was not very important, I was able to escape, but my parents and two brothers died in Nazi camps. Eventually, I came to the United States and in 1940 enrolled at Hope College. How peaceful and pleasant everything seemed. I could understand why people here wanted to remain isolated from the rest of the world. But there could be no isolation while the cancer of Hitler's creed of contempt for the majesty of God and the dignity of the human race was still spreading.

Before long I was back in Europe, this time as a private in the American army. I saw more of the terrible effects of ignorance and intolerance. I learned that I had to fight to preserve the freedom I had found and valued so highly, and then I wondered what would happen if the American people would put the same effort into winning the peace that they had put into the war effort. When I returned to Hope College after the war along with many of my pre-war friends, some of us, who had seen the horrors of war and were convinced that the preservation of peace depended on our individual efforts, organized the first International Relations Club on this campus. Thus, the 10th anniversary of the United Nations is our anniversary, too.

Great progress has been made in these ten years, not only in the United Nations but also in the increasing understanding of Americans for the basic responsibilities of world leadership. On this campus, there is a growing recognition that the noblest ideals of our faith, our country, and our school are worldwide in concept and demand that we employ the wealth, the talents, and the opportunities that God has bestowed upon us in the cause of world peace and brotherhood. Of course, the mere recognition of what we ought to be doing is not enough. The question is: how can we apply these ideals to our life today, and how can we make our own individual contribution to the cause of peace?

First, as students, by studying, by taking advantage of opportunities to learn about other areas, peoples and their problems, be it in a conference like that this afternoon, a lecture like the one scheduled for tonight, or by reading, correspondence, or travel.

Secondly, as Americans we have an obligation to develop our capacity for intelligent examination of facts and conditions, recognizing that world affairs affect us all and that if we want to avoid the dangers of dictatorship, we cannot afford to depend on someone else to tell us what to do. Thirdly, as Christians and citizens of one of the richest nations in the world, we must be prepared to share some of our blessings with those less fortunate than we are. We are people with ten talents and owe accordingly. Finally, we must remember that what we do as individuals is important. What you do counts!

To Rep. Gerald R. Ford Jr., 17 January 1956:

First, I want to thank you again for the interesting hour I spent in your office when I was in Washington. I told some of the students of our conversation and also of your offer to have lunch with the Hope delegation when we come to Washington on April 2 and 3. They were just as enthusiastic as I was when you made the suggestion. I passed the idea on to our national association, so now there may be other peer congressmen who will have to answer questions from IRC delegations.

Next, my sincere thanks for the books that arrived a short time ago. With one exception, I have turned them over to our college library where they will be available for general use. I was happy to add the one duplicate, Admiral Stanley's book on Russia, to my own collection. None of the rest of the books was in the library, and I am sure you will soon receive a letter from Miss Singleton telling you how much she appreciates the gift.

Last, but not least, I have been instructed to inquire if you could come to Holland for two meetings on April 18th. Dean [William] Vander Lugt seemed most interested in the idea of having you speak in the chapel at 11 a.m. (this would be open to the public as well as students) and then having you meet informally with the International Relations Club at 4 p.m. for a question period. This meeting might be conducted along the lines of the "Meet the Press" procedure. The discussion and debate class would be especially primed for the occasion since Professor Reed has offered to assign your topic to his class for study.

In regard to the topic, we wondered if you would like to speak on some aspect of our technical aid to underdeveloped countries or the broader concept of foreign assistance programs. Naturally, we leave the final choice of topic to you, knowing that you would select something that does not involve violently partisan opinions.

I hope your schedule will permit you to accept our invitation. Since we would like to complete arrangements for the second semester program before February 1st, I would greatly appreciate hearing from you soon. Thank you again for your gift, your time, and your interest.

From Rep. Gerald Ford, 19 January 1956:

Ford agreed to meet the IRC delegation in Washington on April 2 but indicated that the two suggested meetings in Holland on April 18 presented a problem because they would come at a busy time in Congress, and he "could not in good conscience" commit himself to anything that would take him away from the capital when legislation was scheduled. Ford wondered about setting up a date in September or October of 1956 but was concerned that his appearance might appear too political in an election year. He assured Paul that he "would make a maximum effort to keep away from any political issues," but that such safe topics as technical aid to underdeveloped countries or foreign assistance programs would be outside partisan politics.

To Rep. Gerald Ford, 6 February 1956:

Thanks for your letter of January 19. We will indeed be looking forward to having lunch with you on April 2, and I shall let you know in time how large a group from Hope College will visit Washington during the spring vacation.

I fully understand your reasons for not accepting our invitation for April 18 and quite agree that September or October will be a better time for your visit. I am not particularly worried about the possibility of having your visit here regarded as political. However, we might even work out the type of program that would involve a member of the Democratic Party in a discussion of foreign assistance programs, if that would be agreeable to you.

Thank you also for your letter of February 1, which I just turned over to our library. The books will be most useful for my course in American diplomatic history. In that connection, I wonder if I can ask you for a further favor. Last year you sent me some material on foreign economic policy. Would it be possible for you to obtain for us a copy of the most recent hearings on that subject (March 9-17, 1955) before the Subcommittee on Foreign Economic Policy? Thank you again for the many evidences of your interest.

To Willard De Pree, 16 March 1956:

I expect to be in Washington from April 2 to April 4. I am taking a group of Hope students to the national convention of IRCs, which will be held in Philadelphia beginning April 4. For April 2 to 4, we have scheduled only a luncheon with Jerry Ford on Monday, a tour of the Voice of America on Tuesday, and a briefing at the State Department on Wednesday. It would be interesting if you should turn out to be the man assigned to brief us on the various phases of the life of a foreign service officer.

To Rep. Gerald Ford, 22 March 1956:

We expect to get to Washington during the morning hours of April 2 and will register at the Willard Hotel. The official program of the IRC does not begin until Tuesday noon, so any time that is convenient for you will suit us. A visit to the Library of Congress would be of interest. I am also planning a get together with several of our recent Hope graduates now in Washington, particularly Bruce van Voorst, Willard De Pree, and Renze Hoeksema. Mr. [Willard] Wichers from the Netherlands Information Bureau has promised to arrange for a visit to the Netherlands Embassy. I have also wondered whether we might not have time and opportunity for a visit to the Georgetown campus and the School of Foreign Service there. I would appreciate having a note from you before I leave or at the Willard Hotel when we arrive.

In April 1956, nine male Hope students from the IRC accompanied Paul to the IRC conference in Washington, DC, and were photographed with Gerald Ford. On 7 May 1956, Ford sent Paul two petitions for signatures so that he might qualify for the Michigan primary election on August 7.

To Rep. Gerald Ford, 31 May 1956:

I am returning herewith the two petitions you sent me. As you will note, one of them has been completed; the other has only a few names on it. I am sorry to be so late with them but I had misplaced them for the last two weeks. I hope they are still in time to be of use to you. Of course, I have not the slightest doubt that you will by this time have more than enough signatures already. You will be happy to know, I am sure, that not a single person hesitated one moment to sign unless he had already signed a petition for you before, or, as in the case of Dr. Lubbers and Dean Hinga, they were circulating petitions themselves. I think you have enough friends in this town to run for US president!

International Relations Club students and
Rep. Gerald Ford in DC, 1956

This is the last day of our examination period, and in the next few weeks I will be off to Europe on a tour with a group of students from here. Before I go, I hope we will be able to complete a tentative schedule for next year's IRC meetings and if we do, I shall contact you again to see what would be the most convenient time for you to speak in Holland.

To Fritz Rüdiger Sammern-Frankenegg, Vienna Summer School employee from 1956 to 1959, 26 December 1956:

We are most concerned about the plight of the Hungarian students now stranded in Austria, and the Hope College International Relations Club has just completed a drive to raise the necessary funds to bring one or more students to Hope College, if possible within the next month.

To Larry Wells, Thanksgiving Day 1956:

Are there some new refugee groups of Hungarians in Munich now, and are the Germans admitting any? The reason I ask is that our IRC is looking for a project and is excited about the Hungarian situation. Perhaps you could establish contact for us with one refugee family. If we found a young student who wants to go to college, we could probably raise the amount necessary to sponsor him for a year here at Hope. I arranged for such a drive in 1947-48 for a German boy from Nürnberg. He has since received his BA from Hope, MA from Michigan State, and is well on his way to the PhD in Physics.

To Larry Wells, 26 December 1956:

The Hope IRC launched a drive which has already brought in enough money to give one student full room, board, and tuition for a year, and there is a good chance that we will raise enough to enable two or three students to spend a year at Hope.

To Willard De Pree, 18 January 1957:

Our drive for the Hungarian Student Fund went over the top; we have more than $1,500. The Cosmos contributed $529.43 earned in their coffee sales.

To Larry Wells, 22 January 1957:

This evening, five Hungarian students are arriving! Three boys and two girls.

To Rep. Gerald Ford, 30 March 1957:

Thank you very much for your letter confirming the 25th of September for your address to the opening banquet of the International Relations Club. Our new program committee was, of course, delighted that you had agreed to come. I was asked to contact you on behalf of the college's cultural program committee, on which I also serve, to ask if you would not like to speak to an all-college assembly either that day, or on the following morning. Usually, our assemblies are held at 11 a.m. Attendance is not required, but for good "attractions" we can count on a good audience. For this type of program, your address would have to be un-political or bi-partisan. One topic that the committee thought of interest to the student body would be something on the inner workings of the Military Appropriations Committee or a report on your own study, here or abroad, of problems related to specific legislation.

Naturally, we would be glad to have your suggestions regarding the specific subject you would like to discuss. I am certain that you have the type of intimate experience in legislation and government which interests our students and that you would be able to make a real contribution. Can you let me know your reaction to this suggestion, and if either the morning of September 25 or 26 would be suitable dates?

As you may recall, I shall be leaving shortly for Vienna, where our Hope College European Summer School will be held this year. If you have not seen the enclosed folder, it may interest you. Thank you again for your generous cooperation.

From Rep. Gerald Ford, 3 June 1957:

Ford agreed to schedule a morning session at the college on Wednesday 25 September, make several visits in Holland in the afternoon, and then return to the college in time for the IRC banquet in the evening. He accepted Paul's suggestion for a topic based on the appropriations committee work and promised to keep his remarks nonpolitical. He also wished Paul "a most successful summer overseas."

To Lothar Sudekum, 6 June 1957:

The 1957-58 program of our International Relations Club will deal with the impact various phases of American life, such as science, industry, labor, agriculture, and business (insurance perhaps), have on our foreign relations. We have generally arranged our program so that when we had a distinguished speaker (and you would certainly be in that category), he would address a college assembly in the morning and then meet with the thirty or forty members of the IRC for informal discussion in the afternoon.

To Charles Lemmen, 12 July 1957:

Dr. Hollenbach is here now in Vienna, and he told me that in Cairo he got to know Sen. [Paul] Douglas and Sen. Humphrey quite well and that he would like to invite them to Hope. (Both are, of course, Democrats!)

To L. Bruce van Voorst, working at the US Embassy in Addis Ababa, Ethiopia, 7 March 1958:

One of my main interests is the International Relations Club. This year we have ninety-eight members who have paid the one dollar registration fee. One of our winter projects was to raise funds for a bulletin board which will be placed in the entrance of Van Raalte and where we plan to put a weekly news map. This map case is finished and will go up in the next few weeks. Another project is to raise enough money to bring an Austrian student to Hope. We have some funds but expect to raise more at the penny carnival with an Austrian sidewalk café selling *Palatschinken* [crêpes]. Mrs. Snow and some girls will make the food, and boys in lederhosen will serve as waiters.

To Rep. Gerald Ford, 18 March 1958:

In view of the large size of the [IRC group of seven women and five men in Washington for the national conference], it might be better if we did not impose on you for lunch, but I do think that the group would very much like to meet with you. I need not repeat how much the group two years ago enjoyed the chance to chat with you and how much an impression the pictures you had taken of the group created when we sent them home.

International Relations Club students and
Rep. Gerald Ford in DC, 1958

To Arthur Frederix, 8 April 1958:

I just returned from attending the national conference of IRCs in Washington. The most pleasant experience was winning first place of five hundred dollars in the national program contest. I am pleased to say that Harvard and Stanford, both of which had very good programs on display, received honorable mention. This display is now exhibited in the New York World Affairs Center across the street from the United Nations building.

To Rep. Gerald Ford, 15 April 1958:

Thank you again most sincerely for the very cordial reception you granted my group and me during our recent visit to Washington. As you may well know, the picture taken at the time has already made the rounds.

I was most amused to receive your note with the enclosed post card by Roger Te Hennepe. It has now duly been forwarded to his father in Wisconsin. I also noticed that a story on your new function as mailman got into one of the Grand Rapids papers.

On the morning following our visit with you, Hope's IRC was named first place winner in the national program contest. Needless to say, our group was more than pleased since this also meant a prize of five hundred dollars that we intend to use towards our club project of helping an Austrian student attend Hope College for a year.

To Rep. Gerald Ford, 23 May 1958:

I am delighted that for once I have been able to be of some small service to you. In the enclosure, I am returning the two petition forms which you sent me. I have, of course, no doubt that the people of this district will re-nominate and re-elect you. Personally, I look forward to seeing you in Washington for a long time to come. I am also most pleased to see that the speaker we discussed during my visit in Washington will be at Hope College for the commencement. I am wondering whether you will be here at that time, too. In case I do not see you, I would like to wish you a very pleasant and restful summer.

To Dr. Wilhelm Schlag, Austrian consulate general in New York and April 1958 IRC speaker at Hope, 11 August 1958:

The Hope IRC is working on a new project connected with Austria. On September 24th, we will have a giant fashion show in Holland, the proceeds of which are to be used for two scholarships to enable American students to spend the summer of 1959 in Vienna on our program. I have little doubt that we will raise the money but would like to discuss with you the problem of selecting winners and of making the awards something quite significant.

In the fall of 1958, Paul delivered these remarks on a topic dear to his heart: "Hope College IRC Provides International Scholarships."

The recent arrival of a personable young Austrian law student from the University of Vienna marked the completion of the second international scholarship drive conducted by members of the Hope IRC. Thomas Nowotny, the top undergraduate candidate who had applied to the Austrian Fulbright commission, will spend a year at Hope College on an IRC scholarship. The young Austrian plans to spend his year in the United States learning as much as possible about contemporary America. He has an excellent command of English and thoroughly enjoys living in the college dorm, going to football games, and being a college boy. His academic subjects at Hope College include American history, American literature, state and local government, and comparative economics. Nowotny expects to return to the University of Vienna next fall to complete his studies for a doctorate in law. He hopes to enter the Austrian foreign service later.

In order to raise the necessary funds, the Hope IRC and other student organizations participating in the international scholarship drive engaged in a variety of activities during the past year. A smorgasbord and the operation of several parking lots during the Tulip Time festival netted nearly $500 for the fund. Another $300 was raised during the annual Penny Carnival at which the IRC featured a Viennese Coffee House, while one of the fraternities contributed $250 of the money they earned through the Frater Frolics.

In selecting a project for the current year, the Hope IRC has reversed the objective of the last two IRC drives. While these had aimed at providing scholarships to foreign students who would study at Hope, the purpose of the present drive is to enable several Hope students to study abroad during the coming summer. One $500 scholarship will be awarded to an outstanding student who wants to enroll in the Vienna Summer School in Austria, and several smaller scholarships will be available to students who plan to invest their summer in other foreign study projects, such as the IRC Seminar at Mexico City College or the Experiment in International Living.

This year's project got off to a good start with a fashion fair held on September 24th in the Holland Civic Center. Attended by over seven hundred students and townspeople, the program [entitled] "Styles for Scholarships" featured the latest fall and winter fashions. Against the backdrop of an Austrian sidewalk café, thirty attractive college girls (selected by their sororities), as well as several faculty wives and children, modeled clothes, hats, shoes, and other accessories supplied by local merchants for the occasion.

A display of Austrian specialties was sent up from Chicago for the occasion by the Austrian trade delegate. This, as well as the inclusion of two musical interludes—one a group of Viennese piano works brilliantly performed by a member of the Hope College music faculty, the other a group of Austrian songs presented by former members of the Vienna Summer School, dressed in the native lederhosen—served to underline the Austrian emphasis and purpose of the project.

Hope's IRC has scheduled several other activities for winter and spring to add more funds to the $500 earned with the fashion fair. All money raised this current year will provide scholarship aid to students who wish to broaden their understanding of international relations by spending a summer abroad living and learning with people in other parts of the world. Awards [administered by the Hope College scholarship committee] will be made on the basis of academic qualification, interest in international relations, and potential campus leadership in the field.

A drive to bring foreign students to the American campus alternated with one designed to send American students abroad should serve as a powerful stimulus to students in the academic and extracurricular aspects of international relations, modern languages, history, art, and literature. At the same time, the personal participation of students in various projects—be it as models, as parking lot attendants, or in another function—emphasizes the direct contribution each individual can make to the cause of greater understanding between people of different nations.

To Rep. Gerald Ford, 2 March 1959:

It was most pleasant to see you in Holland again. Thank you for the most enlightening report on the present state of our defense which we heard that evening. I always appreciate your interest in our activities at Hope College and your readiness to help us. In line with our conversation, I am enclosing a copy of the letter I am sending to the State Department. I am sure your support will add a great deal of weight to our requests.

I am also enclosing some of the material on our Vienna Summer School, and I would like to remind you that a most hearty welcome will await you should you be able to visit Vienna between July 3 and August 15. I would like nothing better than the opportunity to return a little of the generous hospitality you have shown me and my students when we were in Washington.

From Rep. Gerald Ford, 6 March 1959:

Ford expressed great support for the Vienna Summer School and happiness in being able to help Paul with his various projects.

From Rep. Gerald Ford, 10 November 1959:

After thanking Paul for inviting him to participate in a session of the Western Michigan Conference of International Relations Clubs, Ford asked Paul and his students to send him a memo on their observations of the Communist youth program in Austria.

To Rep. Gerald Ford, 4 February 1960:

Paul wrote for help in getting a State Department permit for a visit to Hope by Vadim Ivanovich Storozhko, "a real live Communist" and young English-language instructor from Odessa who was studying methods of teaching English at Indiana University.

To Margaret Mills, 15 March 1960:

IRC is another time-consuming job, but one which continues to satisfy me considerably. I took nine young people to the regional conference in Chicago about six weeks ago.

Included in one folder is a program for "A Link for the Chain," Rolf Italiaander's one-act play in three scenes written to be performed by Hope IRC students at the 14th National IRC Conference in Fremont, Nebraska, on 5 April 1961.

To Dr. Louis E. Lomax, journalist and author of *The Reluctant African, The Negro Revolt*, 16 May 1961:

Just a brief note to thank you again very much for your most impressive performance here at Hope. The students are still talking about your chapel address and about the afternoon talk before the IRC, so I hope that we will be able to have you come back before long and that next time you will be able to stay longer. I have thought a good deal about your suggestion regarding a lecture series on Negro history and have discussed the possibility with the two other members of the department. Both are interested, and we wonder if it might not be possible to do something of this sort next spring.

From Louis Lomax, 18 May 1961:

Lomax told Paul how much he had relished their long talk about racial matters and then said: "When I raised the Eichmann issue, I had no idea that you were somewhat Jewish and certainly did not know that your kin had been lost in the Nazi insanity." Lomax then claimed brotherhood with Paul since both had "suffered at the hands of bigotry." He knew not only that Paul could understand the pain that racked him endlessly, but also that "we must not cut the cake along racial lines. We fight not against white racism so much as we do against a sort of Anglo-Saxon Protestantism." Lomax asserted that if blacks and whites could share their sufferings, they would "eventually be able to pull Western civilization out of the fire and establish a fairly decent world order." Lomax returned to speak at Hope in 1963.

To John Dryfhout, 7 December 1964:

I have just come from an IRC board meeting at which we decided to launch a Hope-type "Peace Corps" program to raise funds to send a few students to spend the summer working in Hong Kong teaching in roof-top schools.

To Dr. Helmut Rückriegel, deputy director of the German Information Center in New York and visitor to Hope in May 1964, 22 September 1966:

I am writing to you primarily in connection with the International Relations Club. The topic selected by the club's officers for this semester is "Nationalism and Internationalism." I mentioned you as a possible speaker, and Jan Huber, a Dutch student who is president of the club this year, was most eager. He felt that your background in political science and your experience as a German diplomat would make you the ideal person to help students understand some of the problems involved. We have approximately 150 members this year, so we would arrange some kind of banquet.

To Rev. David Cassie, 14 December 1994:

The question of what will become of the young people in developing countries who have potential but little or no opportunity to get the kind of education they need to make a significant impact on their country is very important. The answer is difficult. Soon after I came to Hope to teach, I began to agitate for scholarships to students from abroad. I think you may have been involved in some of the IRC fundraising ventures (which included parking cars during Tulip Time) and helped bring Thomas Nowotny from Austria to Hope for a year. He returned to Austria, earned two doctorates, joined the foreign service there, and has been back in the US, first as consul, later as Austrian consul general in New York. He is now in Paris representing Austria at one of the international organizations.

CHAPTER 16

Vienna Summer School

One of Dr. Paul Fried's most enduring contributions to Hope College "beyond borders" was his establishment of the Vienna Summer School. Since its beginning in 1956, this still vital program has introduced more than three thousand students from Hope and other colleges and universities to Vienna and other parts of Europe. Dr. John W. Hollenbach's essay, "Apostle for International Understanding," in *Into All the World*, indicated that the initial program was a German-language offshoot of a summer study tour of Europe set up in 1949 by Dr. Donald Brown, a Spanish professor at Hope. When German students asked "Dr. Brown to set up a German segment of his study tour," he engaged Dr. Fried to lead this effort as tour guide and teacher of "Austrian history, German history, and conversational German" in 1956 (12-13).

Paul's well-organized efforts to educate about one thousand students academically, culturally, and socially in Vienna and environs for the first nineteen years of the program were legendary. Even after his last year (1974) overseeing the actual program in Vienna, Paul continued to implement improvements for the summer school and to mentor me as his successor.

I could write another book solely about Paul's experiences with students in Austria and neighboring countries. Privileged to follow in Paul's footsteps, I have brought more than twenty-three hundred students to Vienna every summer since 1976. This chapter highlights only a few of Dr. Fried's adventures and achievements in this groundbreaking program as he recorded them in letters and published articles.

Letters relevant to Vienna Summer School (1955-58)

To Lotus Snow, 24 November 1955:

Easy [Gearhart] and I have spoken to Dr. Vander Lugt about our Vienna plan, but nothing more has emerged thus far, so I am still biding my time. It may be that we will take tours this time and work toward something else next year. Even then, there would be a chance for you and your mother to book along with our groups as far as passage is concerned. Then you could make your headquarters at Vienna, but all this is still very flexible.

To John and Mary Elmendorf, 10 May 1956:

I will have fourteen students going with me to Italy, Austria, and most of the rest of Europe. We will spend about three weeks in Vienna in concentrated study. It will be a far cry for me from the easy summers in Mexico with a one-hour teaching load; I will be lecturing four hours a day for five days a week.

To Bob Bernen, 9 June 1956:

This summer I will be in Europe. Of course, lest this sound too much like luxury, let me hasten to add that I will have fourteen college students in my group to whom I will be teacher, guide, papa-mama, and wet-nurse (I hope not). Most of them have been in my classes here, so I think it will not be very difficult. But in any case, it will hardly be a vacation.

The Vienna 1956 file contains bills from the Hotel Pension Triest in Nürnberg, the Pension Astra (Alser Strasse 32, 1090 Vienna, where male students lived), and the Pension Baltic (Skodagasse 15, 1080 Vienna, where female students lived). The Austro-American Institute of Education arranged the lodging via Dr. S.F. Richter (15 June 1956).

To Easy Gearhart, 26 July 1956:

All the students have taken to Vienna like a duck takes to water and say that it is a shame we have such a short time here. They have adjusted beautifully. We lived in the pension Dr. Richter reserved for us

Pioneer Vienna Summer School group, 1956

for four days, then moved to the *Studentenheim* [students' residence] on Porzellangasse, which is clean but fairly primitive. We have been to the Augustinerkeller and to an opera at the Schönbrunner Schloss Theater—delightful, rococo, intimate. The opera by Wolf Ferrari was the same, and everyone liked it. We had a cold supper after the opera, and the girls just loved it. We haunted some other Weinkellers—Piaristen, Rathaus, etc. We went to a concert in the Arkadenhof at the Rathaus and had dinner in the Rathauskeller afterwards. It was Jan Evert's birthday, so the kids bought her a blouse, and I gave her some candy and got some roses from the old woman who came around with them. Needless to say, she was delighted with it all. Sunday we took a trip to Melk, going down by train and returning by boat through the Wachau.

To Margaret Mills, 7 October 1956:

In Nürnberg, my old friends, Mr. and Mrs. Schoell (he's the barber whom I helped set up his business in 1949) had made reservations in a truly magnificent tourist home for us. The girls just squealed with delight when they saw their rooms since they had had bad luck with the accommodations in Salzburg. The girls all had their hair done in Schoell's beauty parlor, which is one of the most exclusive in the city.

To Lotus Snow, 4 December 1956:

In regard to the Vienna project, the faculty listened, either politely or they were asleep, and when I finished, there was dead silence. No one

Paul and Frau Schnee (Esther Snow) (on Paul's left)
on transatlantic voyage with students, 1957

even said booooooooo. But then, this was the last item on the agenda, and the poor dears were hungry, so I guess the program is approved. The problem is that Vander Lugt feels we ought to utilize as much European staff as possible in order to conserve funds and give the thing "the continental flavor." I suggested your name, but he did not bite. I am sure your participation would add a great deal to the academic value of the program, so I shall do all I can to include you.

To Kay Stout, 28 April 1957:

The enclosed folder will show you that one of my dreams of long standing is finally taking shape. Getting the project ready singlehandedly, guiding it through faculty committee and discussion, picking staff for this year—all turned out to be more of a job than I had anticipated. But now we are on the way. Some thirty students have registered for this summer—twice the number I had last year.

Later in 1957, Paul received an official acknowledgment from the Greek Line and the Council on Student Travel for his forums and travel tips aboard the TSS *Neptunia*, 10-21 June 1957, from Montreal to Bremerhaven.

With students typing copy for overseas Anchor

To Harriet Cook, 24 June 1957:

My first greetings written from France this year go to you. We had a very smooth crossing—better than any I have ever made—with hardly a ripple in the water—less than you see on an average day on Lake Michigan.

To Huntington Terrell, 17 July 1957:

We were at a SHAPE [Supreme Headquarters Allied Powers Europe] briefing—two generals, an admiral, a French colonel, plus all sorts of lesser fry. That was followed by a cocktail party and a very good lunch. In The Hague, we had coffee at the Noordeinde Palace and heard a lecture on present-day Dutch affairs; the librarian of the Peace Palace showed us around. In Eindhoven, we were guests of the Philips company, who rolled out the red carpet—lunch, reception, guided tour, afternoon tea, lecture. Probably the most interesting experience for some was the visit to Rothenburg, where we were greeted by the city with the traditional (since the Thirty Years War) three-liter wine glass. It took all of us to empty it, and then it had to go around half way the second time.

Mrs. Esther Snow accompanied Paul to Europe as women's chaperone and German teacher in 1957-58, 1960-62, and 1965. Her children collected her beautiful letters to them and presented the volume to Dr. Fried as a gift. They form indelible, scrupulously detailed

*Paul and Frau Schnee with ceremonial three-liter cup
for wine in Rothenburg, Germany, 1957*

impressions of the program for six years and are included in Paul's
files. In an 8 July 1957 letter, Mrs. Snow wrote candidly about trying to
prevent "dumb" Hope girls from going into a dive near the army camp
at Mainz that was a spot for pick-ups. In a 12 August 1957 letter, she
excitedly described the opening of a Bob Hope film when he appeared
and enjoyed having his picture taken with the Hope group that shared
his name. Mrs. Snow's family later endowed a scholarship fund in her
name for Vienna Summer School students.

To Dr. Richard Sickinger, 20 October 1957:

There is a very real esprit de corps among the group, and the
results seem sometimes unexpected. Two people who showed only slight
enthusiasm for what they were doing in Vienna seem the most ardent
advocates of the program now. Last week I attended a New York conference
on student travel at which some hundred different institutions were
present. I came away with the conviction that our program is superior to
most of them. I was urged to write a report on it for publication in one
of the educational journals. I also asked if, for future sessions, students
would prefer European or American professors. Without exception, the
answer was "European. European professors give us a different slant and
point of view."

To Willard De Pree, 14 February 1958:

The most interesting is a new course which I have been planning
to develop for some time. It will be "Europe Since 1939" and will deal

Hope meeting Hope: Bob Hope in tune with
Hope students and Paul

with the Second World War and the readjustment and reconstruction which followed. I hope that we will be able to use a number of guest lecturers as well as take field trips into places which will show students visually the things we are talking about.

To Larry A. Siedentop, 7 March 1958:

There will probably be a change in sailing date since the *Neptunia* will not be on the Atlantic this summer. In its place, the Greek company has purchased the twenty-two-thousand-ton liner called the *Arcadia*. We have been given space on this, and tentatively the departure date has been set for June 7 from Montreal. This will entail an additional cost of fifty dollars since it will mean another week in Europe.

To Dr. Richard Sickinger, 29 April 1958:

Regarding the briefings during the study tour, I am particularly interested in three subjects. In Paris, I would like a visit to UNESCO and perhaps the American Library. In Holland, I would certainly want again the visit at the Dutch Parliament. In Bonn, we talked last year of the possibility of finding a US Embassy official who could brief us either before or after we have had a chance to talk to the German officials. The German Embassy in Bonn is one of the largest installations, and I feel that in view of the present importance of Germany in NATO and in European politics, a chance to talk to the American official who is in constant touch with the situation would be of utmost importance to our group.

Paul's 1958 article on "Hope College Summer School in Vienna"

Paul's detailed descriptions of the 1957 and 1958 versions of the Vienna Summer School not only set the standards for the program for almost two decades but also greatly influenced the formation and development of similar programs by other colleges and universities. His article, "Hope College Summer School in Vienna," appeared in the *Association of American Colleges Bulletin* 44, no. 2 (May 1958): 339-46. Here are several excerpts.

After several years of experimentation, Hope College has evolved a European summer school program which offers its students a unique opportunity to combine the most important aspects of foreign travel and study. While there is no single pattern for foreign study or student travel, most plans currently followed by institutions and individuals fall primarily into one of four categories:

[1] This popular type of educational travel, sponsored by dozens of American universities, features group travel through a number of countries. Usually the group is accompanied by a competent professor who acts as a guide and who lectures on the significance of the historical and cultural sites visited. Students on these tours have little opportunity to escape from the home environment represented by the group on the bus and seldom meet Europeans who are not directly involved in the tourist business.

[2] There are many European universities where summer sessions for Americans are held. Most of the courses offered, however, are geared to the needs of teachers rather than undergraduates, and they are therefore difficult to fit into the average undergraduate degree program. A few universities, such as Chicago, Temple, and Washington, have set up language schools for summer students in cooperation with various European universities. Generally, these programs are of interest only to language students, and they are rarely combined with educational travel.

[3] In its best type, this kind of experiment is probably illustrated by the Experiment in International Living. There can be no doubt that participation in the experiment or in similar plans is of considerable educational value. They do not, however, give the student an opportunity to earn specific course credits.

[4] Travel as such is considered "educational," and every year thousands of American students "do" Europe by car, bus, bicycle, or thumb. They travel alone or in groups and are frequently interested mainly in covering the largest number of countries possible or in just having a good time. While this type of travel may certainly help the student to develop independence in thought and action, it again fails to offer the

opportunity to earn specific course credits, and it does not provide for any kind of educational guidance.

The program of the Hope College Summer School in Vienna represents, I believe, an important innovation in the field of educational student travel because it integrates a carefully planned sightseeing program, study under European professors, extended residence in a European home, and a period of independent travel into one inexpensive, college-sponsored program.

I. The Study Tour

The object of the study tour, which included France, Belgium, Holland, Germany, and Austria, was to introduce the student to the European setting in general and to the beauties and landmarks of the areas visited, and most of all to bring him face to face with the new Europe which has emerged since the end of the Second World War.

While the program included sightseeing in places like Paris, Amsterdam, and Heidelberg, and visits to the Louvre, the Rijksmuseum, and the Rubens House in Antwerp, the real emphasis during the period of travel was on introducing the student to geographical areas and helping him to understand the major political, social, economic, and military problems and issues in Europe today. This was achieved largely through a series of briefings, the first of which were given in Paris, at SHAPE headquarters, followed by a visit to UNESCO, where the group was greeted by a Hope College alumnus (Dr. Samuel Zwemer). Lectures and discussions at the Office for European Economic Cooperation, at the College of Europe in Bruges, and at the Noordeinde Palace and the Peace Palace in The Hague stressed the new trends toward European unification. An extensive tour through the Philips factory in Eindhoven introduced students to European industrial methods and social problems, and briefings in the Dutch Parliament and the German Bundestag brought them face to face with current political issues.

There was, of course, also ample time for sightseeing, souvenir hunting, and picture taking in places like Volendam, Rothenburg, and along the Rhine. The study tour, which began when the bus from Vienna met the group at the pier in Le Havre upon arrival, terminated with a brief introductory tour of Vienna. After that students were assigned to the individual rooms which were to be their homes during the six weeks to follow.

II. Academic Program in Vienna

The academic program was based on the utilization of faculty resources from three cooperating institutions: the University of Vienna, the Institute of European Studies, and Hope College. This combination helped us to solve the basic problem of adapting and evaluating the offerings of a European university and at the same time enabled us to offer our students a choice of six different courses in which they could earn from two to eight hours' credit.

Classes were available in elementary, intermediate, and advanced German; [other classes were] German conversation, music, and European history. Courses were taught by Austrian professors from the University of Vienna and by other European instructors specially appointed for the Hope summer program. In each case, Hope College faculty served as associate instructors and helped in selecting texts, suggesting course outlines, and determining final grades.

The following outline of specific arrangements made in each of these fields will indicate that the academic value of the courses offered in Vienna was equal to that of similar courses given on Hope's campus. At the same time, every course included features unique to the European location.

A. The German Program. Students registered in one of the three basic courses were enrolled in the intensive language program of the University of Vienna where German classes met for three hours every morning. In addition, a German tutor was appointed to the Hope College staff in Vienna, whose main responsibility was to work with these students. On the average, students spent from two to three hours every afternoon working with the tutor. The obvious advantage of living in a city where German is spoken by everyone need hardly be stressed. There is no better motivation for and aid in attaining oral fluency. Aside from the academic program in German, a one-hour non-credit German conversation course was set up at the request of interested students.

B. The Music Program. The course in "Music Literature of the Classical and Romantic Period" was taught by Dr. Carl Nemeth, a prominent young Austrian music historian and conductor. In addition to attending regular lectures, students took part in eight field trips. These included attendance at one symphony concert, one piano-violin recital, and two operas, and visits to four places of music-historical interest: the Beethoven house in Heiligenstadt, the imperial music instrument collection, the music manuscript collection of the National Library, and the Vienna State Opera. In addition, private lessons in voice and piano were arranged for two students, and reserved tickets for the Salzburg Music Festival were available to the whole group. The advantage of studying the music of the classical and romantic period in the city which was the home of Beethoven, Schubert, Haydn, and Mozart is obvious.

C. The History Program. The course in the "History of Europe since 1918" was taught by Dr. Richard Sickinger, a brilliant young Austrian historian and former Fulbright scholar at Yale and in Washington, who currently serves as academic dean of the Institute of European Studies. Aside from regular class sessions, which were augmented by a number of guest lectures by prominent experts in various fields, the course program also included several all-day field trips as well as a number of shorter field trips in the city of Vienna, which served as illustrations for some of the material covered in Dr. Sickinger's lectures.

A feature which deserves particular attention is the term paper which history students were required to prepare. Selection of the topic—within the period 1918-57—was left to the student. The main requirement was that material for the paper was to be collected not from printed sources but through conversation with Austrians who could offer students first-hand information. Thus a paper on the current policy of the Austrian People's Party was based on interviews with government officials, and a paper on youth activities necessitated visits to the city hall and conversation with members of the Catholic and Protestant youth organizations. This oral research had the advantage that it brought students into contact with a large number of native experts in different fields and gave them additional opportunities for practice in German.

III. Social Program in Vienna

During their six weeks' residence in Vienna, students were housed in groups of two, three, or four in private homes with Austrian families. They took breakfast in their respective homes. The entire group had lunch in the modern dining rooms of the Institute of European Studies, where cooks provided a well-balanced diet, adjusted to American standards: for example, milk and iced tea were placed on each table, and the cooks even made a valiant effort to surprise the group with American apple pie. For evening meals, students were given an ample weekly cash refund which enabled them to visit different restaurants of their choice, where they could experiment with Austrian dishes and practice their newly acquired vocabulary.

A series of social events was arranged for the entire group. Highlights of these included a visit to the Austrian Parliament and a reception by the president of the Austrian National Assembly, receptions given by the Hope group for the dean of the University of Vienna and the American cultural attaché, visits to the International Students Club, and a farewell party at the Palais Auersberg. Most of the students also took a lively interest in contributing to the Sunday services of the English Protestant Chapel in Vienna.

These activities helped to mold the esprit de corps of the group. Of even greater importance in this respect was the work on two issues of the European edition of the Hope College Anchor, to which more than two-thirds of the students contributed articles. The family atmosphere was further enhanced by the fact that faculty members joined the group for lunch and that students could invite visiting friends to lunch or to the lounge of the institute. All this contributed to the feeling that they were at home in Vienna.

IV. Independent Travel Program

At the conclusion of the six weeks' session in Vienna, students had ten days in which to travel independently to places of their own choice. A considerable number went to Switzerland and England, which had not been included in the earlier study-tour; several more spent time in Austria and Germany or in other places they had visited before. A number of students utilized the time to visit relatives or friends. Permitting students to plan their own program for the final days of their stay in Europe had the advantage that individuals could visit the places of greatest interest to them and select the group with which they wanted to travel. Having to make their own arrangements meant that they had to think for themselves and that they could develop greater confidence in their ability to use the language they had studied.

Since the cost of travel during this period was not included in the basic price of the program, students were not only able to select the places they wanted to see but also able to adjust plans according to their financial resources. By staying in Austrian homes in the Alps and in youth hostels, two young men spent only about $35 during the ten days. During the same time, several young women traveling in Switzerland, England, and Scotland spent well over $250 each. All arrived safely and on time in Rotterdam for the boat trip home, insisting that this period of independent travel had really been the crowning experience of an exciting summer.

V. Scope and Cost of Program

In the summer of 1957, thirty students were enrolled. Twenty-two of these were Hope College undergraduates or graduates of the last two years, and eight came from other institutions. The group, which sailed from Montreal on 10 June and returned to New York on 7 September, was accompanied by two members of the Hope College faculty.

The basic fee for the 1957 program was $645 for transatlantic passage, study tour, and room and board during the six weeks in Vienna. Tuition, personal expenditures, and cost of travel during the period of independent travel had to be added to this sum. The reported total expenditure ranged from $900 to over $1,300 per student.

VI. Evaluation of Program

While it is possible to measure the results of the academic program in terms of grades, it is more difficult to assess the degree to which the total program contributes to each student's overall development. During the return trip, I prepared a detailed questionnaire in which students were asked to comment on the various phases of their summer's experience and to make recommendations which could be useful for future planning. In the final section of the questionnaire, I asked students in what respect the summer had seemed most profitable to them.

Comments prepared by the majority of the students indicate that they felt that the summer's experience had been of profound importance to them in many ways: in gaining insight into another culture, in bringing academic subjects to life, in learning to live on a budget, in learning to get along with other people, in realizing the important position of the United States in world affairs, and in developing a feeling of self-confidence and independence. All felt that their participation in the Hope College Vienna Summer School marked a real milestone in their lives.

The long-range influence that these students can have on the Hope College community is also of great importance. Their experiences, communicated to other students, should stimulate interest in language study and in the whole field of international relations, history, geography, and current events. The considerable increase in IRC membership this year may be related to this.

From my contacts with many people in Vienna, I can also confidently state that the presence of our Hope College group in the city and their efforts to learn the language and become "at home" there left a very good impression and assured us of a warm welcome next year. At the same time, this individual impression cannot fail to affect the overall estimate of Americans in general, and thus I hope that the Hope College Summer School in Vienna has also contributed something toward the goal of friendship between Austria and the United States.

Letters and reports relevant to Vienna Summer School (1958-65)

Paul also made a major report on the 1958 Hope College Vienna Summer School. Only a few excerpts are included here.

As in the previous year, the Hope group assembled in Montreal, Canada. On June 7, they embarked on the twenty-thousand-ton Greek Line ship *Arcadia* in tourist class cabins for four, five, or six. By prior arrangement, the whole group was assigned to the same sitting and given three large tables. Eating together for over a week helped students become acquainted with one another and facilitated the development of an esprit de corps. Daily meetings were devoted to briefings on contemporary Europe and discussions of the various areas which the group was scheduled to visit during the study tour. In addition, Mrs. Snow taught the group a number of German and Austrian folk songs, several of which the students later sang as their contribution to the passenger talent show. A number of students also participated in language classes and art lectures. On June 15, the group landed at Cherbourg, France, and boarded a comfortable forty-passenger Mercedes bus which had come from Vienna.

The study tour from June 15 to July 3 began at Bayeux with a tour to the Normandy beaches and to the medieval abbey at Cressy. The program in Paris included an extended briefing and luncheon at the SHAPE headquarters, lectures at OEEC, a tour of the city, and attendance at a performance of *Der Rosenkavalier* in the ornate Paris Opera House. In view of the World's Fair, the time spent in Belgium this year was extended, and students attended formal receptions and briefings at the Netherlands pavilion, the Austrian exhibit, and the pavilion of the European coal and steel community. The program in the Netherlands again included a visit to the Dutch Parliament, a discussion of Dutch political issues with Mr. Scheppel (secretary of the Second Chamber), and tours through the Peace Palace and Rembrandt Collection at the Rijksmuseum. Added to the program were attendance at the Holland Festival concerts in the Concertgebouw in Amsterdam and an extended tour of the Zuiderzee project and the newly reclaimed farm areas.

In Germany, students toured the various departments of the Bayern Farbenwerke in Leverkusen, visited the German Bundestag in session, and observed Chancellor Adenauer during the budget debate. Prince Otto von Bismarck (grandson of the famous Iron Chancellor) and Baron von Guttenberg freely answered students' questions on German foreign and domestic policy. Two young members of the opposition party joined the group for supper and helped students recognize some of the controversial aspects of German politics. In Heidelberg, students met with several Hope alumni serving with the US Army in Europe. Other visits with discussions included an American airbase and the facilities of Radio Free Europe.

Students attended classes in Vienna from July 3 to August 15 and pursued independent travel from August 15 to August 25 to such varied places as Rome, Milan, Florence, Barcelona, Madrid, Cannes, Paris, Munich, Hamburg, Zurich, Lucerne, Geneva, Rotterdam, Copenhagen, Stockholm, Edinburgh, and London. For the return trip, the group met at Southampton, England, on the afternoon of August 25 and docked in Montreal on September 2.

Many of Paul's letters in the 1950s and 1960s involved descriptions of courses, events, and other matters relevant to the Hope College Vienna Summer School. Only a few are highlighted here.

To Willard Wichers, who wrote Paul lots of official letters and memoranda from the Netherlands Information Service (Midwestern Division), 6 July 1958:

Just a few lines to let you know that we arrived in Vienna safely and that our program at the Brussels Fair and in the Netherlands was most enjoyable, thanks to your very kind efforts. We did take the group on a conducted tour through the Rijksmuseum in the afternoon, and in the evening we attended the Holland Festival. Thank you for helping us get tickets to the excellent concert. We also took the trip out to the Zuiderzee project again this year by boat. On the way back, we stopped at Kampen, just to emphasize the contrast between the new Emmeloord and the old Hanseatic town.

From Esther Snow, 17 June 1958:

We went to the American military cemetery at Omaha Beach where we saw a most impressive sight. I really had to fight for this because Paul seems to be quite upset by it all, but he finally consented though did not leave the bus himself. We were all very sober and thoughtful after this experience.

To Arthur Frederix, 16 October 1958:

Finally completed the financial statement today for the Vienna Summer School. I spent some $26,666 and came out with a positive balance of a little more than $18.

To Wilford A. Butler Jr., 11 November 1958:

Tell your friend he is crazy if he gets mixed up in organizing a European study program!!

To Dr. Irwin Abrams, 5 January 1959:

[The Vienna Summer School] is one of the regularly budgeted activities of the college. The college absorbs almost all administrative costs for the program. My own salary, as well as that of other American staff members, was paid out of the regular faculty account and not charged to the VSS until last year.

To Dr. Richard Sickinger, 26 May 1959:

I pride myself on the record which shows that we are more selective with admission into the summer school than we are with admission to the college.

A July 1959 Hope College *Anchor* article written by Ralph Wright was headlined: "Austrian Emperor's Son Receives Hope Group in Special Audience." Students found the Archduke Otto von Habsburg (addressed as "Your Imperial Majesty") "an extremely charming and friendly young man who can easily qualify as one of Europe's leading intellectuals." He spoke perfect English at his unpretentious home near Lake Starnberg in Bavaria.

To Harriet Cook, 8 August 1959:

Ordering food, buying tickets, and doing all sorts of other things for a crowd wear me out so that I enjoy very little of the things that we see, worrying if all will go well.

To Larry A. Siedentop, 27 November 1959:

The Vienna project has become a snowball and may turn out to be an avalanche. We have fifty-one registrations and twenty-six pending inquiries of seriousness. This has already had the desirable effect that we have turned a couple of people down flat.

To Wilford A. Butler Jr., 6 August 1960:

Paul wrote about plans for the final Vienna Summer School party in Palais Auersberg with banquet tables, dancing, aperitifs, etc.

In an article entitled "Hope Promotes World Understanding" (Hope College *Alumni Magazine*, January 1960, 1-4), Paul included a few additional observations on the Vienna Summer School.

The unique part of the program in Vienna is that it combines the objectives of international living and cultural immersion with a broad and intensive academic program designed to meet the specific needs of our students. In 1956, when the Hope group spent part of the summer in Austria, students could enroll in one of two courses. Four years later, by the summer of 1959, the enrollment had grown from fourteen to sixty-one students (32 from Hope College and 29 from 18 other colleges and universities), and students had a choice of nine different courses, including

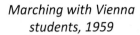

*Marching with Vienna
students, 1959*

art, German, history, literature, and music. The European faculty for the past summer included seven full-time instructors, two tutors, and one regular guest lecturer in art history.

In the four years since its inception, the Hope College Vienna Summer School has enjoyed a growing reputation in the United States and in Europe. Last summer Oberlin College established a program similar to ours in Vienna, and currently Wooster College is exploring possibilities of also following Hope's lead. In Vienna, Hope College has enjoyed the most cordial support of Austrian and American officials. In the past two years, students have been welcomed in Austria by the president of the Austrian National Assembly and by the Austrian foreign minister. Last summer the arrival of our group was noted by four Vienna daily newspapers, by the radio, and in a television TV program called "Welcome to Vienna."

During these three months in Europe, our students gain many new impressions and insights. They are exposed to different points of view and forced to take a new approach to old problems. In the process, they grow to understand and appreciate the values of a different culture and come to see their own responsibility in the shaping of international relations in the future. Perhaps the most significant result of this new experiment in international living has been the effect which this summer program has had on our own campus. It has increased interest in the study of languages, history, art, literature, and music. It has given our students a more profound appreciation of their own country and institutions, stimulated their concern for international understanding, and taught them that they can indeed be at home in this shrinking world.

To Fritz Rüdiger Sammern-Frankenegg, 2 November 1960:

One other new plan for this summer should interest you very much. We will have a two-week-long alumni seminar which will meet in Vienna. The topic is "Tradition and Revolution on European Life and Culture." Dr. John Hollenbach, the vice president of the college, will go along with the alumni group during a three-week study tour and will then lead the discussion in Vienna.

To Dr. Irwin J. Lubbers, 20 June 1961:

Here is a first brief interim report on this year's program. The crossing was calm and restful. Students from other institutions seemed to fit in very well. We held daily briefings on board for our group but otherwise urged our students to take part in the very excellent and extensive orientation and language program put on by the council on student travel. This year's group did not want to wait until we arrived in Vienna before putting out a newsletter to the people back home. A copy of the resulting *Anchor at Sea* has gone to you under separate cover. The council was most cooperative in supplying paper and stencils and running 250 copies for us free of charge.

In Paris, we have had three major contacts in addition to the usual sightseeing. Sunday morning, Dr. Clayton Williams, pastor of the American Church in Paris, arranged a special welcome for the Hope group after the service. Yesterday afternoon, Dr. Ian Forbes Fraser, director of the American Library in Paris, gave a very fine survey of the French political situation for us. This morning the group was briefed on NATO defense and policies at SHAPE headquarters.

To Dr. Richard Sickinger, 29 July 1961:

We are off on a trip to the Burgenland: Forchtenstein, Eisenstadt, Rust, and the "Mosquito Festival" *Czardasfürstin* at Mörbisch this afternoon. Hope the weather will hold out since it generally rains when we go there.

To Margaret Mills, in reaction to the critical tone of her 5 July 1961 letter in which she had told Paul about unpleasant reports from the non-imbibing daughter of a family friend who felt ostracized because of the amount of drinking on the transatlantic ship carrying students to Europe, 3 August 1961:

I hardly think you can hold me responsible for the conduct of some 1,100 students on a student ship, nor for the particular attitudes of any students registered in our program. I am quite certain, however, that at no time has my group been "a disgrace to the United States

Vienna students visiting Supreme Headquarters
Allied Powers Europe, 20 June 1961
(SHAPE photo by Sgt. D. Moore, US Army)

while abroad." My position on alcohol is surely no secret to you. I do not believe that eating or drinking anything, if it is done in moderation, has anything to do with real religious questions. I honor anyone's feeling that he would rather abstain, but I refuse to order abstinence, which could not be enforced anyway, for our students. In the same fashion, I encourage them to attend church, but I would certainly object to an effort to require attendance.

To Dr. Irwin J. Lubbers, 1 August 1961:

The Vienna schedule may look rather hectic, but I think it will assure you an opportunity to get to know our teachers, the staff of the Institute, and a number of Austrian officials. At the same time, I am trying to put in as much contact with the students as possible and a fair amount of sightseeing. You had better sleep on the plane over.

To Edith Lambotte, 29 September 1961:

Did I tell you about my room? True, the apartment belongs to a countess, and she brings my breakfast to me. Her mother, who is about ninety, also lives there, and everything in the room is about as old as the mother.

To David Powell, history professor at Hope, 7 October 1961:

I have now left the countess and, after having looked at innumerable rooms and apartments (ranging from dumps to near palaces), I have settled again in the *Studentenheim* in Annagasse, and my guess is that, after having moved five times since July, I will now stay put, though the place is just a bit Spartan.

To Willard De Pree, 9 October 1961:

Dr. Lubbers seemed most impressed by the school and by Vienna, so he is going to beat the drums for the program.

To David Powell, 1 November 1961:

During the past couple of weeks, I have been busy on the report for the 1961 VSS. The end result is a "Calendar for 1962" with twenty-six very good pictures—half of people, the other half of places. The cover is a beautiful etching of the city from 1720. On every other page, there is a short comment on some aspect of the program, all written in the first person plural. Half are in prose, half in something like free verse! I have had help from one very fine student from Texas but had to learn to write poetry—or what may pass for it—myself.

To Dr. Irwin J. Lubbers, 15 November 1961:

In my negotiations with the printer [of a pictorial report on the 1961 VSS], I found that it would be most economical to print an initial edition of one thousand copies. These are now at the book binder and should be ready in about a week. I plan to send complimentary copies to some 250 former students of the Vienna program, who are really our best agents in recruiting new students.

To Easy Gearhart, 15 November 1961:

Paul wrote a long letter on German offerings in VSS and problems with offering more German courses and separating students. In 1961 four German courses made up half the course offerings but accounted for only twenty students.

To Henry Birnbaum, librarian at Pace University, 29 January 1962:

Even though New York students may be a little more sophisticated than those from the Midwest, I think they would find this program both enjoyable and rewarding as well as very reasonably priced.

From Otto von Habsburg, eldest son of the last Habsburg emperor and pretender to the non-existent Austrian throne, 14 February 1962:

He sent Paul a postcard from Vietnam. Also in the Otto von Habsburg file are three undated Christmas cards (identical) from Bavaria with greetings in seven languages. One in beautiful handwriting said:

Paul with Vienna students, 25 June 1962
(Farbenfabriken Bayer Akteingesellschaft)

"Warmest thanks for your kind words. I so much enjoyed your visit and look much forward to see you again. Warmest regards to you and your students." Eleven other Christmas cards have photographs of the Habsburg family of five daughters and two sons. Some are also signed by Otto's wife Regina.

To Everett Nienhouse, 4 June 1962:

This year we will stop in Düsseldorf for a picnic and swim in Bruce van Voorst's garden and pool with all fifty-seven students plus the usual *Begleitpersonen* [accompanying persons]. The place is so large that I think he plans to invite a couple dozen Germans to fill it up.

To Baron Karl Theodor Freiherr von und zu Guttenberg, 23 July 1962:

Now that my group has safely arrived in Vienna and our summer studies have begun, I would like to express again my sincere thanks for the generous reception you gave us in Bonn. I am sure you know how much you contributed to the understanding of German problems on the part of my students. I sincerely hope that it will be possible for you to include a visit to Hope College on your itinerary when you come to the United States this fall. Since we have a very large and active German department, as well as an overseas program which takes a number of our students to Germany each year, I can assure you of a large and interested audience on our campus.

From Dean William Vander Lugt, in a 1962 statement reported by Paul in an interview with Dr. John Hollenbach:

I have only one criticism of the program. Your students spend too much time looking at books; they're not out enough. They should be out seeing and touching and smelling and feeling, and not spending all that time looking in books.

To Jack Cook, 16 August 1962:

I did carry out your commission to buy a pair of lederhosen. In order to save you the duty which might be charged, I asked my assistant, who is about your size, to wear them for a couple of days. They are well broken in, and you don't have to move slowly in them for the first two hundred miles of walking, as you might otherwise.

To Fritz Rüdiger Sammern-Frankenegg, 27 August 1962:

For next summer, I expect a drastic change from the established pattern of courses. I envision an integrated course which will take the place of all other courses. This would be something like "Europe from the Congress of Vienna to the Treaty of Versailles"—a comprehensive survey of history, literature, music, art, philosophy, and economics. Five or six people would give lectures on different subjects. Each student would receive three hours credit in history and two hours in one related field. He would be assigned a tutor in that area and do a paper based on a topic best done in Vienna.

To Larry Wells, 3 November 1962:

Your question about whether I enjoy my work in the Vienna program as much as I did several years ago is not easy to answer. I think I do, though the nature of the work has changed. I have much less contact with the students now than I had five years ago. On the other hand, the program is better and more distinctly something which I have created and in which I can feel a certain pride.

The 1963 VSS folder has many letters to Paul from Alma Scarlett, the office manager for International Education at Hope, on official VSS notepaper. For close to twenty years, Alma kept Paul well-informed about everything happening on the Hope campus while he was in Vienna.

From Louise Dudley, 25 January 1963:

She wrote to Paul about giving students an impromptu test on geography en route to Europe. She also wanted students to bring Strunk and White's *Elements of Style* ($1 apiece) with them. She complained about the cold weather, the possibility of water rationing, the low coal supply, frozen pipes, and the spread of hoof-and-mouth disease.

To Dr. Richard Sickinger, 11 March 1963:

I was delighted to receive your letter; the first page, describing the beauties of Austrian civil service and the remnants and spirit of Joseph II, had me in absolute convulsions. So much so, that one of the students seeing me read this letter was quite disturbed. Unfortunately, no one here can fully appreciate the fine satire of your letter.

To Dr. Irwin Abrams, 12 March 1963:

As regards Prague, I am certainly hoping that you and Freda will be going. For reasons which have to do with my checkered past, I prefer not to go.

To Lt. Lawrence N. Lup, 28 July 28, 1963:

Everything has grown here. We eat in another building on Krugerstrasse (street of ill repute!), and no meals are served on Sunday. I still have my office on Neuer Markt but hardly see the group except for lunch during the week. Well, this is all part of progress.

To Dr. Wilhelm Schlag, 5 February 1964:

Hope College is planning a Vienna Day on March 5. At that time, we will announce the winners of six five-hundred-dollar scholarships for the Vienna program and also award the one-hundred-dollar prize for the best essay written by a member of the 1963 group. Our public relations man is working out arrangements to bring original *Sachertorte* to the campus. Is this excuse enough to invite you to attend?

To Audrey and Robert Fritts, in foreign service at the American Embassy in Luxembourg, 1 April 1964:

Last year's visit in Luxembourg created great enthusiasm; your brief appearance on the scene sent my stock way up. Naturally, I decided to include a stop in your city again. We have scheduled a visit to the European Community Headquarters and will have lunch there. It would be ideal if we could arrange some kind of party with "native" young people. We would be glad to invite a number to join us for dinner. We could take the bus to Trier, if that is a better place for night life. Perhaps it was the rain, but somehow the streets of Luxembourg seemed to resemble those of Zeeland after 9 p.m.

To John Dryfhout, 16 June 1964:

We have had our daily meetings [on board the *Aurelia*]. After initial discussion about publications, Ruth Wozney and Paul Hesselink took the lead in planning a six-page (three-sheet) ship's newspaper to be sent out to parents and friends as soon as we land. I was asked if I wanted to read the stuff before it went to press, but I declined. I did not want to censor the thing. I hope you admire my restraint. I was concerned enough [about boy/girl liaisons] to ask Marian [Stryker] and Winnie [Hollenbach] to talk to the girls, and I took on the fellows myself to make sure the boys don't experiment with our girls.

The 1964 group posed for a photo with Dr. Otto von Habsburg at his residence in Bavaria. Topics discussed at their meeting included domestic issues in Austria and the country's foreign relations, Eastern European affairs since the war, Khrushchev, German reunification, Vietnam, Castro, and Goldwater.

To John Dryfhout, 28 June 1964:

If Berlin was great, Fulda was out of this world! We arrived in time for supper at the Hotel Kurfürst where Queen Victoria had stayed! Like George Washington, she must have been busy sleeping in a lot of places. This is also where she became engaged to Albert. Zeno Steffens had invited about all of his American associates to the organ recital in the cathedral. Since this was the students' first encounter with Baroque, they were really impressed. It was just getting dark, so the interior was at its mystical best. The organist was very able, and the organ (with some 100 registers which he explained and demonstrated) was magnificent. This was followed by visits to six different homes in groups of four or five. All came back with terrific tales the next day of how nice their hosts had been. Zeno was not feeling too well but took four us (Henry Brown, Bruce Lubbers, Bruce Neckers, and me) to his home, told stories of India, and served fine champagne in quantities. Well, in a short time, we will leave for Vaduz, and everyone is excited about meeting a real prince. I told them not to have too many romantic expectations since he does not look like Douglas Fairbanks.

To Harriet Cook, 6 July 1964:

We had a wonderful time almost everywhere, especially when the Prince of Liechtenstein joined us for dinner in Vaduz, the capital. He even autographed a post card with his picture for every one of the students.

To John Dryfhout, 7 July 1964:

A picture of Prince Emanuel is enclosed. He was charming, and everyone was most impressed with him and the whole stay in Liechtenstein. Otto von Habsburg was the real highlight of the trip. I have never heard a

Vienna Summer School bus, 1964

better and more erudite speaker who could build a completely organized review of world events in one hour or an hour and a half.

To Dr. Helmut Rückriegel, 21 July 1964:

The Berlin visit was a complete and total success. The students were most enthusiastic about our young guide, Hans Heinz Wilke, who met us at the airport and remained with us throughout our stay. The tour of the Berlin Wall made a profound impression. The rest of the program brought students to a realization of the problems Germany faces. I think that those students whom you met in Holland in the spring and who had seen the film *Go to Germany* felt that their visit to Berlin was a high point of the European study tour.

To John Dryfhout, 16 August 1964:

On the way back, we stopped at St. Florian. Cal Vander Werf was so busy taking pictures in the crypt that the tour left and the guide turned off the light and locked the gate! We yelled, pounded, whistled. Finally, after fifteen minutes (which seemed like a couple of hours), a surprised German couple turned the corner. I explained our plight and asked them to find a monk to let us out—or if they could not find one, to send the *Ober* [waiter] from the Kloster Weinkeller! Cal later quipped: what a time to be caught without my skeleton key!

To John Dryfhout, 22 July 1965:

There was little evidence of the Iron Curtain in our trip to Budapest, except at the border, and there seems some evidence that the

Otto von Habsburg entertaining Hope students at Lake Starnberg

Iron Curtain is more like an Emmentaler cheese—full of holes. One gets somewhat the same feeling in Bratislava.

Letters and articles relevant to Vienna Summer School (1966-74)

To Dr. Helmut Rückriegel, 22 February 1966:

With almost five full days in Berlin, I thought that perhaps we could use as an overall umbrella topic the title, "Berlin: Encounter between East and West." Politically, I think our discussion would naturally center on the meaning and significance of the Atlantic Alliance, particularly as it relates to Berlin. Obviously, we ought to look at the economy of the Atlantic Alliance and the economic problems between East and West. Beyond that, I would hope that we could look at education in a comparative fashion and perhaps have not only a visit to the Free University but also some opportunity to meet informally with students there. Obviously, there should be time for a tour of the Wall and for an independent visit to East Berlin. It would be very nice if we could again have as our guide Mr. Hans Heinz Wilke, who served us in such a splendid fashion last year and the year before. Your press office is certainly to be congratulated on having students of his caliber available for visitors.

I hope we can get some fairly substantial aspects of differences in the cultural, intellectual, and philosophical life of the two halves of Germany and have the students attend some musical events, a symphony, an opera, or a play. Perhaps it would be possible to visit the Academy of Art. A session at the city hall with someone familiar with the problems of Berlin would certainly be an outstanding experience. Personally, I have been impressed with the splendid architecture and with the planning that has gone into the reconstruction of West Berlin. Is there someone who can talk about city planning in an interesting fashion in English?

Vienna students visiting Supreme Headquarters Allied Powers Europe,
21 June 1965 (SHAPE photo by Sgt. W. Hartley, RAF)

To Dr. Jaroslav Vachuda, Prague artist who had donated prints of his woodcuts in honor of deceased Hope art professor Stanley Harrington, 25 April 1966:

Since we will have a bus of our own coming from Vienna, we would not have to take the regular sightseeing tour of Prague and would have a great deal of freedom in regard to excursions to the two or three castles you suggest. Incidentally, although I am an historian and agree with you about the importance of the historical foundations of Czechoslovakia, I think that if we can replace at least one of these castles with an opportunity to show the students something of the contemporary life of Prague, either at the university or through a meeting with a workers council in a factory, I would consider this even more important. I would certainly be in favor of getting tickets for a concert in the castle gardens. I hope we can visit the Magic Lantern, but one evening we should let the students go to the Park of Culture, where there is outdoor dancing, etc.

To Harriet Cook, 21 August 1966:

Paul sent her the formal program for the closing convocation of the Vienna Summer School on 19 August. The program included seven musical pieces and five speeches, including a major address by Dr. Paul Grande.

To Felix Molzer, 21 March 1967:

I would like to combine the final concert of Hope's Chapel Choir [first European tour] with our opening activities for the Vienna Summer School. The final concert should, of course, be a gala event. I had thought of

Paul with Vienna students, 1966

arranging it in conjunction with our traditional student-faculty reception. Perhaps we could have either little sandwiches or a regular buffet supper around 6 p.m. and then have the full concert at 8 p.m.

To Dr. Otto Rökker, Institute of European Studies, Vienna, 24 March 1967:

The hotel in Porto Fino sounds fine. We have had a reply from [Yugoslavian] King Peter's office saying that he would be glad to receive our group if he is in Nice at that time. Even without the king, Nice and Monte Carlo might be worth a one-day stop.

To Alma Scarlett, 23 July 1967:

Our crew played a one-sided soccer game against an Austrian club. Though the final score was fully consistent with the performance of the Hope soccer team during the year (we lost), everyone had fun, and we plan to repeat the exercise in two weeks. By fall, all the IES offices will be brought together under one roof in a beautiful old Baroque palace which has not been cleaned for about 150 years. It will look very nice when they get it fixed up; that, I estimate, will take at least five years. This means that we should use up our stationery supply as quickly as possible, unless we plan to buy Lueger Platz. Joke: Lueger was mayor of Vienna who died before World War I. Someone called here Friday asking: "Is this Dr. Karl Lueger?" I did not have the quick reply to say that he was just outside (that is, his statue).

To John Dryfhout, 29 July 1967:

I am invited to drinks with Dr. Schlag of the Austrian ministry of education Monday and to a meeting with him and Mautner Markhof, the richest man in Austria, on Tuesday. In fact, invitations are coming fast and furious. I am having coffee this afternoon with Dr. Stourzh from the Kennedy Institute of the Free University in Berlin.

To Bob Cook, 15 August 1967:

I manage to keep busy here in Vienna. Do you realize that the program you helped get under way is now in its twelfth year? We have the largest group ever, with seventy-one students here for the full program. The Hope Chapel Choir came over for a tour, which ended here in Vienna. I had more than 110 people for our opening party in the Palais Schwarzenberg.

The 1967 folder contains Paul's article entitled "Encounter with History in Vienna."

From Adelheid von Habsburg, sister of Otto, 9 October 1967:

On behalf of her brother, she thanked Paul warmly for sending him the interesting report on the Vienna Summer School.

To William F. M. Hoover, a friend of Debby Klomparens at the University of Michigan, who, on 6 February 1968, had sent Paul four questions about programs in Vienna, 19 February 1968:

I would say that most of the professors with whom I have had contact in Vienna have the kind of qualifications which would make them highly desirable additions to our own faculty at Hope College and probably also at the University of Michigan. As an example, I cite Professsor Dr. Walter Leitsch, who has been teaching there for the last ten years and heads the Institute of East European Studies of the University of Vienna. In November of this year, Hope College was host to a three-state conference on Eastern Europe which brought together some forty or fifty experts on Eastern Europe. I arranged for Leitsch to give the opening address and was congratulated by everyone for selecting him. Almost every one of the senior members of the faculty in Vienna has had invitations to lecture at American universities as a Fulbright or exchange professor.

To Arthur Frederix, 17 March 1968:

Bob Bernen gave a marvelous party for all the students in his studio in Venice back in 1963 when we consumed something like twenty-eight liters of red wine.

Paul's schedule for the 1968 VSS began in Grand Rapids

on 5 June with the ship departure from New York on 8 June, arrival in Southampton on 16 June, VSS program from 5 July to 16 August, group departure from London on 29 August, and Paul's return to the United States from a Yugoslavian seminar on 11 September.

To Kay Stout, 12 June 1968:

Getting ready to leave was hectic, but the ship is restful as usual. New York was horribly hot and with the Robert Kennedy funeral busy and sad.

To Harriet Cook, 13 June 1968:

Last night I was invited to have dinner with the captain and some senior officers. Since this is my seventh sailing on the ship, I have known him for some time, and he is always very nice.

To Alma Scarlett, 14 July 1968:

This weekend we had our first excursion to the Rax mountains not too far from Vienna. One of the boys, Charles Lang, twisted his leg, tore a ligament, and chipped a bone—just horsing around with a ball. This morning, he got a big cast on his leg.

To Arthur Frederix, 14 July 1968:

My landlady, a baroness, sleeps in a little room right next to the entrance door, runs about in pajamas, and comes into the room with barely a knock.

To John Dryfhout, 27 July 1968:

The study tour was great. I enjoyed very much being with just twenty students and getting to know them all rather well. We flew to Frankfurt, were met there by a Vienna bus with IES guide and a representative of the Bavarian state chancery, who remained with us for the first week to make sure that all our arrangements were the best—and they were! He got us tickets to the Mozart Festival (candlelight in the *Residenz-Kaisersaal*), even though it had been sold out for months. He simply told them to put in an extra row of seats. In Munich, he produced tickets in the royal box for nine and in the first eight rows for the rest of the group for *Falstaff* in the National Theater. In Nürnberg, there was a meeting in the city hall with a very nice souvenir book, as well as beer and wine. In Oberammergau, there was a dinner with the mayor, and in Rothenburg we were greeted with the traditional three-liter wine cup.

To Harriet Cook, whom Paul scolded for calling Dr. Vander Werf to tell him Paul had not written letters to her, 29 July 1968:

I write when I can! I am not too happy to have him bothered by private matters! This past weekend I was in Prague with thirty-five students. Things look a lot better than they did two years ago, but they have a long way to go. Bruce van Voorst was there, too, covering the latest political events, so he came over to talk with the students. He may come here on Tuesday or Wednesday as soon as the meetings between the Russians and the Czechs have ended. [In August 1968, shortly after the Hope students left Prague, Russian and Warsaw Pact tanks invaded Czechoslovakia and brought an end to the Prague Spring.]

In the previous letter, Paul's mention of Bruce van Voorst, writer for *Newsweek's* German bureau, brought to mind this 1 September 2006 email read at Paul's memorial service:

Paul several times brought his Vienna-bound students to Bonn. We would party at the famous Dresden Hotel in Bad Gotesburg where, as Paul would explain, British Prime Minister Neville Chamberlain told Hitler that he could have the Sudetenland, whereupon the German Führer promptly told him it was not enough! Exciting stuff, but Paul whispered afterwards that he wasn't sure whether the students were more impressed by the history or by the German beer.

To Alma Scarlett, 26 August 1968:

The final convocation with [Easy] Gearhart as speaker was very impressive, mostly because of the fine musical program Felix Molzer had set up. Kids had tears in their eyes and did not really want to leave.

To Jim Alexander, 1966 Vienna Summer School student, 16 October 1968:

By the way, the Austrian government finally came through with the decoration I had been told I would get, and the Austrian consul general will come up to "decorate" me. As if I were a Christmas tree?

From Otto von Habsburg, 2 December 1968:

He thanked Paul for the booklet of "Hope College Vienna Summer School 1968," praised him for the continued success of the program, wished him a very happy Christmas and New Year, and expressed hope to see him again in 1969.

To Arthur Frederix, 15 May 1970:

The dinner with the Austrian consul general was very nice. He will give us another $1000 for the Vienna Fund, and his wife thinks the Austrian Club in Detroit could also do something to help. She wants me to come down to Detroit in the fall with two or three students to give a program.

Paul receiving Austria's Gold Medal of Merit from Austrian Consul General Norman Birnkrant (left) as Pres. Calvin Vander Werf watches, 18 October 1968 (courtesy Tom Renner)

The 14 August 1970 VSS final convocation involved eleven faculty and staff, thirty-three students, six musical pieces, and speeches by Professors Easy Gearhart and Willibald Kubicek [literature professor].

To Gerben B. (Bonno) Van Dijk, 18 October 1970:

Greetings from the land of the Macatawa Indians, tulips, and Dutch immigrants. You will be pleased to know that last week we were hosts to the ambassador from your country, the Baron Reinhard Bernhard van Lynden, and that I was elected to set up the tea for him and Mrs. van Lynden. I am sorry that you were not here for that occasion. I am planning to invade your country with a horde of American tourists [next summer] and would like nothing better than to house the students in private homes and have them get to know the real Dutchman. I am very anxious that our students will have the opportunity to get together with young people of their own age in the Netherlands.

To Bonno Van Dijk, 10 December 1970:

I also talked with Mr. [Willard] Wichers earlier to see if he could request an audience with Queen Juliana or Prince Bernhard. He is full of reservations if such a revolutionary arrangement could be made, but I followed up with a letter, and I think he has forwarded the request. Another possible visit would be at the Philips plant in Eindhoven, giving us the possible choice between turbines and big wheels in the government for something to do on Monday. I stopped there quite a few years ago and found the reception and the briefings—which included workers' welfare— quite good. I own a hundred shares of stock in the company, too!

To Bruce van Voorst, 26 February 1971:

I have been wondering if I might not be able to get [Simon]

Dutch Queen Juliana (center) attended
by Alma Scarlett and Paul, 1971

Wiesenthal [survivor of Nazi death camps, founder of the Jewish Documentation Center in Vienna, hunter of Nazi criminals] to come to our place in Vienna for an afternoon discussion.

To George Lee, Vienna Summer School alumnus, 10 July 1971:

We were fairly beat by the time we got to Iceland at 3 a.m. Two days in Reykjavik were very restful and helped me get to know most of the kids in the group fairly well. What impressed us most were the clean, cool, clear air and water—so far from polluted civilization and such a contrast from New York the day before. Most of us felt we could have stayed on a bit longer, but this is the way I plan the trip—one should always leave before one gets bored with a place. In the Netherlands, the audience with Queen Juliana went very well. We got there with no more than twenty minutes to spare, having got lost twice. As you can imagine, I was very much on edge. She was most charming; offered us sherry, juice, beer, and wine; and talked with most of the students. We were there for almost an hour.

By the way, I received a most amusing royal put-down. Somehow the conversation had turned to air travel, and Queen Juliana asked if we had been searched getting on the plane since she had heard of all the new precautions because of hijacking. Wanting to compliment her, I said that I was impressed by the democratic trust in the Netherlands and that it seemed easier for us to be admitted into the Royal Palace than to get on a commercial airliner in the United States. Quick as a flash, Queen Juliana retorted: "Well, it would be much harder to hijack a palace." Later, we had pictures taken on the steps with the Queen, and then she waved good-bye to us as we drove off. Mrs. Scarlett said she was not going to wash her hand all summer since it had been shaken by the Queen, but an hour or so later, when we sat down to dinner, she had apparently forgotten her resolve. Just as well, I suppose.

Paul's file on the class of 1946's plans for a 25th reunion in Vienna in 1971 lauded committee members Libby Romaine Hillegonds, Mary Lou Hemmes Koop, Elsie Parsons Lamb, and Elaine Biefeld Walchenbach. The proposed twenty-eight-day trip in three parts would move from Luxembourg to Nürnberg to Chiemsee to Salzburg to Vienna to Bratislava to Budapest to Belgrade to Bucharest to Ismail to Yalta to Kiev. What actually transpired was an 8-15 August program in Vienna with five couples (including the Koops, Lambs, and Walchenbachs) and a 15-28 August trip mostly by boat on the Danube and in the USSR that included seven VSS students.

To Robert Donia, 4 November 1971:

Our study tour next summer will go to Helsinki, Leningrad, Novgorod, Moscow, Zagorsk, Vladimir-Suzdal, Kiev, and Budapest—sort of the longer route from New York to Vienna.

To Randall Miller, 6 June 1972:

Many thanks for your generous and continued support of the Vienna Fund; it is growing, and Mrs. Scarlett watches over it like a mother hen to make sure that all the entries get credited to it—including the interest, which the business office sort of likes to apply to general expenses.

To Jay Dawson, 8 June 1972:

Oh yes, would you believe there is also a Van Raalte great-great-granddaughter [Debby Klomparens Bock] in Vienna doing social work!

To Tom Renner, 11 July 1972:

These excerpts are from Paul's letter to Alma Scarlett about the 1972 Vienna Summer School study tour.

Our activities in Helsinki included (1) the city tour, interesting in regard to architecture and city planning, (2) the visit to Suomenlinna Island with a good historical overview from an excellent guide, (3) a meeting on Finnish neutrality with Mr. Pasi Rutanen from the ministry of foreign affairs (a former journalist who was in Washington a long time and knows Bruce van Voorst), and (4) a choir concert in the Lutheran "cathedral."

The meeting with Soviet young people in Leningrad was only a partial success since not enough of them were male, and too few knew English. In Moscow, we had a much better meeting with young people thanks to a strong chairman who spoke excellent English and arranged five circles for conversation (one in German). In Kiev, we were met by a large group of young people, mostly male, all bringing four or five carnations to each of us. That cheered the girls, who looked a bit bedraggled after the hot day in Moscow and the twelve-hour train ride. The evening's highlight was getting tickets to the ballet performance of *Romeo and Juliet*. The prime minister of Bulgaria was there with the first secretary of the Communist Party of the Ukraine, so policemen and other escorts were all over the place. At the end, the Bulgarian prime minister sent a huge basket of roses to the prima ballerina. The performance was first-rate. The next day we visited a collective farm in the morning and had a most enjoyable afternoon with the young Russians, augmented by a number of additional boys. We were at a pioneer camp, a sort of local Camp Geneva, except that they brought in a very loud band with lots of electronic equipment. We had champagne, wine, fruits, sweets, dancing, exchanging of gifts, walks in the woods, and boat rides. We gave a farewell present to our Russian guide, Adrian. We also gave him some cigarettes and a Hope lighter. He was delighted, and all the girls kissed him good-bye.

On the train to Budapest, after we crossed the border into Hungary, the white-coated head waiter came to our group to find out what time we wanted to dine. The menu: a large glass of cognac for openers, bouillon julienne, stuffed fried mushrooms with rice, tenderloin steak with fresh green beans and small fried potatoes, a small bottle of wine and a mineral water for everyone, *Sachertorte* (without *Schlag* since the cream would not whip; they apologetically showed Karl the unwilling cream), and coffee. After our rather poor Russian food, the kids just went wild, especially since the chef also said, "Seconds for anyone hungry still?" David Bast ended up with a second steak, larger and better than the first.

To Bill Berg, Vienna Summer School student from St. Olaf College, 9 July 1972:

The study tour this year was very interesting, but two weeks in the Soviet Union is a bit more of a strain than travel in the west. I think the students enjoyed the trip and learned a lot, but most of them also lost some weight (as I did). People in Kiev were very friendly; they were colder in Leningrad and Moscow. Everywhere there is the same lack of flexibility in arrangements, which tends to drive me up a wall. Everyone thought Budapest was incredibly luxurious; that was before we came to Vienna.

To Jean and John Bloemendahl, 19 July 1972:

I am back in the little apartment I had last year, so I am reasonably comfortable and undisturbed. At least, I can take a shower every day. Of course, I shall have to see about buying a couple of extra towels since I don't think they will be changed more than once or twice in the summer.

To Mary Herz, 31 July 1972:

More than seven hundred students have been in Vienna with me in the past fifteen years, and they are sort of a special group of friends among all former students.

To Alma Scarlett, 4 August 1972:

The Mexican ambassador is throwing a big formal ball for his niece this evening and apparently had difficulty finding enough young people to invite, so some of ours are going; they even relaxed the black-tie rule.

The twelve-page brochure for the 1973 Vienna Summer School stated that the program had already hosted students from 165 institutions. The brochure included a photograph of Paul and the 1971 students with Queen Juliana at Soestdijk Palace in the Netherlands.

To Klaus Hameyer, who taught German in VSS and by 1972 was teaching at Norfolk State College in Virginia, a predominantly African American school, 24 April 1973:

I would be ready to make one or more special grants to minority students from your school.

To Robert Serum, 31 May 1973:

I am very glad that after ten years your Vienna Summer School experience continues to provide pleasant recollections and stimulation for you. Is it not time for another visit to Vienna soon? You may be sure that there is plenty of red carpet, *Wienerschnitzel*, *Heuriger* [local wine], and *Sachertorte mit Schlag* to welcome you and Cam if you can make your way to my favorite city while I am there.

To Bob Bernen, 4 June 1973:

I sail for Europe with our student group on the *Raffaello*. I am looking forward to the ocean voyage—into the Mediterranean this time with stops at Madeira, Malta, Naples, and Genoa before we get off at Cannes. Saint Paul de Vance will be one of our first stops when we begin the bus tour to Vienna from Monte Carlo.

To Larry Wells, 2 July 1973:

With the dropping dollar and rising costs here, it is much less expensive to live in Holland, Michigan, than in Vienna.

To Alma Scarlett, 9 July 1973:

The Prague trip I had to call off because of the hoof-and-mouth disease in Austria. The Czechs don't want it brought in. The Hungarians don't seem to care—that's where it came from in the first place—so I have just completed arrangements to take everyone to Budapest for three days next week.

To Werner and Ina Heine, 15 February 1974:

For the pre-Vienna tour, I am planning something new—namely, a course called Contemporary Germany, with stops in just four cities: Bonn, Hamburg, Berlin, and Munich. The other major change is that we will begin in Vienna on June 19 instead of our usual first Monday in July. The big advantage is that the opera and many other musical activities will still be available.

From George Lee, 20 February 1974:

[Lee told Paul that he was not] "just the director of the Vienna Summer School program. You are THE VIENNA SUMMER SCHOOL. Just like Charles de Gaulle was France and Winston Churchill was England."

To Arthur Frederix, 10 March 1974:

Speaking of starting a career late in life, I think of Mrs. Snow. Her daughter brought me a file of the letters which Mrs. Snow had written home during the six summers she was in Vienna, and I have had a wonderful time reading all about her impressions. She was fifty-nine when she decided to finish her MA so she could shift to German and sixty-two when she came to Europe the first time. Her letters are fascinating, and I am hoping to have them transcribed since they are very much a part of the history of the Vienna Summer School.

To Debby Klomparens Bock, 23 April 1974:

Basically, I would like to use the first few days in Vienna to give the students a good introduction to the city and the country, emphasizing the modern aspects of life in Austria and particularly in Vienna. This will need to be mixed with enough romantic schmaltz to sell the students on the city.

From Otto von Habsburg, 27 May 1974:

He thanked Paul for a recent letter and commented on how he cherished "the memory of my meeting with the students of Hope College." He regretted that he would not be in Pöcking when the group would be nearby in Munich in 1974; since becoming president of the Paneuropean Movement, he had had several major speaking engagements in other German cities. He hoped "that some other time this opportunity will arise anew."

To Alma Scarlett, 6 June 1974:

Our first day in Bonn yesterday included interesting briefings in the foreign office with a German diplomat just back one week from assignments in Latin America and with two eager young men from the Socialist party; a lunch at the *Mensa* [cafeteria] at the University of Bonn which should help improve the appreciation Hope students have for Saga food; and a most pleasant hour with the mayor of Bonn, who was as gracious as Queen Juliana, offering us excellent wine, juice, and cigars! Everyone received an attractive souvenir. The only difference was that I had to translate the small talk and pleasant jokes, and we stood up the whole time. But the kids were impressed.

To Alma Scarlett, 20 June 1974:

Sunday morning we went to the fish market in Hamburg, which was great fun; to the dress rehearsal of a concert by the Hamburg Philharmonic, which was excellent; and on a boat tour of Hamburg harbor and dinner in a fine fish restaurant. The next afternoon, a trip to the Hauni plant (making cigarette-filter machines) was less impressive than the coffee and pastry in a nearby 12th-century castle with lots of flowers, cognac, cigars, etc., and seats in the first, second, and third rows for the opera *Così fan tutte*.

To Mary Herz, 27 June 1974:

To me, this is one of the most rewarding things about teaching—and about the summer program here. It is fun to watch students grow and to have them return a few years later to see what had become of them.

To Bob Bernen, 7 July 1974:

For the first time in eighteen years, we began our program in Vienna early enough so that we had almost two full weeks of opera and concerts in June before the theaters closed down for the summer. This has given this summer a strongly musical orientation, though the course with the largest enrollment continues to be the art history course, taught by Dr. Spitzmüller, who used to be at the Albertina. She is over seventy but does a great job and spends all of her time in museums or looking at buildings. My Vienna pay has not changed for some ten years—only the number of schillings we get for the dollar has dropped from twenty-five to eighteen.

To Tom Renner, 9 July 1974:

Hope Vienna Summer School is now located in a Baroque mansion, the former Rauchmiller Town Palace, which was built in 1665, at Neuer Markt.

A few letters relevant to Vienna Summer School (1976-98)

To Felix Molzer, 4 June 1976:

By way of requirements, I would ask students taking the course for history credit to prepare a paper, perhaps ten to twelve pages (typed double-spaced) in length. Choice of topics is wide open. Important from my point of view will be a good critical evaluation of sources. This means comments not only on books consulted but also on the people who gave information in interviews, circumstances under which visits were made, or places viewed, etc.

From Felix Molzer, 14 July 1976:

He hoped that Paul would like what he had provided for VSS students in 1976: two visits to the instrument collection (with playing of keyboard instruments); attendance at *Wiener Blut*, *Romeo and Juliet*, *Die Meistersinger*, two Masses, two organ recitals, and the Vienna Chamber Ensemble (his brother-in-law Alfred played the bass); a special demonstration of the new four-manual tracker organ at St. Augustine's by the builder of the instrument; a visit to the archives where students held in their hands the original scores of Beethoven's *Eroica*, Schubert's *Unfinished Symphony*, and Brahms's *Requiem*. Molzer also mentioned attending performances by Leonard Bernstein and the Rolling Stones and enclosed a list of the topics of nineteen papers which his students had written.

From Klaus Hameyer, 8 October 1976:

He reported that Norfolk State student Stephanie Braye had returned from Hope's Vienna program full of stories and enthusiasm. She would soon talk about her Vienna experiences at a German Club party at his home and later speak on "Norfolk State Highlights," a college-produced TV show linked to the local CBS affiliate.

With music professor Felix Molzer
(courtesy Neal Sobania)

To Debby Klomparens Bock, 17 October 1978:

I wish we could find an "angel" to help us offer substantial scholarship assistance to students who find that they simply cannot afford to spend a summer in Austria without some kind of financial aid. Do you know of any Austrian foundations or individuals who might be able and willing to consider something like that?

To Karl Borsai, 4 June 1980:

The main topic on which I had wanted to write to you had to do with our need to find places for three Hope students to work as interns or apprentices after they complete the new economics course which we are adding to the Vienna Summer School this year. We asked them to prepare a resume (copies are enclosed) which might give a prospective employer some background information. All three of these young men are good students and would make a real effort to fit into any situation in which they can be useful. We even set aside a small amount in our budget

To Dr. John Hollenbach, in a 1982 interview:

I think it's important that people who are not language majors, who are going to be physicians or used car salesmen, get the foreign exposure.

To Philip de Velder, 13 February 1983:

Have you been watching *The Winds of War*? I got hooked last Sunday when I noticed that most of the "Berlin" buildings (including the

With Monika Johnson-Schönstädt and Stephen Hemenway
at 25ᵗʰ reunion (1981)

US Embassy) really were filmed in Vienna. One of the sequences even was made in the building which has been serving as home for the Vienna Summer School for more than ten years. In fact, the ballroom [in Palais Kinsky] used for the party "outside of Berlin" was where we had the Hope 25ᵗʰ reunion in 1981.

With Winnie and John Hollenbach
at 25ᵗʰ reunion

Awarding Vienna essay prizes with Howard Plaggemars (center)
to Tom Bamborough (left) and Tom Andrews (right)

To Chris Knecht, 1964 Vienna Summer School student and later the leader of a "Heart of Europe" tour, 15 January 1986:

In 1971 I built a program around the 25th reunion of my class (1946), meeting in Vienna in July and then spending seventeen days going to Hungary, Bulgaria, Rumania, and Yugoslavia—returning to Vienna on a Danube cruise ship. Some time ago, I prepared a memo to the administration proposing that we look at the whole question as part of the continuing education for our Hope constituency and come up with at least one tour per year which would in some way link with established Hope ties—missionaries in Japan, embassy people in various parts of the world, foreign students who have returned to their home countries, etc.—in a word, Hope contacts which no ordinary tour package would include. So far the memo is filed away.

From Michael Koebel, 1972 Vienna Summer School student, 27 December 1988:

Michael told Paul how he and his wife Gerlinde were visiting the *Schatzkammer* [Imperial Treasury] in Vienna that previous summer when they encountered Dr. Anna von Spitzmüller teaching her art history class to Hope students just as Gerlinde was wondering how the cloaks of the Order of the Golden Fleece were made: stitched or woven. Dr. Spitzmüller remembered them from her visit to Hope in 1987 and explained how the vestments were stitched by hand and even indicated who made them.

*Waltzing with art professor
Anna von Spitzmüller*

To Philip de Velder, 28 May 1992:

Our 1992 Vienna Summer School group left Holland about 2 p.m. today. I saw a few former participants bringing their children to see them off. That led to several interesting conversations about past European adventures.

From Dr. David Good, in *Austrian Studies Newsletter* 7, no. 3 (Fall 1995):

My thoughts were sparked by visits to three major capitals of central Europe—Vienna, Prague, and Budapest—between mid-February and mid-June. These stays brought back vivid memories of a similar experience in the summer of 1964 when, after my junior year at Wesleyan University, I attended the Hope College Vienna Summer School and took weekend trips behind the Iron Curtain to Prague and Budapest. The summer turned out to be an important watershed for me in ways I could not possibly have foreseen. I fell in love twice (both times at first sight!): with Austria and the splendor of Vienna, and with a captivating Hope College sophomore, Rosemary Hekman. Rosemary and I were married exactly two years after we met. As I thought back on my watershed summer and its legacies, I realized that the Hope program would be celebrating its fortieth anniversary next year. Founded by Dr. Paul Fried, a pioneer in promoting international education, the program began in 1956, a year after the end of four-power occupation in Austria. Considering its early start, the Hope program may stand as the longest

Stephen Hemenway, Alma Scarlett, and Paul with Dima Vasilenko (far left), designer of 40th Vienna Summer School anniversary poster, 1996 (courtesy Tom Renner)

running of its kind. There is no doubt in my mind that it ranks among the very best, at least judging from my time as a student and a faculty member in the program. The initial summer and my subsequent years in Austria were transforming in fundamental ways.

With (l-r) Neal Sobania, Sharon Adcock, Louke Meulman, and Peggy Bunge in Prague, 1996

*Celebrating with Rita Hartley (*left*) and Ingrid Heyden-Walter at formal ball in Vienna, 1996*

Dr. Paul Grande, a Viennese high school principal and former German teacher in the Vienna Summer School, delivered the keynote address, "First Decade Recollections of the Vienna Summer School," on 6 June 2006 on the occasion of the fiftieth anniversary of the program. He focused on a field trip to Prague in 1962 when students were intimidated by border guards, hammer-and-sickle flags, a fanatic communist guide, striking poverty, and almost inedible food. He praised Dr. Fried's immersion technique in letting naïve Americans benefit from live history lessons. He concluded: "Dr. Fried stimulated

*Sharing wine with Marty Costos (*center*) and Paul Grande (*right*) at 40ᵗʰ reunion, 1996*

Speaking at 40ᵗʰ reunion in Vienna

and triggered mental curiosity in all his students and faculty. His Vienna program enriched not only young American students but also us Austrians."

To Kay Stout, 17 December 1996:

Vienna was a great success for the almost fifty alumni and friends with all kinds of excursions with or without the summer school students. Among the participants were four members of the group which came over on the boat with me for the first Vienna summer in 1956—all well-preserved.

From Ginger Huizenga Jurries, 29 June 1998:

She wrote Paul a nice note recalling with gratitude how he had helped her deal with mumps in Vienna in 1963. The Jurries family also endowed a scholarship fund for Vienna Summer School students.

From Dr. Arthur H. Purcell, Vienna Summer School participant in 1965, as he recalled anecdotes and highlights of his experiences forty years ago, April 2005:

Paul Fried spent a good portion of the trip trying to impart in us the value of trying to blend in and be part of our host environment and the disadvantages of standing out and being viewed as tourists with short attention spans and too much money to spend. He made it possible for us to open our eyes and ears and minds fully to places and cultures different from ours. This was his true legacy.

From Barbara Freggens O'Brien, Vienna Summer School participant and 1964 Hope graduate, who overcame her initial fear of "this professor with the lisp and accent who wanted his students to love his topic as much as he did," a memory in 2006:

Deep within me will always remain the memories of the fabulous summer in Vienna and hearing the life and times of Dr. Fried through his stories and knowing I had a new friend in the professor I was so afraid of as a freshman. From my experiences that summer of 1963, I have the wanderlust that is with me to this day. Dr. Fried instilled in me the knowledge that I could be that independent person not afraid to try new experiences. In visits to his home in Holland, or in notes and cards, he was always interested in where I had been and what I had been doing. Dr. Fried led me away from Hope College to find the world and another Hope.

The Hope College Vienna Summer School was fifty-eight years old in 2014, and its target audience and general features have changed in many innovative ways over this time period. Eight earmarks of the Fried years (1956-1974) are (1) many non-Hope students among the nearly one thousand alumni/ae from 165 colleges and universities, (2) a German-language focus for classes, (3) transatlantic voyages, (4) a lengthy study tour preceding the program, (5) July and August classes in Vienna, (6) elaborate convocations and commencements, (7) occasional Viennese editions of Hope College's newspaper, and (8) partnership with the Institute of European Studies.

Eight characteristics of the Hemenway years (1976-2014) are (1) mostly Hope students—but also participants from at least 135 other colleges and universities—among the more than two thousand alumni/ae, (2) general education courses as focus, (3) transatlantic flights, (4) weekend trips (to Salzburg, Prague, Budapest, Venice, the Alps), (5) May and June classes in Vienna, (6) frequent dinner parties, (7) a poetry/essay contest (now in its thirty-third year) on the Vienna experience, and (8) partnership with the Austro-American Institute of Education. Two major constants throughout the decades have been student residency with Austrian host families and classes taught primarily by Austrian faculty.

CHAPTER 17

Other International Programs

Paul Fried strove for decades to extend "Hope beyond borders" in every sense of those words. In addition to his signature Vienna Summer School, he pioneered extended programs involving students from such places as Germany, Japan, and Qatar. He established scholarship networks to increase the number of international students attending Hope and the number of Hope students studying abroad. In his eulogy at Paul's memorial service on 9 September 2006, Professor Neal Sobania, Paul's successor as director of International Education at Hope, said:

We all know Paul as the founder of the Vienna Summer School, but less well known is the part that he played with the Reverend Gordon Van Wyk to establish the special relationship that the college enjoys with Meiji Gakuin University in Japan. Paul also played a pivotal role in support of international education regionally and nationally. He used his talents to grow the Great Lakes Colleges Association's international emphasis with programs in Beirut, Bogota, Japan, and Yugoslavia. Singlehandedly, he brought to Hope College a national identity in international education.

German students

To Dr. Irwin Lubbers, 27 January 1948:

Paul wrote this letter to get Walter Mayer (originally Meier) admitted to Hope. Mayer, born in 1927, lost his Czech citizenship when the country was occupied by German troops, was sent to an anti-aircraft unit but deemed unsuitable, was drafted into labor service in March 1945, took off his uniform, cycled home, and fled to the American zone in Karlsbad. His family was stateless, but he settled in Bavaria, later got a job as a page boy at the press camp of the International Military Tribune in Nürnberg, and was eventually promoted to desk clerk.

Admission to Hope was a tough process involving many letters from Paul, but Walter enrolled in February 1949, graduated with a degree in physics, eventually got his PhD in physics from Michigan State University, and began teaching at Georgetown University in 1972.

To Don Vandenberg, 23 April 1948:

Had it not been for you and Johnny [De Vries], I think I might have felt pretty well out of place when I came back to Hope at age twenty-six. I would like to make some progress in the matter of getting at least one German boy to Hope for the next year.

To Albert Timmer, director of admissions at Hope College, 19 January 1949:

I think I once told you that in this matter, as in many others, I feel much like a hitchhiker. While we are in college, we stand by the side of the road and hope for someone to pick us up. When we do get a ride, we make the silent promise that when we are older and have cars, we will repay those who were kind to us by picking up someone else who seems in need of a ride.

To Richard Yee, 22 January 1949:

Margaret [Mills] may have told you about my efforts to place a young German student at Hope College. Well, at long last everything was arranged, and I saw him off a couple of days ago. I remembered how excited I was when I started out for the States in December 1939, so I can well imagine Walter's feelings.

To Walter Mayer, 9 September 1949:

Remember what I said about hitchhiking and making returns. [Paul was encouraging Walter to visit an older Hope professor who was lonely.]

To Gordon Van Wylen, president of Hope College from 1972 to 1987, 25 June 1974:

The program [to bring young Germans to Hope for summer study] would focus on contemporary America, along with the opportunity to do intensive work in English. It should include visits to industries (like Ford), a major university (like Michigan), perhaps an opportunity to meet the governor, a trip to the Negro section of Chicago (perhaps with a weekend stay in inner-city homes and similar exposure to American life), and some recreational opportunities. Since we are doing most of these things already in the Japanese program, I foresee no problems in working out details. The group to which this type of program would probably have most appeal would be students who are ready to enter the last year of *Gymnasium* [high school]. The average age would be nineteen, and they should be on a par with American students who have completed the freshman year in college. Professor Italiaander seems certain that he can gain both the moral and financial support needed from school authorities, industry (we talked of 10 full scholarships for children from lower income families), the senate of the city of Hamburg, and the governor of the adjacent province of Schleswig-Holstein. He sees this program as one that would have great public appeal and receive wide publicity. It might be a desirable first step in establishing Hope as an American institution willing and able to offer a worthwhile program for students from Germany. That would be a real asset in the recruitment of students for our regular year or degree program.

To Dr. David and Rosemary Hekman Good, 4 May 1975:

The number of German students expected at Hope for the short summer session has grown to almost sixty. I will go to Germany for about ten days of final orientation and preparation on June 18 and then plan to come back with the group on June 30th. My summer will be busy even without Vienna.

To Lothar Sudekum, 4 May 1975:

There are now almost sixty *Mittelschüler* [secondary school students] from Hamburg and Schleswig-Holstein signed up for the program. When I drew up the basic budget, I cut all the frills to keep the price down. Now that the program has had so much publicity, and Rolf Italiaander has raised so much money in Germany, I feel we ought to have at least a couple of major trips like a weekend at the Stratford Shakespeare festival and a Van Cliburn concert at Interlochen to enrich the experience of the young people. I have just submitted a request for a grant of $3,000 to the Wolfram Foundation in Detroit to help with this. Do you know one or two other small German-American-oriented foundations which might be interested?

To David Havinga, 21 May 1975:

The German high school student program is getting more and more complicated but will, I think, really be very good. I just finished talking with the managing editor of *Ebony* magazine in Chicago about a visit to his offices. One weekend we hope to go to the Sleeping Bear Dunes and also to the Interlochen Arts festival for a Van Cliburn concert. The other major excursion will be to Detroit for a look at the auto industry and Greenfield Village.

To Werner and Ina Heine, 8 September 1975:

The summer project for German students ended up with fifty-nine students. The program went well, though it left me exhausted. Of course, we also had forty-two Japanese on campus most of the time, which meant that we had more than one hundred foreign students in the special summer session. The New York office of German *Fernsehen* [television] sent a six-man team to Holland so they could include something about German students in America in their "New York, New York" series. Some ten minutes of this was shown a week ago Sunday over the German network, and I have had very favorable comments already from Munich, Saarbrücken, Hamburg, and a few other places. As a result of the publicity connected with this program, we now have three German boys enrolled at Hope as regular degree students.

To Hartwig Zipplies, 8 September 1975:

I expect you have heard from friends at home about the TV program shown in Germany a short time ago. It prompted a number of letters from some of the kids who were here this summer, saying they were homesick for Holland. One has already put aside one hundred German marks toward next summer so that he can come back.

To Major (later Colonel) Harley and Gerda Daly, 9 February 1976:

For the past few months, I have been particularly reminded of our luncheon flight to Catalina Island because we have a German student on campus with a pilot's license. He learned to fly before he was eleven (his mother has a plane), and they fly back and forth between Hamburg and Sylt, where they have a really beautiful summer home. I have been up in the air with Peter Matthias Scheer several times. In October, we flew up to Mackinac Island and Traverse City, and later he flew me and another faculty member to a conference in Richmond, Indiana.

To Warren Kane, United States Senate Committee on Appropriations, 30 October 1986:

I have a special request on behalf of one of our international graduates. You may have met Reinhold Grosse, who was a pre-med at Hope and has now opened his medical practice in Everswinkel, Germany, next door to his father's practice. Reinhold's sister Elisabeth also graduated from Hope, and over the years the Grosse family has been most supportive of the college (including a gift for the Dow Center). Most importantly, they have on several occasions provided weekend hospitality for up to thirty Hope students bound for Vienna. I think your daughter Susan was in Everswinkel when she went to Vienna. Reinhold, who is very proud of his American years, asked if he could get an American flag to display. It occurred to me that it would mean a great deal to him if we could send him a flag which had been flown over the Capitol, specifically for Dr. Reinhold Grosse. You were most generous in doing this for me, and that flag, with proper illumination, hangs inside my front porch right now. So, be assured of my thanks again.

The result of this letter was a flag with this wording on the certificate: "This is to certify that the accompanying flag was flown over the United States Capitol on December 15, 1986, at the request of the honorable Ernest Hollings, United States Senator. This flag was flown for Dr. Reinhold Grosse, Everswinkel, Federal Republic of Germany."

To Warren Kane, 26 January 1987:

Thank you for sending the flag for Reinhold Grosse. The whole family will be thrilled to have it flying in front of his house which stands back-to-back to his father's. It will identify both the "old" Dr. Grosse's and the "new" Dr. Grosse's residences.

Japanese students

This piece, entitled "Hope College Has Long Tradition of Hosting Japanese Students," was probably written by Paul Fried in 1976 as a speech.

The first student from Japan arrived in Holland, Michigan, in October of 1869, when Hope College was just three years old. Ten years later, in 1879, two Japanese students graduated with the senior class, which then had a total of six members. An old artist's sketch of the Hope College campus dating back to that period shows that one of the small residences was marked Japanese Hall. It also shows that there were plans for planting a Japanese Grove.

Interest in Japanese students, life, and culture quickly led a number of Hope graduates to go to Japan as teachers, missionaries, and doctors. Soon there was a Hope alumni group of Americans and Japanese who had established firm friendships here in West Michigan. Meiji Gakuin University in Tokyo, which will soon celebrate its centennial, grew out of these early fraternal contacts between Japan and Hope. By the end of the 19th century, the flow of young Japanese who wanted to study in the United States and at Hope had slowed considerably, but the various schools and hospitals established during that period continued to attract young American graduates to Japan, where they became members of an informal circle called "The Messengers of Hope."

During the past decade, contacts between Hope College and the Holland community with Japan, only briefly interrupted during the Second World War, have become more intensive. Since 1965 Hope has offered an annual summer session to introduce Japanese students to contemporary American life. As part of their experience, these young Japanese spend a week to ten days as guests in the homes of American families in Holland. They bring with them gifts and souvenirs which can now be found in many Holland homes. A few years ago, they also began the practice of annually planting a Japanese cherry tree on the Hope campus. There may soon indeed be a Japanese Grove in Holland as a permanent reminder of the close friendships which have been developed over the years.

After eleven years of a summer program which annually has brought some forty Japanese students to the college, Hope has now more than four hundred recent "alumni" in Japan. Partly through their encouragement, there has been a steady increase in Japanese students who enroll as regular degree students. Nor is this a one-way street. In recent years, a number of Hope faculty and students have gone to Japan to study, as well as to teach.

These contacts are not limited to Hope College alone. Not long ago the Holland Rotary Club engaged in a joint project with the Rotary Club of Fuchu in the Hiroshima Prefecture. As a result, the American club paid for planting trees in an area devastated by the atomic blast, and the Japanese club placed valuable books dealing with the history and culture of Japan in the Holland library and the Hope library.

To Mary Jayne Gold, who in 1969 presented to Hope College the Lake Macatawa property known as Gold's Point (a 7.5 acre tract that included a 34-room mansion, Marigold Lodge, built in 1913), 13 August 1969:

*With Alma Scarlett (on Paul's right) and Japanese students
from Meiji Gakuin, 1980
(courtesy Tom Renner)*

Since my own concern is with international students, I can readily see your gift as a center for students from all parts of the world who come to us during the summer for their initial encounter with America. I could imagine no more attractive and meaningful setting than this estate for the type of program we have conducted on our campus for students from Japan during the past five summers.

From Mary Jayne Gold, 21 August 1969:

She was happy that Marigold Lodge might enhance Hope's international programs. She reflected on how she had enjoyed fascinating courses in the first International Administration program at Columbia University during the war. She applauded its aim "to form people to help administer the liberated and occupied territories after the Allied victory," but she was saddened that "somehow our military and the foreign governments didn't like the idea." She found it rewarding that Hope and the whole Holland community (especially the young) might benefit from this new undertaking.

To William Anderson, Hope vice president for finance, 9 May 1975:

In line with your suggestion, I would like to recommend that Hope College extend its longstanding relationship with Meiji Gakuin University in Japan by making available annually one place for a Meiji Gakuin student to spend his or her junior year at Hope College on a tuition-waiver basis.

Several letters to and from Rev. Gordon Van Wyk at Meiji Gakuin University showed concern in Japan about making non-Christian Japanese students participate in Christian services in Holland.

To Jan Evert, 15 March 1995:

Right now I am involved with one of the newer exchange projects with Japan which brings a few students and a teacher from a technical school to Hope for three weeks. They pair up with Hope students who are going to Japan next semester, do field trips, and attend classes. The Japanese instructor is staying at my place upstairs in my old apartment. He is very nice; he has very little English but seems pleased to do his own cooking. I have offered to take him to some antique shops—an interest we share. So I do stay somewhat involved.

This next letter forms a bridge between Dr. Fried's educational interests in Japan and other Asian possibilities with his initiatives in Yugoslavia and other Eastern European locales.

To Keith Taylor, who had just applied to Harvard for the chair in Sino-Vietnamese history, 25 September 1986:

It was interesting to learn of the possibility of your appointment to Harvard, and one part of me certainly hopes that the offer was made and accepted. I not only have a slight residual loyalty to the place but obviously recognize the importance of having Harvard as a base from which to build academic bridges between the United States and the Far East. I agree with you that, if the choice comes down to Harvard or Hope, Harvard is clearly the place for you. Of course, the other part of me hopes that you might end up at Hope. Your "calling to the ministry of conciliation between Vietnamese and Americans" relates to the somewhat broader topic of Asian American awareness and understanding which needs to be addressed much more seriously by educational institutions and the public at large, especially in the United States. The need to foster interest is probably greater here than at any major institution on the East Coast. The possibility of making an impact may be greater at the grass-roots level using a base like Hope College and Holland and the Reformed Church than through the academic community only. I guess what I am saying is that Mike Petrovich helped sensitize Hope students to the Balkans and the opportunities for East-West dialogue in a place like Yugoslavia, just as I hope I have made an impact by taking both students and adults to Vienna for an encounter with an older culture.

Yugoslavian students

To Arthur Frederix, 3 March 1969:

Friday, I managed to talk with the man in the Department of Health, Education, and Welfare who has charge of programs to Europe and found that the request for the Yugoslav program had been approved with only a small cut. We asked for $18,000 and got $15,450.

Paul delivered a report at the 13th annual International Seminar in Dubrovnik, Yugoslavia.

To Prof. Thomas A. Karman, Defiance College, 16 November 1970:

This past summer two young professors from the drama department were members of the Yugoslav American Seminar, and they came back not only with a good play which was performed successfully here, but also with plans for bringing over sculptors and other artists in an exchange program. That same summer a member of our music department was in Yugoslavia and came back with enthusiasm for the scores he had found, and these found their way into the program of the Symphonette which he conducts and also into his own recitals.

To Dr. Nikola Koljevic, comparative literature professor at the University of Sarajevo who taught at Hope two different times before becoming the Serbian member of the presidency of Bosnia and Herzegovina, 3 November 1971:

This long letter describes the proposed exchange arrangement between the University of Sarajevo and the Great Lakes Colleges Association.

To Dr. Nikola Koljevic, 27 November 1989:

Something happened yesterday afternoon "on my way to the forum," or rather to the Holland bus station to see off a friend going to Grand Rapids. The bus from Chicago arrived, and among the passengers getting out was a young man who had trouble communicating with the driver. Thinking he might be a Hope student returning from Thanksgiving break, I went over to see if I could help him. The young man turned out to be from Sarajevo, on his way to visit a girl who had been there with the Grand Valley group last summer and lives in Grand Haven. There is no bus to Grand Haven on Sunday, and the station was closed, so he could not phone her to come and pick him up. I offered to take him to my place so he could phone from there and asked if he knew you. He did, and he recognized the Kovacecic picture in my living room and got really excited when he saw the Sarajevo Exhibit poster and the print that you brought me last time. The boy's name is Tadic Slobodan, and he thinks that you also know the same priest he does. Anyway, he called the girl, and since I had invited one of our Chinese students to go out for a Chinese meal, I decided we might as well go to the China Garden restaurant in Grand Haven and deliver him to his girlfriend. End of "forum" detour.

To John Dryfhout, 3 February 1990:

The big news is that Dr. Koljevic arrived last night *mit Frau und Tochter* [with wife and daughter]. He will be in the United States for about two weeks.

To Chris Knecht, 15 March 1991:

For the past twenty years, Professor Nikola Koljevic, recently elected president of the Yugoslav state of Bosnia, has worked with Hope students both in Europe and on campus as visiting professor. Recently, he spent several weeks in the United States. During one of our conversations about the alumni tour, he suggested we consider a cruise in the Adriatic, visiting islands off the Dalmatian coast. He knows the owner of the ship and has taken the trip with Hope students several times when Dr. Petrovich directed our Yugoslav program.

To Goran Satler, 21 March 1993:

Satler had written in a 19 January 1993 letter about his mother's seventy-two-year-old sister fleeing for her life to a refugee camp in Hungary after thugs had killed most of the males in her neighborhood in the former Yugoslavia. He lamented that Nikola Koljevic had thrown in his lot with [Slobodan] Milosevic and [Radovan] Karadzic (high-profile war criminals later put on trial in The Hague). He viewed Koljevic as "a good example of how much more the human animal relies on emotions than reason in making important decisions." Paul responded: We are much saddened by the role which Koljevic seems to have chosen. I agree with your comment that humanistic education or intelligence is no shield against emotions related to nationalism or religious or racial responses. If they were, the home of Mozart, Bach, Goethe, Schiller, Schweitzer, Mann, and many other great spirits could not have fallen so quickly for Hitler.

To Randy Durband, 18 December 1993:

I am sorry to say that I had offered my guest apartment to Nick Koljevic that last time he was in Holland, but at the time there still seemed at least some possibility of working out peaceful solutions to the situation.

Other international students

To Dr. Wilhelm Schlag, 28 April 1959:

I hope that with your generous assistance, it will be possible to materialize our ambition to have an Austrian student on our campus when the fall semester begins. First of all, we are a Protestant school, and it would therefore be most desirable to have the student be a member of some Protestant church.

To Manzar and Naseem Bashir, from the MS *Aurelia*, 16 June 1964:

Just before I left for Europe, I completed arrangements to have Sir Muhammad Zafrulla Khan come to Hope College on October 9 for a lecture on "World Court and World Peace." We have never, as far as I know, had any students from Pakistan. This seems a great pity to me.

To Willard De Pree, 15 February 1973:

Paul wrote about a scholarship to a young Ethiopian and about his desire to invite one of the official representatives of Qatar to the campus.

To Rev. David Cassie, pastor of United Church of Ponce, 15 October 1973:

While Puerto Rico is not really a foreign country, the culture is sufficiently different to make it desirable for our students to have contact with students from there. Our scholarship resources are limited, but I think there may be federal scholarship funds available for students from Puerto Rico.

To Hilda and Arthur Kloucek, 20 May 1974:

Right now we have sixty-two foreign students from twenty-one countries. The largest groups are from Japan and Qatar, a small oil sheikdom I had never heard of before the first students arrived. They are very nice, have lots of money, and don't like to study too much. I am also chairman of a special committee to raise money and give scholarships to African and Asian students. In connection with my interest in Vienna, I have helped set up two scholarship funds—one to provide money for Austrian students who want to study at Hope and another one for American students who want to study history, art, or music in Vienna.

To Mary Herz, 27 June 1974:

I have tried to increase the interest in having foreign students at Hope, partly by helping raise funds for scholarships and partly by working with them after they come to the United States. It was nice to arrive in Vienna last week and have six or seven Austrians—all former Hope students—attend our reception last Sunday. One [Thomas Nowotny], now in the office of Dr. Kreisky, still speaks with enthusiasm about the year he spent at Hope fifteen years ago.

To Richard and Bev Brown, 26 November 1974:

We currently have sixteen students from Qatar at Hope. One has a $20,000 Mercedes 450SEC here and another one at home. But money or no money, all of them are very nice guys.

*With (*left to right*) Ken Dibi, Alma Scarlett,*
and Tareke Gebre-Hiwot, 1978
(courtesy Tom Renner)

To Wa-el Karachy, who sent letters to Paul over the years from Jordan, Nigeria, Germany, and Abu Dhabi, 20 May 1975:

Your suggestion for developing student exchange arrangements between Hope and Jordan might fit into the general idea I have for the next decade, and I would enjoy talking with you on that and perhaps meeting His Royal Highness Prince Ra'ad bin Zeid when the time comes. [The prince had written Paul on 2 April 1975.]

To Rev. David Cassie, 21 February 1976:

One of my innovations is a course in American history for foreign students. I am now teaching it the second time and still learning just what approach to take. Of the fifteen students in the class, five are from Japan, two from Rhodesia, and one each from Iran, Indonesia, Germany, Qatar, Saudi Arabia, Vietnam, Ethiopia, and Hong Kong.

To Hilda Kloucek, 4 June 1976:

I have become more concerned with import of students and somewhat less involved with export.

To Abdul Al-Mawlawi, 5 January 1987:

You and the whole group of Qatar students were at Hope giving a more exotic flair to the place.

To John Jacobson, president of Hope College from 1987 to 1999, 15 October 1989:

With globe, stressing
"Hope beyond borders"
(courtesy Tom Renner)

This is to follow up on our recent conversation about the use of funds I intend to leave to Hope College. The detailed letter (addressed to my personal representatives and Hope College), which forms part of my revised will, explains my reasons for the establishment of a new endowment fund, tentatively designated as "Vienna II." To make a start, I am enclosing my personal check for $5,000. The primary purpose of the fund is to provide income for "partial scholarship support to carefully chosen young Austrians who could benefit by spending a year or more at Hope College and whose presence on campus could contribute to the education of their American fellow students." A secondary use of the fund might be to assist Hope in bringing Austrian historians or other European faculty in the arts or humanities as guest lecturers to Hope College.

To John Dryfhout, 30 January 1990:

I had lunch with Bob De Young and Dr. Jacobson yesterday. I think I got some encouragement for my idea of a follow-up on *Into All the World* which I would tentatively call *From Many Lands*—in other words, a book dealing with some of the students who have come from abroad to study at Hope and what happened to them.

To Ken Powell, 13 October 1992:

I have long felt that Hope PR efforts tend to focus far too much on domestic and regional activities and that there should be more of an effort to keep up with graduates who live and work outside the United States—be they part of the growing number of Americans living and working abroad or those who came to Hope from some other country and have gone back to live there.

CHAPTER 18

Physical Health

Despite his chubby appearance, Paul was often very physically active. He enjoyed bicycling from his earliest days until long after his retirement. He often took ski vacations, especially during his two post-war sojourns in Germany in 1947-49 and 1951-53. He learned horseback riding during his summer job as a waiter at the Broadmoor Hotel in Colorado Springs. He played tennis and was a lifelong swimmer who raved about German accommodations with swimming pools; he was a devotee of Hope's swimming pool when the Dow Center opened. Hearing problems plagued Paul from the end of World War II until his final days. He never could seem to find his hearing aids, and even when they were in place, he could shut them down if the conversation at one of his many 12th Street soirées got a little tedious. Occasional hospitalizations caused postponed trips and weight fluctuations.

To Margaret Mills, 1 February 1946:

A bit of unpleasant news was given to me a few days ago by the ear specialist. I have had a rather constant ringing in both ears for some time. At first, he thought it was a throat infection and gave me sulfa pills and nose drops to clear it up. Well, the infection cleared away, but the

329

"How do you like this Tarzan pose?"
in Wiesbaden, July 1945

ringing remained. This time he tested my hearing and found that I am probably afflicted with "boilermaker's" deafness. He thinks it may be the effect of the noise of battles. I might have to wear a hearing aid ten years from now. Won't I look good with that!

From Margaret Mills, 19 October 1953:

Margaret advised Paul to see a Christian Scientist practitioner in Holland for his ears.

To Mama Kramer, 18 February 1946:

I am confined to my room, unable to speak, eat, or go out. On Friday, I had my tonsils taken out. They must have been extra-large because, when the doctor tried to take them out with a local anesthetic, I could feel everything. Finally, I just about passed out, so he gave me ether. My government allowance still has not come, and with the hospital and doctor's bills, I am afraid I will have to cash in one of my bonds.

To Lida Imhof, 18 February 1946:

I went to Holland Hospital to have my tonsils removed. [After the ether], I didn't wake up until six hours later, spent a day in the hospital, and then returned "home." Miss Cook has been an angel worrying about my food. Tonight I began taking some Gerber's baby food—spinach and apple sauce.

To Rev. Arthur and Martha Kate Barnhart, 24 March 1946:

In regard to the bicycle, I am sure I can manage the necessary repairs or replacements. As a matter of fact, I found two new tires which I think will fit it at Montgomery Ward—where I work Saturdays—and had

Paul on biking holiday near Nürnberg

them put aside. So, if you can ship it soon, I will use my spring vacation to do the work and get the exercise.

To Rev. Arthur and Martha Kate Barnhart, 28 May 1946:

The bicycle arrived in good condition some time ago. I am enclosing a bank money order for twenty dollars. I am sure the bike is worth that to me, and I could always get that much if I should want to sell it again. I have not done much work on it, but I have enjoyed the few times I had it out.

To Margaret Mills, 15 December 1946:

I am at long last learning about getting along with a little less sleep. I know my mother had that facility; she could rest for five minutes and be quite fresh.

To the Metcalfs and Kramers, 30 January 1947:

Next term, perhaps I shall even have time to go out rowing or cycling. I have a participation card for the Harvard Athletic Association, so I get a chance to go swimming or to exercise when I get tired of sitting over the books or typewriter.

To Don Vandenberg, 31 January 1947:

I am always eager to hear about the games Hope plays—and wins. Now I go swimming about two or three times a week. Usually, I spend a few minutes in the gym before going down to the pool. I hope to take up squash in the next couple of months.

To Harriet Cook, 19 January 1949:

I just had some sort of boil on my arm—probably caused by diet—and enjoyed four or five days rest in the hospital. My staff sent me lots of flowers and candy, and my driver brought over the radio and bed lamp from my room.

To Manzar Bashir, 14 May 1951:

My present boss is all of twenty-one and very intelligent. We play tennis about three times a week together.

To Tom Bennett, 30 June 1951:

Some time ago a few of us went swimming in the tiled pool in the garden at midnight to music.

To Kay Stout, 18 February 1952:

If you still would like to go skiing, I shall be glad to go along for a few days.

To Helen Hathaway, 28 March 1952:

Tonight I went swimming in a newly opened indoor pool, and after that I went to practice bowling, since I have not been doing well in our league. But, of course, sports is only a means to an end, and I much rather sit at home and listen to some good music and read—except on weekends.

To Walter Recknagel, 25 February 1953:

Time out for the dentist and lunch in the warm sun. I am having all my teeth fixed here since I can afford it now.

To Bob and Inge Boelkins, 24 March 1953:

I found a good dentist who is giving me the works. I need two bridges and several fillings, but he is giving me gold inlays instead of the fillings.

To Tom Bennett, 2 April 1954:

I was interested in your plans to learn judo. I never did learn how to defend myself—have not had too much need for it thus far. Of course, there were certain tricks we learned in the army, but you need piano wire for that.

To Edith Lambotte, 4 December 1960:

I had quite a bit of trouble with my insides. I had some X-rays taken; the diagnosis is diverticulitis, which requires careful diet. I lost fifteen to eighteen pounds this spring and would not mind losing a bit more. Then I could get all new suits.

To Manzar Bashir, 13 August 1969:

I think you hinted before that you had rejoined the ranks of the single—welcome to the club, it really has its compensations—like being able to go halfway around the world on leave, and I have not had serious incentive to change my station thus far. Perhaps I will have regrets later, when I need someone to push me around in a wheelchair!

To Bob Bernen, 23 September 1971:

My sabbatical leave in 1969 was spent quite differently than planned. I was vacationing in Nova Scotia when I suddenly had to go into the hospital for an emergency operation for peritonitis which kept me in that place—Yarmouth—for more than four weeks. I returned to Holland for a three-month period of recovery. I then went back for a second operation and three more weeks of hospital residence in Grand Rapids.

To Harriet Cook, from Yarmouth, Nova Scotia, 11 October 1969:

My last tube was taken out on Wednesday, so now I can get about a lot better, and it seems as if the opening is starting to heal. Have a private room with bath and have even rented a TV, so I have more comforts than at home. I have lost fifteen pounds and hope I will not put them on again. The doctor would like to see me get rid of ten or fifteen more.

Surgery canceled Paul's planned trip to Sierra Leone (ca. 1969-70) to visit Willard De Pree, stationed at the US Embassy in Sierra Leone.

To Larry Wells, 4 January 1970:

I am going to the hospital in Grand Rapids to have another operation Thursday, and my "Grand Rapids opening" is scheduled for Friday. I am hoping for a short and successful run, though I expect that I will be in the hospital for two or three weeks.

To Harriet Cook, 6 February 1970:

Paul talked about having twenty-four inches of his intestine removed.

To June Metcalf, 18 February 1970:

Now I am some twenty-five pounds lighter than I was in September, and everyone tells me I look ten years younger. I don't quite believe it, but it's nice to hear.

To Kay Stout, 25 April 1971:

Yes, I am completely well again; i.e., the offending section of my digestive machinery was cut out, and the operation was a complete success.

To Bob Bernen, 23 September 1971:

All is well now, except that I gained back the pounds so unpleasantly lost.

To David Havinga, after Paul had joked about spending two weeks in the Holland Hilton after his December prostate surgery, 12 February 1973:

Most of the time I feel fine, so long as I take my pills for high blood pressure. I eat less and am down to 135 pounds. I hope to stay there since the Dykema brothers, the last real tailors in Holland, are retiring at the end of the month. They have been great about letting out clothes for me in years past and taking them in more recently.

To Arthur Frederix, 5 January 1973:

Paul expressed pleasure at having received three hundred cards while he was hospitalized for the operation on his enlarged prostate.

To Dr. Larry A. Siedentop, 18 July 1983:

Our new physical education center has become one of my favorite spots for late evening swims and sauna—much better than going to Skiles for beer and pizza.

To Mark Christensen, 20 May 1984:

With several luncheon and dinners in my home, I am back to fighting the battle of the bulge.

To Jan Ergenzinger, 15 January 1985:

I remember some American army dentists during the war, but that is better forgotten.

To Ernest and Jessica Lloyd [Ernest had known Paul in Vienna and belonged to the Christian Witness to Israel in England; Paul and Mrs. Lambotte were with Ernest and Jessica when their eldest son was born on 2 September 1939.], 4 January 1992:

What I dread most is the possibility of not being able to read or look after myself.

To Bob Bernen, 19 March 1993:

In December 1991, I fell on the ice in front of the building which has been named for me (a way of adding insult to injury). The fracture had healed, but somehow there were other things, such as weight loss and internal bleeding and continued high blood pressure. I wish I had been wise enough to follow your example and try to find out more about the diabetes, which does not seem to interest many doctors.

In the meantime, I have lost some thirty-five or forty pounds, can wear a thirty-two-inch belt, and seem to be stabilized at 110 pounds. I feel quite well most of the time, but I don't have as much energy as I would like.

To Samuel and Sophia Fumey, 19 March 1993:

Some of my friends are rather concerned when they see that I have lost about thirty-five or forty pounds. At present, I feel quite well and have started to buy new clothing to fit, but I get tired rather quickly.

To Nicolaas Bootsma, history professor at Catholic University of Nijmegen and visiting professor at Hope (1967-68), 14 January 1995:

Yes, after some difficult adjustments, I think I have learned to live with being a diabetic. I lost some thirty pounds and now take part in a rehab program—one hour, three times a week of supervised exercises.

To Kay Stout, 18 November 1995:

I began a regular schedule of one hour every Monday, Wednesday, and Friday at the physical therapy center of our hospital. I use many fancy devices and have blood pressure and pulse checked three times, plus orange juice or fruit. Pleasant nurses and interesting company. I am the oddball in my group since I have never had a heart attack.

To Richard and Bev Brown, 24 February 1996:

I am looking forward to the Vienna Summer School reunion. I just took my tux, made in Vienna in 1963, to the tailor here to have it taken in since I have lost some thirty or more pounds in the intervening years.

To John Dryfhout, 2 July 1997:

I am stuck here for the next two weeks with a not-too-pleasant problem. The key tooth which held my upper bridge collapsed and was painfully extracted, along with its neighbor. Now my face is quite lopsided, and I am told it will be several days before I will be more or less balanced again, as long as I don't open my mouth. I rather expect that I will lose a bit more weight—good thing that I like soups and yogurt.

To Matt Nickel in an oral interview, 12 March 2003:

My need to be needed is gone. I don't have a single relative that I know of.

CHAPTER 19

Food and Beverages

Paul loved to cook, primarily because he loved to entertain people everywhere, especially at his home on 12ᵗʰ Street in Holland. He was the perfect host. In his letters, he often commented, both seriously and humorously, about eating and drinking. From flour and sugar shortages in post-war Europe to culinary extravaganzas for visiting dignitaries, Paul was always aware of the power of food.

From Hilda Kloucek, 19 July 1946:

Hilda wrote about bread rationing in England and how she would appreciate jellies, corn flour, and custard powder.

To Harriet Cook, 2 December 1946:

Thank you for the nice little box of sweets and cookies which came just in time for Thanksgiving.

To Walter A. Scholten Jr., 2 February 1947:

I can fully understand your desire for fresh milk. I never used to drink much before, but when we landed in the States, the Red Cross brought quart cartons to the train. Did that ever taste good.

To Hilda Kloucek, 23 March 1947:

I hope that life in London is again getting a little more pleasant. I was greatly bothered by knowing that so many people had not much fuel or food this last winter, while I have trouble keeping my weight at its proper level.

To Harriet Cook, 30 April 1947:

This letter on an aerogram from Durgin Park said, "Write a note home to Mother from Boston's most famous dining rooms in the shadow of Faneuil Hall."

To Margaret Mills, 6 January 1948:

I think I have discovered the real reason why most GIs and a good many Americans prefer steak, hamburger, and veal to most other dishes. They can't eat holding their forks in the left and cutting with the right at the same time. Thus, any food that can't be easily cut up into little pieces beforehand is additional work—unless they are at home and can pick up chicken with their hands.

To the Metcalfs and Kramers, 20 January 1948:

Regarding the sending of food, your package contained just the right things. What are needed here are fat, flour, sugar, and a few of the things which make life more pleasant, such as coffee or chocolate. I shall only be too happy to distribute the things here; as a matter of fact, I get great pleasure in doing it.

To Dr. William and Ada Schrier, 11 February 1948:

I know a very large number of people who would be happy to receive a small addition to their meager rations. I would suggest a package containing flour, shortening, sugar, and perhaps some dried fruits or raisins, plus anything in the way of canned meat or bacon.

To Harriet Cook, 5 April 1948:

Thanks for the package. I have already had several pieces of the fruitcake. It is a little hard but very good. I shall put some brandy on it to soften it.

To Chet Schultz, 26 June 1948:

I think I shall leave the office and drive out in the country to get some fresh cherries. We get mostly canned stuff at the officers' mess and at the club.

To Margaret Mills, 18 August 1948:

In Salzburg, we met a lot of friends, even our general (not included among my intimate friends). We were invited to lunch in an Austrian place way up in the mountains. The food was wonderful, and there were large quantities of something I hadn't seen for some time and shouldn't be seeing at all—good whipped cream, even in coffee.

To June and Alan Metcalf, 25 September 1949:

Got a royal reception at Holland with a luncheon given by the president of Hope College at the Warm Friend Tavern. I practically had to eat my way through the town. It was nice to see so many of my old friends again after all this time.

To Kay Stout, 7 January 1950:

Tonight I went out to see a movie, *On the Town*, with Frank Sinatra, Gene Kelly, and Vera Ellen, with a fellow from Toronto. Afterwards, we went to an old German restaurant and had beer and pig knuckles! Started talking about Europe, and by and by, I was at once cheered and nostalgic about pleasant times I had there.

To Kay Stout, 10 July 1950:

On Saturday, one of my friends suggested we make a good dinner. Of course, it's not the sort of thing you would make and mostly came ready in cans. We had bouillon with egg, fresh mixed salad, liverwurst with potato salad, fresh red raspberries with sour cream, California fruitcake, iced tea. Then we moved to the "drawing room" and played a game of chess after which we had Gorgonzola cheese and coffee (Nescafé). Anyway, for a first effort, it was not too bad. I repeat my offer to send you spices or other supplies you might need for French cuisine, if they are not available in England.

To Harriet Cook, 19 August 1952:

I was fortunate in finding a nice small furnished apartment with a small kitchen. I can have friends in very easily, but they don't get orange-pineapple upside-down cake or ice cream [as I did at your home]. Tonight one of the fellows from the office came home with me, and we fried some steaks and had canned corn, fresh tomatoes and pickles, and some fresh pastries. It was a pleasant change from eating in restaurants and hotels.

To Samuel De Merit, 14 November 1953:

Even to serve a martini [in Holland] is something very dangerous. Nevertheless, I have invited two women from Hope—one was my history prof when I was here—for cocktails this evening. Both have been very nice to me, taken me out to dinner, etc.; of course, they, like the destroyers that Roosevelt traded off to the British, are overage.

To Frank Buster, 29 March 1954:

Have been wondering if you ever received that beer mug I sent around Christmas and if it arrived in good shape.

To Willard De Pree, 30 July 1954:

You are heartily invited to drop in for a T-bone steak whenever you come to Holland. They are incredibly cheap—less than thirty cents per pound.

On Monday, 2 May 1956, Paul and some of Hope's IRC members had lunch with Gerald Ford, who autographed that day's "Menu from the House of Representatives Restaurant, US Capitol." The special ninety-cent luncheon included a pan-broiled single pork chop, apple fritter, hominy grits, buttered turnips, choice of pie or layer cake, tea or coffee. The recipe on the back of the menu is for Michigan bean soup, a featured item at the restaurant since long before 1904.

To Easy Gearhart, 1 September 1956:

I purchased an espresso coffee maker (six cups) for you before I left Vienna. I also bought one for myself, and in Wiesbaden, I bought a Russian samovar. There are lots of things here which are most enjoyable which I will not have in Holland. I think if we can work out a good summer program which will take us to Europe for two or three months every year, Holland will be a pleasant place in which to rest for the winter.

To Lotus Snow, 21 July 1957:

On Friday, when the institute director gave a cocktail party for us, there were many sad comments that two of the six weeks in Vienna were already past. The group is quite homogeneous; although we all drink wine, no one has been drunk. Most of the kids go to church on Sunday; this morning, Mrs. Snow played the organ, and I donated flowers. The pastor, who came to dinner with us, also wanted me to read the scripture, but here I draw the line.

To Rev. Walter and Harriet de Velder, 21 March 1962:

You may have heard that all four of your children and George Su were over for a meal at my apartment a week ago Sunday. We were going to have a Chinese meal, but I found no one knew how to cook it, so I settled for something I knew I could easily fix— roast beef—with rice, however, just to provide the oriental flavor.

To Arthur Frederix, 3 March 1969:

On Thursday afternoon, I had a cocktail party at the hotel [in Washington, DC] for some twenty-five or thirty people. Congressman

Vander Jagt came and later took us out to his home in Virginia where his wife had prepared a marvelous dinner. Since they have four bedrooms, and it was past 1 a.m. before we finished, we stayed at their place.

To Dr. Robert J. Donia, 6 February 1970:

I just happened to like food more than sports or other ways of burning calories. To make matters worse, I finally have joined the silent majority which sits in front of TV sets every night. The late movies are great, but the commercials, permitting just enough time for a trip to the bar or refrigerator, are very dangerous indeed.

To David Havinga, 22 September 1970:

Your description of the return of the squad and platoon after a beer binge was delightful and, of course, brought back familiar memories.

To Bruce van Voorst, writer for *Newsweek* in Bonn, 24 May 1971:

I look forward to seeing you and getting a bit more firsthand information on SALT, international bankers, and other matters. Your offer to do something informally sounds great. As you may recall, Wa-el Karachy said something about giving a cocktail party or reception for the group at the Jordanian Embassy or at the American Club on Friday afternoon. What about doing something about 8:30 p.m. Thursday? The budget is small, but I am sure it would stretch enough to pay for a keg of beer and some *Bockwüstchen* [sausage]. Just go easy on the Coca Cola and soft-drink department. Remember how much of that stuff was left over in your swimming pool in Düsseldorf!

To George Lee, 10 July 1971:

Most students have taken to drinking wine like ducks to water.

To Arthur Frederix, 4 June 1972:

Paul talked about preparing a dinner for five people with his best silver out: crabmeat cocktails, Gumpoldskirchner 1969 wine, freshly baked bread, stuffed rock Cornish hens (with rice, mushrooms, onion, capers, bacon—his house specialty), three pounds of fresh asparagus tips, a twenty-five-pound watermelon filled with fresh fruit, and brandy.

To Arthur Frederix, 26/27 January 1974:

Paul sent him the menu for a dinner party to celebrate Mozart's 218th birthday: prime rib, hot potato salad, green beans with mushrooms and onions, mixed and jello salads, rolls, four cheeses, fruit, California rosé wine.

To Rick and Hope Brandsma, 6 January 1975:

Thanks for the invitation to have some brandy in your ski cabin. I certainly would be inclined to accept that more readily than deciding to try skiing again—though if Jerry Ford can do it. Well, let's not get into politics. Actually, I would rather try out your new swimming pool, if it is heated, and if I can have brandy after I get out.

To Ingrid Heyden-Walter, 26 October 1976:

We just had October break and, since I figured that quite a few of the students would still be around Wednesday evening, I issued a sort of general invitation. The result: twenty-three guests. A few came early and left early, but most stayed and seemed to have a good time talking, drinking beer, etc. I had about sixty bottles but had to ask Reinhold to go up to Town and Country to pick up more, just to make sure we would not run dry.

To Larry Wells, 9 January 1978:

When I was staying in Fort Worth, I offered to prepare a Viennese dinner on the last evening: *Frittaten Suppe, Wienerschnitzel mit Kartoffelsalat, Grüne Bohnen, und Schwarzwälderkirschtorte* [shredded crêpe soup, pork schnitzel, potato salad, green beans, and Black Forest cherry cake]. All seemed happy and stuffed.

To Arthur Frederix, 22 January 1978:

I just checked the *Kalbsbrust* [breast of veal]; it is almost done, and I am getting hungry. Am using the *Römertof* [glazed clay cooker], so it always takes longer, but the meat is much moister.

Paul also mentioned how Peter Scheer had taught him the best way to bake *Schwarzwälderkirschtorte*.

To Peggy Lubbers, 11 October 1978:

The [international] food fair was a big success. The IRC sold coupons, and you had your choice of meat dishes (like sweet-and-sour pork and a Cuban version of Dutch pigs in a blanket), breads, vegetables, and desserts.

To Arthur Frederix, 4 May 1980:

I just baked three sheets of chocolate cake which I will soon have to put together to make a large *Schwarzwälderkirschtorte* to take to an orientation and dinner meeting for the Vienna-bound students which will be held at Stephen Hemenway's house.

To Duc and Kerrin Browning, 21 June 1982:

Holland will have the honor of a visit by the Queen of the Netherlands at the end of this week. Since I am a member of the committee, I expect I will have a chance to hear her address the distinguished crowd invited to attend the ceremonies in the chapel on Saturday. I doubt if I will have the chance to light her cigarette or have some sherry with her, as I did when I visited her mother some eleven years ago.

To Nicolaas Bootsma, 10 July 1983:

My most recent acquisition has been an outdoor grill which a friend who is visiting from New York helped me initiate last night. The chicken took a lot longer on the rotisserie than we expected, so we did not eat until about 10:30, and the chicken was underdone in Japanese style.

To Bob Bernen, 20 September 1984:

Another chunk of my time goes to entertaining guests. The past three weeks, we have had a group of Japanese students from Meiji Gakuin University on campus. Since this is the 20th year of our exchange program, the university president spent a few days on campus; this meant two dinner parties and drinks at my place since the campus is dry.

On 20 July 1985, Paul and I participated in a "Program for an Imperial Private Meeting with His Imperial Royal Highness Johann S. v. Habsburg/Lothringen (the great-grandson of Emperor Franz Joseph and Empress Elisabeth), Archduke of Austria, Royal Prince of both Sicily, Bohemia, Moravia, and Hungary in the Kaiservilla" in Bad Ischl, Austria. After coffee in the Hofkonditorei Zauner, his highness guided the twelve guests on a tour through the villa before we sat down at a local hotel for a nine-course feast with Austrian wines and music that duplicated the dinner hosted by Kaiser Franz Joseph I for the English King Edward VII on 12 August 1908.

To John Dryfhout, 2 April 1986:

Last night was the final meeting of my Spanish class. We celebrated with a Mexican dinner, but I could not eat most of the stuff brought. I concentrated on the deviled eggs and the *Schwarzwälderkirschtorte* that I had made. Last week I gave a cocktail party for twenty-six people on the occasion of the visit of the education director of the Adenauer Foundation who was here with his wife. The foundation is helping pay for thirty of our Vienna-bound students on a five-day Berlin program.

To Bonno Van Dijk, 3 May 1987:

Tried the Singapore Sling at the Raffles Hotel where, supposedly, it was invented. It did not seem as interesting as the version that I first encountered at the Antlers Hotel in Colorado Springs when I was stationed there in 1942. But I guess memories change in forty-five years.

To Chet and Louise Schultz, 14 June 1993:

I received a telegram-style marzipan cake from friends in Heidelberg that was so large that I still have a small section of it in the freezer.

Paul saved many menus from dinner parties that he hosted. One menu was for a dinner for seventeen people on 18 December 1986 in honor of Jan Evert: deviled eggs with caviar, marinated ocean herring, marinated artichokes, German rye bread, Colby cheese, turkey pastrami, smoked breast of turkey, roast beef, pasta salad, watermelon fruit boat, chicken nuggets and chips, turkey spread, croissants, chocolate cake, champagne/wine punch, German Mosel wine, apple juice, coffee, after-dinner drinks. Another menu, for a birthday party honoring Peter Scheer, listed prices for all purchases, including cabbage for ten cents, avocado for sixty cents, cake mix for eighty cents, and Cutty Sark for $17.50.

CHAPTER 20

World Travels

Paul Fried was an adventurous traveler who genuinely appreciated a variety of cultures, customs, and peoples. He loved to drive anywhere across the United States and Mexico. He journeyed throughout Western Europe during his post-war positions in Germany. He lingered in Europe after many Vienna Summer School sessions to visit old stomping grounds. His sabbaticals always featured new geographic experiences. His early retirement years got him to even more distant places of interest. Although he often ventured forth alone, he preferred journeys with companions. He was at home anywhere in the world because he enjoyed visiting friends and former students globally. He lived "beyond borders." Here are only a few travel observations from thousands found in his letters.

United States—Colorado

To Margaret Mills, 25 August 1945:

Did I tell you my ideas on settling somewhere in the Colorado mountains? Traveling through most of Western Europe, I noted that nearly all the towns have been subjected to heavy bombing and are destroyed. The only houses usually left untouched are ones standing alone somewhere in the woods! Not that I distrust the UN charter, but it would be just as well to be on the safe side. Colorado would be ideal, don't you think?

To Alan and June Metcalf, 2 July 1946:

Paul described his "on the road" experience hitchhiking and advertising for rides to Iowa, Fargo, the Badlands, Denver, and Colorado Springs.

To the Metcalfs and Kramers, 22 July 1946:

I found a job here at the Cliff House. The pay is not good, but I have room and board in one of the best hotels of Colorado and work as a waiter only at mealtimes. The rest of the time I can go swimming, horseback-riding, or I just lie on the roof and get a tan. In other words, I am enjoying my vacation without spending any money.

To Hilda Cook, 1 October 1946:

I put an ad in the paper and made contact with a young man driving to Denver. For the trip across the Dakotas and Wyoming, over one thousand miles, I paid him ten dollars. When I arrived in Colorado Springs, I rested a few days and then went looking for a suitable job. I became a waiter in a very expensive hotel with room and board and about $125 per month. I had enough time to spend an hour in the morning reading, playing tennis, or just sun-bathing, and three hours in the afternoon to go up into the mountains on horseback or down to the lake to swim. Toward the end of summer, one of my army friends in California renewed his previous invitation to visit him, so I gave up my job and took the trip to the Pacific. It was my first trip out there, and I was greatly impressed by the Salt Lake, the vast expanse of prairies in Utah and Nevada, the beauties of California, and especially our visits to Chinatown in San Francisco.

To Edgars Fogels, 1 April 1954:

As for Colorado Springs, I think it is one of the places in the United States which I would readily choose for a home. It has the atmosphere of Wiesbaden or Baden-Baden before the occupation. Mountains within reach and music, art, education, and interest in world affairs far beyond any city of similar size (40,000). I keep hoping for a job at Colorado College.

To David and Betty Dethmers, 22 January 1995:

The fact that I did my infantry basic training at Camp Carson in

Colorado in 1942-43, I fell in love with the area and have gone back a number of times during the past five decades.

United States—California

To Jane Bender, 7 January 1954:

Paul told her that only two places met his standards for permanent residences: (1) Colorado Springs; (2) San Francisco, Berkeley, Palo Alto.

To Frank Buster, 4 February 1953:

I want to go out to California and perhaps settle there if I find the right job.

To Edith Lambotte, 26 August 1953:

In California, I am constantly reminded of the climate in Italy. Los Angeles is like London; it stretches for miles and miles and miles; it is really almost too hot. I like San Francisco better—more moderate climate and a more European atmosphere.

To Lothar Freystatzky, 26 August 1953:

Sunday I was in Hollywood. I like the pictures of it better than the real thing. The ocean is very nice. I just about swam across the United States. I stopped in Rhode Island along the ocean for a swim. Later I bathed in lakes in Connecticut, New York State, Lake Erie, Lake Michigan, a small lake near Omaha, a mountain stream in Wyoming, a swimming pool in the middle of the Nevada desert, and now in the Pacific.

To Reinhard Grond, 20 October 1953:

I went to Hollywood, too, and the symphony under the stars—seats twenty thousand, seats for fifty cents—reminded me of the Roman Bread and Circus Days, but Beethoven's 9th was good all the same.

To Larry Wells, 12 October 1956:

I fully approve of your selection of San Francisco as a headquarters. It is one of my favorite spots, and I would go to Berkeley at the drop of a hat; I wish someone would drop it.

To Larry Wells, 10 April 1959:

We flew to Los Angeles where Herb and Margaret [Mills] met us at the airport. Margaret went all out to show us a good time. We "did" Disneyland on Sunday; she even skipped church to take us there! Monday we drove to Palm Springs and date country.

United States—other western states

To Max Putzel, 2 November 1953:

When I passed through Chicago on August 1, it was ninety-seven degrees in the shade, so I drove as fast as I could to the snowy mountain range in Wyoming. That was really wonderful—to go up to ten thousand feet and see snow on the road. On the way, when I got to the outskirts of Omaha, Nebraska, I picked up a young hitchhiker who was going to Boys Town, so I got a free tour of the place unexpectedly.

To Rolf Italiaander, 25 September 1953:

I passed on into Utah, the state of Mormon settlements, and reached Salt Lake City with its famous Temple Square in the evening. I got there just in time for a very fine guided tour and an organ concert in the tabernacle. I decided to go for a swim in the Great Salt Lake, even though it was almost 10:00 p.m. The water was wonderfully warm, and you cannot sink. The next day came a long and dull drive across the Nevada desert. For miles and miles—about six hundred in all—you see nothing much more than sands and hills. One place, in the middle of nothing, there was a large sign: "Monotonous, ain't it?" I don't know who put it there, but it relieved the monotony for a few minutes.

United States—Midwest

To Arthur Frederix, 24 April 1975:

[Let me] give you an account of our little trip, "Travels with Henry" [Birnbaum]. We went from Holland to Ludington and from there eighty miles by ship and car ferry over Lake Michigan to Wisconsin. When we got to Green Bay, the hotel reservation was mixed up, but the next day we found a lovely motel on the shores at "Sister Bay" in Door County, an area settled by Germans and Scandinavians. One of the specialties is a fish boil, usually held outdoors with freshly caught local fish, potatoes, and onions, all cooked in one large iron pot over a big wooden fire. We enjoyed two fish boils very much. We also took a ferry to Washington Island where the annual summer fair was held that day. Quite unexpectedly, I met a girl (?) whom I had not seen for thirty-three years when we were both students at Hope (1940-42), when I had occasionally dated her. Of course, she is no longer a girl, but we had a pleasant visit. From Door County, we headed north to Upper Michigan, so Friday was a long day of driving for me. We stopped for lunch at some small crossroad which had an Algonquin Hotel (!) and then went on to Calumet and Copper Harbor—most restful and

Skiing in Stowe, Vermont, 1950

quiet. We had dinner there in an excellent German restaurant. The drive along Lake Superior the next morning was very lovely—the scenery a bit like that on Highway 1 between San Francisco and Los Angeles.

United States—Northeast

To Kay Stout, 19 February 1950:

I must tell you a little bit about the ski trip to Stowe. The most striking thing was the cost. For four nights with twelve meals, the hotel bill was fifty-nine dollars. Add to that ski rental, chairlift, bus fare, one lesson, and the total was ninety dollars. I had to think of Garmisch and Switzerland in comparison. If we go into the tourist business, we may well find the truth of the old cowboy expression (or was it an Alaskan gold miner?): "Thar's gold in them thar hills!"

To Jane Bender, 15 July 1950:

In my new convertible, I drove through the Berkshires, New York State, Erie, Cleveland, and then through southern Ohio and Pennsylvania back through the Peekskill mountains to Boston—the first long trip I have taken in my own car in the States.

To the Metcalfs and Kramers, 7 July 1950:

Just outside of Harrisburg, in the rain, I picked up a young hitchhiker who turned out to be a Columbia University law student who had hitchhiked all the way to Mexico and back. We had a very interesting conversation, starting with the people he had talked to, politics, philosophy, religion, faith, and the need for regeneration. The boy was Jewish but seemed quite willing—at least intellectually—to agree with my point of view.

To Kay Stout, 10 July 1950:

I stayed around Boston and then went for a trip to Cleveland with a friend from Vienna whom I had not seen for twelve years and a visit to Aliquippa, Pennsylvania. This was my first trip through the United States in my own car, and I enjoyed it very much. The Berkshire Mountains, the rolling green hills of Pennsylvania, and the very nice country around Bear Mountain, New York, impressed me particularly. Dusty [Paul's car] behaved very well on this seventeen-hundred-mile trip.

To Rolf Italiaander, 25 September 1953:

I arrived in New York on July 11th and found that my car was already there, so all I had to do was to wait endless hours from 7 a.m. until 4 p.m. to drive off into the Land of the Free. It was very hot, so the only thing to do was to get into the air-conditioned Radio City Music Hall. This was my first re-introduction to American "culture," and I was not impressed. The stage show, as in the Apollo in Düsseldorf, was much too *schmalzig*. Broadway, once the center of theater, now looks more like the *Grosse Freiheit* [red-light district in Hamburg] plus the *Oktoberwiese* [annual fair featuring beer] in Munich. There are dozens of stores selling souvenirs, cheap movie houses, and many colorful nightclubs. The place is as crowded at 2:00 a.m. as at noon.

I made a couple of short trips to visit friends. One thing that you would find strange in traveling through the United States is that you pass through no end of cities bearing familiar European names. On my trip I drove through Rome, Milan, Berlin, Frankfurt, Venice, Athens, Prague, Warsaw, Syracuse, Lima, Cambridge, Oxford, Heidelberg, Weimar, and many more of the same type. All of these were of course settled by people from Europe.

In 1977, on a few yellow legal-pad pages, Paul penned notes on "New York—Impressions of an Ever-Changing City, 1939-1977." Paul had just crossed the Atlantic for the 52nd time, and most of the trips included a few days in New York before or after Europe. Over the years, Paul had been impressed with the artistic life, cosmopolitan climate, banking, shopping, and history of New York City; he had not liked the sense of alienation and loneliness or the safety situation.

To Stephen Wilcox, ceramics sculptor, 22 August 1977:

[I enjoyed] a wonderful Sunday of sailing on the Atlantic with Jean and John Bloemendahl in their thirty-seven-foot sailboat which is docked at Kennebunkport, Maine. They've been getting it into shape for a long cruise and plan to spend a year on it.

To Spencer and Marjorie Gouwens Hudgins, 7 January 1987:

Paul mentioned spending the Christmas holidays in DC where he met Paul Wackerbath, attending the National War College, and his wife, Cindy Hill; Tom O'Connell, public affairs officer at the US Embassy in Vienna; Barbara Walvoord, teaching at the University of Maryland; Ingeborg Bauer-Knight, with her husband teaching at Johns Hopkins; Robert Werge, working with the Peace Corps office of planning and policy; and Bruce van Voorst, *Time* magazine's Pentagon reporter. Paul joked: "The place was quite exciting if not exotic, and I hardly noticed that the Reagans were not in town. I would not have had time to stop and see them anyway."

United States—South

To Klaus Liepelt, a German exchange student, 21 July 1954:

I expect to leave [Mexico City] on August 28th and drive by way of Laredo, San Antonio, New Orleans, Memphis, Nashville, Louisville, Indianapolis, back to Holland. My two friends will go along since they want to pick up a car in Detroit and then drive out to Berkeley. If you do not have too much luggage, there would be room for you. Both fellows [Recknagel and De La Camp] are also bilingual.

To Arthur Frederix, 8 September 1955:

The trip back through Mexico with Tom [Wright] was very nice. But, as soon as we had crossed the border in Laredo and stopped at a restaurant where I had eaten on the way down, the manager came over and said, "I am sorry, but we don't serve colored folks." This came as a complete shock to me since I had not traveled through the South with a colored person before. Well, we went without lunch, but I still did not fully understand the situation. We stopped at another place, some miles beyond, and I went in first to ask if they served colored people. "Oh, yes," said the girl, "we have a table in the kitchen where they can eat." Well, that is the way the whole trip went as far as New Orleans. We ate two hamburgers (even there the stands mostly have two windows, one for white, and one for colored). In Corpus Christi, I stayed in one hotel, Tom in another. In New Orleans, I decided to stay in a colored hotel with Tom but felt like a freak since people stared at me and the girl [at the desk] wanted to know if I was white. Tom said, "Only partly." Otherwise, I would not have had a room there either. After that, I suggested that Tom take a plane back since I did not see that we should spoil our vacation and end up with a bitter taste in our mouths after the very nice period in Mexico.

To Hilda Cook, 23 February 1970:

A girl who was in the Vienna program some ten years ago is now living in Key West, where she and her husband own a small hotel. I plan to spend at least a week there.

To Arthur Frederix, 12 March 1970:

By evening, we were in the very charming city of St. Augustine, the oldest city in the United States. It rained, but we had paella in a very good Spanish restaurant and walked around the old city, sort of an American equivalent of Rothenburg. The next morning we stopped to inspect what claimed to be the world's largest alligator and crocodile farm with about two thousand, some more than two hundred years old. From the old to the new, we next stopped at Cape Kennedy to tour the US Space Center. This was fascinating, perhaps more so since I had talked with [astronaut] Frank Borman a week or two earlier.

Mexico

Paul, a visiting professor of history at Mexico City College in the summers of 1954 and 1955, fell in love with the city and its culture. He told John Hollenbach (in notes from his oral history interviews) that his two summers at Mexico City College were a most important start for the philosophy and pattern of the Hope College Vienna Summer School.

To Tom Bennett, 18 June 1955:

I had a wonderful year teaching, with very attentive, attractive classes, so I did not mind that the college took up all my time. The climate here in Mexico City is wonderful. The air is very clear. The city is seven thousand feet up; the college is another three hundred feet above the city and really like a country club. I am not going to give up my first love for Europe and hope I can go there next summer, if I can work out some scheme to make money doing it.

To Rev. Paul Gerhard Diez, 24 June 1955:

I could not withstand the attraction of Mexico City, truly a magnificent place. I found a wonderful furnished apartment with a glorious view just a couple of minutes from the heart of the city. The cost is seventy-two dollars per month, of which I pay half, since I am sharing the place with a fellow from Hope. Steaks are still the greatest bargain, at little more than fifty cents a kilo.

To Peter and Beverly Fuhrmann, 10 July 1955:

You really will have to see Mexico City. It is a beautiful place, located nearly 2,500 meters above sea level, right in the mountains. The climate is wonderful, always cool at night and nice during the day. It is almost like living in the Alps, yet the life of the big city is almost as interesting as that of Paris. There are wide avenues, beautiful shops, lovely modern homes (many with swimming pools and tennis courts), many theaters, and a lot of cultural life. I enjoy nice trips outside the city, where there are many interesting things to see, including pyramids dating back to the period before the Spanish invasion.

To Lotus Snow, 19 July 1955:

I spent that day, most tourist-like, attending a "real" Fourth of July celebration of the American community. It was the sort of thing one reads about but which I have never seen in the United States: bands, booths, speeches, raffle, ice cream, dancing, baseball, tamales, hot dogs, pop, hamburgers, and the American Legion. Spanish by osmosis is not progressing as well as it should because I have thus far not made any Mexican friends who want to speak Spanish.

To Dr. Richard Bennett, 8 August 1955:

I kept in mind your request for additional serapes, and when I went to the thieves market yesterday, I bought two, which I hope will meet with your mother's approval.

To Alice Blum and Ralph Mavrogordato, 12 August 1955:

Mexico City is a mixture of Paris and Vienna with a bit of Tunis thrown in. The architecture is startling and more modern than anything I have seen in the States.

To Kay Stout, 13 August 1955:

Mexico is just as enchanting this year. This may sound like treason to you, but I think I like Mexico City better than Paris.

To John and Mary Elmendorf, 12 December 1958:

Here [in Holland] we have several feet of snow. This, plus the fact that I need a vacation, have not been in Mexico in winter, and hope to bask in the sun at Acapulco, has made me decide to get a plane reservation and to plan for two weeks in Mexico during Christmas vacation. I am also looking forward to seeing you and Mary again.

To Larry A. Siedentop, 10 January 1959:

Mexico was out of this world. I think that, unless I am asked to

Fisherman Fried with a one-hundred-pound sailfish caught near Acapulco

read a paper at the AHA [American Historical Association] meeting some year, my Christmas vacations will probably be spent in Acapulco hereafter.

To Harriet Cook, 22 December 1960:

I went sailing one afternoon [near Acapulco], then fishing the next day. Caught two huge sailfish; one over eight feet weighed about one hundred pounds. I plan to go to the new Christmas oratorio by Pablo Casals and a midnight service after that on Saturday.

To Otto Zeno Steffens, 20 July 1964:

I like Acapulco very much; I have been there about six times. For several years, I stayed at the Hotel del Pacific, directly on the Caleta Beach, where many Mexicans and Europeans of the Mexican community stay. The cost of a room with shower and three meals was about $6.50 per day.

To Rev. Paul Gerhard Diez, 21 January 1974: .

I finally managed to make that trip to Yucatan which I had wanted to make for nearly twenty years now. I really like Merida and was thoroughly impressed by the Mayan sites I visited. I will have to go back again.

To Dr. Everett Nienhouse, 24 November 1975:

In Mexico City, Restaurant Jena is very good, French, not quite as pretentious as the Normandie. One of my favorite spots for dinner on a rooftop is the Hotel Majestic, facing the Zocalo and the cathedral. The hotel is not very expensive, neither is the food, and the view is great. I had paella there for the first time years ago. For the romantic evening with strolling violins, check out the Villa Fontana on the Reforma.

To Abdul Al-Mawlawi, 29 January 1986:

I enjoyed my stay in Mexico enough to feel that it would be good for me to speak the language. So, last week I started in a community education class in introductory Spanish. It will run for ten weeks, and then I hope to go to Mexico again for a couple of weeks in early June for a course in Spanish language and history at Oaxaca.

To Rev. David Cassie, 10 March 1986:

Since I came back from Mexico, I have become a student again. I decided that I should really try to learn the language if I want to go back south of the border. I am taking elementary Spanish through Holland's community education program. The teacher is a Hope graduate whom I helped go to Colombia during her junior year. She is very good, but I am not sure that I am that good a student. Just to give the thing added incentive, I have signed up for another course which will start in June at Oaxaca under the Elderhostel program. There are advantages to being a senior citizen.

Europe

To Hilda Kloucek, 21 August 1947:

Last week, I made a short trip to Prague. I saw Mr. Bradley, one of the first people to teach me English. Later I saw the boy who used to room with me there. In Prague, you can really buy everything you don't see in Germany today.

To Alvin Coox, 19 November 1947:

Last weekend I drove to Berchtesgaden to call on Adolf and Eva, but someone had made rather a mess of their house, so they were not home. There was not even a fire in the big living room, but the snow on the ground made the trip to the mountains very worthwhile. Hope to go back there for some winter sports later. I also drove to Prague some weeks ago and may take the car to Geneva over the Thanksgiving weekend.

To Helen Hathaway, 7 January 1948:

The weather down there in Nice was wonderful—palm trees and sunshine and rooms right on the shore of the Mediterranean.

To Richard Yee, 7 January 1948:

Switzerland is a wonderful country, full of all the good things modern production can provide, lots of food, and best of all, friendly people. While we were in Geneva, we decided to go skiing on a nearby mountain. As we were eating lunch, two Chinese boys came in. They knew even less French than the three of us, so we helped them order lunch. They were members of the Chinese Air Force and are stationed in London. One had a movie camera, and he got so many pictures of me sitting down in the snow in embarrassing positions!

To Margaret Mills, 12 June 1948:

At Linz, Austria, we had to stop to get our grey passes, which permit the holder to go through Russian-occupied areas.

To Hilda Cook, 16 June 1948:

Leslie [Hilda's husband] will be more than welcome to drive the car, as I am frankly afraid of left-handed London traffic. After my return from England, I spent two weeks in Nürnberg trying to catch up with my work. Then I went to Italy for ten days; after I got back, I was away every weekend for six weeks. I made two trips to the Salzburg Festival and in between went to Lucerne, Strasbourg, and Luxembourg City. I had intended to go to Scandinavia for two weeks after that, but when I came back from Luxembourg, my boss suggested that I had better do some work for a change.

To Hilda Cook, 9 January 1949:

I spent a very pleasant Christmas vacation in Engelberg, Geneva, and Paris. Engleberg was very, very English. All the gentleman had dinner suits, and the ladies wore evening gowns—in a skiing resort! I had gone with a friend, Bob Ruggles, and a girl from my office whose home is in London. She had asked her sister to come to Switzerland to join us, so we all met in Basel. The hotel and the weather were not what we had hoped for, so the day after Christmas, Bob and I deserted our ladies and went to Geneva and from there to Paris. Needless to say, Paris was nice. I had not been in Paris since 1945. Paris is full of life.

To Fritz Neumann, 9 February 1949:

Since writing last, I have seen a number of our old friends. Easter 1948, I was in Vienna for the first time since April 1938 when I was so rudely thrown out. I, like so many others, had to sign a statement that I would never return. I thought that called for a celebration on the 10th anniversary, so I had dinner at the Hotel Bristol with Artur Gottlieb and his wife. I met Walter Fürst again. Later in the summer, in Salzburg, I met Leo Lazarowitz (now Peter Jost), an actor who was playing in Schiller's *Maria Stuart* at the time. Since then I also saw him in Innsbruck, where he is now playing Othello. He is quite a good actor and seems to like his profession. He doesn't look a year older than he did as a boy of eighteen when I last saw him.

To Huntington Terrell, 11 June 1949:

A couple of weeks ago I went to Bayreuth on a Sunday afternoon to hear a Wagner concert. I took the car—Dusty II, a 1948 Olds—down to the Chiemsee on the way to Salzburg to sail. Got a real sunburn, but it certainly was fun and a change. On the way back, the driver and I decided to get off the Autobahn a little before Munich and were richly rewarded for taking the country road. We came upon a real Bavarian folk festival, a flag-blessing ceremony. At this little inn, there were perhaps two hundred local people. The men wore black leather shorts and cocky hats and the women their colorful dresses. There were two brass bands, much folk dancing, barrels of beer, and more sausages than you could imagine. Even for an old tourist like me, it was quite an experience.

To Kay Stout, 16 May 1951:

I have taken advantage of some of those privileges which come to the upper or conquering classes and have been in Garmisch to ski a couple of weeks ago.

To John Anderson, 18 April 1951:

Perhaps if you were to visit Hof an der Saale, it might become a more lively place. As it is, there are some dozen beer breweries and about as many textile factories and nothing else. I am sort of blasé about travel in Europe, but only if I have to do it alone. I find nothing stimulates me as much as being able to show others about. I guess I then vicariously enjoy the same thrill you would have seeing something for the first time.

A September 1951 letter from Edith Lambotte told Paul that she recognized Congo "friends" among the trees and plants on Venice's Lido. She lamented that St. Mark's in Venice was a den of thieves that irritated her Protestant spirit too much. Paul left her for several days but came back on foot across the German border to meet her in Salzburg.

To Walter Recknagel, 17 December 1951:

Our first destination was Taormina in Sicily. I had never heard of the place, but the sky was as blue as I have ever seen it and so was the sea. Everywhere there was a profusion of flowers and blossoms, palms, oranges, grapefruit, tangerines, and poinsettias. We stayed at the Hotel San Dominico, the most exclusive, of course. King Farouk stayed there last year. The hotel had been a Dominican convent and is about five hundred years old. In Capri, we transferred to a small motor boat which was to take us to the Blue Grotto. We were rather startled to find that the entrance into the grotto is so small that only a rowboat can get in and only if the people in it lie flat on the bottom! Capri is very lovely and charming but terribly commercialized with junk stands at every corner. It is really amazing to see to what extent Pompeii has been preserved and reconstructed. Perhaps the most remarkable thing is what a high degree of civilization the people had achieved there. It is one thing to read about it in a book and something else to see what their cities looked like.

To Fred Bradley, 3 June 1952:

I found Copenhagen a very nice town, cosmopolitan without being overly big or busy. Most of the people there speak English—or think they do.

To Helen Hathaway, 15 January 1953:

I decided to get back to Austria and went to Kitzbühl, a lovely town in the Tyrolean Alps. There was not much sun but lots of snow, and I enjoyed the change. In Hamburg, I hope to devote some time to preliminary work on a biography of Dr. Hoffmann. I think he has lots of friends there, including the present Lord Mayor.

To Bill Riederer, 26 January 1953:

You wanted a report on the trip to Kitzbühl with _____, but I never did get around to skiing. I had to write so many letters. We stayed at the Grand Hotel, very nice, though a bit ritzy. I had expected that and brought a tux, and _____ had a very nice evening gown, strapless, that she wanted to exhibit, so we were quite content. Saw one exciting hockey game, went to a Christmas midnight Mass in the village church, and went to any number of what pass for night spots in Kitzbühl. She was as pleased as a small child since she had never been in the mountains and hardly ever gets away from her mother. One thing that made the trip pleasant for me was that she insisted on sharing most of the expenses. The day after Christmas we drove to Salzburg and that evening saw a very good performance of *Der Bettelstudent* in the *Festspielhaus* [festival hall]. The next day we climbed by foot to the Burg and later had dinner with a Harvard friend of mine who now works for the Austrian counterpart of our wing.

To Helen Hathaway, 4 May 1953:

Of all the places I have seen in Germany, I like Hamburg by far the best.

To Larry Wells, 5 January 1954:

Your plan about the *Hotelschule* sounded interesting. I am still interested in that field [a hotel and restaurant in Austria], if not as a major project, then certainly as something for the summer for extra income. I wondered about the possibility of buying a place in Lower Austria, not too far from Salzburg. Help is cheap, and we could have someone there during the winter and just run it as an exclusive (well, not too exclusive) summer place. If it works out, there is always a chance to branch out. A nice idea would be a *Landerziehungsheim* [rural boarding school] for Americans who want to spend their junior year in Europe. We would have to find out about taxation in Austria and ownership by foreigners. You might even inquire about real estate prices for a *Gasthof* [inn] in need of fixing up, with a lot of grounds. I like to dream, and I think it is quite possible to do something like this and make it pay. I might even try to get another job in Europe. It would be best to get that sort of thing started while still earning an income from another source. The more I think of this, the more the idea appeals to me.

To Rev. Paul Gerhard Diez, 9 September 1955:

I would like to spend next summer in Europe, if I can work out some sort of arrangement so it won't cost too much. I had just enough Spanish so that I think I would enjoy seeing Spain, too.

To John Anderson, 29 May 1958:

In Vienna, you can stay in a student home for forty cents a day (cold showers after 6 a.m.) or get a room with bath in a good hotel for seven dollars per day.

To Harriet Cook, 30 August 1960:

This letter, on stationery from the Imperial Hotel, Russell Square, London, had pictures of its Winter Garden, Minstrel Gallery, and Turkish Baths. Paul also sent Harriet notes on hotel stationery from all over the world: Roosevelt in New York, Sheraton-Cadillac in Detroit, Caleta in Acapulco, Lexington in Minneapolis, Meran in Salzburg, South Seas Plantation in Captiva Island (Florida), and the Cunard Line's RMS *Carmania*.

To Everett Nienhouse, 10 January 1963:

As for Klagenfurt, my recommendation would be to go a few miles farther to Veit and from there to Hochosterwitz, the largest and most beautiful of the Austrian castles. There are two or three rooms for rent; they have a good restaurant, and you can get something in the village below. I am planning to take the group there for a visit on July 4. You will find the waitresses dressed in medieval garb and the owner of the castle Khevenhüller somewhere about, supervising arrangements. It is an experience that you ought not to miss.

To Ev Nienhouse, 21 March 1965:

Please forgive me for not answering your good letter of February 9 before this. It came while I was still in Europe on my brief but unexpected twenty-one-day trip to France-Holland-Germany-Italy-Riviera-Paris-Yugoslavia-Vienna-Zurich-Paris-New York. Eighteen meals on planes and not much rest, but quite a few contacts for next year.

To Tom Bennett, 21 October 1967:

This past summer I had a most enjoyable encounter with two English fellows who were hitchhiking in Germany. Picked them up at Stuttgart just after I got my new Mercedes-Benz 250S (a beautiful car) and took them all the way to Salzburg. I received a most charming letter from one of them, an accountant in Lancaster, just a few days ago.

To Arthur Frederix, 15 May 1970:

The folder of your hotel in Nice reminds me of the time I stayed there during the Christmas vacation of 1947. It was then still an army rest center, and I think the cost was two dollars per day. It did lack the lustre and atmosphere of a "Grand Hotel," which I imagine it has now recovered.

To David Havinga, 4 September 1970:

At this "let's all praise Lenin" gathering [a Soviet Union congress that Paul called a farce despite 3,500 historians from 46 countries in attendance], he was represented as being considerably more infallible than the pope and more significant than the Virgin Mary. I decided not to waste my time sleeping through dull lectures, so I saw five ballets. Moscow is an impressive city with a great deal of construction going on and the pulse of a busy metropolis. The hotel in which we stayed is considerably larger than the Chicago Hilton and can house six thousand people. It is only a stone's throw from the Kremlin, where we had to go for the opening meeting.

There did not seem to be any overt attempt to control the foreigners, but I'm quite certain there were attempts to supervise us in one form or another. Perhaps the most disconcerting thing was the presence of a floor clerk or night watchman (who seemed to be a retired lady wrestler) on every floor in every hotel. We called them den mothers, the guardians of the keys and of public morality, making sure that no visitors of the opposite sex came into one's room after 10 p.m.

I was tremendously impressed with the beauty of Leningrad and its palaces. The Hermitage is something that defies comparison even with the great museums of Paris and Vienna. What is impressive is not only the accumulation of art and wealth but also the surging masses from all walks of life who walk through this and all other museums in incredible numbers every day.

To Kay Stout, 25 April 1971:

The Canary Islands were nice; the sun was warm, but the wind was cool, and there were far too many Krauts. By the way, have you heard the definition of a German hippie? A flower Kraut.

To Hilda Cook, 5 October 1971:

By far the most relaxing thing I have done in years was the five-day trip up the Danube on the Russian ship *Dnypr* from Rumania back to Vienna. The ship is brand new—built in Austria—and most comfortable with large cabins, a swimming pool on deck, lots of deck space, and a leisurely pace.

To Don Jansen, 18 December 1984:

It was very nice to get your beautiful card with the Austrian village in the snow. It reminded me very vividly of a Christmas some six or seven years ago when I spent Christmas Eve with a Hope graduate and his wife and her Austrian family in a little village at the foot of the Grossglockner. We went to midnight service through the snow, and afterwards we had a family concert at home plus the gifts for the children.

To Albert Lee, 29 August 1985:

I particularly recommend Yugoslavia as a good place to visit. I was there for ten days in July. Prices were most reasonable, hotels absolutely first class, food very good, and the weather cooperated. We stayed three days in Dubrovnik overlooking the Adriatic Sea—swimming in the indoor pool, salt water pool, or Adriatic (with elevator to the sea through the mountain). Then we went on to Sarajevo, Zagreb, and Bled—one of the most beautiful mountain lakes and resorts.

To Bob Bernen, 28 November 1987:

From October 1 to 4, I was very much involved hosting people who came for the opening of the Austrian art show which I had helped bring to Hope. Some 180 Vienna Summer School alumni and friends or spouses came to the special luncheon on October 3. On October 13th, I took off for England, Yugoslavia, Austria, Germany, Denmark, Norway, and Sweden.

To Samuel and Sophia Fumey, 29 November 1987:

My stay in Copenhagen was most enjoyable, mainly as a result of your being there. The trip to Oslo was very long and boring since it rained all the way, and there was almost nothing to see or to eat. By way of compensation, the Sheraton Hotel in Oslo turned out to be a really first-rate place with superb breakfasts as part of the special senior citizens' rate. Once I reached Oslo, the weather turned, so I could walk all about Oslo in sunshine for two days. In Sweden, I ended up staying in Uppsala. I spent part of the time in Stockholm but found Uppsala a very delightful older and smaller university town. Again, meetings with my friends from pre-war Vienna days were most enjoyable.

To Hilda Kloucek, 29 August 1990:

I spent six weeks in the Balkans, plus Czechoslovakia, Austria, and Germany. East Germany was the most exciting since that is where history was really happening every day while I was staying in Dresden with a German couple and their twenty-one-year-old twin daughters. The day we drove to Berlin was the first time that none of the border stations was manned. We drove in and out without any check, visa, or control. A few days later, we found the same thing true at Helmstedt, where I had spent many uncomfortable hours waiting in former years when I was bringing students to Berlin.

To Jan Evert, 28 August 1994:

The trip to Greece was great and helped convince me that there is no reason why I should stay home and live like an old man!

To Martha Kate Barnhart, 10 January 1995:

I was in Europe twice this past year. First, in June with a group led by one of the seminary professors "in the footsteps of Peter and John"— three weeks in Greece. Perhaps just a bit too much church-oriented for my taste. I also ventured a tour on my own and saw friends in Bonn, Nürnberg, Mainz, Frankfurt, and Würzburg.

Africa

To Walter Recknagel, 17 December 1951:

After Tunis, the first place we visited in Tunisia was Dougga, where there had been a Roman settlement in 300 A.D. which had been covered by sand until the early part of this century. The charming thing about this place and most of the other places we saw—in addition to their natural beauty and intrinsic interest—was that it was not commercialized in the least. There was not even a postcard to be had, no stands for souvenirs or anything else. To get to Dougga, we took a public bus to the middle of nowhere and then for the last 8 km the only available "taxi." Man, you never saw any contraption like it; it looked as if it had been excavated together with the city. I felt none too secure in the back with no windows and a few broken springs. But we got there, and it was worth the trouble. Art's [Frederix] nose quivered violently at the sight of the delicacies offered, and we ended up buying two boiled eggs and a flat piece of something that resembled bread from an Arab boy. At Gabes, there were some seventy-five thousand palm trees, mostly full of dates. One interesting spot we visited was an old Jewish village, partly underground, and still inhabited, which dates back to the time of the Babylonian captivity.

To Kay Stout, 10 February 1988:

One reason I want to go to Egypt is to see an old friend who is now the head of the Austrian Cultural Institute in Cairo. He taught in our program in Vienna years ago and later was in charge of the Austrian Institute in New York and then in Poland. I would like to continue from Cairo to Bangladesh, where I also have a good friend from Hope and Harvard days, who recently went out there as US ambassador and urges me to come and visit.

Asia

To Alvin Coox, 5 June 1961:

Having crossed the Atlantic some fourteen times, I am beginning to find the water and view monotonous and would like to see the other side, so there is a fair chance that if you are still in Japan sometime late in December or early in January, I will visit you.

To Bob and Inge Boelkins, 11 November 1961:

I will fly from Amsterdam, after I ship my car, back to Vienna, then to Istanbul, Beirut, Damascus, Jerusalem, Amman, Baghdad, Teheran,

Karachi, Lahore, Delhi, Calcutta, Rangoon, Bangkok, Hong Kong, Tokyo, Honolulu, and San Francisco. I will fly from there to New York to pick up the car again.

To Manzar and Naseem Bashir, 21 March 1962:

The news reports of Mrs. Kennedy's visit to India and the schedule for Pakistan are on the air. I can imagine you and your mother and family getting all involved in the festivities, and I wish I could be in her party! I shall be interested in your reaction to her. My awareness of the non-Western world has vastly increased thanks to the short trip through the Near East and Far East. Also, of course, I have decided that I have only had an appetizer and that I will have to come back for more and longer looks as the years pass. I hope you have a wonderful time with Mrs. Kennedy in the Shalimar Gardens.

To Rev. Walter and Harriet de Velder, 21 March 1962:

I must admit that the more I gain distance from my trip, Hong Kong stands out as the one place above all others I would like to visit again—soon.

To Ike Auerbach, 22 April 1962:

One reason you should come to Holland is to inspect my recently installed Chinese bar [now located in the student lounge in Hope's Martha Miller Center]. It is made of teak wood and painted jet black with colored stone inlay pictures; it is thirty-six inches high, thirty-two inches long, and sixteen inches deep. I was fascinated by it in Hong Kong and purchased it together with the two plaques which hang above it. When I came home, I wondered where I would put it, why I bought it, and where it would fit. It came Thursday, and I am delighted. I had to clean the apartment and rearrange the furniture, but I think it was well worth the effort.

From William Karachy, personal secretary to the prince, on stationery of the Council of Tribal Sheiks in Jordan, 30 August 1972:

H. R. H. Prince Muhammad Bin Talal, the head of the Council of Tribal Sheiks, has directed me to thank you for your willingness to assist us in launching a fund-raising campaign to help in the various projects that deal with the settlement of the nomadic tribes in Jordan.

To Hideo Yamazaki, 19 January 1984:

The two weeks I spent in Japan were great. I particularly enjoyed seeing Kyoto and Nara for the first time. Of course, the activities at Meiji

Gakuin—lectures, dinners, reunions, and the final symposium all went very well and were fun. I then went on to Hong Kong where I spent Thanksgiving in terrific weather—like June here. From there, I went to Korea, which I did not know before. I hope to get back to the Orient before long. One of my German friends was recently appointed ambassador to Thailand and has issued an invitation. I also have friends in Singapore.

To Kaoru Oghimi, whose grandfather was one of two Japanese graduates in the 1879 Hope class of six students, 20 December 1984:

It really was a great pleasure for me to meet you and your mother during my recent visit to Japan. I was delighted to bring back the material about your grandfather [Motoitero Oghimi] which you gave me for our archives. I look with enthusiasm upon the work which we are trying to do in tracing the history of the college and the distinguished alumni of Hope. Certainly, your grandfather belongs to that group. I have located two volumes of *The Excelsiora* (1874 and 1875) which contain numerous articles by your grandfather and his friend [Kumaje] Kimura. These are handwritten volumes published by the students of the upper two classes of the school. They contain an interesting mixture of news items, essays, poetry, and some fun items and "phony" advertisements like those inserted by Kimura, who was offering to sell various items to the "lowest bidder" before going back to Japan on vacation. Included among these were forty-nine used toothpicks.

To Dr. Anna von Spitzmüller, 21 January 1985:

In Seoul, I very thoroughly enjoyed walking all over the place and seeing many of the sites you recommended. On my first day, I attended a really excellent folk opera—quite a bit like the Viennese operetta— with great costumes and dances, good singing, and beautiful staging. As I was leaving, a very pleasant middle-aged couple spoke to me. He was a Presbyterian minister who had been in the United States and was eager to know if I needed any help. As he insisted, I suddenly thought: here is the man who can help me get the topaz earrings you wanted. I hope you received the small package and that I found the right thing. My guide also took me to see a couple of their modern churches, and we went to a Korean restaurant for lunch. Afterwards he went along to bargain for some interesting modern woodcuts.

To John Anderson, 23 January 1985:

Travel continues to be one of my passions. I spent all of November in the Orient—[several] days of lectures in Japan, the rest more or less educated tourism in Japan, Hong Kong, and Korea.

To Suphat Sotthitada, Thai graduate of Hope College, 15 April 1987:

The visit to Thailand and the two days when we could tour together, along with all the conversations, the welcome-to-Bangkok meal with your family, and the chance to meet your colleagues are the real highlights of my trip to the Far East. I might add that when I came back about four weeks ago, I was so disoriented in time that it took me more than a week to get back to some kind of regular schedule and to get over the feeling of being tired all the time.

To Edgars Fogels, 5 July 1987:

I think Bangkok was in many ways the most exciting stop on this trip. The hotel was the most luxurious I have ever stayed in, the weather was perfect, and three Thais—all of whom were at Hope many years ago—were eager to show me all of their country. I gave a lecture at the university and had dinner twice with an old friend who is the current West German ambassador to Thailand. This was my third time in Hong Kong and first time in a luxury hotel. I spent more time shopping (or looking at shops), along with seeing a couple of former students. From there, I went by boat to Shantou, China, to visit the new university where the grandson of one of my former colleagues is teaching English. I gave a lecture there and met twice with faculty interested in knowing more about student exchange with the United States.

To Bob Bernen, 15 September 1987:

In February and March, I joined an AARP group for a trip to Singapore, Thailand, and Hong Kong. I flew out to LA about five days early so I could see a number of friends and former students. In Singapore, I spent most of my time with five former students. My stop in Bangkok was particularly pleasant since a "young" woman who had been in my class the first year I taught at Hope (1953) and her two brothers, who also attended Hope, were eager to show me all of Thailand in four days. I also had the advantage of escaping this intensive tourism for two dinner parties at the German Embassy. The father is an old friend who now has a son at Hope.

To Willard De Pree, 22 November 1989:

Many thanks for your absolutely superb hospitality. Though I have travelled a great deal, this trip [to Bangladesh] is the only one which I will always remember as "a once in a lifetime" experience.

To Janet Riemersma Woods, 4 January 1990:

Particularly fascinating was the time I spent in Bangladesh as the guest of our current ambassador. Bill De Pree comes from Zeeland and

With (top, center)
Tom De Pree, (right)
Ambassador Willard
De Pree, (bottom,
l-r) Anthony Kooiker,
Zwani VanderBurgh,
Beppy De Pree

started at Hope, but we met at Harvard where he finished his BA while I was in graduate school.

To Wa-el Karachy, 27 January 1991:

My greetings also to your mother. I still remember with great thanks the hospitality of your parents, the beautiful gift, the trip to Bethlehem, and the drives with your father to different sections of Jordan. But what I recall most vividly is an evening when we all attended an eggnog party given by someone from the US Embassy and the way the king's brother showed his respect and affection for your mother.

To Rev. Garry Hesser, 1960 Vienna Summer School participant, 1 January 1996:

I would love to see more of China with the kind of personal guide and company you had. I would not mind missing the world's largest McDonald's and Pizza Hut.

To Elisabeth Grosse, 22 August 1996:

Many thanks for your interesting card from Australia. I am glad you liked Hong Kong, which I visited quite a few times and where I found quite a few of the oriental furnishings you may remember from my house. Thus far I have not been in Australia, and am not sure I am quite as interested in the trip since I no longer have friends there.

From Chris Knecht, 29 May 1997:

A native approached me [on the Great Wall of China], offering a sip from a bottle wrapped in a brown bag. I recall being a little apprehensive as to what I was to ingest, but in the interest of international understanding, thought it was only appropriate to ingest this "mystery liquid." I enjoyed the Chinese version of *Bärenjäger* [German honey-based liqueur]!!!

Paul's response to Chris Knecht, 29 May 1997:

I did like your story about the "mystery liquid." I did not get a bottle or other reward for making a tolerable effort to do a steep part of the Great Wall, except a few congratulations from some of our tour for making the effort at my age.

To Goran Satler, 23 July 1997:

Although I do not travel nearly as much as I did in past years, I did take a major trip to China with a group organized by the art museum in Muskegon. The program was very well-organized—very good hotels, one day of rain, lots of interesting people and places. Probably the most fascinating place we visited was the excavation site of the clay soldiers [from more than two thousand years ago]. Also the Forbidden City in Beijing and walking up to the Great Wall. Of course, we were a "first class" travel group bringing in foreign currency. Hotels, food, and organized tours were fully up to the best European patterns.

CHAPTER 21

Writing Endeavors

Thirty-five boxes of Paul Fried's letters (carbon copies of his own, plus actual letters sent by friends) in the Joint Archives of Holland testify to Paul's devotion to this form of communication. Pages of Paul's autobiographical recollections, especially about his life from 1919 to 1949, and jottings relevant to a potential novel dealing with World War II and Germany immediately thereafter (with a main character named Larry Hill) show a desire to use personal experiences as the basis of a fictional story about the war. In addition, Paul's many newspaper articles, journal pieces, speeches, and forays into Dutch history speak volumes about his willingness to educate others about every kind of "hope beyond borders."

Early remarks on the writing process (1945-65)

To Margaret Mills, 6 August 1945:

Truly, you succeed so beautifully in your letter writing, in putting down your thoughts on paper, that I feel I have come pretty close to a chat with you by the time I finish reading one of your letters. Many times, I thank God for giving me such a fine friend as you.

369

From Margaret Mills, 10 January 1947:

She told Paul that when he found the right girl, he should include in his marriage proposal "that you have Margaret on your hands who will forever expect a weekly letter from you alone with perhaps an occasional postscript from her as acceptable."

To Margaret Mills, 15 March 1947:

I have a book report to write for Professor Rudin over the weekend, but at the moment I would rather write to you.

To Huntington Terrell, 3 March 1948:

The trouble about writing postcards is that you can't keep carbons.

To Helen Hathaway, 27 May 1948:

I am doing something I don't like to see others do in my office— i.e., writing personal letters—so I better quit and get back to my job.

To Preston Stegenga, 3 November 1948:

My idea is a series of monographs dealing with the diplomacy of the Hitler period.

To Huntington Terrell, 11 June 1949:

Of course, the real reason why I came down here [to Garmisch] is to see if I can get started on writing that paper for Erlangen. I came in yesterday with a big suitcase full of papers and worked all day, too. Until five, that is, when the lure of the tennis court and the water became too much.

To Margaret Mills, 18 February 1950:

I must show that I am a qualified linguist and thus obscure the fact that I write bad English. Seriously, I need reminders. Ray Baker read my paper on "Law in Nazi Germany" in the second draft and called my attention to a number of unidiomatic terms taken over from the German text on which I was working; I accepted his counsel and rewrote most parts. I got the paper back today with an A on it.

To Kay Stout, 19 February 1950:

You mentioned the term "autobiography," and I confess that I have been doing that, perhaps more in the accepted manner, for some time—writing a few pages now and then when I am tired of reading. When it is completed, I may let you look at it. Up to now, it has made no attempts to leave the cool matter-of-fact narrative style, but sometimes such things take on a life of their own and develop independently of the intents of their author!

To Margaret Mills, 13 December 1950:

I take considerable pleasure from the knowledge that I could stop in many of the large centers of the United States and not feel a complete stranger because I can call up this or that friend with whom I have exchanged greetings [in letters] for years.

To Margaret Mills, 21 January 1951:

I now have assembled all the letters I have from you—with the answers as I have them—in a large binder, and I believe it is an impressive book. It starts in the summer of 1945 with two or three letters written to Heidelberg. Someday, I hope to complete the file from your copies. Bob [Bernen] is terribly impressed by your free and original style.

To Margaret Mills, 25 May 1952:

On my German typewriter, the z is where the y ought to be, so if zou find that sort of thing, zou will know what I mean.

To Margaret Mills, 8 July 1952:

I find I really don't like these air-letters since you are so limited in space, and I shall not use one again in writing to you.

To Walter Recknagel, 7 May 1953:

I realized that when I got back people would ask me, "What about Germany?" If I get a teaching job, I am sure I will be asked to speak at Rotary clubs and other gatherings. I thought I should prepare lectures on various topics of present-day Germany. From that it was about one jump to the idea of a small book, *Germany Today*, which would cover perhaps from twelve to fifteen topics, such as: universities and student life, economic recovery, the German military mind, building/architecture/reconstruction, refugees from the other side of the Iron Curtain, churches, income and cost of living, music and the arts, and the golden cage of the American occupation.

To Margaret Mills, 11 May 1953:

Paul explained that he was helping Professor [Kurt Heinrich] Hansen translate works by Tennessee Williams into German.

To Margaret Mills, 28 May 1953:

In regard to *Germany Today*, I would like to use as much as possible my own experiences (semi-autobiographical) and spin a slight story about it.

To Walter Recknagel, 5 June 1953:

I have been thinking of your remark that I should take up writing. I believe I have some talent, though I have no discipline. The suggestion has been made by others, and, of course, there is some heritage that way. I have given much thought to the question of a book on Germany since the end of WWII. The idea is to put the thing in novel form, based to a large degree on personal experience during this period. I want to have three sets of impressions of Germany: the enemy in 1945, the defeated and recovering nation from 1945 to 1948, and the new center of European politics in 1948.

The story is simple and essentially consists of what I have seen: A young American soldier at the Battle of the Bulge has learned that the only good German is a dead German. A buddy is killed. A few weeks later, on entering Germany, he sees a German officer die and ask, 'Why, why? We only wanted peace also.' Then he notes the early occupation, the arrests, the release of prisoner of war slave laborers, confusion. In between, he sees the beauty of the Rhine, Heidelberg, in 1945, but mostly destruction.

Then as the soldier goes home (by the way, he is of German descent and speaks some German), he decides to study the language and literature of the country and perhaps decides right then that he wants to come back—but not as a GI—so he can live among the people. In 1947-48, he comes back to study at some university. He now has a chance to see the pre-currency reform life and study literary trends, though he actually wants to study economics. He is there long enough to see the blockade of Berlin, the airlift, and the effects of currency reform in Germany.

During this period, he has a love affair, which may later bring him back (of this I am not sure; characters have a way of developing lives of their own, and you just have to see what they want to do). Through an army friend, now an officer in the occupation, he has opportunities to see the occupation life—the golden cage—and travel to Prague in February 1948 and perhaps to other places. Then, when his year is up, he returns, and because he has now qualified as an expert on Germany, he gets a job in a chemical or insurance firm, which will send him to Germany in 1953 to look after some patent rights or something of the sort. In the last section, he is mature and has enough contacts to talk to people who matter in various fields and perhaps form some general conclusions regarding the place of Germany in the present world. This is rough; I am eager to hear what you think of the whole thing.

To Margaret Mills, 8 June 1953:

My new plan for the book: I have decided to let the fellow become a newspaperman who has a real reason to come to Germany again and is perhaps writing a book about Germany. Summary: First, he is in Germany as a soldier, but ten years later he has recognized certain truths about Germany. I may call the character Larry, but I have not asked Larry Wells if it is okay.

To Larry Wells, 11 June 1953:

Together with Rolf Italiaander, I decided to try my hand at writing a novel about post-war Germany (1945-53), which will be mostly autobiographical material based on my own experiences. We decided to call the hero LARRY, if that does not offend you. He is quite a decent chap, even if he is not as good-looking as you are.

From Larry Wells, 22 June 1953:

Wells approved of Paul's plan for writing a novel but was curious to know what sort of character this Larry was or would be.

To Larry Wells, 12 August 1953:

For the time being, the book idea will rest, but I am not giving up the idea. You will be kept informed on Larry's progress.

In a tan folder, Paul included an undated outline of a project called "An American in Germany" with a protagonist named Larry Hill. Astute readers will recognize some of these topics treated in earlier chapters in this book.

Part one had four sections: (a) Battle of the Bulge, turkey dinner in Metz, snow in Luxembourg, violence and death in war, buddy wounded and evacuated; (b) crossing the Rhine, officer dying, people hiding, liberated prisoners of war, Belsen and Buchenwald; (c) end of World War II, death of FDR, rebuilding, long evenings on riverboat; (d) first examination of vanquished, Larry ordered to Heidelberg, preparation for war crimes trials, concerts under the stars, no fraternization, Larry's return to the United States to finish college, Larry's return to Germany after three years.

Part two also had four sections: (a) colony without hope (October 1947), economic conditions, refugees from Silesia and southern Germany, lack of food and energy, Weizsäcker and Krupp, theaters, butter and meat, Czech Putsch (February 1948); (b) currency reform and new hope, reconstruction, change in attitude, still no fraternization, girl in Marburg, trip to Salzburg and Vienna, Berlin blockade and airlift, coffee smuggling and black market; (c) road to recovery, art and literature, concerts, education, end to Nazification, Orwell, new democracy, Larry's return to the United States; (d) Larry's return to Germany three years later, industry in Hamburg and Bonn, new look of Germany, pessimism, "ideas cannot be killed."

To Frederick A. Praeger [Born in 1915 in Vienna, he became associate editor of his father's publishing company until Hitler confiscated it. He escaped to the United States in 1938, trained with Paul at Camp Ritchie, and worked in the intelligence branch after the war. He later published *One Day in the Life of Ivan Denisovich* by Alexander Solzhenitsyn.], 3 October 1953:

I have given a good deal of thought to your suggestion about a serious book on Germany. I may still carry out my plan of working on a novel with Rolf Italiaander, if he gets assurances that it can be published in Germany. In the process of gathering material for the novel, I plan to keep the other project in mind. I also hope to have one of my classes work on post-war Germany. Then, after I have most of the material assembled, I might spend a summer in Germany again to write the thing. But that is a long way off, and someone else may beat me to it.

To Larry Wells, 5 January 1954:

The novel had stopped completely until just a few days ago (New Year's resolution to write two or three pages every day). The thought came up in connection with my recent visit to Cleveland, where the daughter of very good friends [the Kramers] is in the hospital with polio. I told her that she could edit the sheets for me as they come off the machine; that way she will have mail every day, and I will have some incentive to write. If I get my first rough draft done by the time school ends, I may come to Europe for the summer to work it over with him.

To Margaret Mills, 24 January 1954:

I have been trying to write two or three pages every day on my memoirs. I just sent off pages thirty-seven to forty. Since that brings me up to the time I spent in Boppard and Heidelberg in 1945, and my file of your letters begins there, I just had a wonderful time rereading some of these in an effort to see if I was leaving out some things and to what extent my reactions were different from what they were then.

To Margaret Mills, 2 February 1954:

I have been sending installments of two, three, and four pages to Dorothy right out of the oven—without even reading over what I write—and letting her, or rather her mother, do the correcting. I have reached page forty-seven by this time. Of course, I may just throw the thing away when I get done, but I hope I can stick it out and complete it.

To Larry Wells, 28 March 1954:

I did not do anything to continue the story of the fictional Larry, but I hope to get back to him again during the spring vacation.

To H. Stuart Hughes, with the hope that he will write Paul a letter of recommendation for a Fulbright scholarship in Munich, 24 February 1954:

I think you will be pleased to hear that I have been asked to read the paper on Flick (prepared in your seminar) at the next meeting of the Michigan Academy of Arts and Sciences.

To Helen Hathaway, 3 June 1954:

I have sent the Flick paper to the *Political Science Review*, so now I will have to wait and see if they want it.

To Frederick Praeger, 29 October 1954:

I have given some serious thought to the possibility of working on translations, mostly as a way of getting published. You know enough about the academic world to realize that payment for the translation is not the major consideration.

To Frederick Praeger, 21 June 1955:

I have also wondered if there might not be a good opportunity now to study the impact of Communist rule on Austria after the occupation leaves. In other words, what political and social changes have they been able to affect in their zone?

To Margaret Mills, 23 September 1955:

If I want to be perfectly honest in examining the motivations which lead me to write [letters], it has something to do with being lonely, with looking for friendship, and with not being self-sufficient. I am not saying that it is bad to be lonely or to want to be with others. On the contrary—but it is not always comfortable.

In the summer 1956 issue, Paul's book review of Elfriede Brüning's *Regine Haberkorn* appeared in *Books Abroad* (University of Oklahoma Press). Here is a brief excerpt: "The 'thin plot' meets all the requirements outlined by Deputy Minister President Walter Ulbricht for the function of the writer in the Communist state. This dull novel may serve to demonstrate the obvious. While the totalitarian state may prescribe subject matter and doctrine to be treated in the 'new literature,' these requirements hardly encourage artistic creation."

In the winter 1957 issue, Paul's book review of Anton Boehm's *Epoche des Teufels* also appeared in *Books Abroad*. Here is another brief excerpt: "The author attempts to show that the chaos of our time can, in most instances, be traced directly to the workings of Satan. The Soviet state represents a resounding success for Satan. The author's difficult style and abstract treatment will probably appeal more to the theologian than to the average reader."

To Frederick Praeger, 8 May 1958:

The enclosed magazine contains a report I prepared for the Michigan Academy of Science, Arts, and Letters on the church in East Germany. I thought it might interest you and also give you some idea of my style. I have done work on a similar report dealing with education in the Soviet zone.

To Harriet Cook, 28 December 1959:

This is the first letter written with my new pen; I like both the point and the color. However, it does not seem to have improved my handwriting.

To Huntington Terrell, 8 October 1962:

Life here has been very busy for me since I got home. Taking time in the evening for a personal letter is a distinct luxury—one I will gladly indulge.

On 1 November 1962, Paul was one of the keynote speakers at the Twenty-First Annual Institute of World Affairs Conference at Hamline University, St. Paul, Minnesota. His presentation was entitled "Germany between East and West."

To Frederick Praeger, 27 April 1965:

I feel very apologetic and somewhat harassed about the book project. I definitely want to do it and have been collecting material. Hope springs eternal, and I shall take the material and the tentative outline I have with me and find a week or two this summer when I can go into the Salzburg mountains or to Baden to work on a good outline.

The Gerrit Kollen Papers (1970-71)

To Mrs. J. Carleton Pelgrim [nee Estelle Marie Kollen], 17 February 1970:

The college and council records are rather bare of the personal element; they show little of the personal warmth and dynamic which your father [Gerrit Kollen, deceased Hope president] obviously had. This is where I hope you may be able to help me most. I was very interested in your comments on travel with your father and in your reference to his diary. I wonder if you may not also have some letters which he received from Theodore Roosevelt, William Jennings Bryan, and other contemporaries.

To Hilda Cook, 23 February 1970:

I have been given a definite assignment to prepare a short biographical booklet. I have discovered that Dr. Kollen's only daughter, now about eighty-five, is still living and that she has a diary and probably other papers which could be useful in shedding light on his personal life. So I have an appointment to see her in Coral Gables the end of next week.

To Jim Alexander, 5 May 1970:

I am having fun doing research, even reading the microfilm edition of the local paper for 1895!

In spring 1970, the *Hope College Alumni News* published Paul's "Encounter with President Kollen." This brief excerpt indicates Paul's appreciation of Kollen's reach beyond borders.

How did a man like Kollen, who had come to the United States as a boy of eight and had been raised on a farm in Overisel, gain the friendship and respect of men like Theodore Roosevelt, William Jennings Bryan, Woodrow Wilson, and Andrew Carnegie who really had no prior knowledge about Hope College or the small Dutch settlement in West Michigan?

Reconstructing the past, bringing back to life an era which is almost forgotten, makes the historian something of a detective who has to hunt down clues found in all kinds of places. It is fun reading old *Anchors*, going through catalogues printed before 1900, using the microfilm edition of the *Holland City News*, and talking to Dr. Kollen's daughter and other people who remember him. All this, however, falls short of hearing him speak and meeting him in person.

Fortunately, Dr. Kollen occasionally recorded his activities and impressions in diaries. Five of these his daughter graciously put at my disposal, and they add a great deal of life to the material found in our archives. They tell, for example, of Dr. Kollen's first trip to Europe, in the summer of 1906.

In April of 1906, the Council of Hope College congratulated Dr. Kollen on his "brilliant success" in securing endowment and buildings for the college—Carnegie Gymnasium had just been completed, and

Voorhees Hall was about to be built—and urged the president to go abroad for a vacation during the summer of 1906. They even voted him the sum of five hundred dollars to help with the expenses of the trip. That may well have been the first Hope College sponsored European tour.

To Jim Alexander, 16 June 1970:

The research for the Kollen book is going along very well; I have been finding a great deal of material on him. Where there was a dearth of information to begin with, there now is almost a flood. Among the very fascinating things I have found are some sixty letters which he wrote to his daughter during the summer of 1913 when he was first a delegate to a Protestant conference in Scotland and then a United States representative at the International Opium Conference in The Hague and the opening of the Peace Palace. He sent her a great many clippings and other things, and would you believe that prominently among those mentioned in The Hague papers in August of 1913 is one Dr. Fried from Vienna. This is my father's cousin Alfred who received the Nobel Peace Prize back in 1911. It is a small world indeed.

To Randall Miller, 16 June 1970:

Your suggestion of A. J. Muste is excellent, and if the seminar gets underway and I have a really good student, I might turn him loose on Muste. Otherwise, I might want to keep him for future reference. I must say that this whole area of local history has opened up some very interesting new vistas to me. Mostly, I have been surprised at the wealth of material which is available if one really wants to dig. Among other things, I have learned almost to read Dutch and to find my way through the archives of Western Seminary as well as through the storeroom in the Van Zoeren Library. With the help of Dr. Bruins and Miss Schuppert of the seminary library, I even managed to burglarize the Hope College safe in the basement of the Chapel which apparently had not been touched for years. It yielded minutes of the faculty going all the way back to 1866, so by this time I really have material for more than one or two short papers. Perhaps I will have to shift my field completely and become a Dutch Colonial historian.

To Jay Dawson, 19 June 1970:

The transcript of the English part of Gerrit Kollen's 1870 diary has just been completed, so I thought I would send this on to you. I am sure your grandmother will enjoy having you read it to her (perhaps you ought to leave out the part about having beer and ice cream July 21!).

To John and Mary Elmendorf, 23 June 1970:

Just recently, I found a whole trunk full of old letters, speeches, and other papers, including a diary Kollen kept in 1870, the year before he came to teach at Hope College. All of this has made me into something of a local history bug, and I am now offering a seminar in local history during our summer session.

To Bob Bernen, 23 September 1971:

I discovered a delightful new field of interest in working at our college archives and am now at work on a biography of one of Hope's early presidents whose diary and other papers I unearthed. It is nice to know that I can still get excited over historical search and enjoy writing.

To Jay Dawson, 22 December 1971:

I thought you would enjoy the enclosed essay and might be able to read it to your grandmother since you are home. Obviously, it is intended to be followed by the reading of the first section of Kollen's diary. I really wrote this piece for the fall issue of the *Hope College Alumni Magazine*, but it proved too long, and I did not want to cut the diary part. I am now hoping that the editor of *Michigan History* will want to do something with it.

Later remarks on the writing process (1974-97)

From George Lee, 21 January 1974:

Lee was glad to know about Paul's interest in writing his autobiography. He predicted that the historic and humanistic book would show readers the other side of Paul "that was not peeping through with all the maps, gowns, and letters."

On 16 October 1976, Paul dedicated an historical marker for Van Vleck Hall on the Hope College campus. Here are a few of his "Notes for Remarks on the Historical Setting."

Van Vleck Hall had many uses—dormitory, lecture rooms, residence of the principal, dining room or refectory, and students' chapel. Later, during the First and Second World Wars, it was used as the dispensary and sick bay for the army training units stationed on Hope's campus. It would really be interesting to hear some of the stories these walls could tell. But perhaps I had better refer you to the cryptic remarks contained in early issues of the *Anchor* for stories of student exploits or to the *Milestone* of 1930 which contains a poem about Van Vleck Hall written by Philip Tertius Phelps, who was born in the building. We could ask the two young ladies who will unveil the marker what really goes on in Van Vleck Hall these days.

Not too many years ago, I heard Dr. Lubbers say: "Hope College is not a place; Hope College is an idea." Van Vleck Hall, completed in 1858, made physically possible the idea which the founder of this colony had for his people: the idea of a school which would provide vigorous academic preparation for the rest of the young people from this community who were to become the leaders of the future.

We do know that Van Vleck played a major role in charting the course which has served Hope College so well for more than a century. I am happy, therefore, that with the dedication of the Van Vleck Historical Marker during this Bicentennial Year, we are able to pay tribute to one of the college's early leaders who knew that "Hope is not a place, but an idea" and who believed in building for the future.

To Bob Bernen, 2 July 1984:

I hope to work on [writing the history of] the president's house at Hope, which is almost one hundred years old but stood empty (and unfinished for lack of funds) for almost a decade. There are dozens, if not hundreds, of [personal] letters which should be written.

To Douglas Braat, 2 February 1986:

What is needed to complete the picture [of Paul's efforts in international education] is a second volume which might have a title such as *From Many Lands* and would trace the later careers of young people from abroad who have attended Hope College.

To Frederick Praeger, who in a letter dated 11 December 1986 had offered Paul a job translating manuscripts or books from German, 5 January 1987:

I would not be averse to doing some translation work in German history or related fields. As you suggest, a little extra pocket money can be nice to have for pastries, or in my case, the search for interesting old books or prints.

To John Dryfhout, 18 August 1992:

Meanwhile I also completed the outline for the HASP fall course of seven weekly meetings under the general theme of "Vignettes of Holland History."

To Dr. Walter and Gretl Mayer, 12 September 1994:

[Martin Baierl's letter led me] to dig out some old pictures and re-read copies of letters I sent from Nürnberg. Since Martin seemed very interested in hearing my stories of the trials, he urged me to write down some of my experiences. Perhaps I will try in the future. This actually might not be too difficult since I wrote long letters to my friend Margaret Mills in Colorado and have a thick volume of our correspondence.

Included in the Joint Archives of Holland are copies and/or outlines of many other speeches that Paul wrote:

Several Nürnberg trials speeches, including one for the Mr. and Mrs. Club of Holland, October 1953

"Education of German Youth Today—America's Task," 10 November 1953

"Government Policy vs. Christianity" at Hope Church, 20 February 1955

"European Reaction to the UN" for the Grand Haven Women's Club, 19 October 1956

"Political Implications of the Kennedy Tragedy: Is There an Ugly American and Other Questions," 28 April 1959

"Education for World Understanding" in Grand Rapids, 22 October 1959

"A Primer on Undergraduate Study Abroad," 28 October 1966

"Can Christianity and Communism Co-Exist?" at Hope Church, 17 November 1967

"Rotary World Understanding Day," 16 September 1971

"European Images of America: Nürnberg and Vietnam," 20 January 1972

"The Danube Monarchy" to the Monmouth Choir, 20 July 1972

"Hope's International Programs and Vienna" for the Zeeland Lions Club, 11 February 1974

A tribute to Marion Stryker, Board of Trustees luncheon, 4 May 1984

Paul also wrote and delivered eulogies for Hope colleagues Michael Petrovich in 1986 and Charles Powell in 1997.

CHAPTER 22

Art, Books, Music

Paul Fried was a passionate collector of every kind of art. Almost every inch of wall space in his home was covered with a painting or etching or drawing; almost every table top was decorated with an antique or piece of sculpture. Multiple bookcases in his house and office could not hold the volumes of scholarly tomes, first editions, museum catalogs, and garage-sale paperbacks that overflowed onto the floors. His record collection encompassed every known opera, operetta, and symphony as well as humorous recordings from a range of satirists, such as Anna Russell and Tom Lehrer. Today, many walls in Hope College's buildings are festooned with Paul's art treasures, and every floor in the library is filled with Paul's books. Chris Spencer and Charles Aschbrenner, two of Paul's best friends, assisted in saving many valuable personal papers, books, and art works in Paul's collection. They have donated many items to the Theil Research Center.

Art and architecture

To Lida Imhof, 30 August 1945:

I had an afternoon off, so I bought you a souvenir: four rather good reproductions of etchings.

Left to right: *Charles Aschbrenner, Paul Fried, and Chris Spencer, April 1998*

To Walter Recknagel, 31 March 1954:

Thanks for the lovely collection of paintings. Under your tutorship, I shall become an art connoisseur one of these days.

To Alma Scarlett, 30 July 1972:

Speaking of Dubrovnik expenditures, I made a large personal one, buying a very beautiful oil painting by Branko Kovacevic, the man who teaches the painting class. He is really very good as a painter and a teacher and a most pleasant person. He seems to have an international reputation.

To Karl Borsai, 29 March 1974:

Do you remember the painting your father gave me when we visited there a few years ago? It was of a lovely vase and beautiful flowers. I have been looking for a frame for a long time and about a month ago, we asked one of our artistic friends in Grand Rapids to see what he could find. He found a beautiful frame—quite dark wood with a strip of antique gold near the inner edge. It looks just beautiful, and we'll hang it over the organ in the living room. We have thought and talked about you and your family very recently. Please thank your father again and give him and your mother our best and kindest regards.

To Kay Stout, 14 June 1978:

One of my long-range ideas about a second career after retirement (only six years away now) has been to start a small shop for prints, etchings, and rare or old books. Not that it would have to make much money for me, as long as I could justify expenses to go on occasional European hunting trips to buy merchandise and to deduct the costs from the taxes I have to pay. I may decide to do something else, but right now it is one of the few things I feel I would really enjoy. Not the selling, but the hunting and the matching up of interested buyers with worthwhile items rather than mass-produced junk.

To Arthur Frederix, 11 June 1979:

I went to a large antique show in Allegan and found two brass lamps, terribly black and rusted, but with beautifully etched scenery barely visible. I took them home, and after three hours of work, the original beauty was there. I bought new electrical parts, and now they grace my desk. Total cost: $25.

To Hideo Yamazaki, 20 August 1981:

I want you to know how delighted I am with the woodblock print and the most original and useful cloisonné tie pin. I had never seen even this shape or color before, but it is exactly the type of pin I like to wear (when I have to wear a tie). My thanks to you and your mother for your thoughtfulness.

To Jan Evert, 29 March 1982:

Initially, I had made plans for a trip out to the West Coast during spring break, but then I decided to stay here and save the money. Or, rather I spent the money buying a number of old German, Austrian, Dutch, and Italian prints at an estate sale. You will have to come up and see "my etchings" when you get here. One of them is a beautiful picture of Karlskirche [church in Vienna dedicated to St. Charles Borromeo], and there are excellent pictures of Franz Joseph and Elizabeth—almost but not quite life-size.

To Karl Borsai, 8 December 1982:

One request: *Austrian Information* had a story on the *Ver Sacrum* [official magazine of the Vienna Secession movement] exhibition at the Hermes Villa this fall. Have you seen it? If you have not and decide to go before it ends, would you get me a catalog? As you may remember, I have a few books and periodicals from that period—including one issue of the magazine. Earlier this year at an art sale in Grand Haven, I found all kinds of interesting prints—one dating back to 1743 depicting the special coronation meal for Maria Theresa held in Prague. Also included in the forty or more prints I bought is a very large engraving of Karlskirche which

I wanted to reproduce for this year's Christmas card. The printer did not think it could be done, so you will have to come and see it hanging in my guest apartment.

To Mark Christensen, 20 May 1984:

I do the historical research on some of the European prints and graphics which he [Howard Plaggemars, a former VSS student who had recently opened an art gallery in Holland] sells.

To Bob Bernen, 2 July 1984:

The more recent collection more or less started with the large Brandenburg Gate painting I purchased from you in Venice. Since then I have picked up items here and there, in a somewhat unorganized fashion at first, now trying to get some order into what has started to be a collection. With retirement came the offer by a former student who is starting an art gallery here in Holland to become a "consulting historian" for his business. I am supposed to provide brief historical, biographical, or socio-political materials for some of the works he hopes to sell.

To Dr. James W. Hawkins, psychiatrist, Vienna Summer School alumnus, 8 July 1984:

I am already somewhat involved in working with an art gallery here. My role will be to dig up material on old prints, which will add to their romantic attractiveness and thus make them more saleable at a higher price. It allows me to indulge in my taste for looking for art materials and reading about them.

To Dr. Randy Miller, 6 January 1985:

The other thing I have been working on is trying to develop an architectural history research program for Hope College. I am starting to learn more about where to look for information. Hope Church has asked me to become the church archivist. I will have to take lessons from Elton Bruins, but this may turn out to be rather interesting.

To Dr. William Waggoner, 6 November 1986:

The day after I saw you, I visited a New York print shop at 2nd Avenue and 52nd Street and found a very attractive hand-colored print of Vienna, dated 1713. It was not too expensive, but since I was not too certain if it was what I thought it was (namely, by Fischer von Erlach), I did not buy it then. I went to the New York Public Library on Friday morning and did find quite a bit of information on this, so I went back and made the purchase. The curator of the Muskegon Museum of Art liked it so much that he borrowed it for a show that will open on Saturday.

To Kay Stout, 29 June 1987:

I have developed an increasing interest in art and art history, partly in connection with my hobby of collecting prints.

To Jan Evert, 9 September 1987:

John Dryfhout has helped make the Saint-Gaudens historical site a real monument. Did you see the large book on Saint-Gaudens which John put out ten years ago? It sold for seventy-five dollars and was fully worth it!

To Bob Bernen, 15 September 1987:

I go antique hunting. You helped me get started in collecting art to the point that many people claim that my house is a museum—three floors of pictures and books.

To Jean and John Bloemendahl, 13 July 1988:

Last Saturday, I went to the antique sale at Saugatuck and happened to find another good etching of a Vienna view, probably from the 1920s. I already have a picture of the Opera and St. Stephen's by the same artist but still can't read his signature.

To Dr. Gerda Ungar and Jack Joseph, 20 February 1989:

I did stop at one of the antique malls and found a print of Neuer Markt ["square" in the inner city of Vienna] for three dollars. Add a mat and glass (I had a good frame), and for just over ten dollars, I have one more Vienna view hanging in my dining room. I hope that my dinner guests tonight, an alumnus of the 1959 program and his wife, will properly admire the thing.

To Kay Stout, 28 December 1991:

I am much involved in preparing for the opening of our new Holland Museum in October 1992. My other contact is with the nearby Muskegon Museum of Art, which has a Salzburger as curator. I was asked if I would lend them some of my older European prints for an exhibit. Getting material ready for this show, which ran from early September to the end of October, took a great deal of research and quite a few trips (40 miles each way). The gallery looked very professional, and I learned a lot that may help as I try to inventory my collection, which has grown and grown.

To Nicolaas Bootsma, 12 January 1992:

I have been quite involved working with two museums. First, here in Holland where the old Netherlands Museum will soon move to the much larger old post office building. As president of the Holland Historical Society, I have served on the Holland Historical Trust, which is responsible for raising the money and making plans for the new Holland Museum. We have some very competent people working on this. My other involvement has been with the Muskegon Museum of Art. I have served on their collections advisory committee for about five years and am learning more about art. This past spring I was asked if they could have on loan some forty or forty-five old engravings for an exhibit. There are several pieces they would like to have as gifts, and in time I may turn over some of them to the museum.

To John Mulder, 15 April 1992:

It occurred to me that you might like to have one or two items which were in the Muskegon Museum of Art show for your seminary and that they might more appropriately find a home there. In particular, I have in mind the work of Jan Luyken, Dutch engraver and poet (1649-1712), whose *Berühmteste Bilderbibel* [Most famous picture bible] appeared in 1712. The two-volume work contains 208 engravings by Jan and 131 by his son Caspar. The vellum binding on both volumes is badly worn, and the last five pages of volume two, though complete, have been damaged. As you can see from the enclosure, the other item is a good copy of *The Signing of the Edict of Nantes*.

To Peter and Beverly Fuhrmann, 23 May 1993:

I am starting to work on ways for orderly disposal of things I have collected over the years. I made a start by donating a number of art pieces—mostly older prints—to the Muskegon Museum of Art and to Hope College. The museum did have a very nice exhibit of some forty prints from my collection. Most of them are back in the house, but others were gifts which allowed me to use some deductions on my income tax.

To Rev. Paul Gerhard Diez, 30 May 1996:

One of my recent fruits is a colored woodcut, *Marktplatz in Mittenberg*, signed C. Thiemann.

In 1996, Paul celebrated John Dryfhout's gift of an original bronze bas-relief by Augustus Saint-Gaudens to Hope College.

To Jan Evert, 30 November 1996:

The Muskegon Museum of Art and the Grand Rapids Museum are collaborating in plans for a tour of the People's Republic of China scheduled for next spring. Special guides are Dr. David Ihrman (prof at Grand Valley) and his wife, who is a native. They have an incredible

Hard at work amid walls of books (courtesy Tom Renner)

collection (prints, mainly) in their home here in Holland and are very, very nice people. So, I just sent in my five hundred dollar deposit!

The Joint Archives of Holland contains many folders on art (along with accession data entry forms) that Paul collected, exhibited, and donated. Hope College and the Muskegon Museum of Art received huge donations of art works from Paul.

Books

To Hilda Cook, 6 March 1948:

Have you finished reading [G. M.] Trevelyan's *English Social History*? I would be interested in it and in your reaction. How about [Arnold] Toynbee? Have you read his *Study of History*? I should like to take time for it, but for the present, I don't see how I can.

To Gustav (Gus) Wieman, 7 December 1948:

By now the shortage of goods is back again, the prices are up and keep going up, and to get the least amount of work done—like on the car—you have to bribe the men with candy and tobacco. The only thing which still keeps me interested is the chance to pick up some good books. I just bought nice editions of Goethe and Schiller.

To Annabelle Werley, 12 February 1950:

If you have some time to spare, I highly recommend *Walden Two* by B. F. Skinner, a utopian novel by a psychology prof and very interesting. Skinner's book is a good reply to George Orwell's *1984*.

To Lothar Sudekum, 19 May 1955:

Thank you for [shipping] the books that will fill a very decided gap in our college library. They certainly caused some excitement on our campus arriving in five big boxes all marked "LIQUOR" (or something similar) and sitting in plain sight in the library hall and addressed to Dr. Fried. You should have seen all the grinning student faces during the next few days. Our campus is supposed to be completely dry, so I thought I should explain to the wife of the president about the joke. She is a real WCTU [Woman's Christian Temperance Union] supporter and said, without a smile, "I suppose they are good strong boxes." The dean and the rest greatly enjoyed the idea, especially when I suggested that all this was in preparation for a party at our next library committee meeting.

To Al Coox, 10 February 1977:

In view of the unusually severe winter, I am really happy to be sitting home with books—even if the temperature in the house sometimes makes sweaters and fur-lined boots desirable attire. But that is still better than going outside.

To Jean and John Bloemendahl, 28 January 1978:

I am still thinking about eventually starting a small book and print business. Talked about that with a friend in Texas, who is all for doing this kind of thing on a mail-order basis. Also talked with Bruce Neckers, my attorney, who suggested that I ought to try doing something like this for a couple of months in the summer. We talked about Saugatuck, but my friend in Texas reported on one of the people whom he knows who clears some $20,000 in two months every summer in Provincetown. Perhaps I ought to think about Maine or Key West, which at this point seems more attractive.

To Brigitta Kowallik, who helped Paul with transactions related to the disposition of his rare books, 7 November 1978:

I would very much like to see you again and talk about your new enterprise. Since I have given some thought to becoming involved in the same kind of business when I retire, I have gradually built up a small collection of books and prints, many of them dealing with European subjects.

To Henry Birnbaum, 8 March 1982:

Anyway, Camp Ritchie training and my natural bent toward the detective novel always prompt me to try to track down people, especially if they were interesting or have done interesting things.

To Kay Stout, 29 June 1987:

You asked about my reading. It could mostly be called: history, mystery, and a mixture of novels and classics which I have never read or can remember only vaguely.

To Nikola Koljevic, 20 February 1988:

I have lots of books written for young people. Many deal with American history and biography; others are stories by Mark Twain or Daniel Defoe. Do you think Bogdana [Koljevic's daughter] would find them of enough interest? Let me know what you would like to have me send. There also is a series called *The Hardy Boys*, which is sort of a male counterpart to the *Nancy Drew* stories. They are kind of fun to read but not too profound.

To Nikola Koljevic, 27 January 1989:

Should I start sending young people's books which deal with American topics—Indians, Lincoln, Washington, the Pilgrims, the gold rush? Most of these seem to be written more with boys in mind. Do you think that would make much difference?

To Kay Stout, 12 October 1988:

My big find of the year was a two-volume work by Jan Luyken, Dutch poet and etcher, who died in 1712. This is a poetic rendition (in Dutch) of the Old and New Testaments with some 340 well-preserved engravings. Even the vellum binding is still in reasonably good condition. One of my friends in the Netherlands said that the books would bring between six hundred and twelve hundred guilders, which is a great deal more than I paid here.

To Kay Stout, 28 December 1991:

I ought to try to get help in cataloguing books—probably more than ten thousand spread over three floors, twelve rooms, and several hallways.

To John Dryfhout, 18 August 1992:

The big event today was the completion of the German book project for Van Wylen Library. Twenty boxes stand ready to be picked up. Total count: about 550 items. Estimated appraisal value: just under $4,000. Russia and England are next on my list.

To Xin (Andrew) Chen, 12 May 1994:

The project of transferring books to Van Wylen Library has continued. So far this year, I have packed and sent over to them twenty-four large cardboard boxes.

To Wilford Butler Jr., 23 February 1996:

I wish to come up with a simple system of organizing forty years of correspondence, pictures, articles, etc. As an historian and participant in that history, I am reluctant to burn the stuff.

Music

Dozens of letters to Arthur Frederix, as well as to others, began with references to what Paul was listening to on Saturday afternoon radio broadcasts of the Metropolitan Opera.

From Chet Schultz, 27 March 1993:

Chet recalled Paul taking him to the outdoor horseshoe theater at the Broadmoor Hotel in Colorado Springs and explaining great music to him. Paul got tickets for both of them by laying down money, rolling the dice twice, and winning both times.

To Lida Imhof, 15 August 1945:

We got four-day passes to Paris. The first evening I went to the opera and saw the ballet *Coppélia*. The next evening I was really bold and went to the Folies Bergère, supposedly a must in Paris. I can't say that I was too impressed, except by the prices!

To Harriet Cook, 23 December 1946:

Paul enclosed the program from the Boston Opera House's "Sunday at 4:30" Eightieth Program with Arthur Fiedler conducting.

To John De Vries, 11 August 1948:

In the evening, we went to see *Aida* in an outdoor theater [in Rome]. John, I wish you could have been there. I have never seen anything so impressive. In the second act, during the triumphal march, there are some fifteen hundred people on the stage.

To Margaret Mills, 1 September 1948:

In Lucerne, we went to a concert to hear Artur Schnabel play a Schumann concerto and to enjoy a Brahms symphony. Monday night in Nürnberg, we went to the opera and saw *Tiefland*, a modern German work which deals with the danger that comes to an Alpine shepherd when he moves into the low country (Tiefland). The pleasant part about this evening was that not only did we see a good opera but we had seats in (and were the only occupants of) the Führer Loge, Hitler's personal box.

To Huntington Terrell, 23 September 1951:

This summer, I saw both of our flames: Irmgard Seefried singing the lead in *The Magic Flute* in Salzburg and Elisabeth Schwarzkopf singing the role of Eva in *Die Meistersinger*. Both were even better than I remembered them but had gotten much bigger, too! Well, that seems to be the fate of opera stars.

To Dorothy of the Kramer-Metcalf clan, 14 August 1952:

I have about seventy LP records, mostly classical music, which I can play any time of the day or night.

To Bob Bernen, 21 September 1952:

I have bought a large ($300) radio-phonograph in which I replace the German player unit with an American three-speed job, so I have plenty of good music when I want it. Just a few hours ago, I played both of your records, Beethoven's 3rd and 6th. Then some Rachmaninoff, then Tchaikovsky—all mixed up. Violetta is still keeping her youth and does a fine job of dying whenever I call on her, which is quite frequently. I never did get *Bohème* again, though I meant to do so a number of times. The nearest I have come to it has been the purchase of a record with some of *Butterfly*! But I got the complete recordings of *The Marriage of Figaro* and *The Magic Flute*—both of which I heard in Salzburg—as well as *Salome*. If you drop in for a Sunday afternoon, you will find enough to choose from.

To Hans-Joachim (Hajo) A. Robert, 12 February 1953:

I sold my Kuba *Musikschrank* [music cabinet] in Essen, so I had to go to Bremerhaven last week to buy a new radio.

To Mary Herz, 25 February 1953:

I have found that since the mass production of LP records, I have been able to accumulate quite a large library of classical music, so that I have little incentive to go to concerts.

To Walter Recknagel, 25 April 1953:

Since Wolfgang always wants me to diet or do something else for my health, we walked for about an hour through the woods. I got quite a tan. In the evening, we saw a not too good performance of *Carmen* in the Hamburg State Opera. *Elektra* was very good, though the women were very fat. None of this comes up to Salzburg.

To Huntington and Carolyn Terrell, on the birth of their son Nathan, 27 January 1954:

It seems to me that Nathan ought to have a welcome to initiate him into the world of pleasant things. So now the question is: what he would like? My own suggestions are based on association with pleasant hours spent with the father: (1) Beethoven's 9th Symphony: I have the Toscanini recording and like it very much. I recall one early morning at Stein castle when Hunt got up, walked over to my record player without a word, put on the last movement of the 9th, and claimed that he had dreamed the first three movements—when I rudely awakened him; (2) Mozart's *Requiem*: There is a Mozarteum recording made in Salzburg. I did not hear it but remember how much you praised it; (3) D'Albert's *Tiefland*: This may remind you of the Hitler box in Nürnberg. I read somewhere that this recording is not too good, though; or (4) any other record you might like to have for Nathan and his family.

To Walter Recknagel, 10 April 1954:

A Mozart opera, *Così fan tutte*, is playing, so I feel in the mood for writing to you. I have to think of that very lovely opera house in Bayreuth, but I couldn't imagine the singers doing their roles in English. I still associate my Mozart memories with *The Magic Flute* and *The Marriage of Figaro* and *Idomineo*.

To Margaret Mills, 12 July 1954:

Yesterday we went to the symphony concert [in Mexico City], which turned out to be a complete flop. Beethoven's *Emperor Concerto* would not have been recognized by its composer. It was a good thing he was dead so he could not hear it murdered.

To Rand Carter, 20 September 1954:

I had to think of you yesterday as I was listening to the rebroadcast of Strauss's *Ariadne auf Naxos* from Salzburg. I thought you might be listening, too. [Metropolitan Opera star] Hilde Gueden sounded wonderful. I had seen the opera in Hamburg last year, but the performance was not nearly as good. We will have Gueden here in Holland for a concert on November 13th. In January, the Vienna Boys Choir will be here, and in March, Boris Goldovsky is coming to town.

To Rand Carter, 15 November 1954:

Hilde Gueden gave a truly brilliant performance which impressed even our otherwise dull Holland audience. Afterwards I went backstage and, being almost last in line, greeted her in German since I knew she was Viennese. She was quite pleasantly surprised and, after a few minutes of conversation, I asked her if she had made any plans for the evening and, if not, if she would not like to come to a little party. She said she would be delighted, if she could have a glass of beer. I took her and her accompanist back to the hotel to change and quickly got some beer and a couple of other people before picking her up. It was really a most successful evening for everyone. Then yesterday, I drove her from the hotel to the Grand Rapids airport, so we had about an hour to chat. I received an invitation to look her up next time I come to Vienna or Salzburg. She is married; darn it. As you can guess, I was most thoroughly charmed. I think my friends here considered Saturday's party quite a scoop, too.

To Willard De Pree, 7 December 1954:

My two major events in Holland were the Trygve Lie lecture which was a success with some thirteen hundred tickets sold and the concert by Hilde Gueden, soprano of the Met, Salzburg, Vienna, and Milan. The second rates as a major event because I had arranged a little party for some of my more enlightened friends after the concert, and finding that no plans had been made to entertain her, boldly asked her over. She not only accepted but was obviously the center of the party. She is thoroughly charming and not a bit "prima donna."

To Walter Recknagel, 17 January 1956:

Thank you so much for sharing your new-found taste. I love that Vivaldi record and have played it a great many times. In fact, it is on now. Of course, if you really wanted a long letter, you would have to send me something like *Die Meistersinger* or *Götterdämmerung*, so there would be a great many sides to play.

To Felix Molzer, 5 December 1961:

There will be a three-and-a-half-day weekend trip to Salzburg in August 1962. The musical offerings are ample; I have ordered a block of tickets for *Figaro*, *Entführung*, *Iphigenie*, and *Troubadour* as well as one Kammerkonzert and one Orchesterkonzert. Also, I expect to repeat the Saturday evening trip to the candlelight concert at Chiemsee.

To Bruce van Voorst, 15 April 1968:

By the way, do you like Wagner, and do you have part or all of the recordings of *The Ring*? If not, you might be interested in the new complete London set of the entire cycle. There are nineteen records in it, and the darn thing weighs half a ton. Having just bought the thing for myself as a birthday present (with a check I received for giving a lecture at the Grand Rapids Women's City Club), it occurs to me that this set might appeal to you also.

To Arthur Frederix, 13 April 1969:

I first watched Karajan conduct in Salzburg in 1948—*The Marriage of Figaro* with Schwarzkopf, Seefried, and Kunz—and I have been a fan ever since.

To Karl Borsai, 29 October 1969:

The very beautiful book on Vienna's opera has arrived, and I am delighted. I have an idea that you were at least partly responsible for the selection, which could not have been better, so thanks. The author Marcel Prawy is another Viennese whom I know from my days in the army. He and publisher Fred Praeger and I were in the same room and unit back in 1943.

To Bruce van Voorst, 7 December 1969:

I am listening to the Cleveland Symphony's excellent performance of the Tchaikovsky violin concerto. I hope the program is not interrupted again, as it was twenty-eight years ago [attack on Pearl Harbor] when I was listening to the New York Philharmonic.

To Arthur Frederix, 24 March 1970:

Thanks for the two lovely recordings and your thoughtful wishes for my birthday. The Beethoven 6th is a wonderful recording which has the added attraction that I heard Herbert von Karajan and the Berlin Philharmonic perform this in Dubrovnik in September 1968.

To George Lee, 10 July 1971:

In Milan, I discovered that Margot Fonteyn was dancing at a special ballet summer festival inside the courtyard of the medieval Sforza castle. She did *Swan Lake* and another Tchaikovsky ballet, and there was also a full performance—orchestra, piano soloist, and ballet—of Gershwin's Concerto in F.

To Arthur Frederix, 11 July 1972:

My plan is to leave Vienna early Saturday and get to Salzburg about noon. The festival in Hellbrunn is from 3 to 9 p.m.—music, dance, oratory, *Wasserspiele* [water games], and fireworks. I have tickets for the Mozarteum concert the next morning, for *Jedermann*, and for the evening Orchesterkonzert conducted by Seiji Ozawa, who is fantastic, with a Liszt piano concerto played by Shura Cherkassky, Mendelssohn's 4th, and a modern Japanese piece.

To Mrs. Janet Riemersma Woods, 24 June 1974:

Today is the first day of our classes in Vienna and, for the first time in nineteen years, we are here a week before the Staatsoper and

Volksoper close. We have already had, as part of our orientation to the city, a visit to the Volksoper for *The Land of Smiles* and to the Staatsoper for *Tannhäuser*. Tonight some students will go to *The Marriage of Figaro*, and later in the week, we have tickets for *Die Fledermaus, Don Carlos, Rigoletto*, and *The Gypsy Baron*. I am not sure how much studying the students will do this week.

To Arthur Frederix, 6 October 1979:

Hope's music department does not like Felix Molzer, or rather, they do not like the fact that I have been hiring people to teach music in Vienna without always checking with them in advance.

To Julia Herrick White, 13 February 1980:

I enjoyed seeing you and your husband on Saturday and hearing you read some of your poems. I particularly liked "In Praise of the Lord's Suitcase" and was interested to know that the poem had been set to music. I suggested to Dr. Kooiker that he might want to consider this piece for Hope's women's choir. He liked the words and would be interested in seeing the music.

To Bob Bernen, 2 July 1984:

How about a visit to beautiful Holland? I can offer you the comfort of a complete guest apartment equipped with hi-fi and hundreds of classical records. I have not counted lately but had to move them to make room for the recent addition of some thirty operatic records. I still have the three-record *Traviata* as well as the Brandenburg Concerti and other items which fell to me when we split the collection we began at 3 Athens Terrace [in graduate school at Harvard]. The records, as you might remember, made the trip to Europe and back.

To Debby Klomparens Bock, 3 January 1985:

Tuesday, 25 June, is the official alumni gathering to which we want to invite as many friends of Hope College as possible. We have a star pianist for the occasion. Norbert Frühwirth is a young Austrian pianist selected by the Austrian government to play for the opening of the Washington exhibit this fall. We had him [at Hope] for one of his six American concerts (his next and last one at Carnegie Hall was sold out). He was pleased with his reception here and has agreed to give a *Klavier Abend* (piano evening) for us that Tuesday.

To Jan Evert, 17 March 1996:

Yes, I have read Alma Mahler's memoirs and also heard Tom Lehrer's [satiric] record [about Alma], which you may even have heard

Hamming it up with Albertus Van Raalte descendants
(l-r) Debby, Patrick, and Margret Bock, mid-1980s

here. I have also heard most of Mahler's symphonies, but that is a long time ago. My record player is now semi-retired since I did not update my equipment. I envy you being in San Francisco and able to attend all these concerts with little expense and excellent company.

CHAPTER 23

Philosophical and Religious Insights

Many of the already included excerpts from Paul's letters, speeches, and other writings are ripe and profound with his philosophical and religious thoughts, and most of the passages in this section would fit neatly in earlier parts of the book, but these paragraphs seemed particularly appropriate for the next-to-last chapter celebrating Paul's vision of "Hope and hope beyond borders."

Philosophical insights (1946-55)

25 May 1946, a paragraph not addressed to anyone:

During the past ten or fifteen years, I have been in almost constant contact with current history. When I was thirteen, I saw Hitler come to power in Germany. In Vienna, I missed school the day Dollfuss was killed and landed in prison at the time of the *Anschluss*. I saw angry crowds in the streets of Prague after Munich, and I heard the first air-raid alarm in London. In this war, I served with the US Army Intelligence Service in England, France, Belgium, Holland, Luxembourg, and Germany. Out of all these experiences has come the firm conviction that this is "One World" and that we are doomed if we do not learn to live together in peace. If the United Nations succeeds in its present task of bringing order into international affairs, that field will be the most important in the world; if the UN does not succeed, nothing matters very much. It is my hope that I may eventually perform some service in this field.

To Margaret Mills, 22 March 1947:

I value my citizenship perhaps a great deal more than many natives just because I know how rare the kind of life we live here is in the world of today.

To Margaret Mills, 30 March 1947:

I am most afraid of the internal effects a strong anti-Russian policy and a planning for the inevitable war will have on this country. Once we begin with the suppression of the Communist party here, it will only be a short step to a certain amount of censorship and to the suspension of civil liberties for atomic scientists and newspapermen, to the supervision of colleges and teachers. Before we know it, we might find ourselves living in a police state. The answer to Communism is found not in the suppression of liberties, but in the demonstration of working democracy. Nothing is as hard on the Communists as a period of prosperity and happiness for the working classes of a country. If we can give enough assistance to any country in Europe to give the workers a high standard of living, we will not have to fear Communism from that country. Two big powers like the United States and the USSR are bound to make each other nervous, but the world is large enough for both.

To June Metcalf, 23 September 1947:

I don't think you should worry about giving me anything for Christmas, but I shall give you the answer I am going to give most of my friends. I have about everything I need and can easily afford to buy the rest. What matters is that I am remembered, that a card can do.

To Margaret Mills, 20 May 1948:

I had mentioned the question of war guilt. At present, when there is so much talk of democracy, of the responsibility of the individual, and at the same time so much of the horror of the Nazi period is being uncovered and shown to the German public, many people (especially those who were not the fanatical Nazis) have started to search their souls and ask themselves if, in some way, they do not bear part of the responsibility for those things that happened. For instance, should the schoolteacher have kept quiet to keep his job and feed his family, the officer to keep his rank, or should they have spoken up against those acts of inhumanity, even if it would have meant the loss of position, freedom, and even life? Yes, there are quite a few Nazis still, some in high places and able to bring influence to bear on the American administration here. Those Germans who lived abroad (also in the US) saw only the "good" Hitler did—development of roads, reduction of unemployment, etc., but did not see the cost of dictatorship.

To Ike Auerbach, 25 May 1948:

I must confess that I have never been to a DP camp; neither have I visited any of the former concentration camps. You may think that funny, but I have fought for ten years not to hate, and I am afraid still. It is too painful to be reminded of the past, so I rather leave it alone.

To Frank Zvonar, 17 November 1948:

Frank, you should not get the idea that to be up in the air with one's plans is something unusual. It happens to me about every couple of years or more, and most people have the same trouble.

To Ike Auerbach, 7 November 1949:

Toward the end of the summer, as the Korean settlement seemed on its way to settlement, I tried to take stock of the situation and the way it related to my own affairs. I wondered if most people in the United States (including myself) were indulging in the sort of thinking which I have always regretted in my father and his friends: the idea that "it can't happen here." When, from the historian's point of view, the signs of war and persecution to come were as clear as day, my father persisted in his hope that "it will all blow over." If there is to be a war—or a continued state of unrest or emergency—my hope for a quiet career as a teacher at some small college would probably be frustrated. Sooner or later, I expect that I will have to go back to some form of service.

To Margaret Mills, 26 December 1949:

I think I have given you an indication of this feeling of lack of purpose, so much so that I find relatively little pleasure in any of the things I do. Perhaps I am now reaping the reward for my attempt to recapture experiences which I thought I ought to have had by the time I was twenty or twenty-one. That is the time to have doubts and *Weltschmerz* [concern about changing the world and the inability to do so]. Yet, the realization of the uselessness of our present set of values and aims may be the first step toward doing something to bring about an improvement.

To Kay Stout, 28 January 1950:

There is also the problem of next year: general examinations and a thesis and a teaching job, and tied with them the problem of life as such and the future. One thing I have gained as a result of fairly careful self-analysis—brought on by this feeling of restlessness and depression—is the conviction that I really ought to start thinking about a family and marriage. Somehow I have always thought too much of the European idea of having to attain some safe place in life first, and where do you find that today? Mixed with that was the romantic notion, produced or at least strengthened by the Hollywood conception of LOVE, which is certainly something quite unrealistic. Perhaps I should hope for it to come someday, but I am thirty and cannot say that I have ever been in love. It would probably be very unrealistic to think that I must find it, and even then I wonder if it would be more than an infatuation. I would rather think of marriage as a down-to-earth comradeship in which both partners have an equal investment of affection and interest in home, work, and family.

To Margaret Mills, 18 February 1950:

Only lately have I come to the realization that success depends almost exclusively on a single-mindedness of purpose. I do not mean that other things, such as talent or opportunity, are unimportant, but even where these are present, the lack of a single purpose leads to a dissipation of energy. Up to now, my interests have been diverse to the extreme, and I am wondering if I should narrow them down. I confess that for the present I have no strong incentive in any direction. I would like to do something and have a comfortable and secure life. I sometimes wish I had retained some of the religious interests of earlier days or that I could become more interested in making money. Then again, I don't really mean that. I don't think I ever got over the shock of finding out how much money meant to some of my friends.

To Kay Stout, 19 February 1950:

I was struck by your phrase that you have "attempted to gain immunity against getting hurt." I have been doing much the same and for years have not permitted myself to become involved in anything or any emotion. As a result, I have gained a certain amount of assurance, a "good-natured indifference" to most problems, and somewhat of a balance as far as the outside world is concerned. But just lately, I have come to realize that the final result of this struggle against involvement with other people or in causes is isolation and (once the basic needs of life are provided for) indifference towards things which were once important to me. I find less enjoyment in theater, skiing, or travel when I do them alone. I have the impression that this is a natural reaction and not the result of some sort of neurosis.

Your comment on the difference in our attitudes towards "settling down and sinking roots" made me examine that part of my plans a little more carefully. Somehow, ever since my family was forced to leave Germany in 1933, and later Austria, the ideal of a stable home and residence has been one of the major parts of my general ambitions. Add to that the fact that the two years I spent in Holland, Michigan (1940-42), and the time I spent there after the war were among the happiest (or the most peaceful) periods of my life, and you will understand why this dream has persisted. On the other hand, Hope College, which had provided the setting for these pleasant years, has twice offered me opportunities to join the teaching staff there. The first time, in 1947, just before I went to Nürnberg, I was offered but declined a position as instructor of German. In September 1949, when I came back from Germany proudly flourishing my new PhD from Erlangen, I was given to understand that I could have a job there any time, along with the casual comment by the president that the chair of the Department of History was getting rather old and would retire within a couple of years. I did not feel that I wanted to accept the opportunity then. I concluded that I had no intention of accepting a lifetime position in a small, if pleasant, community. The wanderlust which has plagued me for as long as I can remember will never leave me. My experiences in Europe have made me only too well aware of the danger of having all of your eggs in one basket (in this case, the USA). For the present, my aim has been to gain a certain professional standing through an appointment to a larger university.

I have no great interest in accumulating large amounts of money. I will probably never be a success in the material meaning of the word. That does not mean that I could not work hard to achieve certain desirable goals, both in the intellectual and material fields. I hope this has not grown too much into a self-analysis.

I had thought of the possibility of buying or building some sort of resort hotel or camp. I have heard of a very lovely mountain camp, owned by friends in Colorado, which is for sale. At the same time, while I was in Stowe, Vermont, Ike Auerbach and I talked about this sort of plan; he assured me that he would always be interested in putting money into something like the building of a ski lift. That, too, is a "dream" for the present. But I seem to ramble on and on.

To Margaret Mills, 26 February 1950:

I should probably hasten to reassure you that there is little danger of my conversion to anything even remotely related to Communism. On the other hand, I am glad that you noted that the label is frequently attached to anything different from the accepted pattern and to everyone who sees room for improvement in our system. I am afraid that sort of attitude will lead to stagnation or the danger of eruption on a political or social level. Fortunately, our government is progressive, and both parties are fully aware that there is room for improvement in our social and economic conditions.

To Kay Stout, 18 March 1950:

We have to decide at some time or other whether to live only for the present or plan ahead as if there were to be a future. I will admit that I have often been more than tempted to ignore the future almost completely and live only from day to day. The war has probably taught me that.

To Fred Bradley, 10 September 1950:

I was much interested in your comments on the danger of war breaking out in earnest. Perhaps your way of saying that we should go in as if war couldn't come is best, yet I feel that I ought to prepare for it in the best way possible. In the past, I have always held my father responsible to some extent for the fate which befell the whole family. I felt that as a journalist, he should have foreseen the developments in Germany and acted in time to get his own family into safety, which would have been easy in 1933 or 1934.

It seems that we are now in just about the position the world was in in the mid-1930s. Of course, I have no family and am really indifferent as to what will happen to me. But, looking at things realistically, I have the feeling that for at least ten or fifteen years, we will not have anything resembling peace or normalcy. In other words, whether there is a shooting war or just a state of continued mobilization, it will be difficult, if not impossible, to live a normal life or even to plan a career as one would have ten years ago.

To Huntington Terrell, 1 July 1951:

As I see it, it is hardly a question of communism versus capitalism but of freedom of the individual versus dictatorship. There was a lot of noise about the hanging of the war criminals, and we received special advance warnings to look out for trouble. Nothing happened. People felt that those hanged fully deserved it but should have been hanged long ago instead of dragging out the case over years. There is a lot of anti-American feeling, and only last night five GIs in a taxi were stopped by a truck blocking the road and beaten mercilessly with lead pipes. Two are in the hospital now, but Germany is now almost our ally, and there is little that will or can happen to punish that sort of thing.

To Bob Bernen, 14 July 1951:

But if you have mastered the art of meeting people and adjusting yourself to their minds, etc., I think you have achieved a great deal which will be valuable in making you a good teacher in addition to being a good scholar.

To Gerhard Muller, 10 April 1953:

What do you think of McCarthy and the investigation of colleges and other antics? I don't like it a bit. If he has his way, everyone in the whole country will be afraid to speak his mind, and we will be on the road to dictatorship.

To Gerhard Muller, 7 May 1953:

You may be sure that wearing glasses will not make you an inferior human being. I have been wearing them since I was thirteen. As far as pressing suits goes, I fully agree with you that the man inside is the important thing. All the same, I am sure taste and breeding are something that goes with the man inside. While it is true that the man inside matters, many people will not take the trouble to look at him to discover what is inside if the outside is not such that they would want to be seen with him. In England, when I was still quite young, Mrs. Lambotte told me: "Shined shoes are the mark of a gentleman. You may have old clothes, but they must be clean. But everyone can have shined shoes if he takes the trouble."

To Margaret Mills, 29 June 1953:

Paul told her that he felt like the main character (merchant) in Thomas Mann's *Buddenbrooks* who just becomes the shell of his former self.

To Edgars Fogels, 1 April 1954:

Despite the many valid criticisms which can be made of materialistic tendencies and of the various political trends in the United States, this is still the most desirable country for permanent residence. To be a citizen of the United States is today what it was to be a Roman in the time of Christ.

To Margaret Mills, 3 May 1955:

Communism, as any other form of totalitarianism, will in the long run move to exterminate all individualists or deviationists; thus, the threat is personal.

To Margaret Mills, 23 September 1955:

The idea of a happy home and a good upbringing is to produce a degree of self-sufficiency so that a young person does not have to "depend," does not have the feeling of "loneliness," does not have to run to the movies or get drunk whenever he is alone (because he is afraid to face himself). The eternal paradox is that you cannot have both: freedom and self-sufficiency with child-like affection and dependence. Admittedly, there is a happy medium, but that is generally a product of maturity and experience. It is essentially the focal point of controversy between Protestantism and Catholicism. Read the little legend of the Grand Inquisitor in Dostoevsky's *The Brothers Karamazov*. It is only about twenty pages but very important. End of lecture.

"Adjustment or Adventure"

On 27 May 1960, Paul delivered a talk entitled "Adjustment or Adventure" as the Honors Assembly address at Hope College. Here is a slightly abbreviated version of that talk.

I count it a real honor to speak here when we pause to pay tribute to the outstanding students in our college. I particularly want to congratulate those of you whose scholastic achievements we are recognizing today. You represent the elite of our college, and in the best sense of the word, you represent Hope. Not only the college so named, but more importantly, the hope that this country and our Western heritage are not in immediate danger of being buried by Khrushchev and his friends.

That this danger of a decline in the West does indeed exist, we all realize only too well. What we often fail to see, however, is that, if Western civilization should fall, its decline will be due not so much to foreign aggression as to our own complacency. It seems tragic to me that, in the years since the end of the Second World War, conformity, complacency, and adjustment to our surroundings—an attitude which makes the average seem much more desirable than the outstanding— have become almost synonymous with the American way of life.

I am not sure just what that phrase means to you. I only know that all too often it seems to refer to an economy of plenty, with well-paying jobs, split-level homes, cars, refrigerators, television sets, and automatic washers for all. More importantly, it seems to mean being part of a well-organized community, getting along well with everyone, and being like everyone else.

What is tragic about this superficial definition of the American way of life is that it indicates an unwillingness to assume the responsibilities of the freedoms which we now enjoy. The inherent danger of this trend toward conformity is perhaps best expressed in the title of Erich Fromm's famous book, *Escape from Freedom*. In this study, Fromm shows how German democracy succumbed to Hitler, primarily because in their search for security, the German people were willing to abdicate their freedoms to a man who offered to lead them. What happened in Germany is not unique. It happened in Italy, in Spain, in Portugal, and, more recently, in France. There are dictators in Asia, in Africa, and in Latin America, as well as behind the Iron Curtain.

We deceive ourselves if we assume that it cannot happen here. Talking of a crusade for freedom to liberate Poland or Hungary, we forget that dictators rise and stay in office not only through terror, but because to a great many people freedom seems a burden rather than a blessing. Is this true also in the United States? Perhaps not in the same measure as elsewhere, but ask yourself how often you have said in recent weeks: "I'll go along with that" or "I'll do whatever the rest decide." This is the same desire for conformity which leads us to buy grey flannel suits or white buckskin shoes and to change our hairstyles or automobiles to keep up with the Joneses.

In reality this almost frantic search for security, the fear of being thought different, and the willingness to submit to the norms set by the majority are almost diametrically opposed to the spirit of those who have made America what it is. America was built by men who left the security of their homes on the other side of the Atlantic because they desired freedom; they refused to adjust to the demands of the society in which they lived and went out to build a New World. When that world—New England—became too crowded with rules and restrictions, they packed up and went on to Ohio, Michigan, and Kansas. Each time they were willing to give up security and to face the adventure of standing alone, as individuals, not as organization men.

This spirit of adventure, which we associate with the early settlers of our country, differs profoundly from the docile acceptance of facts—which apparently cannot be changed—found almost everywhere else in our Western world. Maybe I can illustrate this difference. One of my first impressions of America, when I came to this country twenty years ago, was not the Statue of Liberty, but a sign in a little tailor shop in Cleveland. It read: "The difficult we do at once; the impossible may take a little longer." I am sure you have seen this sign often, and it may seem very trite to you. But to me, it seemed a summary of one essential difference between Europeans and Americans. I found this same difference later in the army. Millions of Americans wore the same uniform and lived by the same regulations, but they were not uniform; they were individuals who sincerely believed that nothing was impossible. If a river was in the way, they built a bridge or a dam; if a truck broke down and there were no spare parts, they stripped an old German car or made the necessary part. I don't know what has happened in the meantime, but today there seem to be more Americans who wear different clothes, but follow a uniform pattern of behavior. Little remains of the spirit of the frontier.

Of course, there are not many wide open spaces left in America. The days of the frontier are past. But other frontiers beckon to those who have the courage to leave the crowd and stand alone. There are the frontiers of learning and research, more challenging perhaps today than ever; there are opportunities for the discovery and contact with other cultures and societies which could not even have been imagined fifty years ago. Nor do we need to bury ourselves in a laboratory or travel to India in search of this adventure of seeing frontiers open. To many of you, especially the freshmen, this past year at Hope has been an exciting adventure, and I hope that even some of our sophisticated seniors have experienced the challenge of unanswered questions and the thrill of new discovery.

This adventure of discovery does not always have to be profound. But there has to be a willingness to venture into unknown territory and to take the risk of being thought odd. Two years ago, two Hope students in our [Vienna] summer group decided to keep a careful record of all the places they had visited. So, everywhere we stopped, they tried to obtain maps. Shortly after we entered Belgium, we stopped to get gas for our bus. They were soon trying to get a map from the station attendant, even though they knew no French and only very little German. Trying to get the message to the Belgian, one student said something like "Avez vous . . . haben sie . . . eine . . . Karte . . . you know . . . map?" The attendant looked at him for a moment and then asked, in perfect English: "What's the matter with you? Can't you speak English?" This may not be a great tribute to our friend's linguistic ability, but while the others remained securely in the bus, he exposed himself to the adventure of talking to a stranger—and he got his map.

Our survival as a free people depends on this spirit of adventure. The writer of Proverbs said, "Where there is no vision, the people perish" (29:18). Faust, in making his deal with Mephistopheles, agreed that he would let the devil have his soul when he had reached the point where he had seen and experienced everything, when he had no more unanswered questions, no more curiosity, and was content to live only in the present. Toynbee and other historians who have written about the rise and fall of civilizations point to the similarities between the late Roman Empire, with its wealth and love of comfort and splendor, and our own civilization. History does not have to repeat itself, but it might be well to remember Winston Churchill's warning that "those who will not learn from history are bound to repeat it."

I urge you to greater independence of mind, to give freer play to your imagination, and to worry less about security and conformity. I realize that both you and I are caught up in a paradox of contradictory objectives. We, your teachers, would like to see in you more spirit of adventure. We would like to see you develop ingenuity and give free range to creative thought. Yet we insist that you display these desirable attributes regularly third hour Monday, Wednesday, and Friday, and that you conform to academic and social regulations and become good, well-adjusted citizens. We know that all worthwhile advances in history have come through the work of a creative minority, yet we treat with suspicion anyone who differs from the majority.

This same paradox appears when we look at the United States in the world today. We would like to support all those who seek freedom. We are opposed to imperialism and colonialism and speak with great earnestness about the moral and spiritual values of our Christian heritage. Yet, in practical politics, we are allied with dictators and former colonial powers; we find it impossible to aid those who revolt against their oppressors and export not ideals but primarily guns, tanks, and planes, as well as cheap movies.

Is there any way out of this dilemma? I believe there is, but I have no ready answer. I know that we must look at ourselves much more critically than we have in the past and that we cannot afford to limit, complacently, our concerns to physical comfort and security. Before all else, we must come to the realization that there is no escape from freedom if we sincerely accept the precepts of Christianity and democracy. Both demand that we stand alone. There is no escape into togetherness or the anonymity of belonging when we are asked to account for our actions as individuals. Nor is there the comforting excuse that we have done no more and no less than other people. The parable of the talents clearly suggests that some of us have been given more ability and responsibility than others, and that we are under obligation to make the fullest use of all our abilities.

In concrete terms, there is always an elite which must lead. Without it, our society would soon resemble a committee of third graders deciding on their own curriculum. Americans have always shied away from the idea of an intellectual elite; they are quickly ridiculed as eggheads, while a left-handed pitcher becomes a national idol. Perhaps the time has come for change.

You, whom we have honored this morning for your academic achievements, are the elite of our school and our nation. If you are willing to accept the challenges and responsibilities of this position, if you are able to risk standing alone in a crowd as you search for new frontiers and forgo the security of being just one of the boys, if you will choose the adventure of the mind instead of the adjustment of the body, then you will truly represent our best Hope.

Philosophical insights (1965-94)

To Robert Donia, 28 October 1965:

All work and no play makes Jack a dull boy; I hope that you are taking full advantage of the opportunities to visit the opera, theater, concerts, and museums. If the occasion arises, take off a weekend or even a bit longer to visit Venice or Dubrovnik.

To George Lee, 21 May 1972:

Your last letter sort of raised the questions: what is reality? what do we feel about ourselves and other people? I find it easier to talk and write on pragmatic subjects rather than to articulate ideas in this area. All the same, I shall try to answer some of your questions. First, I think you should not have to feel any regrets about anything you have done in the past. Money, to me, has very little value except in relation to what it can buy—either the things you need or the things which make life pleasant. Things have very little value except as they can give me and others comfort and pleasure. A beautiful day like today and a beautiful convertible in which to drive about have little or less meaning to me if I have to go by myself. I don't think it should worry you too much what others think, so long as what you do gives you and others pleasure and does not inflict pain or hardship on someone else. You willingly give of yourself and of your things, and I greatly admire you for this and admire your parents who have given you this heritage and outlook on life. Real friendship and human involvement cannot be static in what we expect from each other. We do not remain the same, and if we expect others to remain as they were when we first met them, we are only inviting disappointment.

To Duc Nguyen Browning, 5 January 1982:

As you may know, I have helped start several [scholarship] funds at Hope. In each case, I had in mind trying to pay back either money or friendship which had been given to me when I was still very much in need of outside help. I feel a little like a hitchhiker who is now able to offer transportation to others.

From Paul's oral history interview with Professor John Hollenbach, 16 November 1982:

It isn't so much whether you get your input from something you see or from something that you read, but it's what you do with it; in other words, it's the mind reflecting upon what you do and the insistence then that this be something of an intellectual experience.

To Frank and Charlotte Buster, 21 March 1988:

It is difficult to believe that over forty years have passed since Frank and I drove our little VW in Nürnberg! As one of my friends wrote, forty years is no age for a cathedral but a long time for being friends.

To Frank and Charlotte Buster, 31 December 1994:

I decided I wanted to write to Frank and tell him again how much I appreciated his friendship and his company, as well as his good nature, which made him such a pleasant companion.

In a document entitled "The High Adventure of Teaching" (no date), Paul singled out his friend Rolf Italiaander:

Ideally teaching is a joint adventure of discovery and exploration carried on together by a professor and his students. A good teacher not only has real knowledge of his field and enthusiasm for it, but he knows how to transmit the reality of his subject to the student and how to stimulate him to continue the journey of discovery and exploration independently.

Three Special Letters to _____ _____

In large portions of these next three letters, Paul went to great lengths to give advice and help to someone in need. I have chosen to keep the recipient anonymous.

To _____ _____, 2 December 1949:

Thank you for your long and interesting letter of November 1ˢᵗ. I had really just about given up hope of hearing from you again. But I can well understand that studies must be quite hard, especially after the long interruption and with financial worries.

I am sure that you still have not quite understood my philosophy of life. You are doing me a great injustice by saying that I could not understand your situation. What I tried to explain to you was that it is more important to try to secure some income than to cut expenses down to where the body doesn't get enough food. But I thought that I had made it quite clear that I wanted to continue to help you on the way through school. Perhaps I was not too clear on that because I wanted you to explore other avenues of getting help, too. Not in order to leave out my share of it, but so that you would have more to live on.

But this is a Christmas card, and I don't want to preach a sermon. I was truly sorry to hear that you had to move down to the cellar and more so that you had to go to bed hungry at times. As I had intended, I sent off a care package to you. It would have been sent earlier had I heard from you before. I think I can make some arrangement to have a small amount of German marks sent to you now and then, but I wanted to hear from you first. So you see that it doesn't pay to brood too long. Letting friends know what you need is one of the avenues I had in mind.

I think more than power, most people want security in our age. I know that is one of the things that you and I look for. Of course, it comes in different forms. Perhaps the simplest way is to be a farmer and live on the land. Or you may get a civil service job with *Pensionsberechtigung* [right to a pension], or you may trust in your own skill and knowledge as an investment which will always, even in bad times, pay its dividends. That would be my Christmas wish for you—that you find yourself and your self-confidence.

Don't think I am talking about something I don't understand. I would wish the same for myself; even though I may have a little more already, it's not much. We all need something to believe in and to strive for. In that respect, you are better off than I am. I spent ten years trying to get out of poverty and trying to gain a place for myself. Now that I have almost reached the point of "being somebody," I find I have no good goal to fight for. You still have that ahead of you, and the hope for a tangible and physical improvement of your situation can do much to help you over periods of disappointment. Anyway, I make this wish for you: that you see the hope of progress and find the power to fight for what you want.

To _____ _____, 3 January 1950:

My thanks to you for your two letters of 14 and 23 December. I think you said that you would not mind getting letters in English, so since I can express myself more fluently in that language, here goes. I wonder if, in the meantime, you have received a transfer of money from a friend of mine. I don't know how much he sent, so please tell me if he has and how much. (He owes me money, and that is one of the ways he has to pay it.)

I am glad that my letter helped cheer you up a bit and the package arrived in time for Christmas and provided some extras for the occasion. That is one thing I don't have to complain about; there is always too much to eat and too many invitations. I wish I could send you some of them or simply take twenty or twenty-five pounds and send them to you. Well, at least I don't have a masseur come twice a week to keep me from gaining weight.

I am very glad to know that on the quota you will have preference, and I hope that before very long something will work out regarding an affidavit for you. I have written to one of my friends about you but have not heard from her as yet. If I had a job or owned a house or something, I could sign the papers myself, but as it is—as far as the government is concerned—I am poor. But never so poor that I have to save to eat. Anyway, don't tell me whether I can afford a food package for you or not! As you admit, your judgment may be clouded as to whether you deserve it or not!?? (This is in fun—don't take me too seriously.)

Now, as to your studies, I was glad that you plan to go on for the next term at the school. I can well understand the difficulty you must have trying to adjust, and it is possible that other fields would be better for you; for the time being, I think that there is little point in changing to anything else. The question you ought to keep in mind is the long-range plan after you get here. That you will get to the States, fairly soon, is a foregone conclusion for me. The question is: what do you want to do to earn a living? There is no point in thinking that you will have to work two years for your passage. Washing dishes in a restaurant, you can earn enough in three months to pay that back, but there are other ways of making a living. Of these the intellectual is the lowest paid. Whether you have a degree or not, nobody cares, if you do your job well. Perhaps radio and television repair would be in demand. I really don't know, but there is always something to do, so you don't have to worry about that too much. The main thing is that you find the kind of occupation you will enjoy, so that you don't have to slave all day to enjoy spending the money you have earned. My idea is the kind of job which gives me enough enjoyment so that I would hate to go home in the evening and would look forward to getting down to it in the morning. Of course, I don't mind admitting that this is not the way I feel about my work here right now.

I don't think you have to worry too much about that feeling of insecurity or lack of confidence; that is, you don't have to regard it as something specifically wrong with you. Certainly there is something wrong, but it has affected almost our whole generation. Our great-grandparents still believed in God and the devil. Our grandparents had Darwin and his materialism and the theory of progress, and our parents had hopes for a much better world, social security, plenty of food, etc. Now that is almost here, at least for us, and it was well on the way and could have been in Germany. Suddenly we have discovered that material progress is not enough, that men need something more; they are seeking for mental and spiritual security. I envy the good, believing Catholic farmer; I can even at times wish for the fanatic faith of a good Communist or Fascist!!! That is part of the secret of Hitler's success. He told people: "You don't have to think for yourself. I am the Führer; follow me."

Unfortunately, we always find it easier to follow someone with materialistic aims than for instance to accept the challenge of Jesus who also said: "Follow me." I honestly think that if we could, that would solve the problem. Are you looking for a temporary solution? Well then, find out how best to use your life. But the point is that life can seem really useful only if we are being of use to others. I can see little or no excuse for a plan which is concerned only with my own advance in the world, money, prosperity, etc. Happiness, which, after all, is what we are really after, at least for me, always depends on being together with others and sharing both joys and sorrows. The contradiction lies in that having once been severely hurt by others—which applies to both of us—we are ambivalent. While wanting to have others with us, we are afraid to give of ourselves, lest we become again emotional (fall in love, marry, have people who really depend on us and can make claims against us) because being so involved we have again exposed ourselves to the danger of being really hurt. Strangers can anger us, but most of the time we are really hurt only by the people we love, or we imagine we are hurt by them.

The only solution is to turn away from concern about our own person and to think about someone or something else; whether this is a friend, wife, children, parents, or institution, such as a political party or social cause, or a spiritual force, such as faith in God. Whether such concern is altruism or not is a philosophic question which is really not very material. Writing to you, or thinking about your problems, or sending a package to you diverts my thoughts from myself and gives me the assurance that—since I may be able to help you in some way—I am doing something worthwhile. Consequently, I feel better than I did before. You might as well call it a selfish concern, but that doesn't matter. Nor does it have to take this particular form or have to involve material values at all. But enough of all that. (Am I getting too involved?)

I really have to work. My paper on "Nazi Ideas about International Law" is due on the 11th, and I have not started to write it. More next time. Write again soon.

To _____ _____, 9 March 1950:

Thanks for your two letters of February 2 and 29. Here in the States, February had only twenty-eight days this year, but I suppose in Bavaria things are a bit different! I was glad to hear from you and to know that you are up and about, even if the doctor did not give you permission. But I might as well start my letter with a reproach and then pass on to more pleasant subjects.

Since I wrote a six-page letter to _____ and told her that you would call her, I would feel very foolish if you did not do so. That does not mean that you have to ask for help, but at least you should call her, or see her, or write her a note. Otherwise she will wonder what on earth is the matter with me. My motive in this is selfish. At the same time, I am sure you will like her and spend an interesting hour or two talking to her, if nothing else. One of my best friends in Colorado I met after the wife of one of my professors had written to introduce me and to tell her that maybe she could invite me for dinner one Sunday. We have been corresponding for seven years now. I don't care if you talk to her about anything but the weather, but I hope you will call on her. If you don't, you will deprive me of the advantage of having a good friend in Munich whom I can ask to do favors for me since she will not take my requests seriously.

I certainly enjoy writing to you and getting your letters. As I explained to you a short while back, I get a certain feeling of usefulness if I can assist you now and then. You are quite correct; you should certainly not develop a feeling of dependence. On the other hand, I really don't think the danger is as great as you claim. Ultimately, we need to feel that we are part of a larger pattern of friendships and relations than our everyday life might indicate. I think philosophically that there is a flaw in making autocracy, either of the state or the individual, the goal of life. Perhaps in the medieval pattern of life, it was possible to withdraw into a monastery and forget the world outside; theoretically that is still possible, but today it would be utterly impossible without a very, very strong faith as a motivating factor. Even there, I think that to the thinking individual of our age, especially if he has faith in the power and reality of God, there are too many things to be done on the outside which would make it impossible for him to lock himself up in a cell.

Now the same thing, in a different way, applies to the physical aspects of life. It is impossible to be economically self-sufficient the way a caveman was or after the fashion of Robinson Crusoe. You can't make your own shoes, clothes, and books, or build your own house, or produce your own food. In short, we are utterly dependent in our needs on the cooperation of a great number of others, and we would needlessly complicate or make impossible our lives if we were to try to return to some primitive state of independence. I think you will understand what I am driving at. The whole ideological struggle over the word "socialism" has to do with the realization that we do have a responsibility toward the community as a whole, and for the welfare of the country. Thus, we pay a school tax in every community on the basis of the value of our property (house), regardless of whether or not we have children. A man with a large home may pay a lot and a poor family with five children nothing. Yet those children go to school, and the rich man may not have any children at all. Of course, this is only a very mild example of what I mean.

By now I am in the middle of the term again and busy working on a paper on the "Role of Industry in German Politics, 1930-33" with particular attention to Flick's case. I am sorry I didn't think of working on something like that while I was in Nürnberg and had all the material at hand, as well as plenty of help for typing. Ah well, life is full of missed opportunities, isn't it? Another paper I have to write will be on Philip of Hesse and the Reformation. I am also taking a course in modern Italian history, but I don't have to write a paper there, thank God. Now I better get busy and do some reading for tomorrow's class. I trust you have recovered fully from your illness and that you have managed to find a better place to live. Let me know as soon as you move what your new address is. And write again soon!

Religious insights

From Edith Lambotte, 5 May 1940:

Mrs. Lambotte advised him to "place your confidence in the entire word of God, Paul darling; it is being fulfilled before our eyes, and God is working His purpose out, and soon His glory (and not Hitler's) will cover the earth."

To Margaret Mills, 25 August 1945:

To a man who does not believe in God, or in a great cause, or at least in himself, freedom is the greatest burden. Being unsure of himself and of the why of life, he is always ready to surrender his freedom in return for security or membership in a group.

Many of Paul's early letters on religion were written to the members of the Cleveland Hebrew Christian group which got him to the United States as a missionary. He had divided loyalties to the group.

To Lida Imhof, 9 September 1945:

Of one thing I am reasonably certain: I am not cut out for missionary work. During the last twelve years, I have had a continual guidance in my movements—as if there was no other alternative in each of the steps that I took. I am sure there must have been some Divine purpose to all that. [However], it seems to be the curse of the Jewish Missions that they split and get into internal difficulties. Perhaps my parents gave me too liberal an education. I can always see the other fellow's point of view. That's why I could never be a missionary.

To Hilda Kloucek, 3 June 1946:

It was interesting to read your comments on the lack of Christian ideals in the UN. That is exactly the feeling some of us have here. If the delegates now in New York would devote some of their time to the consideration of Christ and his teachings instead of investigating the well-stocked American bars, things might go a bit better. While I was in Cleveland, I heard much teaching and preaching on the pre-millennial Second Coming. Now at school, I have the chance to hear the other side. It would be presumptuous to say who is right. I doubt whether we are meant to know too much about it. I have a very short time before leaving Hope College. By the way, is there anything I can send you from here? I have more money than I need and shall be very happy to mail you a package of things which you can't buy in England.

To Margaret Mills, 12 March 1946:

Sunday night we had a Christian Scientist as our speaker at Hope Church. It was especially interesting, especially to Bob Snow and myself. I think everyone was much impressed by the simplicity and clarity of his presentation.

To Margaret Mills, 21 April 1946:

Does it seem possible that three years ago this Easter we attended the Easter sunrise service in the Garden of the Gods?

To Margaret Mills, 15 October 1946:

On Sunday morning, I went to the Mother Church [for Christian Scientists, in Boston]. I was greatly impressed by the size and architecture.

It seems to combine the outside of St. Paul's in London with the interior of the Paris Opera. I am wondering if what I said about the difference between Hope and Harvard would not also apply to churches. Of course, it is up to us to bring with us an attitude of worship, but there is something to be said for stimulating it and against creating too great a diversion. The American ideal of "the bigger the better" seems to affect not only cars and iceboxes but also churches, schools, and wars.

To June Metcalf, 17 October 1946:

The Old Cambridge Church is right near the campus, and there is a very pleasant group of young people there. Wish I could get there as frequently as I would like. The services at the Memorial Church are usually quite interesting, though they present a variety of speakers from various denominations.

To Margaret Mills, 23 November 1946:

Yes, I go to church fairly often, usually to the Baptist church.

To Margaret Mills, 15 December 1946:

I think, in the final analysis, you would find that we are not poles apart in our religious thinking.

To Dear Folks (the Metcalfs and Kramers), 8 January 1947:

I would like to ask you a favor. My [Jewish] roommate is getting his MA this month. We have had quite a few long conversations about religion, Christianity, and the Bible. He said he had never owned one, and if he had one, he would read it as a literary master work. I would like to give him one. Knowing that you might be able to get him something much nicer for the same money, I wondered if you would be able to send me a really good King James edition. I would be willing to pay up to five or six dollars.

To Dear Folks (the Metcalfs and Kramers), 30 January 1947:

The Bible came a couple of days ago, so I will be able to give it to Bob when he leaves tomorrow morning. I pray that he may find it more than a literary masterpiece as he reads it.

To Howard Kramer, 15 March 1947:

The boy who has asked me to go to Philadelphia with him is Jewish, so I would like to give him one of the New Testaments put out by the Million Testament League. Do you have any on hand? I had one but gave it away last summer.

To Margaret Mills, 8 February 1947:

I do want to send some things to Czechoslovakia, so I am wondering just what sort of contacts the Christian Science relief organization has there.

To Margaret Mills, 10 March 1947:

I have often wondered just what our attitude toward the spending of money ought to be—that is, whether we should try to live like Tolstoy and divide our goods until there are no more, or whether it is better to remain in a position where we can continue to earn and to contribute money. If everyone were willing to live in poverty and our society would not consider it a stigma to be poor, then I think we should follow the example of Tolstoy and interpret the gospels literally on that point. Since, however, we do not live in that kind of society, our ability to do good would be impaired and eventually reduced to nothing, once the means of earning had gone. This could, of course, be nothing more than rationalization on my part. I don't know what got me off on this subject, unless it is your new upholstery.

To Hilda Cook, Christmas 1949:

The comment about the loss of Christian ideals and social conscience is more than pertinent to our time. I have been reading quite a bit on the matter lately, and I am convinced that the general loss of purpose in life—combined with either extreme poverty as in Germany after World War I or with prosperity which makes striving for one's livelihood less of a struggle—has resulted in the kind of psychological mess we are in now. I don't know which of these is worse. I think that to most people the challenge of making a living in adverse circumstances still serves as a purpose and those to whom things are given are worse off if they have nothing to set up as a goal. That is the real problem of socialism and the welfare state; there is little beyond the material ideal, and that is probably the reason why people turned to such terrible beliefs as Nazism because it is a faith, just as Communism claims to be. I am less afraid that the latter will ever take the place of a religious ideal as Nazism did. Where are we going? That is the burning issue of our day. Is return to the unsophisticated faith of our parents possible for the great masses? I imagine this must sound a bit improper for a Christmas message, but I am glad there are at least people like you who think about the matter.

To Margaret Mills, 12 January 1950:

I came to the conclusion that law and Nazism were totally incompatible, and therefore they tried to eliminate law. At the bottom of the whole system, there was not only disrespect for law but also for all moral or ethical values, for man, and for God.

To Harriet Cook, 20 January 1950:

I met another Hope fellow who is student pastor at the Park Street Church in Boston, so I promised I would go there this Sunday. I had been there once before, but it had been very full with people standing to hear the evangelist Billy Graham.

To Margaret Mills, 18 February 1950:

I was very much surprised when he [Pakistan's foreign minister who had just addressed a Harvard audience] spoke of the new constitution which is being drafted and will contain many of the social teachings of Islam, the most startling of which is that the earnings of industry are to be divided in equal parts among (1) labor, (2) capital, and (3) the community. Since Islam states that the wealth of the earth comes from God and belongs to all people in the community, and since nothing could be produced without natural raw materials and natural power, nothing could be more reasonable. This is going to be an interesting experiment.

To Margaret Mills, 26 February 1950:

When I was about sixteen or seventeen, I had no doubts that my own brand of religion was the only true way to heaven.

To Margaret Mills, 29 June 1950:

I do find that in twelve years my interests have shifted, and I am unable to accept the very narrow opinions of some of my friends (who would count Christian Science as a heathen religion or worse)!

To Harriet Cook, 9 July 1950:

My friends, the Kramers, have moved to a very nice new home in Cleveland Heights, and they gave me a fine welcome. Their middle daughter, who lives in Oklahoma, was home with her husband and two sweet little children, so it was a grand reunion. I was treated like the prodigal son returned!

To Lida Imhof, 5 December 1952:

I have always had the feeling that the Mission as such has not paid enough attention to the physical needs of the people it deals with. I am not saying that we should feed them, but that we should be human and humane in our contacts. [Paul enclosed a money order from Essen, Germany, for $25 as a "Christmas treat to Hebrew Christians"—a phrase used in the receipt from Lida.]

To Lida Imhof, 24 February 1953:

Just now I received a very interesting letter from a young man who escaped from the Soviet zone a few months ago but plans to go back there now in order to help continue the Catholic youth movement in which he had played a prominent part. It sounds like a very daring undertaking, but I must say I can only respect a man who will risk his life—whether he is a Catholic, Protestant, or Jew—for the sake of his faith.

To Hans-Joachim (Hajo) A. Robert, 4 March 1953:

Your new interest in the Old Testament and the story of David did not surprise me. I like the story very much.

To Frank Buster, 23 November 1953:

I have been thinking of a good [wedding] present for you, and perhaps also a reminder of Nürnberg and Germany. Anyway, I found just the thing and shall mail it soon. It's not new, but it is what a real present should be, something I like enough to want to keep it; that is, I would want to keep it, if I were not sending it to you with all the best wishes. The inscription in German is: "Him, to whom God would show real favor, him he sends into the wide world." I think in that respect, as in many others, He has shown us both real favor.

From Alan Metcalf, 8 December 1953:

Metcalf thanked Paul for his article for *The Star of David* and requested "information on your conversion as to place and time as well as your background in Judaism (Orthodox or Reformed) before you came to know Jesus as Messiah."

To Alan Metcalf, 9 December 1953:

Sorry I can't oblige with background in Judaism (Orthodox or Reformed). My parents on both sides were of Jewish race, but my grandparents on both sides had been converted. My father's family was Reformed (Calvinist), my mother's Lutheran. I was brought up Lutheran and did not even know of my Jewish ancestry until shortly before Hitler came to power in 1933. Of course, all people of Jewish race, regardless of religious affiliation, were persecuted by the Nazis, and my parents were no exception. As non-Aryans, we were expelled from Germany in 1933 since my father was Austrian by birth. In Vienna, I began to attend the service of the Swedish Mission to the Jews, led by Dr. Frederick Forell, now head of the Newcomers Christian Fellowship in New York. Through him, I came to recognize and accept Christ on a personal basis in the summer of 1936. Today, as I teach Western civilization to college freshmen, I am more convinced that our only hope for survival as a civilized nation lies in the personal acceptance of Christianity by more of our population.

Paul's article for the *Star of David* was rejected on 6 February 1954. Verda Kramer said that it needed to be edited to "make it more acceptable to the taste of our constituency."

To Verda Kramer, 27 February 1954:

I think the *Star of David* was very nice, and I am not at all hurt that you did not use my article. I dashed it off in a hurry when Alan wrote that he wanted it that week.

To Margaret Mills, Thanksgiving Day 1956:

In June, I was appointed by the general synod of our church to the committee on international justice and good will. In November, at a meeting in New York, I was elected chairman for the coming year. I am flattered but also a bit worried since it is a great responsibility. We are supposed to help the denomination determine its stand on questions of international affairs.

To M. Eugene Osterhaven, 16 July 1957:

There is some talk of establishing an American church in Vienna [the English-language Vienna Community Church is still in existence], similar to those which exist in Paris, The Hague, Cairo, and other places. I have been invited to a meeting on that subject for next week.

To Harriet Cook, 22 October 1961:

Today I went to church twice. First, I went to hear the Vienna Boys Choir sing a Beethoven Mass in the Imperial Court Chapel. It was very good and inspiring. I wish we could have more music like that in our church. Later I went to the Vienna Community Church. The music was not as good as at the Catholic service.

To John Dryfhout, 7 January 1965:

I have agreed to speak to the Hope Church young people Sunday night on Jewish history and persecution.

To Edith Lambotte, 16 November 1970:

Yesterday morning, I went to the student church and heard a very fine guest preacher. I think you would have enjoyed him. He reminded me of Dr. Lord in his accent and gestures and also in his sermon. There must have been nine hundred or a thousand students to hear him. Later that day, I had seven young people over for dinner.

To Arthur Frederix, 1 December 1971:

You gave up your lunch and nap in order to write your last letter to me, so the least I can do is to sacrifice going to church this morning in order to write a reply. As a matter of fact, I did go last Sunday, and it must have shocked the minister to see me. Anyway, he wanted to know if I would light the Advent candle this morning; they wanted someone living alone to do it. I quickly said I did not think I would be in town.

To Alma Scarlett, 24 June 1974:

A lot of our group went to the Vienna Community Church yesterday, and about five even sang in the choir. That ought to count for something. At church Sunday, I was trying to recruit a very nice young Nigerian whose father is high up in UNIDO here. I don't think he would need any Geneva funds!

To Arthur Frederix, 10 April 1975:

The Qatar program will be that evening [same day that Paul hosted a luncheon party for Harriet Cook's 96th birthday], and I will serve as MC for the Qatari raffle! I am not sure what my good Jewish grandfathers are thinking in Vienna's *Zentralfriedhof* [central cemetery] or wherever they are.

A tan folder holds a four-page unsigned and undated document, but the written words look exactly like Paul's handwriting. Here is a small portion of the message:

To man who does not believe in God, or in a great cause, or at least in himself, freedom is the greatest burden. Being unsure of himself and of the why of his life, he is always ready to surrender his freedom in return for security or for membership in a group. The first and most obvious solution lies in the acceptance of the Christian doctrine of God the Father and the God of Love who cares for every single individual. For this faith, there is no real substitute, and in it alone lies the key to man's freedom. True faith is something which can only be advanced individually, and though it is the only true solution to man's problems, it is not something which can be brought about by government action or law. It is therefore necessary to create at least the external prerequisites for the growth of Christian faith and practice.

CHAPTER 24

Memorial Service

On Saturday, 9 September 2006, Paul's friends gathered at Hope Church in Holland for a memorial celebration of his life. From his early days at Hope College to his last days at the Warm Friend, Paul had been a devoted member of Hope Church, where he worshiped many Sundays in thanksgiving for the chance to survive and succeed in Holland. At the memorial service, several letters and emails were read, and three eulogies were delivered. Brief excerpts from a few letters and emails and a few sentences from each eulogy are included here.

From Dr. Eva Nowotny, Austrian ambassador to the United States, 28 July 2006:

The gains in that long era [since 1945] of expanding wealth, democracy, and increasing international cooperation were contingent not just on the actions of resolute and far-sighted statesmen. They were contingent on the interests, moods, and perceptions of a wider public that had to be educated and brought to understand the advantages of empathy and international solidarity over the material and emotional benefits of narrow and mutually antagonistic nationalism. Professor Paul Fried was one of these leaders and educators. Austria, in particular, owes him recognition and gratitude—all the more so, as his efforts and successes in building bridges have to be set against the background of the tragedies in his early life, when his family was sent from Austria to their extermination in concentration camps. Yet he became a pioneer in the academic exchanges between the two countries.

During my student days at the University of Vienna, Paul engaged me to teach courses in Austrian and European history for the summer school; that began a friendship which continued over many years. When I was working at the Austrian mission to the United Nations, I lectured at Hope College; when I became foreign policy advisor to the Austrian federal chancellor, I had opportunities to assist the Vienna Summer School. I witnessed Hope's proactive opening to the world to which Paul contributed so much and which was an essential component of his life and work. He lived in two worlds and sought to bring them closer together in a sense of shared values, goals, and responsibilities. I wish for what he has sown to ripen and to endure.

From Dr. Thomas Nowotny, Hope graduate, husband of Eva, prolific author with multiple positions in the Austrian Foreign Service, 28 July 2006:

I was probably the first beneficiary of his efforts to bring Viennese students to Hope (1958-59). Had it not been for this year and for Paul, I certainly would not have been launched into a career as diplomat, academic, and banker. Hope was different with its open intellectual atmosphere mixing American optimism with a Calvinistic sense of moral obligation. Paul was certainly most instrumental in adding to this mix the element of world openness and internationality. He looked forward to making the future better than the past and inspired me to do the same. Marc Antony, you were wrong. The good that men do *does* live after them. So let it be with Paul Fried.

From Dr. Brigitte Marcher, Hope graduate and head of European Political Department at Austria's Renner Institute, 16 August 2006:

I am grateful to have known Paul in his best days. He lived a long life rich with academic and personal rewards for his tremendous engagement in networking European and American people.

From Bruce van Voorst, 1 September 2006:

Who was Paul Fried? Our model? Our prototype? Both and more. Paul was our internationalist, and more importantly, he was the world spirit for Hope College. Paul was from another planet, one called Europe, one called European intellectualism. Those of us who had Paul in his first-year teaching assignments knew little about his background but did notice both his accent and his intense familiarity with European history. His tongue still tended to say, "Vee have to go home," and "quick" came out "kvick." But it didn't matter. When Paul talked of Europe, Metternich was his George Washington; Bismarck was his Abe Lincoln.

From Mag. Margareta Weissgärber, director of the Austro-American Institute of Education, 4 September 2006:

The commitment of Paul Fried has always been a shining example. He and his family suffered incredibly during the Third Reich, but rather than ending up in bitterness and despair, he built bridges through cultural exchange. To us, Paul Fried ranks with another great Austrian, Viktor Frankl, the founder of logotherapy, who also dedicated his life to better international understanding. Frankl's *Man's Search for Meaning* is a manifestation of his own belief, and his ideas and ideals apply equally to the life of Paul Fried.

From Ingrid-Heyden Walter, 1978 Hope graduate, 6 September 2006:

For the many international students, Paul was a good friend, and for us German students, he was a substitute father. He was always there when we needed help and gave us the feeling of home when we were thousands of miles from our families. I am enormously proud and thankful that our friendship has lasted for thirty years and that I could see him a last time during my visit to Holland this April.

From Brian Gibbs, former student and lifelong supporter of the Vienna Summer School, 8 September 2006:

I had Paul for European history (he was what he taught, a very special gift for any professor), and he encouraged me to apply for a Fulbright in Austria. I got to know him more closely after I had graduated from Hope. Visiting his house, I marveled at how his books stretched wall-to-wall and floor-to-ceiling, and I contemplated the single, lone picture of his family in a small frame perched on his bedroom dresser. [When Paul's family members were forced out of Germany in the 1930s], they crossed the border back into Austria at Schärding, the place where I would teach some fifty years later at Paul's encouragement. Were it not for Paul, I would not be where I am in Europe, doing what I am doing, married to whom I am married. Nor would my children be half-Austrian.

My own eulogy (with ample examples mirrored in the previous pages of this book) focused on how Paul's life embodied several virtues

One of the last photos of Paul as he enjoys talking
with Ingrid Heyden-Walter at Resthaven, April 2006

lauded in Aristotle's *Nicomachean Ethics*: courage, justice, practical wisdom, and generosity.

Those of us who saw Dr. Fried often in the past few years recall his use of the bittersweet phrase, "the need to be needed." No matter how often I reassured Paul that he was still needed, he never really believed me. As I reflect on his incomparable life, however, I see how the world needed Paul Fried to invigorate those four Aristotelian virtues and how Paul never let us down.

Courage: On the day Paul died, I imagined his soul reuniting in heaven with his parents and brothers who had lost their lives in concentration camps. I sensed their pride as they heard more about his circuitous journey to Hope College and his brave enlistment in the US Army. Paul, in humility, seldom mentioned these events that compelled him to make his family's unjust deaths count for something. The Allies, in general, and Paul's family, in particular, needed Paul Fried, and he answered that need with courage.

Justice: Interrupting his graduate studies to serve as a translator at the Nürnberg war trials, Paul played a major role in an event that defined accountability and moral witness. Paul, without an ounce of bitterness in his being, was forgiving, but he knew that the world must never forget.

The world, recovering from the mad atrocities of World War II, needed Paul Fried, and he answered that need with a sense of justice.

Practical wisdom: In 1956, the summer after Austria had regained independence, Paul started introducing American students to Vienna as a practical outlet for his wisdom about war, peace, and international relations to flourish. "Education," he said, "ought to let you back up, so you can see things in perspective, be less parochial. I wanted to build bridges between Americans and Austrians." He insisted that the bridges go both ways and spread his gospel with vigor and creativity. Hope needed Paul Fried to launch this mission in international education, and he answered that need with practical wisdom.

Generosity: Most of us have benefited from Paul's generosity and hospitality. We have received his etchings and prints as gifts. We have dined on his deviled eggs, *Wienerschnitzel*, Farmer's Market vegetables, and signature *Schwarzwälderkirschtorte*. We have imbibed his Austrian wines during bridge games and receptions for visiting dignitaries while Mozart concertos serenaded us. My dad, now ninety-three, recalls the sterling silver and china foretelling a six-course gourmet dinner. Ample scholarship funds from Dr. Fried still support Hope students in global endeavors. Paul Fried saw the need of students to have a teacher who put his money where his mouth was, and he answered that need with generosity.

The long-lasting results of Paul's courage, justice, practical wisdom, and generosity constitute his magnificence. His spirit and propensity to teach were legendary. Paul's "need to be needed" admonition has challenged me to visit and listen to those with memory losses. When the Resthaven staff spoke of Paul as friendly, sweet, and uncomplaining, he twinkled his eyes and graciously acknowledged the compliments. He is probably groaning at these eulogies but politely accepting our tributes with patience. Paul Fried saw our need for him to build a house befitting his riches, and he answered that need with magnificence.

Paul Fried brought Hope (small and large H) into all the world.

Professor Neal Sobania, Vienna Summer School participant and 1968 Hope graduate who succeeded Paul as Hope's director of International Education, spoke of Paul's unique value to the entire Hope College community.

Paul's influence went well beyond Holland and Vienna. What Hope College provided was a springboard from which to bring to reality Paul's imaginings and dreams. Patiently and persistently, he was ever moving the college, its administrators, faculty, and students toward a deeper understanding of the world. As he enjoyed describing it, all alike needed a medicinal dose of anti-parochial pills.

His life experiences woke many of us to the new, ever-changing global realties. Paul taught us about the world of ideas and inspired us to become idea people because ideas are agents of change. He knew the world needed to be changed. He made us think about sobering and unsettling questions; he drove our curiosity. From Paul we learned, in the words of Gandhi: "Be the change that you wish to see in the world."

Paul played a pivotal role in support of international education regionally and nationally. He used his time and talents to grow and shape the Great Lakes Colleges Association's international emphasis with study abroad programs in Beirut, Bogota, Tokyo, and Yugolsavia—how prescient! At the Institute for European Studies and with the Council on International Educational Exchange, he gave national leadership to help insure the academic foundations of the first study centers they ran. In the process, he singlehandedly brought to Hope College a national identity in international education.

German was always an important part of who Paul was, so let me burrow into my limited German and mine three words: *Ausblick, Durchblick and Einblick. Ausblick* means perspective, what Paul had for higher education generally. *Durchblick* translates as "seeing through" something or gaining comprehension, the goal Paul had for all his students and colleagues. *Einblick* translates as "gaining insight," the way Paul lived his life and challenged us to do the same, whether through history (first and foremost, he was an historian), art, music, good food, wine (or his favorite, Scotch), and academic travel.

When Paul retired, he took great fondness and a certain degree of pride in telling people that it took three people to replace him: Marc Baer to teach European history, Stephen Hemenway to direct the Vienna Summer School, and me to oversee international education. Behind this was always that distinctive glint Paul sometimes got in his eye that said, this is my view of Hope College: significant programmatic growth led by well-trained and broadly experienced faculty—*Ausblick*—perspective.

Finally, Glenn Lowe, Paul's official guardian in his final ten years (1997-2006), talked lovingly of his "Saturdays with Paul" (a Holland version of Mitch Albom's *Tuesdays with Morrie*, an account of the author's weekly visits to see a former college professor). After Paul had moved into the Warm Friend senior living community, Glenn showed up every Saturday at 9 a.m. to listen to Paul "reflect on his travels, his former students, and his life so richly blessed."

Commencement with (l-r) Larry Penrose, Marc Baer, Paul Fried,
Stephen Hemenway, and Neal Sobania, 1984

We would sort through the mail, often including wonderful letters or postcards from former students or friends. We would pay bills. I took over that process after I discovered he had been writing multiple checks to *Time* magazine for subscriptions. I told him that, at this rate, his subscription would last another twenty to thirty years! He smiled, and with that distinctive impish grin, said: "Do you suppose *Time* will forward them to me?"

I will always remember Saturday, June 6, 1998. After moving Paul into the Warm Friend, it became my job to dispose of all the items in his three-story house on 12ᵗʰ Street. I arranged for an estate sale, and hundreds of collectors and buyers streamed into the home. In mid-afternoon, I glanced up, and there stood Paul. I tried to direct him back to the Warm Friend, but he calmly said, "It's okay. I want to watch." He sat in his favorite striped velvet chair in the corner. After a period of time, I approached him and said, "Paul, isn't it just tearing you apart to see your collections of a lifetime being carried out the front door?" He looked at me and said, "When you've lost your possessions, your home, and your family, this becomes just stuff."

In 2003 Mitch Albom wrote another book, *The Five People You Meet in Heaven*. In heaven, a carnival worker notices some people whose presence created an influence, a shift, that changed the course of his life. When we get to heaven, how many of us will see Paul Fried as one of those who influenced us? How many of us will realize that our understanding of other cultures and traditions is broader and deeper because of Paul? How many of us will set aside bitterness because we heard the story of Paul rising above his past to create for us a bright future?

Dr. John Hollenbach called Paul an "apostle of understanding." [As Paul lay dying in Resthaven's Good Shepherd Center], I reminded him of that title. Paul smiled and said "I like that." These words are etched on his gravestone in the hope that future generations will walk by, wonder about the man behind such an interesting title, and learn the story of Dr. Paul George Fried.

Index